HEMP

Lifeline to the Future

The Unexpected Answer for Our Environmental and Economic Recovery

by Chris Conrad

"Turn this hempen paper page
— enter a new Emerald Age."

Title page printed on 70% hemp / 30% cotton paper.
Paper courtesy of American Hemp Mercantile, Seattle Washington

Remainder of the book on tree pulp paper, with apologies to the Earth.

Creative Xpressions Publications
Los Angeles, California
© 1994, 1993 by Chris Conrad. Second edition, December 1994

HEMP, LIFELINE TO THE FUTURE

ISBN 0-9639754-1-2
© 1994 by Chris Conrad

Edited by Roy Richard

Revised edition, December 1994. ISBN: 0-9639754-1-2. Unabridged first edition: © March 1993 by Chris Conrad. ISBN 0-9639754-0-4. First reprint: March 1994. Second edition, revised and updated: December 1994. Printed in USA.

ACKNOWLEDGMENTS:

We apologize if any copyrights have been accidentally infringed regarding any article or graphic in this book or its appendices. We have endeavored to stay within all federal and international copyright laws and guidelines in the use of excerpted material, and have given credit whenever possible. Thank you for your understanding.

The author would like to acknowledge the following information sources: Ernest Abel (*Marihuana, the first 12,000 years*); Dr. Michael Aldrich & Trans-High/Stonehill Publishing (*High Times Encyclopedia of Recreational Drugs*); AP; Athens News; *Bible*; Biologue; S.S. Boyce (*Hemp*); Cato Institute; Christic Institute; Common Sense for America; Consumers Union; Mary Cooper (*Congressional Quarterly*); The Ecologist; Encyclopaedia Brittanica; Jack Frazier (Hemp Paper Reconsidered, *The Great American Hemp Industry*); The Guardian; Harper & Row; Hash Info Museum; Hearst Co.; Jack Herer (*The Emperor Wears No Clothes*); Herodotus; High Times; In These Times; John Kaplan (*Marijuana, the New Prohibition*); *Koran*; LA Times; Library of Congress; Dr. Tod Mikuriya (*Marijuana: Medical Papers*); Brent Moore (*Hemp Industry in Kentucky*); Dr. David Musto (*The American Disease*); The Nation; Newsweek; NY Times; NIDA; Omni; Orange County Register; NORML; Pacifica News; Popular Mechanics; Public Citizen; Reason; Reuters News Service; San Francisco Examiner; San Francisco Chronicle; San Jose Mercury News; Science; Scientific American; Larry Sloman (*Reefer Madness*); David Solomon (*The Marijuana Papers*); Time; United Nations; *Upanishads*; UPI; USA Today; USDA; US Government Printing Office; Utne Reader; *Vedas*; Wall Street Journal; Washington Post; & all the media & researchers that chronicle history.

Special thanks to all BACH representatives, the American Hemp Council & everyone who helped gather and prepare this information over the years, including: Dr. Michael Aldrich, Julian Alexander, Walt Bender, Edward Brecher, Ken Breeding, Randy Davis, Lyster Dewey, Ben & Alan Dronkers, Genie Erstad, Henry Ford, Gatewood Galbraith, The "Governor", Lewis Cecil Gray, Dr. Lester Grinspoon, Steve Hager, Dr. Roberta Hamilton, Linda Hendry, Jack Herer, John Horgan, Thomas Jefferson, Ellen Komp, Floyd Landrath, el Lorenzo, Lynn McIntosh, Dr. Tod Mikuriya, Dr. John Morgan, Carl Olsen, Lynn Osburn, Judy Osburn, Dr. Jeri Rose, Ed Rosenthal, Barry Stull, Larry Serbin, Jon Schultz, Alex Shum, Eric Skidmore, Paul Stanford, Barry Stull, Dr. Donald Tashkin, George Tyson, George Washington, Lennice Werth, Donald Wirtshafter, Judge Francis Young & others too numerous to mention by name. You know what you did, and I appreciate you for having done it.

Finally a negative acknowledgement to all journalists, editors & media "watchdogs" of government, who failed so miserably to uncover or present the facts about cannabis hemp, & to those who, when faced with this information, hide their heads in fear rather than bring truth to light. To all DEA, "Justice" Department & other bureaucrats, to Mr. Anslinger, Bennett, Bensinger, Bush, DuPont, Hearst, Heath, Lawn, Lungren, Mellon, Nahas, Wilson, & their lackies; may they be fully compensated and remembered in proportion to their crimes against humanity & nature.

Creative Xpressions Publications
PO Box 1005, Novato, California. Postal Code: 94948
Book orders: 1-800-Hemp Man / 1-818-376-0671

Contents

Dedication

To this amazing herb, cannabis hemp, and to the source from whence it sprang; to all the individual men and women who play a role in this never-ending saga of discovery; to all hemp advocates; and to the spirits of curiosity and invention that advance humanity.

I wish to extend a special dedication and profound gratitude to my wife, Mikki Norris, for her unwavering support; to my niece Marisa for asking me after that fateful 1988 Thanksgiving dinner, "Why did they make marijuana illegal in the first place?"; and finally to my parents and family for making me the kind of person who could not rest until I had uncovered the truth.

Editor's Note

Chris Conrad has provided policymakers—which really can include any active citizen—with the best compendium available on the history, present worldwide status and future potential of our planet's premier plant: hemp. He charts, with much insight and humor, a very clear and practical course to a world liberated from the toxic influences of petrochemical polluters and prohibitionist politicians.

— Roy Richard, February 1993

About the Author

Chris Conrad is president of the Hemp Industries Association, founder of the Business Alliance for Commerce in Hemp (BACH), director of the Family Council on Drug Awareness and founder of the American Hemp Council. He designed and edited Jack Herer's landmark book, *Hemp and the Marijuana Conspiracy: The Emperor Wears No Clothes*. He is a curator of the Hash – Marihuana – Hemp Museum (a.k.a. Hash Info Museum) in Amsterdam, and a member of the Indian Hemp Drugs Commission Centennial Committee, 1993–94.

An acknowledged expert on the industrial, ecological, medical and social uses of cannabis hemp, Chris appeared as the character 'Johnny Marijuanaseed' in The Hemp Show #1 produced by *The Nineties* (PBS) in 1990. He has since become a popular guest on broadcast and cable interview shows and speaks on college campuses and at events across the United States. He wrote and produced the play *Marijuana!*

Mr. Conrad is a businessman, consultant, lecturer, writer, editor, fine and graphic artist, researcher, community activist and philosopher.

THE MANY USES OF HEMP

The World's Most Valuable & Versatile Natural Resource

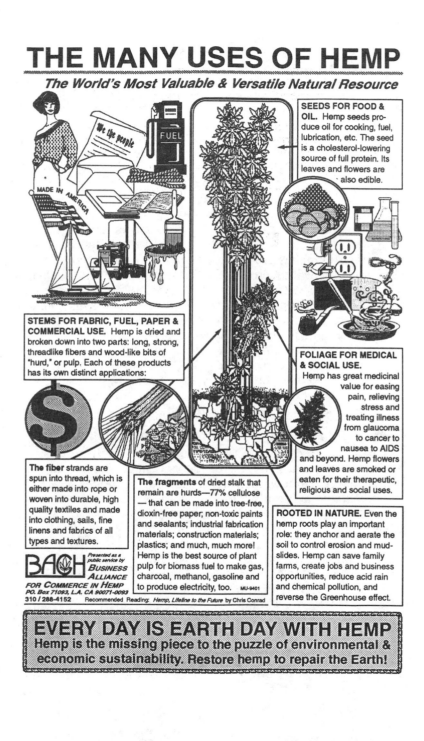

SEEDS FOR FOOD & OIL. Hemp seeds produce oil for cooking, fuel, lubrication, etc. The seed is a cholesterol-lowering source of full protein. Its leaves and flowers are also edible.

STEMS FOR FABRIC, FUEL, PAPER & COMMERCIAL USE. Hemp is dried and broken down into two parts: long, strong, threadlike fibers and wood-like bits of "hurd," or pulp. Each of these products has its own distinct applications:

FOLIAGE FOR MEDICAL & SOCIAL USE. Hemp has great medicinal value for easing pain, relieving stress and treating illness from glaucoma to cancer to nausea to AIDS and beyond. Hemp flowers and leaves are smoked or eaten for their therapeutic, religious and social uses.

The fiber strands are spun into thread, which is either made into rope or woven into durable, high quality textiles and made into clothing, sails, fine linens and fabrics of all types and textures.

The fragments of dried stalk that remain are hurds—77% cellulose — that can be made into tree-free, dioxin-free paper; non-toxic paints and sealants; industrial fabrication materials; construction materials; plastics; and much, much more! Hemp is the best source of plant pulp for biomass fuel to make gas, charcoal, methanol, gasoline and to produce electricity, too.   MU-9401

ROOTED IN NATURE. Even the hemp roots play an important role: they anchor and aerate the soil to control erosion and mudslides. Hemp can save family farms, create jobs and business opportunities, reduce acid rain and chemical pollution, and reverse the Greenhouse effect.

BACH
Presented as a public service by BUSINESS ALLIANCE FOR COMMERCE IN HEMP
P.O. Box 71093, L.A. CA 90071-0093
310 / 288-4152   Recommended Reading: *Hemp, Lifeline to the Future* by Chris Conrad

EVERY DAY IS EARTH DAY WITH HEMP

Hemp is the missing piece to the puzzle of environmental & economic sustainability. Restore hemp to repair the Earth!

INTRODUCTION

Self-Destruction Is Not the Price of Progress

Life begets hope. Understanding life is the key to survival. Today, however, we see our economic and biological support systems crumbling beneath us. The industrial revolution led to a level of consumerism unparalleled in human history—a "throw-away" society with a hidden price tag. Did you ever wonder how people used to survive without all the things we take for granted? How did they get by without plastic packaging, fat newspapers, traffic jams, synthetic fibers and pills, bottled water, electricity, photocopies, television, smog and junk mail?

The natural healing processes of this planet are being tested and, all too often, overrun by the pace of pollution. The cumulative devastation of the environment is accelerating at a calamitous rate. In the words of President Bill Clinton, "Economic strength will increasingly depend on sound environmental policy. ... If we do not find the vision and leadership to defeat the unprecedented new threats of global climate change, ozone depletion, habitat destruction and desertification, then those threats may well defeat us."[1]

We need a lifeline that society can grasp onto, to keep us from falling into chaos, deprivation and possible extinction.

Human Nature in Harmony With Natural Law

We humans are part of a vast biological web of life. Our biosystem consists of the myriads of interdependent life forms. Nature has given us a fragile but wonderfully balanced planet where plants use the earth, water and sunlight to provide the oxygen animals breathe and the food we eat. Animal waste fertilizes the plants. Natural selection ensures survival of the best-adapted species.

To discover our future, we must first recover our past. Our forebears built great civilizations and powerful empires without using fossil fuels or toxic chemicals. Of course, people were fewer and life was simpler. But they had ample metals, ceramics, glass and nature's wondrous bounty to provide for their needs. What they lacked was the technology that's been developed over the past few

---

[1]Clinton, William Jefferson. 'Caring for nature is good business.' in *Los Angeles Times*. CA. Nov. 8, 1992

generations. What we lack is their awareness of how nature can meet our needs while supporting the Earth's ecosystems.

Logic demands that we face our problems and start repairing the damage. What is available to shift civilization back onto the road to survival while maintaining our standard of living? How do we motivate ordinary people to freely undertake the journey to a viable future? Can we get there using existing technology, institutions and infrastructure? Where is that sustainable resource, or group of resources, capable of fulfilling this vital mandate?

Historical and current data suggest there is such a resource. One that will help us not only to survive, but to thrive and even flourish on a global scale. The Bible holds that God created and gave us "every seed bearing herb" to use.[2] Farm crops meet a vast array of human needs in addition to food, often with less processing than synthetic substitutes. Plants produce fresh, clean air and yield the same or improved consumer products at a better price.

Does money grow on trees? Imagine a plant that is fast and easy to grow and, at this moment, ounce for ounce, is more valuable than gold. There is such a plant. It's been here all along. It's hemp.

This book will demonstrate that cannabis hemp is the ultimate green industry. There are many long-term ecological benefits which can be reaped by using hemp. Anything made of wood or petroleum can be made more economically with hemp. Hemp is so easy to grow and use that it lends itself to the most primitive handicrafts and the most sophisticated high-technology applications.[3]

Make no mistake about it: this is not an overnight miracle cure for all our ills. Hemp is part of a long-term process of repairing our economy and environment. Hemp restoration will yield permanent financial benefits that will reverberate throughout the economy for generations to come. Given the scope of today's environmental and economic crises, it is time for national and global crash programs to restore hemp and explore its vast potential.

Hemp: Earth's Premier Sustainable Resource

We are convinced that people want to build a secure and sustainable future; they just don't know how to go about doing it. Hence this book. Our goal is to strip away the misconceptions about hemp which have been foisted on our society over the past few decades and take a fresh, new look at this amazing plant.

---

[2]*Bible, The.* King James version, et al. Genesis 1:12, 29-31

[3]True both today & yesterday. "The hemp plant is the most simple and the most widely adapted to cultivation in all climates, the most susceptible to the manipulations of chemical and mechanical processes, and the most universally adapted to ... production." Boyce, S.S. *Hemp.* Orange & Judd. New York NY. 1900

This volume contains practical and technical information useful to researchers, environmentalists, farmers, investors, students, teachers, cottage industries, multinational corporations and all sizes of business in between. When people regularly use hemp paper, wear hempen clothes and eat hemp-based foods, they will recognize the importance of fully restoring the hemp plant and will become empowered to take the initiative and bring it back. We take a common-sense look at the various applications and implications of the industrial and medical uses of cannabis, as well as issues of personal and social consumption. This approach places the issue in its real context, for reasonable formulation of hemp policies.

The text is designed to be read through, skipped around according to interest, or used as a reference. It is broken into three general sections. *Part I: Future Prosperity, Rooted in Our Past* is the broad vision of hemp in the historic and future human experience. *Part II: The Premier Plant of the Planet* deals with some of the practical aspects of utilizing hemp in the real world. *Part III: Beyond the Marijuana Smokescreen* is an excursion into an amazing aspect of civilization: How America was subverted and hemp suppressed on a global scale —and how we, the people, can still win it back.

Nonetheless, *Hemp: Lifeline to the Future* remains a work in progress. Curious, creative people will continue to explore and expand upon the many uses of our precious natural resources like hemp, so there will always be more information to add. To this end, we would like to hear from you about any information you have to add to our database regarding cannabis hemp.

When all these issues are held in perspective, there can be no doubt that hemp is, indeed, our lifeline to the future. It is time that we grasp this and make the most of this opportunity for new growth, for therein lies our best real hope.

Part I
—
Future Prosperity Rooted in the Past

HEMP
Lifeline to the Future

1

THE HOUSE THAT HEMP BUILT

This is the story of two very special species. One is a plant and the other is an animal. To understand this relationship, we must understand those involved. The plant is *cannabis sativa*, or hemp. The animal is *homo sapiens*, or human beings. The best way to see how hemp is intertwined with a biosustainable society is to visualize a day in a typical household in the not-too-distant future.

Hemp will be used in almost all the component parts of the house itself: the construction boards, insulation, finishes, paint and plumbing. Hemp is incorporated into the desk and all the papers in it, the clothes in the closet, the fabric of carpets and curtains, and all the plastic components of phone and entertainment systems, computers and accessories. Hemp biofuel provides the household's energy supply. You might say hemp has built the house and garage, and even put a car in it—complete with a tankful of gas and a bagful of groceries.

It's a long story that begins with simple vegetable cells and works its way to the height of technology and into 50,000 consumer and commercial products. We pick up our tale in everyday life.

A Day in the Life: The Morning

You wake up in the morning, shut off the alarm clock, rub your eyes and slip out of your cozy, hempen bed sheets and blankets and into a soft, warm hemp robe. The shower water is good and hot, and these new hemp towels are so soft, thick and absorbent.

What a wonderful day!

Open the window and take a deep breath. You notice how fresh the air is, blowing over the hempfields, scented with new flowers.

Over breakfast you can't help but notice how good the eggs are. Whatever they're feeding those chickens sure makes them tasty. You pick up the newspaper and leaf through it. There's a small notice that today's edition is printed on recycled hemp paper. It's about time! DEA investigators located and destroyed another illegal stockpile of chemical weapons. The FBI finally caught up with that illegal dumper who poured toxic waste into the nearby stream last month. Good riddance. Violent crime and property theft are at a record low since all those police resources have been diverted from prohibition enforcement to focus on serious crime. They could have done that long ago. Another forest is officially preserved for posterity. Excellent. When you stand up, you notice your leg is a little sore from that hike through the reforested zone yesterday. "Honey, can you hand me the cannabis balm out of the medicine cabinet," you ask. "And the antibiotic cannabis cream, too; I've got a few scratches here."

"Okay. Remember to take your edestin dietary supplements. And don't get home too late; you don't want the hemp nut loaf to dry out."

As you head out the door, you smile to remember how you only recently discovered you are allergic to synthetic fibers and had to have the carpets replaced with hemp weave. And you thought you had hay fever all those years! What a relief that turned out to be.

Out to the garage now. Those fiberboard beams are great, especially since they've been freshly varnished with nontoxic seed-oil sealant. Should you have used one of the color paint versions? No; it's a neat looking pattern with all those fibrous threads still visible through the lacquer—kind of high tech and natural at the same time.

You drive the car out of the garage and wave goodbye, then head down the road, past tall stands of hemp alternating with alfalfa, corn and other crops. It's great that the community industrial center is not too far away, yet you can still feel like you live out in the country. Since most of the car is made of lightweight re-fabricated vegetable matter instead of steel, it doesn't use much fuel, and that new hemp-ahol blend works great. What will they think of next?

The Afternoon's Business

Most of the morning and afternoon are spent meeting with a group of clients to review their proposal. They plan to convert an old steel mill and make PVC plumbing components, electrical insulation and fiber-optic cables out of recycled plastic and cellulose from that big new hemp processor they use at the re-opened textile mill. You're confident the project will be approved. After all, the plan is consistent with the local raw-material exchange programs, where waste products from one industry are used as raw materials at another operation located nearby. Those programs have really come on strong over the past few years. Looking over details of the reports is meticulous but interesting work.

You resolve a few minor technical problems, reprint the report on the laser printer and make a stack of photocopies. Now that the duplication equipment uses seed oil inks instead of toner, the type quality is as good as real printing. Since the proposal is still on the drawing board, you use blended hemp and recycled paper for copies today, saving the 100 percent hemp paper for the final version after the plan has been approved. That's when they will be archived in the permanent file, so you want to use paper that does not have to be treated with preservatives.

The Evening's Relaxation

You get home just in time for dinner—delicious, as usual.

Tomorrow is your turn to cook, so you start planning the menu now. Luckily, there are plenty of hemp sprouts ready for a salad and hempseed oil for the dressing. Your mother will be coming over, so you decide to pick up a packet of barbecue-roasted hemp seed for her to munch on, to help her digestion.

"Your cousin just got a job over at the textile mill, and they're opening up a new hempseed coffee shop near the civic center. Did you notice the neighbors installed a backyard biofuel unit for their garden clippings? Oh, by the way, we got the electric bill."

You decide to visit the herb garden, water the houseplants and have a nice, hot cup of hemp flower tea to relax before you look at it. Settled back in your soft hemp tow-upholstered chair, you open the bill. Just above the "hemp paper" symbol is the amount due. You breathe a sigh of relief. Not so bad since they decommissioned the nuclear reactor and converted it to use biomass fuel. The utility company saved so much money on transport and insurance that rates have actually gone down for the first time you can remember. They enclosed a self-congratulatory note about passing the savings on to you. That frees up a little more pocket money.

You take a little stroll out through the night to enjoy the cool air of the evening breeze. You hear birds and wildlife rustling through the woods and fields. Hard to believe the city is just over the hill there, across the "green belt" of farmland designed into the city plan. Tomorrow there's no presentation to make, so instead of driving you can bicycle into town to get some exercise and enjoy the view.

When you get back to the house, you notice the lights are dim. An incense-like fragrance drifts out from the bedroom. You freshen up in the bathroom and smile at the sexy music that's playing.

This, you tell yourself, is how life is meant to be. And if other people have different ideas about how to live, so be it.

After all, it's a free country.

2

THE MANY HISTORIES OF HEMP

"Agriculture is the foundation of manufactures, since the productions of nature are the materials of art," wrote historian Edward Gibbon in *Decline and Fall of the Roman Empire*.[1] There is no clearer case of the connection between agronomy and culture than that of cannabis hemp agriculture. While some may regard it as little more than a footnote in history, actually hemp has always been a primary element of world economics.[2]

The hemp plant is like a complex thread that weaves through the rich tapestry of time. It begins in prehistoric and ancient ages, runs through the millennia in Africa, Asia and Europe, and eventually winds its way to the Americas. It's been used for textiles, cordage, paper, seed oil, food, fuel and more.[3] Many and separate histories run concurrently—and occasionally intertwine. Women, religions, music, cultures, languages—all have special connections to hemp; the herb's medical legacy stretches back thousands of years. As Carl Sagan writes, "It would be wryly interesting if, in human history, the cultivation of 'marijuana' led generally to the invention of agriculture and thereby to civilization."[4]

Early Industrial History of Cannabis Sativa

The essence of manufacture is the transformation of material. So it was natural for people to seek a fiber plant to craft into products. The earliest civilizations sprouted along the banks of great rivers: the Tigris[5] and Euphrates in Mesopotamia, the Hwang-Ho in China, the Indus in India and the Nile in Egypt. The soil along these river banks was highly fertile and particularly suited for agriculture.

---

[1]Gibbon, Edward. *Decline & Fall of the Roman Empire*. Moses Hadas, ed. Fawcett Crest/Random House. New York NY. 1962. p. 8
[2]"It was also the material of great other works for which there was a very great demand ... as may be seen in Aulus, Gellius, Columella, Cato, Hesychius, Pliny, Titus Livius, Xenophon, Cinegius, Pollux, Catullus, Aetius, Paulus Aeginetus, etc. Since that time, have we not still extremely multiplied the uses of it, by paper & cartoons, the consumption of which is so very great?" Marcandier, M. *A Treatise on Hemp*. Edes & Gill. Boston MA. 1766. also Boyce, S.S. *Hemp*. Judd & Orange. New York NY. 1900. also Dewey, L. 'Hemp.' in *USDA Yearbook, 1913*. USGPO. Washington DC. 1914
[3]Other historical details are found in related topic sections of this book.
[4]Sagan, Carl. *The Dragons of Eden*. H&S Pub. London England. 1977
[5]Fabric that may be hemp, recovered near the headwaters of the Tigris from about 7500 BC, may have been used to cushion the handle of a harvesting tool. Bailey, M. 'Rag trade caught in time warp.' in *Manchester Observer*. Aug. 15, 1993

Hemp was the first plant known to have been cultivated. About 10,000 years ago, hemp industries appeared simultaneously in China and Eurasia for the production of a textile fiber.

The oldest relic of human industry is a trace of hemp fabric from about 8000 BC[6] in the "Cradle of Civilization" at Çatal Hüyük, ancient Mesopotamia, an area in modern Turkey. Archaeologists also unearthed an ancient village site on the Island of Taiwan, off the coast of mainland China, dating from about the same time period. Pottery fragments were found with sides decorated by pressing strips of hemp cord into the wet clay before it hardened. Also found were elongated rod-shaped tools, like those used for thousands of years to loosen cannabis fibers from their stems.[7]

Hemp agriculture and industries spread quickly around the world. The Egyptians spun hemp in the region of Badarian around 4000 BC,[8] but still used papyrus for paper. Mention of hemp is made in texts of the Babylonians, Persians, Hebrews and Chaldeans. Hemp again appears as fiber marks on pottery around 4000 BC from the Neolithic village of Pan P'o in Shensi Province, China.[9] The *Lu Shi*, a Chinese work of the Sung dynasty, contains the statement that in the 28th century BC, the mythic Emperor Shen Nung taught his people to cultivate *ma* for making hempen cloth. Its name occurs in the earliest Chinese caligraphy, designating a plant with two forms, male and female, used for fiber.[10]

During the Bronze Age, the Scythians probably introduced the textile and social use of the plant to Europe during their westward migration around 1500 BC, along with the long-handled cutting tool that is still used to harvest hemp, known as a *scythe*.

The Egyptians made a heiroglyph of a coiled up piece of rope that went through the Semitic and Greek characters to the Romans, who adapted it into the letter *H*.[11] The Akkadian root word for cannabis hemp –*an*– went East and up through India, wound over the Black Sea then back down through the Greek and Latin languages. When modern languages began to develop, these two ancient symbols for the plant merged into the French *chanvre* and the German *hanf*, which led to the English word *hemp*.

[6]*Columbia History of the World.* Harper & Row. New York NY. 1981. p. 54
[7]Old Stone Age, or Paleolithic times. Chang, K. *The Archeology of Ancient China.* Yale U Press. New Haven CT. 1968. pp. 111-112. also Kung, C.T. *Archeology in China.* U of Toronto Press. Toronto Canada. 1959. a:131
[8]Mercer, John. *The Spinner's Handbook.* Prism Press. Dorset England. 1978. p. 16
[9]Aldrich, Dr. Michael, et al. *High Times Encyclopedia of Recreational Drugs.* Stonehill Publishing. New York NY. 1978. pp. 116-144
[10]From about 500 AD. in Dewey, Lyster. 'Hemp.' in *USDA Yearbook, 1913.* US Government Printing Office. Washington DC.1914. pp. 288-291
[11]'History of the letter H.' in *World Book Encyclopedia.* Vol H. 1972. p. 1.

The Classical Era

According to the Greek "Father of History," Herodotus,[12] writing about 450 BC, the Scythians carried hemp with them when they rode into Europe from beyond the Caspian Sea. The world's "linen" has been made of hemp as often as flax. Herodotus stated that hemp cultivated in Thrace was used for fine cloth as well as ropes:[13]

> There is in that country *kannabis* growing, both wild and cultivated. Fuller and taller than flax, the Thracians use it to make garments very like linen. Unless one were a Master of Hemp, one could not tell which it was. Those who have never seen hemp would think it was flax.

A cargo of hemp stalk was dredged up from a Carthaginian galley which foundered on a shallow reef off Sicily and sank around 300 BC. These plant stalks were still identifiable after being in the salt waters of the Mediterranean for over 2300 years.[14]

The Romans utilized much hemp[15] and periodically issued instructions on how to farm it, so as to create a domestic supply.[16] Nonetheless, Rome imported a substantial amount of hemp, especially from the city of Sura in Babylonia.[17] Hemp was used in all Roman ships, adorned their great temples and theaters and covered their streets and public places. Their laws and annals were sometimes written on hempen cloth.[18] They left hemp ropes and such behind in the ruins of their vast empire's scattered forts and settlements. A well rope believed to be hemp was taken from the Roman fort on the Antonine Wall at Bar Hill, Dumbartonshire, Scotland, occupied between 140-180 AD.[19] In sites in eastern England, pollen and macrofossil data indicate the soaking, or *retting*, of hemp prior to fiber extraction around 400 AD.

Meanwhile, paper had been developed in China using a "mixture of flax and hemp."[20] The oldest paper documents are Buddhist text from the first century BC, made of a mixture of bark and old rags,

---

[12]Roman statesman & writer Cicero gave him this title.

[13]Herodotus. *Histories IV*. University Press. Cambridge MA. 1906. pp. 74-76

[14]Morphological exam by archaeologist Honor Frost. in *Natural History*. 1987. also Latimer, D. 'Crimes of the Ancient Mariners.' in *High Times*. May 1988. p. 21-22

[15]"Packthread, girths, ladders, bridges, trousers, cloaths, helmets, bucklers, armour, urns, baskets, cabling & tackling for ships etc." Marcandier. *op. cit.*

[16]"Besides the use formerly made of hemp, for cloth, thread & cordage, it was also the material of other great works, for which there was a very great demand, such as fishing lines & nets, hunting nets & gins [machinery]." Pliny the Elder (Caius Plinius Secundus). *Natural History*. 23-79 AD. 19.57

[17]Frank, T. *Economic Survey of Ancient Rome*. Pageant. Patterson NJ. 1959. 4:131

[18]Sackett & Hobbs. *Hemp; A war crop*. Mason & Hanger. New York NY. 1942

[19]Godwin, H. 'Ancient Cultivation of Hemp.' in *Antiquity*. no 41. 1967. pp. 42-49. also Edwards & Whittington. 'Palynological evidence for the growing of cannabis sativa L. in medieval & historical Scotland.' in *Inst. British Geography*. 1990. p. 60

[20]Blum. A. *On the Origin of Paper*. R.R. Bowker Co. New York NY. 1934. p. 16

primarily hemp. The Chinese developed the first printed book in 770 AD, a book of prayers called *Dharani*, "composed 100 percent of hemp ... of a light tan colour, as would naturally be the case with unbleached hemp as the material."[21]

In Japan, the aristocrats wore silk. But until the introduction of cotton in the ninth century AD, hemp, or *asa*, was the cloth used by everybody else.[22] Hemp was the primary material in clothes, bedding, mats and nets. Hempen clothes were worn especially during formal and religious ceremonies because of the plant's traditional association with purity. Gifts of hemp were traditionally sent as wedding gifts by the groom's family to the prospective bride's family, to show that they accepted her.[23]

Back in Europe, the French queen Arnegunde was buried in Paris around 570 AD in a tomb draped in a hempen shroud.[24] Pieces of cloth and fishing line made from hemp have also been discovered in Viking graves in Norway, and cannabis seeds have been found in the remains of Viking ships that date back to 850.[25]

Following the decline of the Roman Empire and the onset of the Dark Ages, the use of cannabis continued to spread throughout the Mediterranean with Islam, beginning in the eighth century. In 1150 Moslems established the first Western paper mill, using hemp, in the city Xativa[26] in present day Denia in the province of Alicante, Spain. Soon mills were also located in Valencia and Toledo.[27]

Threading Through Post-Medieval Europe

Pollen records from two sites in Fife, eastern Scotland, reveal that hemp cultivation was an important part of the local farming economy during medieval and later historical times.[28] Up to the time of the Black Death, flax seems to have been practically unknown in England, although the use of hemp was almost universal.[29]

In Italy, hemp was *quello delle centro operazioni*, "the substance of a hundred operations." In the 15th century, girls broke hemp stalks and pulled the fibers out, preparing hemp for the craft in-

---

[21]Hunter, D. *History & Technique of an Ancient Craft.* Knopf. NY NY. 1947. p. 70
[22]Sackett & Hobbs. op. cit.
[23]Joya, M. *Things Japanese.* Tokyo News Service. Tokyo Japan. 1963. p. 23-24
[24]Werner, J. 'Frankish Royal Tombs in the Cathedrals of Cologne & Saint-Denis.' in *Antiquity.* no 38. 1964. pp. 201-216
[25]Godwin. op. cit. pp. 44-47
[26]Note the linguistic connection to "sativa."
[27]Abel, E. *Marihuana: The first 12,000 years.* Plenum Pr. New York NY. 1980. p. 9
[28]Spatial & temporal variation in the palaeo-ecological record may have resulted from differences in land & labor availability, market factors or, indirectly, climactic change. Godwin, H. 'Pollen-analytic evidence for the cultivation of cannabis in England.' in *Review of Palaeobotany & Paynology.* no 4. 1967. pp. 71-80
[29]Rogers, Thorold. *Economic Interpretation of History.* p. 281

dustries.[30] Columbus's ships each carried over 80 tons of hemp rigging and sails. Hempseed may have come to the New World on his ship. It certainly made its way as a crop from Spain to Chile by at least 1545.[31] With the Moslems and Jews driven out of Spain and the New World under Spanish control, King Philip in 1564 ordered that cannabis, or *cáñamo*, be grown throughout his domain to provide for his ships and textiles.[32]

It was not until the beginning of the 16th century that the materials composing various canvas and linen goods began to be specified. After that we find frequent mention of "hempen," "hempen cloth," "hempen table cloth," "hempen towels," and so forth. Untold varieties of canvas are mentioned for windmills and ship sails, for altar cloths, fine napkins, sheets, meal bags, horse blankets, flags and so forth.[33] French philosopher Rabelais wrote of hemp, "Without it, how could water be drawn from the well? What would scribes, copyists, secretaries and writers do without it? Would not official documents and rent-rolls disappear? Would not the noble art of printing perish?"[34]

The "Golden Age" of the Netherlands was the 16th and 17th centuries. Much of her prosperity came from the shipping that passed through her ports, sustained by a strong hemp, or *hennep*, industry. One region boasted at least 28 *hennipkloppers*, or windmills, used to process the hemp crop.[35] The power of the wind was captured by sails drawn over the wooden frames of the mill's four blades. They used a fabric known as *canefas*, derived from the Latin *cannabis* and leading to the English *canvas*. Other wind and water mills were used to press oil from the seeds, and so on. Such mills were also common in Germany to process *hanf*.[36]

In the 1580s came this British farming rhyme:[37]

Now pluck up thy hempe, and go beat out the seed,
and afterward water it, as ye see need.
But not in the river where cattle should drinke,
for poisoning them and the people with stinke.

[30]Lane, F.C. 'The Rope Factory & Hemp Trade in the 15th & 16th Centuries.' in *Journal of Economic & Business History*. no 4. 1932. p. 834
[31]Dewey. op. cit. pp. 288-291
[32]Herer, Jack. *Hemp & the Marijuana Conspiracy: The Emperor Wears No Clothes*. HEMP Publishing. Van Nuys CA. 1991. p. 42
[33]Moore, Brent. *The Hemp Industry In Kentucky, A Study of the Past, the Present & the Possibilities*. Press of James E. Hughes. Lexington KY. 1905. pp. 9, 11
[34]Rabelais, Francois. *The Histories of Gargantua & Pantagruel*. c. 1550. in Thompson, W. *At the Edge of History*. Harper & Row. New York NY. 1971. p. 124
[35]Goudsbloom, J. in Husslage, G. *Wind Molens*. Uitgeterij Heijnis nv. Amsterdam Holland. 1965. p. 114
[36]Weber, Friedrich Wilhelm. *Die Geschichte de pfälzischen Mühlen besonderer Art*. Verlag Franz Arbogast. Kaiserslautern Germany. 1981. pp. 215-229
[37]Tusser, T. *Five-Hundred Points of Good Husbandrie*. London England. 1580. p. 152

Soon, Britain's mighty navy and merchant marine fleets were consuming vast amounts of hemp.[38] This played a strategic role during the Napoleonic Wars, when access to global sea lanes was linked to the hemp fields of Russia and America. Britain blockaded France and controlled access to both the Atlantic and Mediterranean by its grip on Gibraltar. Napoleon sold the fledgling United States the Louisiana Territory to raise revenues, then struck a deal with the Baltic States to deprive England of its vital supply of hemp. After Russia failed to live up to this agreement to stop selling hemp to England, Napoleon made a desperate move. He invaded Russia. The severe winter destroyed his once mighty land forces, leading ultimately to Napoleon's own downfall and defeat.[39]

To protect their colonial sources in 1777, Spain sent hemp experts to various outposts throughout America and the Philippines to teach the fine points of growing and preparing hemp for market.[40] When Spain opened the Mississippi to international trade in 1795, hemp and hempen goods were specifically mentioned among the articles which were to pass freely.[41] Swedish royal botanist Carl Linnaeus[42] grew cannabis on his window sill to scientifically confirm the sexuality of plants. The Italian Trade Commission list of 1930s factories devoted to hemp manufacturing included over 20 Italian "manufacturers of hemp fabric for various purposes."[43] Italy did important research on hemp as a non-wood paper source in the 1970s and exported hemp into the 1980s. In Europe there is an official subsidy on hemp, reaffirmed by a 1986 decision that it would be anti-competitive to disallow hemp production from the market.

A Long & Distinguished Medical Career

Medical cannabis has been ubiquitous in human history, and its use was advised in virtually all ancient and medieval medicinal texts.[44] This would doubtless be true today, too, and its use as medicine much more common if not for political reasons.[45]

---

[38]Russell, Richard. *The Rope-maker's Guide; or a complete key to the art of rope-making: comprised in a set of tables & instructions. ... for the use of His Majesty's royal navy.* Heather & Dale. London England. 1804

[39]Crosby, A. Jr. *America, Russia, Hemp & Napoleon.* Ohio State U Press. OH. 1965.

[40]Hill, H. 'The Ganja Problem in Singapore.' in *International Criminal Police Review.* no. 23. 1968. p. 211

[41]Moore. op. cit.

[42]Linnaeus invented genus/species classification in 1753 & listed *cannabis sativa* in *Species Plantarum.* Aldrich. *op. cit.*

[43]Six sources of hemp, 7 "manufacturers of hemp canvas for camping/beach tents or sails, 7 manufacturer of hemp fabric for clothing," & over 12 "manufacturers of hemp fabrics for clothing & furnishings."

[44]Dewey. op. cit.

[45]"The chief opposition to the drug rests on a moral and political, & not a toxicological foundation." *Merck Manual of Diagnosis & Therapy.* Rahway, NJ. 1992

Hempseed and flower-tops were frequently recommended for difficult childbirth, menstrual cramps, rheumatism and convulsions, earaches, as well as fevers, dysentery, epilepsy and insomnia, also to soothe nervous tension, stimulate appetite and as an analgesic and aphrodisiac.[46] It is described in the *Pen Ts'ao* of the mythic Chinese Emperor Shen Nung, compiled during the Han dynasty[47] based on traditions handed down for millennia. It classified *ta-ma* among the "superior" immortality elixirs. The female plant was said to possess *yin* energy (as opposed to the male plant's *yang*) and was prescribed for "female weakness," along with rheumatism, beri-beri, malaria, constipation, *gout* and absent-mindedness, among other ailments.[48]

The 16th century BC Egyptian Ebbers papyrus records medical use of cannabis.[49] One of the earliest surgeons, Sushruta, recognized that cannabis dried up mucous membranes and prescribed it as an antiphlegmatic during the third century BC in India. A tomb near Jerusalem yielded physical evidence that cannabis smoke had been used to help a young girl survive an unsuccessful childbirth in the fourth century AD.[50]

Roman Emperor Nero's surgeon, Dioscorides, labelled the plant *cannabis sativa*, the name it still bears. He praised it for making "the stoutest cords" and for its medicinal properties.[51] Half a millennium later, a revised codex of Dioscorides' *Constantinopolitanus* gave us the first botanical drawing of the plant.[52] Biblical scholars concluded in 1860 that "the gall and vinegar, or myrrhed wine, offered to our Saviour immediately before his crucifixion, was in all probability a preparation of Indian hemp."[53] In the second century, another Roman, Pliny the Elder, prescribed hempseed for constipated farm animals, the herb for earache, and hemp root, boiled in water, to ease cramped joints, gout and burns.[54] His contemporary, Galen, wrote that it "eliminates farting and dehydrates. ... Some squeeze its juice when fresh and use it as an analgesic for ear pains," and adds a

---

[46]Mikuriya, Dr. Tod. *Marijuana: Medical Papers, 1839-1972.* MediComp Press. Oakland CA. 1973

[47]206 BC-220 AD

[48]*Lu Shi*, a Chinese work of the Sung dynasty from about 500 AD refers back to Shen Nung. op. cit. p. 288. Nung described cannabis c. 2737 BC, but no original text survives. Schofield, M. *The Strange Case of Pot.* Penguin Books. Middlesex, England. 1971. p 17. also see Abel. op. cit. p. 10-12

[49]Mechoulam, R. *Cannabinoids as Therapeutic Agents.* CRC. Boca Raton. 1986

[50]Zlas, Stark, et al. 'Early medical use of cannabis.' in *Nature.* May 20, 1993. p. 215

[51]Dioscorides. *Materia Medica.* 70 AD. 3.165

[52]*Anicia Juliana.* 512

[53]Ohio State Medical Society. *Transcript of 15th Annual Meeting.* White Sulphur Springs OH. June 12-14, 1860. pp. 75-100

[54]Plinius Secundus, Caius. *De Historia Natura.* 20.97

culinary note: "There are some who fry and consume the seed together with other desserts."[55]

Bhang was classed as a seed oil in ancient Persia and valued in treating miscarriages. It is described in the pharmacopeias of the Persian doctor Avicenna. Islamic medical texts use *qinnab* as the botanical term for the plant.[56] Cannabis is discussed in the 13th-century Moslem works of Ibn Beitar, and again in the 16th-century Chinese *Pen Ts'ao Kang Mu* of Li Shih-chen.

Africans in Southern Rhodesia have long used the cannabis plant, combined with others, to treat malaria, blackwater fever, dysentery, blood poisoning, anthrax and as "war medicine." Sotho women smoke the herb during childbirth and feed children ground-up seed with bread or mealie-pap for weaning.[57] The Hottentot have not only used the plant for snakebites but apparently as a mood elevator for centuries. The one reference to possible maternal problems from cannabis smoking was a vague observation by a traveller that some Eastern Ugandan tribes forbade married women to smoke because of "some evil effect it is said to have upon her or her child, should she be about to become a mother."[58]

Portuguese physician Garcia da Orta practiced medicine in India, grew cannabis, and wrote a scientific accounting in 1563.[59] The *Compleat Herbal,* compiled in 1645, recommends the herb for hot or dry cough, jaundice and ague, fluxes, colic, worms and earwigs, inflammations, gout, "knotty joints," hip pains and burns. The *New English Dispensatory* of 1764 recommends boiling cannabis roots and applying them to skin inflammations.[60]

The plant is a common folk remedy for the swelling of joints, childbirth, inflammation, fever, and to prevent convulsions and cure jaundice and rheumatism. In Mexico, leaves soaked in alcohol are wrapped around aching, arthritic joints. In Poland, Russia and Lithuania, peasant farmers inhaled the vapors of smoldering hemp seeds thrown onto hot stones to relieve toothache.[61]

The *Edinburgh New Dispensatory* of 1794 notes that the water in which stalks are retted was "violently poisonous, and to produce

[55]Galen, Claudius. *De Facultatibus Alimentorum.* 100.49

[56]Avicenna, 980-1037 AD. *Banj* was popular parlance for both hemp & hembane, while *hashish* originally simply meant "grass" or "herb."

[57]Watt, J.M. & Breyer-Brandwijk, M.G. *The medicinal & poisonous plants of southern Africa.* E&S Livingstone. Edinburgh Scotland. 1932

[58]Purvis, J.P. *Through Uganda to Mt. Elgon.* Fisher Unwin. London England. 1909. pp. 336-337

[59]DaOrta, Garcia. *Colloquies on the Simples & Drugs of India.* (translation of original. 1563.) Henry Southern. London England. 1913

[60]Abel. op. cit. p. 119

[61]Benet, S. 'Early Diffusion & Folk Uses of Hemp.' in *Cannabis & Culture.* Rubin, V. ed. Mouton. The Hague, Netherlands. 1975. pp. 43, 46

its effects as soon as drunk," but that the oil from the seeds is added to milk to form an emulsion useful for treating coughs, "heat of urine" (venereal disease), and "incontinence of urine."[62] It closes on this note: "Although the seeds only have hitherto been principally in use, yet other parts of the plant seem to be more active, and may be considered as deserving further attention."

Culpeper's *Complete Herbal* summarizes the known medical effect of cannabis, and says in part:[63]

> Being boiled in milke and taken, helps such as have a dry, hot cough. ... Very good to kill the worms in men and beasts; and the juice dropped into the ears kills worms in them, and draws forth earwigs or other living creatures gotten into them. ... Emulsion or decoction of the seed stalls lasks and continual fluxes, eases the colic and allays the troublesome humours in the bowels and stays bleeding at the mouth, nose and other places. ... Decoction of the root allays inflammation of the head or other parts; the herb itself, or the distilled water thereof, doth the like. The decoction of the roots eases the pains of the gout, the hard humours of knots in the joints, the pains and shrinking of the sinews and the pains of the hips. The fresh juice mixed with a little oil and butter, is good for any place that has been burnt with fire, being thereto applied.

A Modern Medicine for the Scientific Era

When Napoleon invaded Egypt, French doctors were sent to North Africa and learned about the medical value of cannabis. Physician Louis Aubert-Roche published his 1840 book on using hashish to treat plague and typhoid fever. Psychologist Jacques-Joseph Moreau de Tours "invented" modern psychopharmacology and psychotomimetic drug treatment in 1845 with studies on datura and hashish, and documented both physical and mental benefits.[64]

The British East India Company surgeon in Calcutta, William B. O'Shaughnessy, introduced the telegraph to India and cannabis to Western medicine with a monograph on the topic.[65] Fresh out of Edinburgh Medical School Scotland, he investigated Indian medicine carefully, experimenting with it on himself, animals and patients, and recommending *gunjah* for a great variety of therapeutic purposes. He established his reputation by successfully relieving the pain of rheumatism and stilling the convulsions of an infant with this strange new drug. O'Shaughnessy's most spectacular success came when he quelled the wrenching muscle spasms of tetanus and rabies

[62]*Edinburgh New Dispensatory*. W. Creech Co. Edinburgh Scotland. 1794. p. 126
[63]Culpeper, N. *Complete Herbal*. Richard Evans Co. London England. 1814. p. 91
[64]Moreau, J.J. 'Lypemanie avec Stupeur: Tendence á la demence, traitement par l'extrait Guerison, resineux de cannabis indica.' in *Gazette des Hopitaux Civils et Militaires*. vol. 30. 1857. p. 391
[65]O'Shaughnessy, W.B. 'On the Preparation of Indian Hemp, or Gunjah.' in *Translations of the Medical & Physical Society of Calcutta*. v. 8:2. 1842. pp. 421-461

with the fragrant resin. He gave some to Peter Squire, whose pharmacy began to prepare "Squires Extract" commercially. In 1857 the Smith Brothers of Edinburgh obtained a highly active extract of indica that became the basis for innumerable tinctures marketed thereafter, and well into this century.

In 1839, the homeopathy journal *American Provers' Union* published the first of many reports on the effects of cannabis.[66] The *United States Dispensatory* first listed cannabis in 1854, along with a cautionary note on the variable potency of the commercially available preparations. It read in part,[67]

> In morbid states of the system, it has been found to produce sleep, to allay spasm, to compose nervous inquietude and to relieve pain. ... Complaints to which it has been specially recommended are neuralgia, gout, tetanus, hydrophobia, epidemic cholera, convulsions, chorea [spasticity], hysteria, mental depression, insanity and uterine hemorrhage. Dr. Alexander Christison, of Edinburgh, has found it to have the property ... of hastening and increasing the contractions of the uterus in delivery. ... For this ... it acts very quickly, and without anesthetic effect.

By 1896, several new cannabis derivatives were developed, among them cannabin, cannabindon, cannabine and cannabinon. Cannabis was also included along with other drugs in various preparations, such as Brown Sequard's Antineuralgic Pills. At least 30 different pharmaceutical preparations contained cannabis. Among the companies manufacturing these over-the-counter remedies were Eli Lilly (Dr. Brown Sedative Tablets, Syrup Tolu Compound, Syrup Lobelia), Parke Davis (Casadein, Veterinary Colic Mixture, Utroval), and Squibb Co. (Corn Collodium, Chlorodyne [a stomach remedy]).[68]

Sir John Russell Reynolds, during his 30 years of experience as Queen Victoria's personal physician, found it useful for menstrual cramps, dysmenorrhea, migraine, neuralgia, epileptoid convulsions and senile insomnia. He wrote in 1890, "When pure and administered carefully, it is one of the most valuable medicines we possess."[69] A cannabis extract was reported to be *"Par excellence*, the remedy for ... controlling menorrhagia (excessive menstrual bleeding) that is a valuable aid to diagnosis, in cases in which it is uncer-

66Allen, T.F. ed. *Encyclopedia of Pure Materia Medica.* Boericke & Tafel. New York NY. 1875. p. 448
67Wood, G.B. & Bache, F. *Dispensatory of the United States.* Lippincott, Brambo & Co. Philadelphia PA. 1854. p. 339
68Sassman, M. 'Cannabis Indica in Pharmaceuticals.' in *Journal of the Medical Society of NJ.* vol. 35. 1938. pp. 51-52.
69Reynolds, J.R. 'On the Therapeutical Uses & Toxic Effects of Cannabis Indica.' in *Lancet.* vol. 1. 1890. pp. 637-638

tain whether an early abortion may or may not have occurred."[70]
Other conditions for which the drug was often prescribed in the late
19th century were loss of appetite, inability to sleep, migraine
headache, pain, involuntary twitching, excessive coughing, and
treatment of withdrawal symptoms from morphine and alcohol addiction.[71] Between 1840 and 1900 at least 100 major articles were
published recommending cannabis as a therapeutic agent for various
health problems and disorders.[72] By the 20th century, it was
common in corn plasters, veterinary medicine and nonintoxicating
medicaments.[73] Eli Lilly and Parke Davis, as a cooperative venture,
developed a very potent indica strain called *cannabis Americana*. In
early 20th century pharmacology texts, "extracts of cannabis were
about the only compounds that could be used for pain relief and
anxiety," noted one researcher.[74]

During the period 1964 to 1965, Dr. Rafael Mechoulam of Hebrew University in Jerusalem, Israel, isolated pure delta-1-trans-
tetrahydrocannabinol and identified it as the principal psychoactive
and medicinal ingredient. THC represented a new class of
compounds structurally different from any other drugs.[75]

In the 1970s researchers at Pfiser Laboratories, a Connecticut-
based pharmaceutical drug company working with synthetic analogs
of THC, claimed to have produced analgesics 100 times more potent
than cannabis. These cannabinoids also had that much stronger a
"high" connected with them. The company eventually dropped research because of this effect and the fact that opiates already controlled the heavy-sedation market.[76]

In 1973 Tod Mikuriya, M.D., compiled major medical works on
cannabis into the book *Marijuana: Medical Papers, 1839–1972*.[77]

America's leading cannabis researchers attended the Asilomar
Conference in November 1975, sponsored by the National Institute
of Drug Abuse (NIDA). The seminars and compiled reports indicated that cannabis was destined to be one of the world's major
medicines within a decade. The next year, Dr. Sidney Cohen and
Richard Stillman produced a hopeful prognosis for using cannabis
in numerous medical applications, *The Therapeutic Potential of Mar-*

[70]Batho, Dr R. 'Cannabis Indica.' in *British Medical Journal*. May 26, 1883. p. 1002
[71]Abel. *op. cit.* p. 169
[72]Walton, R. *Marijuana: America's New Drug Problem*. Lippincott. Phila. PA. 1938
[73]Musto, David F., M.D. *The American Disease: Origins of Narcotic Control*.
Colonial Press. Clinton MA. 1973. pp. 216-217
[74]Allyn Howlett, pharmacology professor at St. Louis U Medical School. in Wallach,
Leah. 'The Chemistry of Reefer Madness.' in *Omni*. August 1989. p. 18
[75]Aldrich. *op. cit.* pp. 140-143
[76]Wallach. *op. cit.*
[77]Mikuriya. *op. cit.*

ijuana.[78] To date 30 or 40 cannabinoids have been identified, along with many congeners, synthetics and metabolites. In 1990, when special receptor sites uniquely suited for THC were charted in the human brain, the director of the National Institute of Mental Health, Lewis Judd, announced, "Now scientists may be able to develop (synthetic) drugs that possess marijuana's positive medicinal effects without its negative effects."[79] In December 1992 a simple protein binder was identified that attaches to these sites.

A Cultural History of the Cannabis Herb

No one knows how it first happened. Perhaps one cold night a group of primitive people huddled together in a small enclosure for warmth. They ran out of wood and tossed dried hemp plants into the fire, and the smoke's effect was felt in the course of the night.

However it started, throughout human history, hundreds of millions of people around the globe have put their brain receptors in touch with cannabis alkaloids—some using it as medicine, some as sacrament; others for fun. Many diverse cultures of people share this common link with related words and customs.

The origin of social and religious cannabis use seems to have been in Central Asia. The name *bhanga* occurs in the Hindu Sanskrit philosophical text, the *Atharvavéda,* around 1400 BC. Most of the time, people have referred to hemp flowers and leaves as cannabis indica, sometimes simply called *Indian hemp.* It offers an amazing effect: a symbiotic link that heals the body and expands the mind. Several strains of cannabis sativa also offer this benefit. Cannabis use has been integral to many of the world's cultures. It has also, when convenient, served as an excuse for political and social persecution of ethnic groups in intolerant societies. Attempts to eradicate these distinct cultures by arbitrarily prohibiting the use of a valued plant are genocide.[80]

Cuneiform descriptions of cannabis that were found in Babylonian Emperor Ashurbanipal's 650 BC library "are generally regarded as obvious copies of much older texts," says Dr. Robert Walton. They "project the origin of *hashish* back to the earliest beginnings of history."[81] Around 1980, etymologists at Hebrew Uni-

78Cohen, Dr. Sydney, Stillman, Richard, ed. *The Therapeutic Potential of Marijuana.* Plenum Press. New York NY. 1976
79"... intoxicated feeling, disorientation & impaired perception & memory." Booth, W. 'Marijuana receptor exists in brain.' in *Washington Post.* Aug. 9, 1990.
80Among 5 definitions are "deliberately inflicting on (an ethnic, cultural, etc.) group conditions of life calculated to bring about its physical destruction in whole or in part." *UN Genocide Convention.* in *The Nation.* NY. Oct. 19, 1992. p. 432
81Brecher, Edward M. & the editors of Consumer Reports. *Licit & Illicit Drugs.* The Consumers Union Report. Little Brown & Co. 1972. pp. 397-398

versity in Jerusalem confirmed that cannabis is mentioned in the Bible by name: *kineboisin* (also spelled *kannabosm*). This occurs in a list of measured ingredients for "an oil of holy ointment, an ointment compound after the art of apothecary" to be smeared on the head. It was mistranslated in King James' version as "calamus."[82]

The original "Johnny Marijuanaseeds" were the Scythians, proto-Turkish nomads who wandered the steppes of present-day Cossack Russia in great ox-wagon trains. Herodotus said they invaded Thrace and Europe. He described one of their activities:[83]

> After a burial, those involved have to purify themselves, which they do in this way: First they soap and wash their heads. Then to cleanse their bodies, they make a little tent, fixing three sticks in the ground, tied together and tightly covered with felt. Inside a dish is placed, with red-hot stones and some hemp seeds. The Scythians take *kannabis* seed, creep in under the felts and throw it on the red-hot stones. It smolders and sends up such billows of steam-smoke that no Greek vapor bath can surpass it. The Scythians howl with joy in these vapor-baths.

Both men and women consumed cannabis. A smoking apparatus like Herodotus described was excavated from prehistoric Scythian tomb-barrows in the Siberian Altai Mountains.[84] Two sets of implements found next to an ornately tattooed male corpse and a mummified female body included a copper cauldron, censer and leather medicine bag containing hemp seeds from about the fourth century BC. Botanists identified them as cannabis.[85] Four hundred years later, Plutarch wrote that Thracians still threw hemp tops (which looked like oregano) into the fires after the meal, inhaled the fumes deeply, became drunk and finally fell asleep.[86]

In medieval Asia it was given colorful Hindu nicknames like *ganja* (sweet smelling), *vijayá* (victorious) and *siddhi* (that which bestows magic power). Spiced bhang milkshakes were consecrated to the goddess Kali and drunk in her honor. Bhang drinks and sweetmeats are still used on festive occasions by all classes. Ganja made only from cultivated female flower-tops is preferred for religious purposes or simply to please the senses.

A 15th-century document refers to bhang as being "light-hearted" and lists among its virtues stringency, heat, the capacity to "remove wind and phlegm," as well as inspiring mental powers, ex-

---

[82]Exodus 30:23. also Latimer. op. cit.
[83]Herodotus op. cit. pp. 74-76
[84]About 18 inches high, with 6 sticks, not 3. The seeds found were c. ruderalis.
[85]Rudenko, S.I. *Frozen Tombs of Siberia*. UC Press. Berkeley CA. 1970. p. 90
[86]Plutarch. 'Of the Names of Rivers & Mountains, & of such things ...' in *Essays & Miscellanies*. Simplin, Marshall, Hamilton, Kent & Co. London England. vol. 5

citability and speech. In a 17th-century Indian text, the *Rajvallabha*, cannabis is described in similarly glowing terms:[87]

> Indra's food is acid, produces infatuation and destroys leprosy. It creates vital energy, increases mental powers and internal heat, corrects irregularities of the phlegmatic humor and is an *elixir vitae*. ... Inasmuch as it is believed to give victory in the three worlds and to bring delight to the king of gods [Shiva], it was called victorious. This desire-fulfilling drug was believed to have been obtained by men on earth for the welfare of all people.
> To those who use it regularly, it begets joy and diminishes anxiety.

A Moslem-Arab History of Cannabis

While the discovery of how to sift the resin out of harvested and cured cannabis flowers and compact it into hashish has been lost to antiquity, the art of rubbing the resin off living plants to produce *charas* was developed around 1000 AD by Islamic Sufis.[88] The Sufis stayed above the fray of schismatic Islam into Shia and Sunni, emphasizing scholarship and non-violence (including vegetarianism in imitation of Prophet Mohammed's diet-style). They, like Jewish Essenes and Christian Gnostics, considered direct and personal ecstatic union with the Supreme Being in divine love the real standard of religious life. [No wonder charas proved to be a sacramental ingredient of their culture!] Charas is still most popular in Islamic areas of Sufi influence, like Afghanistan, Pakistan, Kashmir, Nepal and other Himalayan kingdoms.

Mohammed's teachings prohibit alcohol,[89] but cannabis is allowed[90] — a cultural distinction between Moslems and alcohol-consuming Europeans. Islam adopted many earlier Roman customs, such as public bath houses and use of hemp for industry and medicine. In keeping with the medieval church's war on all things Islamic, Pope Innocent VIII condemned bathing as witchdraft and issued a papal fiat in 1484 proclaiming hashish use as a "Satanic mass."[91] In 1492, the last of the Moslems were driven from Spain. The public bath houses were shut down and cannabis was suppressed by the Inquisition.

---

[87]Grierson, G. 'On References to the Hemp Plant Occurring in Sanskrit & Hindi Literature." in *Indian Hemp Drugs Commission Report*. vol. 3. Simla India. 1894. p. 247

[88]Latimer. op. cit.

[89]"Satan seeketh to sow dissension & hatred among you by means of wine & lots, & to divert you from remembering God, & from prayer; will ye not therefore abstain from them? Obey God." *Koran*, chapter 5

[90]"Forbid not the good things which God has allowed you; ... that which is lawful & good." *Koran*, ch. 5

[91]DePasssquale, A. 'Farmacognosia della *Canape Indiana*.' in *Estratto dai Lavori dell'Institute di Farmacognosia della Universita di Messina*. Italy. v. 5. 1967. p. 24

Cannabis was, indeed, linked to Islam. Use of hashish became pervasive and popular, along with the baths and gardens that typified Moslem luxury in Asia, Africa and Europe. The shape of pipe bowls discovered in the Alhambra palaces of Granada, Spain[92] suggest that inhabitants of these castles smoked cannabis resin in pipes like those still seen in present-day Morocco.

The *al-Mukhassas* of Ibn Sidah[93] offers clear proof that smoking resin was commonplace, both for pleasure and to combat seasickness. The Cordoban fleet was the master of the western Mediterranean and ruled the Atlantic from the coasts of the Rio de Oro to Brittany.[94] In the words of a Turkish poet, cannabis was "the friend of the poor, the Dervishes and the men of knowledge, that is, all who are not blessed with earthly goods and social power." In other words, those most easily victimized by tyrants! As such, cannabis and its devotees were subjected to periodic persecutions, especially in Egypt.

Traders visited Ethiopia and carried home a piece of smoking paraphernalia for which the human lung has been ever grateful: the water pipe, or hookah. Smoking cannabis became closely associated with drinking coffee. A medieval Sufi tale holds that a Lebanese mountain man first taught the women of Tripoli how to brew coffee by erecting his coffeepot on a tripod over the bowl of his long pipe.

Drugs and spices, including cannabis, were made into chewy medicinal confections called *ma'joun*; hundreds of recipes are still passed along in the Arab world.[95] Customs surrounding the social use of the herb in modern Morocco appear to be of a secular nature, in contrast with those of the holy men of India who use cannabis as a religious sacrament.[96]

An African History of Cannabis

Pygmies in the equatorial forest believe they have "smoked hemp since the beginning of time."[97] Some Pygmy tribes have domesticated only hemp.[98] Cannabis smoking appears to have been common and widespread throughout Africa for ages. Most tribal histories have never been written down. But "earth smoking,"

---

[92]*Al-Andalus: The Art of Islamic Spain.* Metropolitan Museum of Art. New York NY. 1992. ISBN 0-87099-637-1. pp. 177-178
[93]Murcia Spain. Died in 1064AD/AH458
[94]*Al-Andalus. op. cit.*
[95]The secret was shared by thousands of Sufis, esp. Haydari & Qalandari sects. Cherniak, Lawrence. *Great Books of Hashish Vol. 1.*
[96]Carstairs, G.M. 'Daru & Bhang: Cultural factors in the choice of intoxicant.' in *Quarterly Journal of Studies on Alcohol.* 1954. vol. 15:2. p. 228
[97]Watt & Breyer-Brandwijk. *op. cit.*
[98]Sagan. op. cit. p. 191. also in *High Times.* April 1991. p. 40

building up a mound of clay and sucking smoke directly through a hole in the mound, is an ancient custom on the continent.

The connection to Indo-European cultures is evident in the variations on the words bhang and *bangi*, such as *mbange* and *lubange*, that are common among Bantu- and Swahili-speaking east African tribes. As cannabis penetrated the interior, its name was transformed. In central Africa the sound was reversed into *chamba, riamba* or *diamba*, eventually reaching the west coast of Angola with these names. To the south, the Sotho call it *matokwane* or *lebake*, titles that also worked their way west. To the Zulus, whose gourd water pipes are justly famed, it is mighty *ntsangu*.[99] Young Zulu warriors under the "exciting stimulation" of *dagga* were said to be capable of "accomplishing hazardous feats."[100]

Two ceramic pipe bowls from about 1320 AD excavated near Lake Tana, Ethiopia, contained cannabis residue.[101] One of the first European books about Africa to mention cannabis was in 1609 by Dominican priest João dos Santos. He mentioned a plant called *bangue,* cultivated throughout Kafaria, near the Cape of Good Hope; the Kafirs had a custom of eating its leaves.[102]

Europeans brought tobacco to Africa, where people adopted an herb/tobacco blend. In the words of one observer, "In order to procure the pleasure more speedily and deliciously, he mixes his tobacco with hemp chopped very fine."[103]

The Hottentots were said to be descendants of Bushmen mothers and Egyptian soldiers who had deserted their posts in Ethiopia back in 650 BC. By 1705, both the Hottentots and the neighboring Bushmen were smoking, having been taught the art by the white man.[104] Influenced by "the fumes of the dagga, ... devotee commenced to recite or sing, with great rapidity and vehemence, the praises of himself or his chief during the intervals of coughing or smoking."[105] Hottentots had no pockets, so they carried dagga in leather pouches tucked under ivory rings worn on their arms.[106]

---

[99]Aldrich. op. cit.
[100]Bryant, A.T. *The Zulu People.* cited in T. James. 'Dagga: A review of fact & fancy." in *Medical Journal.* 1970. no 44. pp. 575-580
[101]Van der Merwe, N.J. 'Cannabis Smoking in 13th-14th Century Ethiopia.' in *Cannabis & Culture.* op. cit. pp. 77-80
[102]Abel. op. cit. pp. 138-139
[103]Thunberg, C.P. 'An Account of the Cape of Good Hope & Some Parts of the Interior of Southern Africa, 1795' in *A General Collection of the Best & Most Interesting Voyages & Travels in All Parts of the World.* Pinkerton, J., ed. Longman, Hurst, Ries, Orme & Brown. London England. 1811. 16:31
[104]Abel. op. cit. pp. 138-139
[105]Stowe, E.W. *The Native Races of South Africa.* Juta & Co. Capetown, S. Africa. 1910. pp. 52-53
[106]Schreyer, J. 'Diary.' in *Cape of Good Hope.* R. Raven-Hart, ed. A.A. Balkewa. Capetown, South Africa. 1971. p. 126

On holidays or important occasions, such as the conclusion of a treaty or alliance, the Baluba tribe smoked hemp in gourds up to one meter in circumference. In addition, the men gathered each evening in the main square, where they solemnly smoked hemp together.[107] A delinquent individual among the tribe was compelled to smoke potent cannabis until he lost consciousness. He would wake up rehabilitated, having seen the error of his ways.

The Bashilange tribe was transformed from savagery to civilization by Chief Kalamba-Moukenge's introduction of cannabis.[108]

> One tribe with another, one village with another, always lived at daggers drawn. ... Then about 25 years ago [c. 1850], ... a hemp-smoking worship began to be established, and the narcotic [sic.] effect of smoking masses of hemp made itself felt. The *Ben-Riamba*, Sons of Hemp, found more and more followers: they began to have intercourse with each other as they became less barbarous and made laws.

The decision to promote social equality by banning people from wearing the trappings of wealth and power led to an uprising of the nobility, and ultimately to the downfall of this cannabis king.[109]

In 1910, South Africa set about outlawing cannabis and teamed up with Egypt in an unsuccessful bid for a League of Nations ban on cannabis. In the 1980s, the autonomous Sutu homeland in modern South Africa, Transkei, became a major cannabis producer that is a kind of a resort center for South African youths. While the use of cocaine and other hard drugs is lower there than in surrounding areas, dagga use is still very high.

So we look to the past in search of our future, and thereby find out even more about our connection to this earth.

IN GOD WE TRUST
DECLARATION OF INDEPENDENCE 1776

[107]Reininger, W. 'Remnants from prehistoric times.' in *The Book of Grass*. Grove Press. New York NY. 1967
[108]von Wissman, H. *My Second Journey Through Equatorial Africa*. Chatto & Windus. London England. 1891. p. 312
[109]Abel. op. cit. p. 145

3

HEMP IN THE UNITED STATES

There are various theories as to when people first migrated to the Americas. Likewise, it is uncertain when hemp arrived here. Could the Vikings have carried cannabis seeds to the continent; was the plant native; or did hempseed arrive with the Spanish?

When the first waves of the Age of Discovery washed European explorers onto American shores, many observed that hemp was already there. Hemp, or *hempe*, was already the primary English name for cannabis. John De Verrazzano described natives as early as 1524 using "threds of wilde hemp."[1] Jacques Cartier called Canada a land "full of hempe which groweth of itselfe,"[2] — rather like telling the folks back home that the streets were paved with gold.

Were they cannabis? The Smithsonian Institution reported that fiber from prehistoric burial sites "has been identified as that of *cannabis sativa*, or wild hemp. That the well-preserved fabrics just illustrated represent fairly the textile work of the mound-builders is practically demonstrated by the evidence furnished by the mounds themselves."[3] Were they indigenous? While no pollen-count evidence supports this claim, the hemp patches Thomas Hariot described when he wrote about Virginia in 1585[4] were not dense enough to leave measurable amounts of pollen behind.

A Dutchman named DuPratz wrote that "hemp grows naturally on the lands adjoining to the lakes on the west of the Mississippi."[5] DuPratz was a farmer who identified the plants botanically. "The stalks are as thick as one's finger, and about six feet long. They are quite like ours in the wood, the leaf and the rind." Given his expertise, it is quite probable that these plants were true cannabis.[6] But that was 1719, long after European hemp was established on the continent, so even his remarks are inconclusive.

---

[1]Hakluyt, Richard. *The English Voyages.* Glasgow Scotland. 1903. vol viii. p. 429. cited in Frazier, Jack. *The Great American Hemp Industry.* Solar Age Press. Peterstown WV. 1991
[2]He also went in 1536 & 1541. Sauer, Carl. *Sixteenth Century North America: The land & the people as seen by the Europeans.* Berkeley CA. 1971. p. 96
[3]*13th Report of the Smithsonian Institution's Bureau of Ethnology, 1891-1892.* USGPO. Washington DC. cited in Frazier, Jack. *op. cit.* pp. 27, 40
[4]"Of hempe & flaxe there is no great store in any one place together, by reason it is not planted but as the soile doth yeeld of itself." Hakluyt. op. cit. p. 268
[5]In 1719. *Ibid.* p. 354
[6]Frazier, J. *op. cit.* p. 6

The first Europeans who came to America invariably carried hempen goods, hempseed and hemp industries with them. Given the diverse qualities of this plant, it seems hemp would have been entrenched in the indigenous cultures were it a native.

The European Powers Rewarded Hemp Growers

The Spanish brought cannabis to Mexico, Central and South America. The French traded hemp cloth with Natives in the Louisiana Territory. The English settlers planted it beside the Union Jack, in the area now known as the United States and Canada. From the Puritans[7] to the present, hemp has always been important to United States economics. Hemp was exchanged as money throughout most of the Americas from 1631 to the early 1800s.[8] Tradition holds that hempen paper was used to draft the Declaration of Independence and the Constitution. Hemp fiber was woven into uniforms for our troops and used to reinforce American flags.[9]

Both flax and hemp were important in the American colonies. Practically every farm had a field devoted to their cultivation.

The production of these fiber crops was of particular interest to the British government, which had ended its domestic hemp industry and was eager to escape from its dependence on the Baltic countries and Holland. Parliament set a bounty[10] on imported hemp in the Naval Stores Act that lasted 16 years. In 1721, hemp from British plantations in America was exempted from import duty, followed by a series of farm subsidies to reward hemp growers.[11]

A mid-18th century French treatise described hemp as the most important product of the settlement, except for "bread corn."[12] However, at times France discouraged items to protect its domestic industries. As early as 1721 it formally prohibited development of the colonial wine, hemp and flax industries (allowing home use). And at other times the governor of Louisiana was urged to encourage hemp production and even to supply free hempseed to colonists.[13] Near the end of the 18th century, a traveller reported that hemp grew so

---

[7]Dewey, Lyster. 'Hemp.' *US Department of Agriculture Yearbook, 1913*. US Govt. Printing Office. Washington DC. 1914. p. 291
[8]Clark, V.S. *History of Manufacture in the US*. McGraw Hill. 1929. p. 34
[9]Herer, Jack. *Hemp & the Marijuana Conspiracy: The Emperor Wears No Clothes*. HEMP Publishing. Van Nuys CA. 1991. pp. 5-7
[10]Of 1704-05. £6 per ton. A bounty is a subsidy or reward offered by a government.
[11]1764 to 1778. An argument in favor of the 1764 bounty was that importing hemp & flax into Britain would prevent the Colonies from manufacturing naval store products. Gray, Lewis Cecil. *History of Agriculture in the Southern US to 1860*. Carnegie Institution. Washington DC. 1933. vol. 1. pp. 179-180
[12]Sackett & Hobbs. *Hemp; A war crop*. Mason & Hanger Co. New York NY. 1942. The word *corn* refers not just to Indian corn, *maize*, but to wheat or any food grain.
[13]In the years 1736 & 1752.

well that a large ropewalk, or hemp cordage factory, had been established in New Orleans. Vessels to the port were assured they would be able to provide themselves abundantly with the product.[14]

To encourage immigration, numerous bounties were set on products believed to be suitable as staples for the back country of the several colonies, especially hemp, flax and wheat.[15]

The Colonial Hemp Industries

The first settlers of New England, New York and Virginia immediately introduced the cultivation of hemp. The "mother countries," England and Holland, hoped their American colonies would furnish enough for their great navies. With her domestic hemp industry weakened by reliance on imports, England was precariously dependent on her European rivals or their colonial possessions. In 1608, some 50 men worked in the Jamestown, Virginia colony clearing land and planting crops. Hemp, wine, flax, cotton, spices, and medicinal herbs were most desired.[16]

Colonies promptly made the production of hemp compulsory. The Virginia General Assembly in 1619 officially did "require and enjoine all householders of this Colony that have any of those seeds to make tryal thereof in the nexte season."[17] This was reiterated several times.[18] Hemp farming was introduced into New England when Puritan settlements were established. It was grown on Manhattan Island by 1626 and in Massachusetts by 1630.[19] Thomas Morton wrote in 1632 that hemp grew "twice so high" in his superior American soil as in old England.[20] In 1640, Connecticut ordered every family to plant hemp.[21]

Consumption soon outpaced the supply, and hemp soon began to be imported here, too. *The Calendar of State Papers for Colonial Virginia* declared in 1665, "Hemp is so useful that (the tariff) may well be dispensed with ... from any parts."[22]

---

[14]Gray. op. cit. pp. 75-76

[15]*Ibid*. pp. 88-89

[16]*Ibid*. p. 16

[17]Aldrich, Dr. Michael, et al. *High Times Encyclopedia of Recreational Drugs*. Stonehill Publishing. New York NY. 1978. p. 127

[18]in 1633. Lack of seed hindered the programs. Similar acts were suspended in 1661 and 1662 and the colony sent to England for seed, but mandatory cultivation resumed in 1673 and 1691. Gray. op. cit. pp. 179-182

[19]*Facts for Farmers*. Robinson, S., ed. Johnson & Ward. New York NY. 1865. p. 965

[20]Morton, Thomas. *New English Canaan*. 1632. p. 64

[21]Rasmussen, Wayne D., ed. *Readings in the History of American Agriculture*. U of Illinois Press. Urbana IL. 1969. p. 296. Mandatory cultivation laws were first enacted in MA in 1631 & CT in 1632. Herer. op. cit. p. 1

[22]Hening. *Compiled Statutes of Virginia*. vol. 1-11: 1619-1780. in Moore, Brent. *The Hemp Industry In Kentucky*. Press of James E. Hughes. Lexington KY. 1905. pp. 13-14

By 1690, sufficient hemp was being produced to take care of the domestic market and the first paper mill was built in Pennsylvania by the Rittenhouse firm. Using flax and hemp rags as raw material, a network of mills and publishing houses soon arose.[23]

A Boston paper set out "arguments to encourage the sowing of hemp." *The Loyal Post* predicted a good return on "hemp for cordages and other uses in ... Her Majesty's dominions."[24] Farmer, philosopher and traveller Jared Eliot said that 1000 acres would supply the needs of Massachusetts Bay. "If I should presume to hint anything to the legislature ... to promote the interest of it, I hope the good of my country ... will excuse me."[25]

The ideal of establishing a closely settled colony led the Georgia promoters to base their economy on tropical or semitropical products that required intensive cultivation or processing. Greatest emphasis was placed on crops including hemp, cotton and medicinal plants.[26]

As early as 1723 South Carolina placed a bounty on hemp, and a salary was voted in 1733 for Richard Hall to write a book and promote the production and growth of hemp and flax for three years. Hall travelled to Holland to buy seed. William Byrd II wrote in 1737 that hemp "thrives very well in this climate," and bounties were set in 1744. After the middle of the century, the settlement of upper South Carolina led to another series of bounties and provisions for the inspection of product. In the late colonial period, North Carolina paid substantial bounties on hemp and flax for export, and provided warehousing and inspection services.

Dutch settlers brought their hemp working expertise along with them to Pennsylvania, which offered bounties in 1730 to encourage hemp growing.[27] In 1770, homespun manufactures of the Province, especially Lancaster County, produced 4091 yards of flax linen and 8877 yards of "hemp linen."[28]

"I am informed by my worthy friend Benjamin Franklin, Esq, of Philadelphia, that they raise hemp upon their drained lands," reported Jared Eliot.[29] Owner of a flourishing printing business, Franklin was also the most active paper merchant in the colonies.

---

[23]Landegger, Karl. 'Growing with the paper industry since 1863." Address to the Newcomen Society. 1968

[24]*The Loyal Post, with Foreign & Inland Intelligence.* no. 23. London England. Jan 11-14, 1705. p. 2

[25]Gray. op. cit. pp. 158-159

[26]*Ibid.* p. 101

[27]*Facts for Farmers.* op. cit. p. 965

[28]American Philosophical Society. in *Pennsylvania Gazette.* June 14, 1770. Klein, H.M.J. ed. *Lancaster County Pennsylvania: A History.* Lewis Historical Publishing Co. Inc. Philadelphia PA. 1924

[29]Gray. op. cit.

A Barometer of American Economic Growth

Hemp farming moved West with the American frontier. Conestoga wagons and prairie schooners of pioneer days were covered with hemp canvas or its lightweight version called "duck."[30]

In the 1750s, hemp homespun was being worked in Kentucky which signalled the beginning of an era filled with commerce and competition. A touch of elegance reached the Blue Grass State when "Flanders fine hemp linen" was advertised for sale there.[31]

Georgia provided free seed and instructions to farmers in 1767, and set bounties on hemp and flax in 1768. As the American Revolution approached, Virginia's mandatory cultivation laws returned "as a preparation for war."[32] In 1775, American patriot Thomas Paine insisted that the colonies were strong enough to break free from old King George's oppression and rise to its own greatness, in part because "hemp flourishes" here.[33] The policies of economic resistance and exclusion of British goods before and during the Revolution so greatly increased the hemp supply that South Carolina repealed its bounties, noting they were no longer needed.[34]

Spain launched a massive effort to increase its colonial hemp supply beginning in 1777. California produced 12,500 pounds of hemp fiber in 1807. About 40 percent came from Santa Barbara, but good harvests were also reported for San Jose, Los Angeles and San Francisco. California was producing over 220,000 pounds of dressed hemp by 1810.[35]

Competition With Tobacco

In the South, hemp was in competition with a tenacious adversary: tobacco. Concern about the detrimental physical effects of tobacco use and the fact that tobacco monoculture did not meet the prevailing ideals of colonization led officials to favor diversification for the first three quarters of the 17th century. The British Committee for Trade and Plantations recommended sending flax and hemp seed to Virginia in the crisis of 1681. Two years later, England began to encourage tobacco instead, fearing that production of hemp or other agricultural industries would compete with British goods.

30*Hemp for Victory*. USDA film. Washington DC. 1942. Cotton duck began to be used in the 1860s.
31in *Kentucky Gazette*. Lexington. 1810. Moore. op. cit. p. 31
32"Each tithable ... is bound to deliver every year one pound each of dressed hemp & flax or two pounds of either ... under oath that it was of his own growth."*Ibid*. p. 14
33Paine, Thomas. *Common Sense*. Pamphlet. 1776
341778. *Ibid*. pp. 179-182
35Abel, Ernest L. *Marihuana: The first 12,000 years*. Plenum Press. New York NY. 1980. p. 120

Maryland set bounties on flax, hemp or both.[36] By 1695 inhabitants of Dorchester and Somerset counties in Maryland, largely Scottish-Irish immigrants, were clothing themselves in their own hemp linen and wool. However, in 1697 it was reported that "tobacco swallows up all others," and the region lost its self-sufficiency. An act of 1706 permitted the use of hemp and flax as legal tender at specified rates to pay for one fourth of all debts. An act passed in 1727 set a bounty of 100 pounds of tobacco for every 100 pounds of hemp. A number of additional measures encouraged the manufacture of cloth from hemp or flax between 1730 and 1740. Interest in these crops increased during periods of economic depression, but planters abandoned their cultivation whenever the price of tobacco recovered.

In four Maryland counties south of the James River, the inhabitants were clothing themselves in hemp and even "sold great quantities." but it was noted in 1711 that tobacco was "so rooted in the affections of the people" that they returned to it with the earliest improvement in prices.[37]

The controversy raged right through the Revolution and into the coming decades and centuries. In 1791 Thomas Jefferson made this comparison of the two crops:[38]

> The culture [of tobacco] is pernicious. This plant greatly exhausts the soil. Of course, it requires much manure, therefore other productions are deprived of manure, yielding no nourishment for cattle, there is no return for the manure expended. ...
> It is impolitic. ... The best hemp and the best tobacco grow on the same kind of soil. The former article is of first necessity to the commerce and marine, in other words to the wealth and protection of the country. The latter, never useful and sometimes pernicious, derives its estimation from caprice, and its value from the taxes to which it was formerly exposed. The preference to be given will result from a comparison of them: Hemp employs in its rudest state more labor than tobacco, but being a material for manufactures of various sorts, becomes afterwards the means of support to numbers of people, hence it is to be preferred in a populous country. America imports hemp and will continue to do so, and also sundry articles made of hemp, such as cordage, sail cloth, drilling linen and stockings.

Hemp production has a long and profitable heritage in the economic and agricultural history of the tobacco-growing region. Records of St. Louis for the years 1848 and 1849 reveal hemp commerce at $1,820,970, exceeding tobacco at $1,061,347.[39]

---

36 1671, 1682, 1688 & 1695. Gray. op. cit.
37 Ibid. pp. 179-182
38 Jefferson, Thomas. Farm Journal. March 16, 1791
39 Tobacco Leaf, $900,930. Finished products: $160,417. Lead, $3,193,751; Wheat, $2,960,380. Commissioner of Patents Report. 1849. 31C 1S no 20. p. 566

Early American Republic to the Civil War

Most of the "Founding Fathers" were also hemp farmers. Particularly well known were Presidents George Washington and Thomas Jefferson, who often wrote about hemp. Jefferson also invented a number of new machines and systems to process hemp.[40]

Rhode Island removed import barriers from hemp in 1785, and in 1786 declared, "It is of great importance to this State to encourage the growth of all raw materials, more especially those that supply clothing to the inhabitants and duck and cordage for carrying on commerce," and set bounties for "each and every pound" of hemp.[41]

How to maintain the supply of hemp was discussed at the highest levels of government in the formative years of the Republic.[42] A protective tariff was placed on imported sailcloth, and soon-to-be President John Quincy Adams went to Russia to report on hemp manufacturing techniques there.[43]

The War of 1812—the inspiration of the National Anthem of the USA—was provoked by the discontinuation of American smuggling activities involving hemp on behalf of England. Hemp was the "fuel" (sails capturing wind) of international transportation—the "gasoline" of earlier times—and governments then, as now, were eager to go to war to insure their energy sources.

In 1829 and 1830, hemp became a leading agricultural enterprise in Vermont, with whole farms given over to its cultivation. E&T Fairbanks Company built three machines for dressing hemp. They invented and perfected the Fairbanks platform scale to weigh the bounty of their fertile farmland, and the scale was marketed on a national and, eventually, a worldwide basis.[44]

With growing rivalry from both north and west, Virginia led the States in its 1840 hemp yield. Missouri followed, with Kentucky third.[45] One farmer bragged in 1845 that Kentucky and Missouri produced more hemp than all the other states, "and 10 times as much

---

[40]See appendix: Writings of Washington & Jefferson.

[41]*Records of the State of Rhode Island & Providence Plantations.* Providence RI. vol. x:16 pp. 120-121, 180-181

[42]President Washington asked "How far ... would there be propriety, do you conceive, in suggesting the policy of encouraging the growth of cotton & hemp in such parts of the United States as are adapted to the culture of these articles? The advantages which would result to this country from the produce of articles which ought to be manufactured at home is apparent." October 1791 letter to Sec. Treasury Alexander Hamilton. in *Writings of George Washington.* Library of Congress. vol. 31. p. 389

[43]Adams, Hon. John Q. 'On the Culture & Preparing Hemp in Russia.' March 1810. in Fairbanks, E., editor. *Compilation of Articles Relating to the Culture & Manufacture of Hemp in the US.* Jewett & Porter. St. Johnsbury VT. 1829. p. 5

[44]Simpson, W.A. in 'Green Mountain Heritage.' St. Johnsbury VT. 1969

[45]Moore. op. cit. pp. 46, 61, 112

as Ohio, Indiana or Virginia."[46] Another called hemp "the great staple of the whole of northwestern Missouri."[47] The New York Farmer's Club said hemp was "very interesting as a crop for our country."[48] A new rivalry emerged, this time between imported Russian hemp and the domestic crop. The hemp tariff won by Henry Clay raised Kentucky to a kind of economic supremacy over the other States. They brought together the whole of the Ohio Valley but angered practically everybody else, who still used foreign hemp.

These trade barriers and price supports led to a search for cheaper alternative fibers, which in the 1850s also began to be referred to as *hemps* so as to sound more desirable.[49] But cannabis sativa retained the name *true hemp*.

Meanwhile, other powerful factors were turning the States against each other, and war loomed on the horizon.

During an early battle of the American Civil War, hemp was used in an unusual way. In the summer of 1861, the State of Missouri had not yet formally seceded from the Union, but rebels had set up their own government-in-exile. Confederate General Sterling Price led nearly 7000 Missourians north to the Missouri River in a bid to split the Union east from west. At Lexington, Missouri, 3000 federal troops of Mulligan's "Irish Brigade"[50] converted an old college on the biggest hill in town into their fort. They dug trenches and laid the first land mines of the war. At the bottom of the hill, hemp factories had bales lined up, ready to be fashioned into rope. Fighting began September 18 and continued through the next day. Price's men encircled the Yankees and cut off their water and supplies. On September 20, Union troops awoke to see a line of more than 100 hemp bales snaking across the hill. Three or four Rebels pushed behind each bale, firing over the bales. Return fire could not penetrate the thick bundles of hemp stalk.[51] The Yanks tried to set the bales on fire, using hot shot in their cannons, but the hemp had been soaked with water and would not ignite. Missouri forces kept working their way forward until the Union men surrendered.[52]

---

[46]Cist, Charles. in Bidwell, Percy Wells, Ph.d. *History of Agriculture in the Northern US, 1620-1860.* Carnegie Institution. Washington DC. May 1925. pp. 363-365
[47]Samuel, G.W. of Savannah MO. Oct. 26, 1849. *Commissioner of Patents Report, 1849.* 31C, 1S, no 20. pp. 328-329. "Missouri is now the great hemp state & will probably remain so." Gallagher, W.D. letter in Kentucky Statesman. Dec. 27, 1859
[48]*Commissioner of Patents Report, 1845*
[49]Frazier, Jack. *Great American Hemp Industry.* Solar Age Press. Peterstown WV. 1991. p. 13
[50]Ad for Civil War Centennial Commission, 'est. by Act of Congress to increase awareness of our historical heritage.' in *National Geographic.* April 1961. p. 7
[51]"Casualties were low because men pushed wet bale of hemp ahead of them for protection." Ibid.
[52]Kinnison, Guy. 'Battle of the Hemp Bales.' in *High Times.* August 1989

Despite this early victory, in a very real sense the Civil War marked the end of the hemp industry's power in America.

Kentucky Hemp: A Long, Illustrious History

Kentucky was for many years the nation's largest producer of hemp. A comprehensive 1810 survey of the United States economy concluded that, "The ability to produce hemp is enjoyed by every state in the American Union (and) ... to the greatest height in the State of Kentucky."[53] The first commercial hemp grown in Kentucky was that of Archibald McNeil, near Danville in 1775. The industry came to be a fair and consistent indicator of the general prosperity of the commonwealth, and reflected its great social, economic and political changes.

When settlers arrived in Kentucky, they carried hempseed and scythes for tending the crop. Hemp was, literally, Kentucky's first "cash" crop. It was used for money due to its relative uniformity and freedom from deterioration, the universal and steady demand for it,[54] and its proven value—which exceeded all other raw produce. Trade with Spain began when the Mississippi River was opened in 1795. Since there was practically no coin or paper money in the region, even home trade was carried on mainly by barter. Hemp was the standard commodity of exchange for the state's first decades.[55]

Here, as elsewhere, encouraging the industry quickly became a governmental concern. In 1797, *The Monitor* newspaper discussed crops suited for export and stated that hemp offered the most money-for-weight of all crops. It demanded an official inquiry into "whether the last legislature acted wisely when they refused to lend the public aid to enable a citizen to carry on the business of manufacturing duck." Ads in 1800 showed land sold for "cash or hemp," and firms settling accounts in "hemp, wheat, flour or tobacco."[56]

In 1802, 65 prominent Kentuckians petitioned Congress to protect the hemp industry from foreign competition in the matter of overall production, especially cordage and sail duck.[57] The pace of Kentucky's progress was measured by its hemp output. Hemp commerce at Lexington ran to $900,000 in 1811,[58] a year after the

---

[53]Coxe, Tench. *Statement of the Arts & Manufactures of the US.* 1810. in Moore. op. cit. p. 34
[54]Ads in the *Kentucky Gazette:* "Will receive linen & hemp in discharge of book accounts," June 8, 1793. "Generous price in cash or merchandize for all good clean hemp delivered," June 14, 1794. "Will purchase all clean good hemp that may be brought." also "Quantity of well cleaned hemp wanted," April 16, 1796. *Ibid.* p. 22
[55]*Ibid.* pp. 16, 17, 91
[56]*The Monitor.* Dec. 6, 1797. *Ibid.* pp. 24-25
[57]*American State Papers.* 7Cong, 1Sess, HR. no. 173. Feb. 18, 1802. *Ibid.* p. 27
[58]Warden, D.B. *Statistical Account of the USA.* 1819. *Ibid.* pp. 37-38

"cultivation and manufacture of cotton have suddenly and greatly interfered with the manufacture of this raw material."[59]

Hemp was everywhere. An industrial survey in 1819 reported that Lexington had three steam paper mills, an oil cloth and carpet manufactory, a steam rope manufactory, several ropewalks for making cordage, and bagging factories which consumed 14,000 tons of hemp each year. At Danville, several mills, factories and ropewalks were operating. There were still more hemp manufacturers at Frankfort. One ropewalk stretched an impressive 1250 feet.[60] Maysville shipped 3000 tons of hemp in 1844.[61]

Brief New Hope & Rapid Decline of an Industry

Another group of businessmen petitioned Congress in 1809 to protect the Kentucky industry, which was "capable of producing hemp for the whole supply of the United States. ... (Hemp) cannot easily be procured in times of war. If the manufacturers of Kentucky were sufficiently encouraged, they would induce the farmers to cultivate it, so as to furnish a never failing resource, whether in peace or war."[62] The formidable one-man political force Henry Clay joined them and proposed an amendment to a bill in the United States Senate, instructing the Navy to give preference to American-made cordage, sailcloth, hemp and so forth, in buying.[63]

Both the growing American mercantile industry and Navy depended on hemp. "For the sailor, no less than the hangman, hemp was indispensable. A 44-gun frigate like our cherished Old Ironsides (the USS Constitution) took over 60 tons of hemp for rigging, including an anchor cable 25 inches in circumference."[64] Counting sails and caulking, the total ran to over 100 tons.[65]

While steam ships began to travel against the currents of the nation's rivers, the seafaring Navy continued to rely on its hempen sails until after the Civil War.

---

[59]Coxe. op. cit.

[60]Warden. op. cit. pp. 37-38

[61]Moore. op. cit. p. 94

[62]June 1809. "The non-importation act, which was passed ... as much to change the direction of the national capital from commercial to manufacturing pursuits as with a view to bringing a great foreign power to a sense of justice, by prohibiting the introduction of foreign linen, etc. into the US, gave being to their manufactories, & with the further patronage of your honorable body will, beyond doubt, rapidly increase in the western country. ... (Hemp is) an article perhaps as much wanted as any other, both by the government & by private citizens engaged in every pursuit of life & which, to an enormous amount, is annually imported from the northern parts of Europe." John Allen, et al. HR Doc. 11C 1S no 302. in Moore. op. cit. pp. 28-30

[63]April 6, 1810. Ibid. p. 32

[64]That use ran through the age of the steamship & continues into the modern Navy, at a reduced level, using imported hemp. Hemp for Victory. USDA film. 1942

[65]Crosby. op. cit.

Virtually all naval hemp was being imported from Russia. Secretary of the Navy Alexander Hamilton reported that "American water rotted hemp is no doubt in all respects equal to the best Russia hemp; indeed, I rather incline to think it superior."[66] The topic became so important that President James Buchanan spoke to Congress about the virtues of Kentucky hemp.[67] The influential *Niles Weekly Register* reported on an experiment at Boston navy yard showing water-retted American hemp yarns to be stronger than Russian yarns of the same weave. "We look to Kentucky for a full supply of such sail cloths, sheetings and linens as were heretofore received from Russia."[68]

In 1842, the Kentucky General Assembly called on Congress to build a retting facility for hemp as a national defense measure. Money spent abroad would thus be saved, and an abundant supply of top quality fiber assured, in case of war.[69] A Louisville manufacturer said cordage could be made there "as cheaply as in the east."[70]

In 1849, the Kentucky agent reported on a milling machine which softened and refined hemp for fine fabrics. "Common dew-rotted hemp may be cheaply and expeditiously prepared to make fine linen." Farmers could get to market early with "a very superior article, having a rich, oily, lively appearance." The Navy then consumed 800 tons of water-retted hemp a year, less than half of which was produced at home. Kentucky expected a great financial boon, because all Navy cordage would soon be made in Memphis Tennessee, where the government was building "the best and most perfect ropewalk ever."[71]

From the Civil War to Late 19th Century

Cotton and cheaper imported fibers of a lower quality ate away at the hemp market. Nonetheless, use and production of hemp grew until the Civil War. Then the hemp industry was stripped of its major markets one by one. The invention and gradual perfection of the mechanical cotton gin made cotton textiles so cheap that hemp could no longer compete until a machine was designed to inexpensively

---

66Sen. Doc. 27C 2S no 6 Feb. 21, 1809. Moore. op. cit. pp. 34, 35

671828. *Ibid.*

68Cited p. 43. Feb. 6, 1830 Register cited *Ibid.* p. 44. March 27, 1830. *Ibid.* p. 35

69Using the Kentucky river, hemp could be shipped directly to points on the Ohio & Mississippi rivers & manufactured hemp exposed to much less danger from shipping accidents then when in bulk. Sen Doc 26C 2S no. 91. April 1842. *Ibid.* p. 48

70Forman, T. 15 yrs. as hemp farmer & manufacturer. in *Patent Office Report.* USGPO. Washington DC. 1845. *Ibid.* pp. 53-54

71Saunders, L., KY hemp agent. Invention of J. Anderson of Louisville. "durability is insured from the fact that the albumen is ... cured by the natural heat generated in the mass in bulk." in *Commissioner of Patents Report.* USGPO. Washington DC. 1849. 31C 1S no 20. pp. 328-329

break and dress hemp. Following Elias Howe's 1845 invention of the sewing machine, factory-sewn woven goods of cotton or wool steadily replaced hempen "homespun" for clothing.

Hemp was used by the cotton industry as binding and baling twine and for "cotton bagging," made of hemp, to wrap the cotton bale. The price of hemp rose on the tides of war. In 1861 and 1862, advertisers offered the "highest prices."[72] The Civil War was primarily a land war that did not increase the market for naval stores. The Confederate Congress forbade growing cotton, except for home uses. Thus bagging and bale rope, the market for hemp, was promptly destroyed, and little hemp was grown during the 1860s.

Initially, the War sparked demand for hemp, but it ultimately devastated the Southern agricultural economy and placed firm control of national policy into the hands of the industrial North. After the War, cotton retook control of the fiber market, and ravaged hemp farms could not supply enough bagging for the cotton crop, which by 1870 created an opening for jute to take over that market.

Then came another brief surge and the hemp industry began to rebound. It spread to Champaign, Illinois, and a cordage mill was established there about 1875. Hemp was grown in Nebraska at Fremont in 1887. A federal report on irrigation in California noted that, "Hemp being the mosts valuable crop, receives attention first if it needs it, which is seldom the case." [73] It was grown in Butte County and the lower Sacramento Valley, and later under irrigation near Bakersfield in 1912.[74] Much tow was also used by the eastern cities for making paper for several years after hemp bagging disappeared.[75] But timber pulping processes, introduced in the 1850s, began to flood the market with low-grade paper to feed the presses of the pulp novels and "yellow journalism" newspapers.

Wire cable was introduced into the cordage market, but it could not be used for sail rigging. Hemp ropes yield somewhat, distributing the strain of a storm, while steel cables are rigid. This inflexibility allowed the wind to search out weak spots in the sails, and many ships wrecked while using wire rigging. Metal cable did, however, find other applications that continued to erode the hemp market. The gradual 19th century substitution of steam engines in place of sails, even at sea, decimated the market for rigging. Locomotives replaced canvas-covered wagons. Then steel ships replaced wooden ones, which reduced even the caulking market.

---

[72]Moore. op. cit. p. 62
[73]Alexander, Mendel & Davidson. *Report of the Board of Commissioners on the Irrigation of ... the State of California.* USGPO. Washington DC. 1876. p. 71
[74]Dewey. op. cit. pp. 293-294
[75]Moore. op. cit. pp. 62, 63, 106

The wheat harvester created a considerable short-term market for hemp in binder twine, but cheaper abaca from the Philippines, called "Manila hemp," cut into this market. Twine made of hemp tow still competed successfully until the introduction of still-cheaper sisal.[76]

Petroleum entered the oil market, but did not win initial acceptance because of its dirty character and inferiority to vegetable oils. However, through aggressive marketing along with the heavy taxation and eventual prohibition of alcohol fuels,[77] petroleum gained early control of a whole new market: liquid fuel for the growing automobile industry. Petroleum's link with government, coal and banking industries created the notorious "Robber Barons."

20th Century: Bottleneck, Boom ... & Ban

And so it went. Hemp, once the mightiest industry on the continent, had fallen into decline mainly due to the one weak point in hemp production: separating out, or *breaking*, fiber from the pulp by hand. While Eli Whitney's cotton gin, invented in 1793, drastically reduced the price of cotton fiber, no comparable equipment existed for hemp. All the laborious work continued to be performed by hand. This had one advantage for the farm: It provided year-round work for the hands. During most of the winter, cleaning hemp was the only work to be done. If the hemp could be broken out early, workers had the rest of the season for hackling, or combing out the long fiber. But this was also an insurmountable disadvantage: the cost of "breaking" the hemp was nearly two-thirds of the total expense of raising and preparing the crop for market.[78]

This was the downfall of the industry. Despite the inventions of Jefferson and others, no satisfactory method was found. Until this problem was solved, the hemp market could not rebound. By 1905, demand for hemp was largely confined to cordage, commercial wrapping twine and carpet thread.

The decline of the hemp industry hurt the home, farming and manufacturing sectors of the domestic economy. But while hemp occupied by this time only a small corner of the fiber market, overall demand had grown until this corner equalled nearly the whole fiber market of earlier periods.[79] At the turn of the century, hemp was a well-known but underused commodity. Its supply was assured. Its markets were once again expanding.

---

[76]*Ibid.* pp. 63-64
[77]Morris, David. 'Alternatives to oil, paper get the kiss of death.' in *St. Paul Pioneer Press*. MN. also in *News Herald*. Dec. 9, 1990. p. 7-D
[78]Moore. op. cit. pp. 86, 91, 98
[79]*Ibid.* pp. 63-64

Hemp was still used more extensively than any other soft fiber, except jute, in 1913. The Agriculture Department decided to encourage the industry anew. Fiber specialist Lyster Dewey reported that the drop in domestic production was primarily due to increasing difficulty in securing sufficient labor to care for the crop; secondly, to the lack of labor-saving machinery; and, thirdly, to the increase in livestock, tobacco and corn production. Meanwhile jute, "inferior in strength and durability and with only the element of cheapness in its favor, is usurping the legitimate place of hemp." He noted that new machinery for harvesting hemp and preparing the fiber, "together with the higher prices paid for hemp during the past three years," had aroused new interest in the industry.[80] New uses for hemp pulp, known as hurds, were being developed for paper, plastics, explosives and so on. In 1916 the Department proposed making paper from the waste pulp instead of using timber from the forests. *Bulletin 404* proved the value of hurd, which was very important for industry, because "without a doubt, hemp will continue to be one of the staple agricultural crops of the United States." Better yet, hemp produces four times as much pulp per acre as does forest land.[81]

A few years later, a technological revolution of processing equipment began. Farmers and industrialists poised to get in on the resurgence of the hemp industry. For a brief period around 1917 the Scripps newspaper chain considered using hemp hurds grown in California's Imperial Valley for their paper, using a decorticator invented by G.W. Schlichten.[82] Unfortunately, the economic impact of the First World War caused the company to cut the project and kept it from moving beyond the research scale.

Product research and development continued. By 1929 and throughout the thirties, Ford Motor Company was planning to build and fuel a fleet of cars using hemp and other plant matter.[83]

Then came hemp's big break—literally: Efficient breaking equipment came onto the market, making hemp industrial feedstocks simultaneously far more affordable and much more valuable than fossil fuels or even timber. Almost overnight, the cost of clean hemp fiber plunged from 50 cents per pound to one half cent.[84] Cellulose-rich hurds were ejected into a container as a virtually free source of

[80]Dewey. op. cit. pp. 284-285

[81]Dewey, L.H. & Merrill, J.L. 'Hemp Hurds as Paper Making Material.' *Bulletin 404.* USDA. US Government Printing Office. Washington DC. 1916

[82]McRae, Milton. letter to E.W. Scripps. Aug. 28, 1917. in Wirtshafter, Don. *The Schlichten Papers.* Ohio Hempery. Athens OH. 1994

[83]'Auto body made of plastics resists denting under hard blows.' in *Popular Mechanics.* December 1941

[84]'New Billion-Dollar Crop.' in *Popular Mechanics.* February 1938. pp. 238-39, 144A

raw material for industry. The long-awaited hemp revival had arrived. Businesses sat up and took notice. A 1937 *Industrial Arts* report predicted, "Hemp will bring a new industry to the Corn Belt
this year and provide rope needed for the Navy."[85]

A technical report to the American Society of Mechanical Engineers in 1937 noted the rapidly growing market for cellulose,
"especially in the plastic field, which is growing by leaps and
bounds." It predicted that hemp hurds would meet "a good part of
that need" and that "this hitherto wasted material may be sufficiently
profitable to pay for the crop."[86] That new market, along with the
historically valuable hemp fiber, meant that hemp "can make American mills independent of importations." *Mechanical Engineering*
magazine declared hemp "the most profitable and desirable crop that
can be grown."[87] *Popular Mechanics* magazine dubbed hemp the
"New Billion Dollar Crop" and predicted a bonanza for farmers and
industry alike. The surge in new uses for cellulose, along with new
processing equipment, meant that hemp "will not compete with other
American products. Instead, it will displace imports of raw material
and manufactured products produced by underpaid coolie and peasant labor, and it will provide thousands of jobs for American workers throughout the land."[88]

Hemp offered America a road out of the Great Depression.

Except there was this one small problem. A few years earlier,
hysterical articles had begun to make their way into the newspapers
about a new mystery "drug" called *marijuana*, which was said to
drive Negroes and Mexicans criminally insane and violent. In the
spirit of the Roosevelt New Deal, a federal "alphabet agency" was
designated to solve the problem. The Treasury Department's Federal
Bureau of Narcotics, the FBN, took on its new assignment.

The domestic hemp industry, focus of over 150 years of federal
encouragement, was abruptly terminated in 1937 by the Marijuana
Tax Act, a single bill that passed through Congress in just 10 weeks
without a roll call vote.[89] As historian Thorold Rogers said, "The
favors of government are like the box of Pandora, with this important difference; that they rarely leave hope at the bottom."[90]

85*Industrial Arts Index, 1937.* [UCLA Library]. 131:3. May 3, 1937.
86Lower, George A. 'Flax & Hemp: From the Seed to the Loom.' in *Mechanical Engineering*. February 1938
87Ibid.
88'New Billion-Dollar Crop.' in *Popular Mechanics*. February, 1938. p. 238.
89House Ways & Means Com. April 27-30, 1937. Senate hearing. July 12, 1937
90Rogers, T. *Economic Interpretation of History*. p. 378 in Moore. op. cit. p. 112

4

A BRIGHT PROMISE ASSASSINATED

The *Virginia Law Review* analysis of the 1937 hearings on the Marihuana Tax Act described them as a "near comic example of dereliction of legislative responsibility" and "a case study in legislative carelessness."[1] It noted that "no primary empirical evidence was presented about the effects of the drug ... (only) hearsay and emotional pleas" from the "Federal Bureau of Narcotics and a few state law enforcement agents." The law "was tied neither to scientific study nor to law enforcement need." The legislative review concluded that Congress had been "hoodwinked."

The scene: America in the early 1900s. Two powerful rivals faced off over several multi-billion dollar markets—this time in the form of petroleum and timber versus hemp. Fortunes would be made ... and lost. When Rudolph Diesel produced his famous engine in 1896, he assumed it would be powered by "a variety of fuels, especially vegetable and seed oils."[2] Like most engineers, Diesel realized that vegetable fuels like hemp are superior to petroleum.

The promise that hemp held for the rest of the world was quickly perceived as a threat by a small core of powerful people in the elite special-interest oligarchy dominated by the Du Pont petrochemical company and its major financial backer and key political ally, oil man and Treasury Secretary Andrew Mellon.

Through careful bureaucratic control of both legislation and enforcement, the hydrocarbon interests[3] achieved market supremacy by turning a blind eye to the poisons generated by industrial hydrocarbons, while imposing extreme obstacles on natural carbohydrates,[4] supposedly because the latter cause physical pleasure. And, ever since the release of *Bulletin 404*, the Hearst newspaper/timber interests had supported the petrochemical campaign against hemp. In just a few years, Hearst newspapers and allies[5] generated enough confusion and hysteria to ram a "marihuana" prohibition bill through

---

[1]"Lawmakers assumed that the drug was addictive & caused crime, pauperism & insanity." Bonnie & Whitebread. 'The Forbidden Fruit & the Tree of Knowledge: An inquiry into the legal history of American marijuana prohibition.' in *Virginia Law Review*. vol. 56:6. p. 971

[2]Downs, Hugh. 'Dope hope for oil imbroglio?' on ABC radio. November 1990.

[3]First coal, followed by petroleum & so called "natural" gas

[4]Alcohol & hemp

[5]Herer, Jack. *Hemp & the Marijuana Conspiracy: The Emperor Wears No Clothes.* HEMP Publishing. Van Nuys CA. 1991

Congress in less than three months. Over the decades, an entrenched "Marihuana Bureaucracy" has used its influence to demand ever more prohibition enforcement power and money. Canada's LeDain Commission Report of 1972 lamented that the debate on non-medical cannabis use "all too often has been based on hearsay, myth and ill-informed opinion about the effects of the drug."[6]

The question has since been raised: Was the enactment of cannabis hemp prohibition under the contrived name *marihuana* a colossal bureaucratic blunder—or was it actually a high level criminal conspiracy to violate antitrust laws?[7]

Mellon: A Textbook Case of Corruption

The Mellon Bank of Pittsburgh, Pennsylvania, was the sixth largest in the United States in 1900, when it financed an oil well in Spindletop, Texas. The gusher paid off in a big way. Petroleum spraying into the air rained down on the town for nine days. It was known as the 'Klondike' of the Texas oil boom. A few years later, a *New York Times* editorial complained that "It is only the heavy tax imposed by the United States that has prevented the use of a large number of vegetable products for the manufacturing of an exceedingly cheap and available alcohol (fuel)."[8]

Andrew Mellon, the well-connected multi-millionaire banker, bought out his partners and took over Gulf Oil Corporation. In 1913, Henry Ford opened his first auto assembly line, and Gulf Oil opened the first drive-in gas station, in Pittsburgh.[9] In 1919, with ethanol fuel again poised to compete with gasoline, Alcohol Prohibition descended on the nation. Lucky Mr. Mellon. When wheeler-dealer Mellon was sworn in as President Warren G. Harding's Secretary of the Treasury, he was considered the richest man in America. Despite this obvious conflict of interest, repeated scandals and the economic collapse of the nation during his tenure, he held this influential bureaucratic post for 20 years over several different Presidential administrations.[10] During this time Mellon laid the groundwork for hemp prohibition.

In the 1920s, Mellon arranged for his petroleum-rich bank to loan his friends at Du Pont the money to take over the automobile

---

[6]*Report of the Canadian Government Commission of Inquiry into the Non-Medical Use of Drugs.* Canadian Government Printing Office. Toronto Canada. 1972
[7]Herer. op. cit. pp. 21-26
[8]*New York Times.* May 22, 1906. in Morris, David. 'Making Fossils of Fossil Fuels.' in *Utne Reader.* St. Paul MN. May/June 1991
[9]Solberg, Carl. *Oil Power: The rise & imminent fall of an American empire.* New American Library. 1976. pp. 58-59, 73
[10]Malone, Dumas & Rauch, Basil. *War & Troubled Peace: 1917-1939.* Meredith Publishing Co. 1960. p. 106

manufacturer General Motors. Du Pont had developed new gasoline additives for gasoline and other petroleum fuels, as well as toxic sulfate and sulfite compounds used to pulp trees for paper.

The Oil Depletion Allowance that Mellon forced through Congress gave such huge tax rebates to Gulf Oil that a later Congressional investigation reported "gross unfairness."[11] During Senate investigations into the Teapot Dome scandal, it was revealed that Mellon had been aware of the illegal sale of public oil leases all along, as well as the bribery and secret campaign contributions of the 1920 Presidential election. This paid public servant told the Senate that "neither then, nor during a Presidential Prosecutor's investigations" had he felt called upon to say anything about it.[12]

Mellon publicly encouraged "easy money" policies that were designed to profit speculators like himself and close acquaintances. This led to the 1929 Stock Market Crash that threw America into the Great Depression and bankrupted millions of ordinary Americans.[13]

President Herbert Hoover later summarized Treasury Secretary Mellon's formula for American recovery.[14]

> Liquidate labor, liquidate stocks, liquidate the farmer, liquidate real estate. ... People will work harder, live a more moral life.
> Values will be adjusted and enterprising people will pick up the wrecks from less competent people.

After Mellon was removed in 1932, his policies and influence remained a powerful force within the Department. Mellon did not like competition, nor did his friend Du Pont. In the 1930s, the Ford Motor Company operated a successful biomass fuel conversion plant, using cellulose at Iron Mountain, Michigan. Ford engineers extracted methanol, charcoal fuel, tar, pitch, ethyl-acetate and creosote from hemp.[15] However, these same fundamental ingredients for industry could also be made by fossil fuel-related industries.

Du Pont's Dream: A World Without Nature

The Du Pont Company, under various names, has been instrumental in developing much of the plastics, synthetic materials and toxins we use today. Thomas Jefferson had urged a young French refugee[16] to start a gunpowder company to provide the struggling new nation with powder for hunting, clearing land, quarrying, mining and defense. As a result, the Du Pont Company was

---

[11]Solberg. op. cit. p. 80
[12]*Ibid*. p. 107
[13]Malone & Rauch. op. cit. 1960. p. 145
[14]in *Oxford History*. London England. vol. 3. 1961. p. 292
[15]Downs. op. cit.
[16]Eleuthére Irénée Du Pont de Nemours

founded in 1802.[17] Its development of smokeless powder from cellulose led the company to research other cellulose products like nitrocellulose for lacquers, belt cement, leather finishes and so on.[18]

Cellulose continued to be the crux of the companies production from then on, first from vegetable matter, then from fossil fuel.

In 1917 Du Pont entered the petrochemical industries and turned out 40 percent of the smokeless powder fired by Allied guns in World War I. The ammonia department's work on explosives and fertilizers led to the development of cellophane, nylon and dacron. Favors of the federal government soon placed much of the domestic textile production in the hands of its chief munitions maker. Nitrocellulose lacquers and neoprene synthetic rubber were developed. The firm became a leader in such diverse industries as paints, rayon, plastics, electrochemicals, photographic film, insecticides, fertilizers and other agricultural chemicals.

The late 1920s and 1930s saw continuing consolidation of power into the hands of a few large steel and petrochemical manufacturers, primarily the munitions companies. However, amid the lingering Depression, the financial situation did not appear so good. The 1937 Du Pont *Annual Report* took stock of the situation and warned, "The future is clouded with uncertainties. ... Funds for the development of new industries or for the expansion of established lines must be provided out of savings."[19]

Two years later, an upbeat corporate president Lammont Du Pont wrote in *Popular Mechanics* magazine, "Synthetic plastics find application in fabricating a wide variety of articles, many of which in the past were made from natural products." By synthetic, he meant items made from mineral, chemical, petroleum and fossil fuel deposits. "But what of the significance of these things to the nation?" he asked. "Consider our natural resources. The chemist has aided in conserving natural resources by developing synthetic products to supplement or wholly replace natural products."[20]

17It became a corporation in 1899. Artificial leather was added in 1910, pyroxylin nitrocellulose plastics in 1915, rubber coated textiles in 1916.
18Colvin, James. 'Du Pont.' in *American Peoples Encyclopedia*. Sponsor Press. Chicago IL. 1953
19Du Pont Corporation. *Annual Report*. 1937. Wilmington DE. p. 25
20"Today, American chemical industry & industries ... employ one-fifth of all factory workers & one-fourth of all industrial capital investments. Chemistry underlies not only such patently chemical industries as the manufacture of acids, alkalis, dyestuffs, explosives & plastics, but also such giant industries as leather tanning, petroleum refining, pulp & papermaking, the smelting of metals & soap making. ... The idea must be developed on progressively larger scales until it can be operated as a factory process." Du Pont, Lammont, president of Du Pont. 'From Test Tube to You.' in *Popular Mechanics*. June 1939. p. 805

Du Pont lavished praise on this dreamy, petrochemical world he envisioned. For industry to create this artificial paradise, he noted with supreme optimism, "Supplies of raw materials must be assured; outlets determined; and the product introduced to the public." As examples, he cited the "petroleum refining, pulp and papermaking" chemicals used by his good friends Mellon and Hearst. The Depression was not over, but something had changed in that brief period. A clue is found in the 1937 report: "The revenue-raising power of government may be converted into an instrument for forcing acceptance of sudden new ideas of industrial and social reorganization."[21] A new tax law had gone into effect.

Enter Mr. Hearst, Master Propagandist

When it came to forcing acceptance of sudden new ideas, like a ban on hemp, William Randolph Hearst was the ideal point man. His company was a major consumer of the cheap tree-pulp that had replaced hemp paper in the late 19th century. It was also a major logger and producer of Du Pont's chemical-drenched, tree-pulp paper, which turned brittle yellow and fell apart after a short time.

His newspaper chain stretched across the nation and had already demonstrated its power to turn public opinion and federal policy. Its biased reports on Cuba had led directly to the Spanish American War in 1898, and spawned the expression "yellow journalism."

Fueled by the advertising it sold to petrochemical and related industries, the Hearst newspaper chain was known for sensational stories and prohibition politics. It railed against cigarettes, alcohol, cocaine, heroin, dancing, popular music and other things. The rhetoric hit such a level that the Associated Physicians' Economic League of New York referred to a 1916 criminalization plan as the "Towns-Hearst Bill" because of its strong support from grandstanding political lobbyist Charles Towns and the Hearst chain.[22]

Hearst despised poor people, African Americans, Chinese, Hindus and all minorities. Most of all, he hated Mexicans, especially since their revolutionary hero Pancho Villa's cannabis-smoking troops had reclaimed some 800,000 acres of prime timberland in Mexico from Hearst, in the name of the peasants.[23] And Hearst Paper Corporation was not happy with hemp, either. All the low-quality paper the company planned to make by deforesting its vast United States timber holdings might be replaced by low-cost, high-quality paper made of waste hemp hurds.

---

[21]Du Pont. op. cit.
[22]The 'Boylan Bill.' Musto, David F., MD. *The American Disease: Origins of narcotic control.* Yale U Press/Colonial Press Inc. Clinton MA. 1973. p. 110
[23]Herer. op. cit. p. 24

Hearst had his work cut out for him. The bigoted fanatic had always supported virtually every form of prohibition, and now he wanted cannabis added to every "anti-narcotic" (sic.) bill. Never mind that cannabis is technically not a *narcotic*.[24] Facts were not important to his agenda — the important thing was for hemp to be completely removed from society, doctors and industry.

Around 1920 or so, a new word entered the English vocabulary by way of screaming headlines and horror stories: *marihuana.* Columnist Winifred Black unveiled Hearst's "New dope[25] (sic.) lure, marihuana," mourned its "many victims" and cheered for Italian Fascist leader Benito Mussolini, who "leads way in crushing dope evil: Italy jails smugglers and peddlers for life with no hope of pardon." Black heaped praise upon the fascists and fretted that America was moving "too late" in adopting his policies.[26]

Defining the Enemy: Marihuana

The name that the special interests used as a smokescreen was not, as many people think, the Spanish word for hemp, which is *cáñamo.* The first known reference to "maryjane," dates only to the 1890s.[27] "*La cucaracha, la cucaracha ya no puede caminar / Porque no tiene, porque se falta marijuana[28] que fumar.*"[29] With poetic vengeance, Hearst plucked the little-known slang term from this drinking song after Pancho Villa's men sang it to celebrate their 1913 victory at Torreón. The word slipped over the border from Sonora into Texas, where it was promptly misspelled. The town of El Paso, Texas passed the first local ordinance against *marihuana* in 1914. The pretext for the law was a fight said to be started by a Mexican.

The scientific community protested the manipulations. The news reports had switched the name of the plant from cannabis hemp to

---

[24]In medical terminology, *narcotic* refers to a specific class of drugs that cause *narcosis* & can lead to death; originally the opiates. While cannabis does relieve pain & aid sleep, there is no fatal dosage; hence, its listing as a narcotic is a legal fiction.
[25]Another tactic to confuse the public. *Dope* was slang for opiates, not cannabis.
[26]If the US sponsored an international prohibition conference, "I shall come in person to attend it in America," promised Benito Mussolini. Black, W. 'Mussolini Leads Way in Crushing Dope Evil.' in *Herald Tribune*. NY. March 9, 1928
[27]Oxford unabridged dictionary. *Marijuana* was defined in a memo by USDA Bureau of Plant Industry Economic Botanist W.E. Safford as a "drug used by the lower class of Mexican in certain localities ... cannabis indica, the hashish of the Orient, in Mexico called marihuana." in 'Narcotics & Intoxicants Used by American Indians.' prepared for the US Indian Service. May 10, 1921. in Musto. op. cit. p. 330, note 18
[28]The name *marihuana* may be a corruption of the Portuguese *mariguango,* meaning intoxicant, from Brazil. Grinspoon, Dr. Lester. 'Marihuana.' in *Scientific American.* vol. 221:6. December 1969. Or it may be a corruption of *ganja* or *ma'joun,* while its other Mexican nickname, *mota,* may come from *matokwane*. in *High Times Encyclopedia.* Stonehill Publishing. New York NY. 1978. p. 26
[29]Translation: "The cockroach, the cockroach, already he cannot walk / because he has not, because he's lacking maryjane to smoke!"

gunjah, then *hasheesh* or *hashish,* and now *marihuana.* News reports did not square with the facts.

As more and more horror stories popped up in the headlines, experts tried to sort out the confusion and bring reason to the discussion. Bureau of Plant Industry scientists said, "Recent reports ... of the effects of the drug on Mexicans, making them want to 'clean up the town,' do not jibe very well with the effects of cannabis, which so far as we have reports, simply causes temporary elation followed by depression and heavy sleep."[30]

The National Herbarium urged that all the various names of the plant should by rights be reduced to a single one for clarity's sake. Cannabis sativa was the accepted title for this plant.[31]

The United States Bureau of Plant Industry reported that,[32]

> Though they have had ample opportunity, workers in the hemp fields have never become addicts. The hasheesh producing varieties of hemp were introduced extensively into American culture a few years ago through the efforts of the Department of Agriculture, for cannabis has a large and legitimate use in veterinary medicine. The cultivation of the drug hemp was carried on mainly in South Carolina. Large numbers of Negro laborers were employed in the business, yet no cases of hasheesh addiction were reported.

Undeterred, Hearst continued to drum racist horror stories into the public mind, and criminalization into the political arena. Eventually, virtually every marijuana story reported in the campaign for its criminalization would be proven false; but, alas, too late.[33]

The spectacular stories raised bizarre expectations of behavior. A Texas prison warden gave one inmate a *reefer* to smoke so an AMA investigator could witness the transmutation, but "to the surprise of the American Prison Physician and the jailer, who assured me three whiffs would drive fellows so wild that they became exceptionally difficult to subdue,"[34] the prisoner remained calm and quiet.

Every time new hemp processing equipment appeared on the market, the marihuana problem was made to seem more terrible. Hearst newspapers sponsored speeches by the most influential prohibitionists, like Charles Towns and Harry Anslinger.

---

[30]Bureau of Plant Industry , Dr. W.W. Stockberger said, "I suspect the Mexican bravo doesn't take his marijuana straight, but mixes it with something else, possible cocaine or a couple shots of mescal or bad whiskey. That combination could easily bring on fighting madness." Science Service. in 'Our Home Hasheesh Crop.' in *Literary Digest.* April 3, 1926. pp. 64-65
[31]Ibid. Killip, E.P.
[32]Ibid. Stockberger, Dr. W.W.
[33]Sloman, L. *Reefer Madness: Marijuana in America.* Grove. New York NY. 1979
[34]Ball, Dr. M. V. report to American Medical Association. 1922

Rise of the Marihuana Bureaucracy

Andrew Mellon had a nephew-in-law named Harry J. Anslinger, the former assistant Commissioner for Alcohol Prohibition.[35]

When the Federal Bureau of Narcotics was formed in 1931, Anslinger was appointed its head, a job in Mellon's Treasury Department which was designed just for him. Mellon was removed from his post in 1932, but his influence continued—Anslinger held his post at the FBN until forced out by President Kennedy in 1962.

The stated intention of the Harrison Act of 1914 was to create the Narcotics Division of the Internal Revenue Bureau as a bookkeeping department to supervise collection of tax stamp monies.[36] But Congress got more than it bargained for.

The police bureaucrats who moved into the department had their own agenda in mind. They set out to create an issue that Congress could march behind, and see a need to subsidize the enforcement budget. They began with a media campaign on the alleged evils of *narcotics* and *dope*, lumping cannabis in with opium. The Bureau launched a second front to increase the scope of its power through judicial reinterpretation of its terms. Many reputable physicians were closely watched by overly zealous Treasury agents. Harassment was inevitable; humiliation was commonplace. Careers were destroyed.[37]

Deep in the throes of the Depression, Congress began to examine all federal agencies. The Bureau's budget was cut by $200,000 and the number of agents on the payroll was reduced. Anslinger began to fear that the Bureau was in danger of emasculation.[38]

When the idea of the prohibitive tax law was first broached to Anslinger, he called the idea "ridiculous." Even after the decision was made to recommend it to Congress, he did not believe it could pass. Worldwide, hemp was still big business. The Bureau had avoided cannabis, which, Anslinger ruefully pointed out, grew "like dandelions" and still had legitimate commercial uses.[39]

Nonetheless, the Treasury Department began secretly drafting a bill in 1935. The Department's general counsel, Herman Oliphant, was put in charge of writing something that could get past both

[35]Anslinger was a hardliner who sought to make purchasing alcohol for non-medical use a crime, with a first conviction penalty of a fine of at least $1000 & imprisonment for 6 months or more. For subsequent offenses, he sought fines from $5000-50,000 & imprisonment for 2-5 years. Musto. op. cit. p. 211
[36]Abel, E. *Marihuana: The first 12,000 years*. Plenum Press. New York NY. 1980. pp. 196-197
[37]Sloman. op. cit.
[38]Dickson, D.T. 'Bureaucracy & Morality: An organizational perspective on a moral crusade.' in *Social Problems*. vol. 16. 1968. pp. 143-156
[39]*Worcester Telegraph*. MA. Oct. 11, 1936. in Musto. op. cit. p. 223

Congress and the Court.[40] His staff essentially conceived, wrote and engineered passage of hemp prohibition, disguised as a tax revenue bill. Anslinger knew that Congress was not very interested in the matter. "The only information they had was what we would give them in our hearings."[41] He set to work and sent a confidential 1936 memorandum to the Assistant Secretary of the Treasury.[42]

> The State Department has tentatively agreed to this proposition, but before action is taken we shall have to dispose of certain phases of legitimate traffic; for instance, the drug trade still has a small medical need for marihuana, but has agreed to eliminate it entirely. The only place it is used extensively is by the veterinarians, and we can satisfy them by importing their medical needs. We must also satisfy the canary bird seed trade, and the Sherwin Williams Paint Company, which uses hemp seed oil for drying purposes. We are now working with the Department of Commerce in finding substitutes for the legitimate trade, and after that is accomplished, the path will be cleared for the treaties and for federal law.

Addressing the exclusive group invited to the planning session on the Tax Act, FBN counsel Alfred L. Tennyson stressed that every detail of the bill would have to be worked out well ahead of the hearings. This was not "a fishing expedition," Anslinger told the group—296 cannabis seizures had been made in 1936 alone. He complained that traffic showed up in almost every state. A member of the Treasury legal staff asked the commissioner, "Have you lots of cases on this? Horror stories; that's what we want."[43]

Anslinger promptly produced just such a collection of hysterical news articles — mostly pulled from Hearst newspapers.

Anslinger's Gore File

Anslinger had been busy for some time clipping news stories which he had, coincidentally, also helped to write and generate.[44]

> Under my direction, the bureau launched two important steps: first, a legislative plan to seek from Congress a new law that would place marihuana and its distribution directly under federal control. Secondly, on radio and at major forums, ... I reported on the growing list of crime, including murder and rape. ... I believe we did a thorough job.

---

[40]Bonnie & Whitebread. *The Marijuana Conviction.* University of Virginia Press. Richmond VA. 1974

[41]*Ibid.* p. 225

[42]Memo to Stephen B. Gibbons. Feb. 1, 1936. Musto. op. cit. p. 224

[43]Jan. 14, 1937. *Ibid.* p. 227

[44]"At major forums, such as that presented annually by the [Hearst] NY *Herald Tribune*, I told the story of the evil weed of the fields & riverbeds & roadsides. I wrote articles for magazines; our agents gave hundreds of lectures to parents, educators, social & civic leaders [and in] network broadcasts." Anslinger & Oursler. *The Murderers: The story of the narcotics gangs.* Farrar, Strauss & Cudahy. New York NY. 1961

The reason his crime list kept growing was that his staff made it up as they went along, fabricating stories on demand. Anslinger attributed all manner of spectacular crimes to the helpful cannabis plant, even crimes which had never even occurred.[45] In the words of Adolph Hitler, "The great masses of the people ... will more easily fall victims to a big lie than a small one."[46]

During the Daniel Committee hearing on the Narcotic Control Act of 1956, Senator Welker asked Anslinger, "Is it a *fact* that your investigation shows that many of the most sadistic, terrible crimes, solved *or unsolved* (our emphases), we can trace directly to the marihuana user?" The apparently psychic Anslinger replied without missing a beat, "You are correct in many cases."[47]

Canada's anti-cannabis laws were forged by an overzealous judge named Emily Murphy. Among her proposals to punish drug use were long prison sentences, public whippings and deportations, if the offenders were aliens. She described people on cannabis as "immune to pain. ... They become raving maniacs and are liable to kill or indulge in any form of violence to other persons, using the most savage methods of cruelty without, as said before, any sense of moral responsibility."[48] Her sources were the same as those presented to the United States Congress: Anslinger's Gore File, which continued to be cited well into the 1960s.

A Closer Look at the Stories in the File

And so, in 1937 Anslinger went before the poorly attended Congressional committee hearings and called for a total cannabis ban, stating under oath, "Opium has all of the good of Dr. Jeckyll and all the evil of Mr. Hyde. This drug is entirely the monster Hyde, the harmful effects of which cannot be measured."[49]

After the hearings, psychiatrist Dr. Walter Bromberg conducted an independent investigation of the major crimes Anslinger blamed on cannabis. He clearly demonstrated the carelessness of the police in attributing criminal activity. Here are some samples.

One prisoner confessed that while on marihuana he murdered a man and put his body in a trunk. Bromberg discovered that the man had made up the story as an insanity defense. The police accepted it as true, although there was "no indication in the examination or his-

---

45The opening scene in his story 'Marijuana, assassin of youth,' in this chapter.
46Hitler, Adolf. *Mein Kampf*. Berlin Germany. 1924
47Cited in King, R. *The Drug Hangup*. Charles Thomas. Springfield IL. 1974. p. 91
48Murphy, Emily F. *The Black Candle*. Coles Pub. Toronto Canada. 1973. pp. 332-333 Murphy wrote for *Macleans* in the 1920s as 'Janey Canuck.' She considered any & all drugs associated with minorities as tools for the seduction of white women.
49Committee on Ways & Means, House of Representatives. 'Hearing Transcript.' 75c 1s. HR 6385, April 27-30, May 4, 1937

tory of the use of any drug. The investigation by the probation department failed to indicate the use of the drug marihuana."[50]

In another case, two men were drinking heavily one night and at some point smoked a reefer. A fight erupted later. One of them was killed. Newspapers blamed the marihuana and completely ignored their use of alcohol, which is known to lead to violence.[51]

A 1927 *New York Times* report said an impoverished Mexican woman went insane after she fed her family marijuana leaves,[52] adding, "there is no hope of saving the children's lives, and that the mother will be insane for the rest of her life."[53] Her husband had just been killed and she had no food or money to support her family, so the *Times* blamed cannabis, of course, for her troubles.

The most sensational crime attributed to marijuana was the death of a Florida family. Anslinger cited this case during the Marihuana Tax Act hearings in 1937: "In Florida a 21-year-old boy, under the influence of this drug killed his parents and his brothers and sister. The evidence showed that he had smoked marihuana."[54] Here are the facts: On October 16, 1933 Victor Licata axed his mother, father, two brothers and a sister to death in their Tampa home. There was no evidence whatsoever that he was under the influence of marijuana. His family had a history of insanity, and Tampa police had tried to commit Licata to an asylum a year before the crime—a full half year before he first tried marijuana.[55] Nevertheless, a *Tampa Times* editorial raved that, "Whether or not the poisonous, mind-wrecking weed is mainly accountable for the tragedy, its sale should not be and should never have been permitted here or elsewhere."[56]

So it went in each and every case. The role of marijuana in the Gore Files was either assumed, exaggerated or directly fabricated.

Prohibition: Assassin of Truth

Anslinger did not even stop there. He also contrived a dramatic and highly imaginative account of a medieval legend for Congress at the 1937 hearings: the tale of the *Assassins*. A Louisiana judge had recited a version of the legend of the Assassins to support his finding in 1931 that cannabis posed a threat to the community.[57] His

---

[50]Bromberg, Dr. W. 'Marihuana: A Psychiatric Study.' in *Journal of the American Medical Association*. vol. 113. 1939. pp. 4-12

[51]Kolb. Dr. Lawrence. *Addiction*. Charles C. Thomas. Springfield IL. 1962

[52]More likely it was the seeds she was using, although if she used the foliage to extend the meal, it could conceivably have caused her a temporary panic attack.

[53]'Mexican family goes insane: 5 ... stricken.' in *New York Times*. July 6. 1927

[54]'Hearings on HR 6387.' House Com. on Ways & Means. 75C, 1S. 1937. p. 24

[55]Kaplan, John. *Marihuana*. Pocket Books. New York NY. 1972. p. 98

[56]'Stop This Murderous Smoke.' in *Tampa Times*. Oct. 20, 1933

[57]State vs. Bonoa. in Bonnie, R.J. & Whitebread, C.H. 'Forbidden Fruit.' in *Virginia Law Review*. vol. 56. 1970. VA. pp. 1022-1023

story was widely adopted and embellished by prohibitionists. One early propagandist equated cannabis with opium, and described the Assassins as "stupefied with hasheesh ... and exalted by the delicious opiate (sic.)."[58] We could not put this exotic tale in the history section since it is essentially a romanticized legend.

Here is a more accurate account of the tale. A bold revolutionary named Hasan-i-Sabbah captured the Persian mountain stronghold of Alamut in 1090. The word *hashish* at the time meant simply "grass" or "herb," and only later came to refer to cannabis resin.[59] Hasan's followers fought in the Near East for several centuries, according to Marco Polo and other travelers.[60] The outlaw band mixed religious intrigue with stealthy political murders[61] and avoided pitched battles. Hasan's band called themselves the Devoted Ones, and shared some drug. No one knows what it was.[62]

This mystery drug was not even used for their missions, but to initiate new members into the band by sharing a 'moment of paradise' here on earth. Their enemies called them Assassins, a name that worked its way into fictional works of literature, like Boccaccio's *Decameron* and Dante's *Inferno*.[63]

Anslinger co-authored a magazine article that was republished in many forms and magazines over the years, often under the infamous title, "Marihuana, assassin of youth."[64]

> Not long ago the body of a young girl lay crushed on the sidewalk after a plunge from a Chicago apartment window. Everyone called it suicide, but actually it was murder. The killer was a narcotic [sic.] known to America as marihuana, and to history as hashish. ...
> How many murders, suicides, robberies and maniacal deeds it causes each year, especially among the young, can only be conjectured.

Or, in this case, simply invented.[65] No such suicide has ever been documented, but Anslinger's mixture of fantasy and conjecture was laid out before the United States Congress as evidence.

---

[58]Robinson, Dr. Victor. 'An Essay on Hasheesh.' in *Medical Review of Reviews.* vol. 18. 1912. pp. 159-169

[59]Frenchman Sylvestre de Sacy came along in 1809 as the first to attempt to derive the name *Assassins* from *hashishiyyun*. *High Times Encyclopedia.* op. cit. p. 129

[60]All their records were destroyed by the Mongol hordes. Crusaders used the tale to stir up racial hatred for Moslems & to recruit knights to fight in the Holy Land. *High Times Encyc.* op. cit.

[61]From which we derive the modern term *assassination*.

[62]It may have been the fly agaric mushroom, *amanita muscaria*. Allegro, John. *Sacred Mushroom & the Cross.* Bantam/Doubleday. New York NY. 1971. pp. 188-189

[63]The French Romantics patterned their 'Club des Haschischins' after their own image of the medieval cult and its exotic trappings. *Ibid.* p. 13

[64]Anslinger, H.J. & Cooper, C.R. 'Marihuana, assassin of youth.' in *American Magazine.* vol. 124. 1937. pp. 18-19, 150-153

[65]It was, however, depicted in the classic propaganda film, *Reefer Madness.*

The Petrocriminal Coup of 1937

The bureaucrats agreed on a plan for the hearings. The Public Health Service was not invited, since its Division of Mental Hygiene[66] had refuted the Treasury Department claims months before the April hearings, stating that "marihuana is habit forming, although not addicting in the same sense as alcohol might be with some people, or sugar or coffee."[67] To avoid discussion by the full House, Treasury officials and Anslinger brought the measure in the guise of a revenue tax bill to the six member House Ways and Means Committee, chaired by key Du Pont ally Robert Doughton of North Carolina. This would bypass the full House without further hearings, then hand the bill to the Senate Finance Committee, controlled by their ally Prentiss Brown of Michigan, to rubber stamp it into law. Once on the books, Anslinger would "administer" the licensing process to ensure that no more commercial hemp would ever grow in the United States. Assistant General Counsel for the Treasury Department, Clinton Hester, kicked off the attack before the House Committee.[68]

> The leading newspapers of the United States have recognized the seriousness of this problem and many of them have advocated federal legislation to control the traffic in marihuana. ... In a recent editorial, the *Washington Times* stated, 'The marihuana cigarette is one of the most insidious of all forms of dope [sic.], largely because of the failure to the public to understand its fatal [sic.] qualities.' ... The purpose of HR 6385 is to employ the federal taxing power not only to raise revenue from the marihuana traffic, but also to discourage the current and widespread undesirable use of marihuana by smokers and drug addicts [sic.] and thus drive the traffic into channels where the plant will be put to valuable industrial, medical and scientific uses.

"The $100 transfer tax in this bill is intended to be prohibitive," he acknowledged, and would work by being added to the price of cannabis, which at the time was "about a dollar per ounce, as a drug." Anslinger testified that the harm caused by the herb was "beyond measure" and required absolute control by the FBN.

The First Wave of Resistance Rises

A last-minute witness, Ralph Loziers of the National Oil Seed Institute, representing paint manufacturers and high quality machine lubrication processors, showed up at the hearing to disagree. He stated that the seed was an essential commodity used in all the Asian

---

[66]Now the National Institute of Mental Health.
[67]Musto, D. *The American Disease*. Colonial Press Inc. Clinton MA. 1973. p. 226
[68]Transcript. 'Committee on Ways & Means, House of Representatives. 75c 1s. HR 6385.' April 27-30, May 4 1937

nations and in parts of Russia as food. Furthermore, he pointed out the need for hemp seed by American industry.

> It is grown in their fields and used as oatmeal. Millions of people every day are using hemp seed in the Orient as food. They have been doing that for many generations, especially in periods of famine. ... The point I make is this—that this bill is too all inclusive. This bill is a world encircling measure. This bill brings the activities—the crushing of this great industry under the supervision of a bureau—which may mean its suppression.[69]

Dr. William C. Woodward, long-time legislative counsel for the American Medical Association, spoke in defense of cannabis medicine and also to protest the way the bill was handled. "The law simply contains provisions that impose a useless expense and does not accomplish the result." Dr. Woodward said it was uncertain from the data that cannabis use had increased at all, but if it had, the "newspaper exploitation of the habit has done more to increase it than anything else." Asked point blank, "Don't you think some federal legislation necessary?" Dr. Woodward replied, "I do not.... It is not a medical addiction that is involved."

Doughton snapped back, "If you want to advise us on legislation, you ought to come here with some constructive proposals, rather than criticisms, rather than trying to throw obstacles in the way of something that the federal government is trying to do."

Switching Hats, or the Name Game

Woodward still had other criticisms to make, namely that the use of the term "marihuana" was deliberately misleading and that the bill had been prepared "in secret."

> The term *marihuana* ... has no general meaning, except as it relates to the use of cannabis preparations for smoking. It is not recognized in medicine and hardly even in the Treasury Department. Marihuana is not the correct term. It was the use of the term *marihuana* rather than the use of the term *cannabis* or the term *Indian hemp* that was responsible, as you probably realized a day or two ago, for the failure of the dealers in Indian hemp seed to connect up the bill with their business until rather late .... In all that you have heard here thus far, no mention has been made of any excessive use of the drug by any doctor or its excessive distribution by any pharmacist. And yet the burden of this bill is placed heavily on the doctors and pharmacists of the country, and I may say very heavily—most heavily, possibly of all—on the farmers of the country. ...
> We cannot understand yet, Mr. Chairman, why this bill should have been prepared in secret for two years without any initiative, even to the profession, that it was being prepared. ... No medical man would identify this bill with a medicine until he read it through, because *marihuana* is not a drug, ... simply a name given cannabis.

---

[69]"... Last year [1936], there was imported into the United States 62,813,000 pounds of hempseed. In 1935 there was imported 116 million pounds."

A few days later, Representative Fred Vinson of Kentucky was asked to summarize the AMA's position for the full Congress before the final vote. He lied outright that the medical group's spokesperson "not only gave this measure his full support, but also the approval from the American Medical Association."

The Act passed without a roll call vote. Today, we well understand why it was kept secret. Passage of the Act put all hemp industries firmly within the iron fist of the very special interests that most benefited from its repression over the years: prohibition police and bureaucrats, working in collusion first with the petrochemical and the timber industry, later the alcohol and tobacco industries, the pharmaceutical drug industry and, more recently, the urine testing, property seizure, police and prison industries.

The Case Presented to the Senate Hearings

Two months later, Treasury Department representative Clinton Hester appeared before the three members who bothered to attend the Senate Finance Committee hearing.[70]

> Not only is marihuana used by hardened criminals to steel them to commit violent crimes, but it is also being placed in the hands of high-school children in the form of marihuana cigarettes by unscrupulous peddlers. Its continued use results many times in impotency and insanity [sic.]. … As an additional means of bringing the traffic in marihuana into the open, the bill requires all transfers of marihuana to be made in pursuance of official order forms issued by the Secretary of the Treasury.

The Treasury Department had generously offered that its agents would simply refuse to issue any permits. Hester described the technicality used to get around the fact that prohibition laws had repeatedly been declared unconstitutional by the Supreme Court.

> You would have to prohibit it entirely, and of course you would put all of these legitimate industries out of business. The Supreme Court has held that where on the face of the act, it appears to be a taxing measure, the fact that it happens to be prohibitive in character will not affect the Constitutionality.

Next, Anslinger took up the attack. Although not a doctor, he nonetheless announced that its medical use could be abandoned without any suffering. He perjured himself to the effect that the herb's effects lasted "48 hours before they returned to normal," and "we have heard of them smoking the seed." He told of two men who "stripped the plants on a hemp farm" to sell the foliage, which he claimed was worse than opium. He failed to mention the fact that

---

[70]'Hearing before a subcommittee of the Committee on Finance, US Senate, 75c 2s. HR 6906.' Library of Congress transcript. July 12, 1937

it would take smoking a couple hundred pounds of commercial hemp to get high, if even then.[71] "The States are asking for help."

Chairman Brown cautiously noted, "I read with care the supplemental statement which you placed in the record before the Ways and Means Committee in which you brought out quite clearly that the use which will be 'illicit,' if we may describe it that way, in the event this bill becomes a law, has been known to the peoples of Europe and Mexico and the United States for centuries." He asked why no one had heard about it "until the last year or so." Anslinger said, "I do not know just why the abuse of marihuana has spread like wildfire in the last four or five years." Brown asked what dangers, if any, this bill had for those engaged in "the legitimate uses of the hemp plant?" Anslinger answered under oath that "they are not only amply protected under this Act, but they can go ahead and raise hemp just as they have always done."

Hester assured the committee that this measure was fair and came "strongly recommended" by the Treasury Department.

The Loyal Opposition Emerges

By this time the hemp industry had begun to catch on that something was amiss. A number of important witnesses now came forth to challenge the bill before the committee.

Mr. Rems of the Rems Hemp Co. bluntly charged that the tax was designed to put hemp manufacturers "out of business." Farmers harvested hemp while it was "still green, with no seed in it, and we field-wet it. All these leaves are gone. There is no marihuana drug there." He cut to the heart of the matter and demanded, "The real purpose of this bill is not to raise money, is it?" Brown replied, "Well, we are sticking to the proposition that it is."

Mr. Moksnes represented the AmHempCo., organized just three years earlier in New York to refine hemp fiber for textiles and use the hurd for plastics. "The capacity of the plant is 15,000 acres. We have to contract our seed from the growers in Kentucky. ... That tax is going to be prohibitive. We are going to lose the small growers, and it is the combination of growers that we have to depend on."[72]

Mr. Johnson, representing Chempaco, Inc. and Hemp Chemical Corp., agreed that the small grower would be eliminated. "And why shouldn't he be?" he asked pointedly. "But here is a great industry." The business group he represented planned to plant 20,000 acres of

---

71Wood, Ian. Fiber crop expert, Commonwealth Scientific & Industrial Research Organization. Brisbane Australia. in DaSilva, W. 'Australians want to make paper from pot.' *Sunday Punch*. Sydney Australia. March 24, 1991
72"Three years ago we planted 1200 acres, last year 4200 acres, & this year 7000."

hemp all over the country, because "big industries use the fiber and use the hurd." Johnson defended the integrity of the farmer.

> He knows definitely that he is not growing anything that has marihuana on it. He does not want to grow marihuana, and yet we might lose an industry. ... This is not the sort of measure that people here are saying it is, a regulatory measure under the guise of a tax measure. We do not need to run around the corner to the hemp industry in order to stop the sale of the flowers or of the leaves. It can be taxed like the automobile industry, like the domestic industry, like the fur industry and we do not need to use any legal sophistry in this to sustain this statute because hemp is produced in the United States. ... Be fair to industry and the farmer. ...
>
> People making paper, and the finest grades of paper, which you cannot make in this country without the use of hemp at the present time, and which is being imported—even a great deal of the paper that goes into our money is being imported—must have hemp fibers. It is just a ridiculous situation, because it can be made out of our local products in this country. The paper manufacturer, when he gets the plant, simply blows these leaves away. They disappear when dried. They are gone.
>
> As a matter of fact, these people in Minnesota did not know until two months ago that the hemp which they grew there contained marihuana ... and they were as surprised as anyone else.

The AMA's Dr. Woodward wrote to the committee with one last appeal to reason. "The obvious purpose and effect of this bill is to impose so many restrictions on the medicinal use as to prevent such use altogether. ... It may serve to deprive the public of the benefits of a drug that on further research may prove to be of substantial value." The committee then went into executive session, approved the law and forwarded it to the Senate for final passage, which occurred without further debate.

The Grasping Tentacles of Prohibition

It is significant that when hemp was "controlled" by the federal government, it was outlawed for almost every use except birdseed, which was mostly imported and did not compete with any of Du Pont, Mellon, Hearst or their allies' financial interests. The imported seed was required to be sterilized. The regulations for use of the herb by physicians were so complicated that they were not likely to prescribe it, which opened the market for synthetic drugs to replace the more efficacious and benign cannabis, a natural medicine.

That same year, 1937, Du Pont filed its patent on nylon, a synthetic fiber that took over many textile and cordage markets that normally would have gone to hemp. More than half the American cars on the road between 1922 and 1984 were built by General Motors which guaranteed Du Pont a captive market for paints, varnishes, plastics, rubber, etc. Furthermore, all GM cars would be designed to use tetra-ethyl leaded fuel exclusively, which contained chemical additives that Du Pont manufactured.[73] Du Pont was able to use its control of the entire sphere of the auto and fuel industries to keep out competitive technologies. It made little difference to them that Henry Ford built his hemp-mobile and secretly grew fields of hemp, hoping to become independent of the petroleum industry. He could not long keep it up long under the state and federal bans.

Finally, the public attitude toward the cannabis user changed overnight once he became a criminal. This activity that had been merely a pleasant pastime was now perceived to be a moral pestilence—a plague that destroyed the spirit and left the body to rot. Latinos and the African American blues and jazz culture soon fell under a systematic racist attack by prohibition bureaucrats who used the cannabis ban to imprison minority community leaders and undermine the positive role models they provided. With their new police power, the entrenched marihuana bureaucrats had a clear field to enforce their economic, political and social agendas.

---

[73]Colby, Jerry. *Du Pont Dynasties*. Lyle Steward. New York NY. 1984

5

REPRISE: HEMP FOR VICTORY

Around this time over in Europe, Hitler's Nazis seized power in Germany and Mussolini's Fascists overtook Italy. Germany invaded Poland and Holland, plunging Europe into the Second World War. In Asia, military industrialists took power in Japan and invaded China. The United States remained neutral, selling arms, fuel and supplies to all sides of the spreading conflict.

In late 1941 Japan bombed Pearl Harbor, Hawaii. It then seized control of the Philippine Islands, the source of the United States' tropical fibers, used to replace true hemp. That meant war.

Once again, when the nation needed help, it turned to hemp. Only a few short years after being prohibited, hemp made a strong but short-lived comeback. *Business Week* reported that hemp had been grown in a small way in Wisconsin for a few years, "but 1943 will find it an industry in the Middle West because of the loss of Philippine fibers. ... The Bureau of Internal Revenue will police the six states concerned, and require that each grower register."[1] Little known to most people, hemp had already returned in a big way in the previous few years. Farmers had earlier received a government-issued booklet, titled *Hemp, a War Crop*.[2]

> In normal time rope and twine made from Manila fibers [abaca] imported from the Philippines constituted a large portion of the supply. ... Hemp imported from Italy, Russia, France and Holland, together with a small amount grown in Wisconsin and Kentucky, was used for medium grade wrapping twine and rope. Because we do not have climactic conditions conducive to the growing of Manila or jute, ... thousands of acres in the Midwest will be planted and new factories built to handle the crop.
>
> Hemp growing in the U.S. ... is now apparently going to be allowed and even encouraged as a result of the war. This is seen from a War Productions Board order prohibiting the use of domestically produced hempseed for any purpose except the growing of hemp fiber or the growing of additional hempseed.

A stirring Department of Agriculture film, *Hemp for Victory*, was being shown in farm houses and Grange Halls across the land.[3]

[1] 'It's a hemp year.' in *Business Week*. April 24, 1943
[2] Sackett & Hobbs. *Hemp; A war crop*. Mason & Hanger Co. New York NY. 1942
[3] *Hemp for Victory*. USDA film. Washington DC. 1942

In 1942, patriotic farmers at the government's request planted 36,000 acres of seed hemp, an increase of several thousand percent. ... Thus hemp, cannabis sativa, the old standby cordage fiber, is staging a strong comeback. ... The power breaker makes quick work of it. ...
The old Kentucky river mill at Frankfort ... has been making cordage for more than a century. All such plants will presently be turning out products spun from American-grown hemp: twine of various kinds for tying, winding armatures and upholsterer's work; rope for marine rigging and towing; for hay forks, derricks and heavy duty tackle; light duty firehose, thread for shoes for millions of American soldiers; and parachute webbing for our paratroopers. As for the U.S. Navy, every battleship requires 34,000 feet of rope, and other crafts accordingly. So here in the Boston Navy Yard, where cables for frigates were made long ago, crews are now working night and day making cordage for the fleet. ...
Today, even the ropewalk is mechanized: 160 fathoms to go.

Soon the renaissance was in full bloom. *The Herald Tribune* trumpeted, "Hemp Cultivation in the United States: Long neglected American crop takes over 240,000 acres in Mid-West, in program to replace lost import from the Far East." The government-financed corporation in charge of the program, War Hemp Industries, Inc., built 42 new mills to process the hemp, each employing about 100 people, and trained the operators. The mills, with about 60 harvesting machines each to rent to farmers, were built by Defense Plant Corporation at $350,000 each, totalling almost $15 million. The "polo farmers," mostly Republicans, referred to the mills as juicy political "plums" in the hands of the politicians.[4]

Most of their products were allocated for the war. The rest found "many civilian and indirect uses, such as thread for shoes and harnesses, fish nets, carpet warps and packing for pumps and ships' seams." More than 20,000 farmers in Illinois, Indiana, Iowa, Kentucky, Minnesota and Wisconsin contracted with the government to grow hemp in "the largest annual increase of a major crop in American history." Some 55,000 acres were grown for seed. The 185,000 acres of fiber hemp yielded 75,000 tons of fiber that year.[5] By war's end nearly a million acres of "marijuana" had been cultivated to support the troops in their struggle for freedom.

Even the 4-H Clubs were promoting traditional agriculture and boosting the hemp team effort. They encouraged schoolchildren in rural areas to plant their own hemp patch, which "gives 4-H Club

4'Hemp Cultivation in the US.' in *NY Herald Tribune.* May 30, 1943
5Under 10,000 acres in 1941, & 50,000 in 1942 for seed. The area planted in 1943 was 5 times that of 1942; 25 times more than 1941. "An old but long-neglected American crop, hemp, is sprouting again this spring on almost a quarter of a million acres of the richest corn land in the Mid-West ... to ease the critical shortage of strong & durable fibers needed for the war." Ibid. It calls this "exactly the output of the largest previous crop in the US, in 1859." However, the 1859 crop was greatly overstated due to a clerical error. Hopkins, James F. *History of the Hemp Industry in Kentucky.* U of K Press. Lexington KY. 1951

members a real opportunity to serve their country in wartime. Grow at least an acre of hemp; one to two acres would be better."[6]

The nation was in a race with Germany over who could boost hemp production to the highest level to produce the most war goods. German youngsters studied the value of *hanf* at an early age, in the pamphlet *Die Lustige Hanffibel*, which reads in part:[7]

> In today's world ... crops should not only provide food in large quantities, they can provide raw materials for industry. Among such raw materials, hemp is of especially high value. What it provides, where it is planted, what is made from it and how to grow it can all be learned from this primer. ... The wood ... can easily be used for surface coatings for the finest floors, ... paper and cardboard, building materials and wall paneling. Further processing will even produce wood sugar and wood gas. However, all the above pale in comparison to the usefulness of its fiber. ... Sixty years ago German ground produced much more hemp.[8] ...
>
> In short, anything sown in hemp's fields will bring rich harvests and much money. ... because hemp, useful as it is, will be purchased in unlimited amounts.

All this interest was quietly buried at war's end. American mills were quietly phased out over the next decade. By 1957, prohibitionists had reasserted a total ban on the domestic hemp industry, which has been in effect ever since. In 1961 Anslinger helped design the United Nations *Single Convention Treaty on Narcotic Drugs*, to further cripple the global industry. Hemp is the natural competition that the timber and synthetic products industries don't want you to know about. But you can't keep a good plant down.

The searches for clean, abundant energy, tree-free paper and sustainable natural resources converged with the cannabis reform movement in the late 1980s. More and more people have come to see the vast potential of a restored hemp industry. In 1991 Australia began growing hemp for paper. In 1993 the United Kingdom issued its first hemp farming permits. In 1994 the Irrigated Desert Research Facility, USDA, planted a joint research crop with Hemp Agrotech, Inc., a division of the Hempstead Company, in Brawley, California. Their field was invaded and destroyed by prohibition agents just a week before its planned harvest.[9] That same year Hempline, Inc., was allowed to grow and harvest a legal hemp crop in Canada.

Today we are perched at the edge of what could be a new era of prosperity and justice—the revival of the American dream. And the hemp renaissance will be at its heart.

---

[6]Edwards, Don. 'For 4-H Clubs, Patriotic pot patches.' in *Herald-Leader*. Lexington KY. Jan. 25, 1983. p. B-1

[7]*Die Lustige Hanffibel* Reich's Nutritional Institute. Berlin Germany. 1943

[8]21,000 hectares in 1878. By 1932 it was only 200 hectares, but in 1939 production was 16,000 hectares. During the war years, production continued to climb. *Ibid.*

[9]*Hemp Today*. Quick American Archives. Oakland CA. 1994. pp. 189-195, 257-260

Part II

—

The Premier Plant of the Planet

HEMP
Lifeline to the Future

6

MEET THE HELPFUL HEMP PLANT

Cannabis hemp is a versatile, attractive plant with three listed species, scores of strains and three essential characteristics: It is a survivor; a builder; and a healer. The plant has been endowed with an exceptional measure of the life force, but also with an identity problem. Botanists still debate whether it is *monotypic,* with only one species, or *polytypic,* having several. Hemp has scores of subspecies and hundreds of regional names, while at times its own name is misapplied to a dozen or so other fiber plants.

The hard-working hemp plant's official Latin name is *cannabis sativa,* L, from the Greek *kannabis.* This double name was first listed in 60 AD by Dioscorides,[1] and adopted by Carl Linnaeus for his 1753 compendium, *Species Plantarum.*[2] Monotypists argue that this is the only species. However, Jean Lamarck's 1783 *Encyclopedia* listed another species, *cannabis indica,* to honor the resinous herb's presumed homeland, India.[3] While not universally accepted, a third species was published in 1924, *cannabis ruderalis.*[4] All cannabis seed lines, or *cultivars*, can be cross-fertilized.

The herb's trail through the world lexicon lies in its word fragment "an," a relic of its ancient Accadian (in the modern Middle East) root name, *Quanuba.*[5] It traveled east into Asia, in names like *ganjah* in India. It went west through the Greek *kannabis* to Latin *cannabis* into the Romance languages, where we find *canapa* in Italian, and *cáñamo* in Spanish. The "an" tied into the Egyptian hieroglyph for rope, now transformed into the Roman letter "h," forming *chanvre* in French, then made its way north into the German *hanf,* through the Dutch *hennep* into Old English *hænep,* where it turned first into *hempe* and, finally, our modern *hemp.*[6]

In this book, we use its English name, hemp, or its scientific name, cannabis, unless the context calls for one of its other names.

---

[1]Dioscorides. *De Materia Medica.* 60 AD

[2]Leonhart Fuchs of Basel had already revived the name *cannabis sativa* in his herbal catalogue *De Historia Stirpium.* 1542

[3]Lamarck, Jean. *Encyclopedia.* 1788. vol. 1. p. 695

[4]Janischewsky. 1924. Also, a potent & consistent yielding strain of medical cannabis indica was naturalized to North America & registered as *cannabis Americana* by the US drug company Parke Davis. We have not determined if this line still exists.

[5]There are numerous spellings used to translate this cuneiform word.

[6]The spelling *h–e–m–p* was first defined & listed (along with *cannibum, hænep* & *henep*) in Wm. Wulcker's *Vocabularium.* London England. 1000 AD

A Brief Description of Cannabis Hemp

The cannabis hemp plant is an annual herbaceous crop that is grown from seed each year.[7] It is included in the botanical order *Urticales*, along with the hops plant, used to make beer, in a distinct family called *Cannabaceae*.[8] Some botanists prefer to assign it to the *Moraceae* family, which includes the mulberry.[9]

Hemp grows to heights of one to five meters (three to 16 feet) or more in a season and produces a long *bast*, or bark, fiber. It has a rigid stalk that is round or obtusely four-cornered, more or less fluted or channeled, with well-marked nodes at intervals of 10 to 50 centimeters (four to 20 inches).[10] If crowded, as grown for fiber, the stalks have no branches or foliage except at the top, and the smooth stems are six to 20 millimeters (1/4 to 3/4 inch) in diameter. When not crowded, as grown for seed or herb, a hemp plant produces many spreading branches on a central stalk with a mature thickness of three to six centimeters (one to two inches) and a rough, fibrous bark near the base.

The familiar cannabis leaf pattern is palmated, compound with five to 11 serrated leaflets, usually seven. The leaflets are rich green, lighter below, lanceolate,[11] five to 15 centimeters (two to six inches) long, and one to two centimeters (1/4 to 3/4 inch) wide.[12] The leaves grow in lateral opposite pairs, except near the ends of branches, where they often alternate sides. Side branches begin at the leaf node. Most of the nutrients used by hemp are stored in the foliage and returned to the soil as mulch at the close of the season.[13]

The genus is *dioecious*, meaning it has two distinct sexes. The flowers of hemp are highly developed, with the pollen-bearing staminate, or male, flowers, and the seed-producing pistillate, or female, flowers, blooming on separate plants. However, individual plants can also be *monoecius*, or hermaphroditic.[14]

Since most people cannot recognize the female flowers, the males are often called "flowering hemp." A male flower consists of five greenish yellow or purplish sepals in small radiating clusters

---

[7]In tropical zones or in greenhouses, this cycle can be extended to 2 years or more.
[8]Urticales includes *humulus lupulus*, or hops. in *Historia Natural*. Carroggio, sa, de ediciones. Barcelona Spain. vol. 3. p. 198
[9]Cannabis has been associated with the mulberry plant in China since ancient times.
[10]Indoor growing techniques can reduce this gap down to 1–2 centimeters.
[11]Lance shaped; tapered or pointed at both ends.
[12]Described by Dewey, Lyster H. Chief botanist, fiber plant specialist. 'Hemp.' in *Yearbook of the United States Department of Agriculture, 1913*. Government Printing Office. Washington DC. # 53C, 2S no 989. 1914. pp. 286-287
[13]Harvesting methods, like early cutting or uprootings, affect these proportions. Use for seed, herb or biofuels consume more nutrients & thus require more fertilizer.
[14]Werf, Hayo van der. *Crop Physiology of Fibre Hemp*. Proefschrift Wageningen. Wageningen Netherlands. 1994

that open wide at maturity, when five stamens discharge abundant pollen. The inconspicuous female flower is small, green, solitary and stemless. It consists of a calyx—a thin, green pouch—that is pointed with a slit at one side. The calyx is nearly closed over the ovary and merely permits two small white stigmas to protrude at the apex, like feathers on a cap, to collect airborne pollen. Nestled hidden in the axils of the small leaves near the ends of the branches, they are often so crowded together as to appear like a thick, spiked club. Males die soon after their pollen is shed, but females remain alive and green two months later, until the seeds have sufficiently developed. The one-seeded ovary develops into a tiny, smooth, nearly spherical "achene," or seed kernel, each in its own pod.[15] The oil-rich fruits grow together in clusters along the flowering stalk.

The relative proportions by weight of the different parts of the thoroughly air-dried hemp plant are approximately as follows: stems 60 percent, leaves 30 percent and roots 10 percent.[16] When grown for seed, about half the weight of the dried plant will be fruit.

A Netherlands study of 200 hemp cultivars found 97 varieties in the .06 to 1.77 percent THC flower content range, whereas the potency of strains grown for herb are four percent or above. Furthermore, dense growing patterns reduced the occurence of potency levels so as to have no psychoactive effect. [17]

A Comparison With Cannabis Indica

Although similar in appearance to sativa, cannabis indica is shorter and more densely branched, with thick, tropical foliage. Its leaves bear seven to 11 (usually nine) leaflets that are wider[18] than those of sativa. United States Department of Agriculture botanist and hemp expert Lyster Dewey described cannabis indica in 1913 as "different in general appearance from any of the numerous forms grown by this department from seed obtained in nearly all countries where hemp is cultivated."

Its resinous foliage remains green until after the last leaves of even the female sativa plants have withered and fallen. This medicinal variety was known to Europeans and Americans as *Indian hemp*. Dewey said it was "very attractive as an ornamental plant, but of no value for fiber."[19] That is because its stem is too short (just over a

---

[15]2.5-4 mm. (1/10-3/16 in.) thick, & 3-6 mm (1/8-1/4 in.) long. Seeds range from dark gray to light brown & mottled & weigh from .008-.027 gram, with dark seeds generally being much heavier than pale ones of the same batch sample. *Ibid.*
[16]*Ibid.*
[17]Meijer, E.P.M. de.. 'Hemp variations as pulp source researched in the Netherlands.' in *Pulp & Paper*. July 1993. pp. 41-43
[18]Dewey said "very narrow," but our study found the reverse to be true. op. cit. p. 302
[19]Dewey. *Ibid*. p. 302

meter, or four feet) and too lignified to produce long, high quality bast fibers. Indica has a nearly solid stalk.

The Country Cousin of Cannabis

This breed epitomizes the rugged survival instincts of this adaptable plant. Ruderalis means "roadside,"[20] which is where you are likely to encounter this wild plant. Its special characteristics enable it to spread without much human help. In southern Russia, ruderalis is a very short, sprawling, unbranched or slightly-branched hemp with fat leaves. Its seeds detach easily and can survive a freezing winter to germinate the next spring. It can grow in marginal conditions and still prove valuable for a variety of uses.[21]

Some of the Ways Hemp Is Used

The hemp plant, primarily the sativa strain, has many special characteristics. Each part of the plant has its own distinct uses.

Its leaves and roots build and improve the soil. Its stalk wraps nature's finest soft fiber around a readily available source of wood for cellulose, or $C_6H_{10}O_6$, the building block of modern industry. Cellulose, used to manufacture paper, plastic, film, rayon, etc. is the chief component of cell walls in the woody parts of plants. The seed of the hemp plant is a complete and highly digestible source of nutrition for human and animal and is also the source of a valuable oil. And hemp is an aromatic, decorative herb that can be bred for the therapeutic and psychological effects of its flowers.

The Herb That Makes People Feel Better

Cannabis foliage, seed and roots have scores of medical uses, both traditional and clinically demonstrated, with potential for more.

The leaves and flowering tops of certain plants constitute an effective herbal medicine and a mild intoxicant.[22] The chemical THC and its related compounds are concentrated in the female flower. They are less pronounced in sativas traditionally grown in temperate climates, and higher potencies are frequently considered characteristic of indicas.[23] Very little THC occurs in ruderalis.

[20]*Ruderal* is a German term for "weeds of old fields & roadsides," which grow where natural vegetation has been disturbed. Webster's *New Collegiate Dictionary*. 1974
[21]*High Times Encyclopedia of Recreational Drugs*. Trans High Publishing, Stonehill Publishing Co. New York NY. 1978. p. 120
[22]We use this word guardedly, since cannabis is nontoxic; however, no suitable word is available in the English language. Furthermore, people speak figuratively of "intoxicating beauty" & other pleasurable things which are nontoxic. The term *narcotic* is pharmaceutically inaccurate. The effect of cannabis deserves a word of its own, & is often referred to as "getting high."
[23]*High Times Encyclopedia*. op. cit. p. 118

CANNABIS SATIVA
Leggy female flower
Taller plant
Longer stalk
Sparse foliage
Slender leaflets

CANNABIS INDICA
Dense, resinous flower
Shorter plant
Branchy stalk
Heavy foliage
Wide leaflets

Male in Flower

Over 60 synergistic therapeutically active compounds are among the 421 components of the cannabis herb. The human brain has special receptor sites for some of these that are a unique part of our genetic design and put the human mind and the cannabis plant in direct contact.[24]

The Life Story of the Common Hemp Plant

Spring rain moistens the soil. Sunlight warms it.

Just below the surface, a tiny seed starts and awakens, as from a deep sleep. It stirs. It moves. It bursts open its ashen woody shell.[25]

The curious youngster takes two opposite courses: the white, fibril-tapered root turns away from the sun and burrows deep into the nourishing bosom of the Earth; the tiny stem, bearing two small, shield-like leaves, ascends bravely and gracefully up through the soil to peer out into the bright sunlight.

The soil all around is covered with the bright green flush of thousands of other yawning, stretching seedlings. Brilliant, saturated with blazing sunlight, they radiate a rich green as they scramble out of the ground, thrusting skyward, first opening and then shedding their serrated multileafleted foliage as they race side by side, standing taller and prouder every day. They dance together in the breeze throughout the hot summer. The weeds try to keep up, but fail and then fall.

Only a hundred days it takes to rise out from those tiny seeds, these powerful woody stalks—hollow, hairy, covered with their tough fiber with the strength of anchor cables. The field sparrow nests among the bushes along the edge of the crop while the vigilant crow keeps a keen eye out around the roots to catch a tasty cutworm nematode, hemp's major pest enemy. A hundred days after the sowing, the shorter male plants shed their pollen, then begin to yellow and die.

The air is filled with a rich, balsamic perfume as the tall, slender females toss their luxuriant flowering heads in the autumn breeze. The farmer recognizes that fragrance and knows it is time to harvest the fiber hemp. The seed hemp still needs time to mature.

Then comes the cool of autumn and, one fine day, the slice of a cutting tool and the mighty stalk comes crashing down, down onto that rich mulch of its season's bounteous leaf growth. Stronger still is the aroma of the fresh cut stalks and flowers, spreading far throughout the air: the fragrance of the harvest.

---

[24]Matsuda, Lisa. National Institute of Mental Health. in Booth, W. 'Marijuana receptor exists in brain, study confirms' in *Washington Post*. DC. Aug. 9, 1990
[25]Based on the description of: Allen, James Lane. *The Reign of Law: A tale of the Kentucky hemp fields*. MacMillan Co. London England. 1900.

It lies there a week or more, drying, until the sap is out of the stalks—until leaves and blossoms wither and drop away, giving back to the soil the nourishment they have drawn from it. Then the rakers gather the stalks up and take them away. They are carried by truck to the market, where people select and buy the crops for the mills and factories. There they will be processed and manufactured into all manner of products that make life a little better for everyone.

Winter time. All the hemp is gone now, except for the seeds that the farmer held back for next year's crop. The fields are plowed—stubble, mulch and manure adding to the topsoil, now tilled and smoothed over, ready for the next planting—a cycle that has been repeated each year for 10,000 years or more.

Springtime.

The farmer looks out at the fertile land and sky heavy with rain and knows it is almost time to sow the hempseed once again.

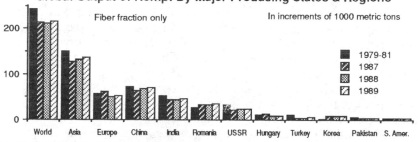

Global Output of Hemp: By Major Producing States & Regions

[56]*Hemp Traders.* 2130 Colby Ave. #1, Los Angeles CA 90025. 310-914-9557
[57]350% profit after expenses. *Facts for Farmers*; editor Solon Robinson. Johnson & Ward Pub. New York NY. 1865. p. 967
[58]Moore, Brent. *The Hemp Industry In Kentucky, A Study of the Past, the Present & the Possibilities.* Press of James E. Hughes. Lexington KY. 1905. p. 92
[59]'Hemp Cultivation in the United States.' in *Herald Tribune.* NY. May 30, 1943

7

FOR THE HEALING OF THE PLANET

Human beings, like all living creatures, have a survival instinct. Unlike most creatures, however, we exert a great deal of control over our destiny. Dinosaurs, for example, became extinct not due to any activity of their own but were victims of climactic change. Yet now it is our own industries that are causing environmental and climactic changes that may lead to our extinction.

This is not a wholly new problem. Loss of topsoil is the historic cause of the demise of many great civilizations,[1] and has been a topic of concern throughout the ages. The ancient Mesopotamian text *Epic of Gilgamesh* describes emperor Nimrod's destruction of a mighty forest. Today his empire is gone, and the region is a virtual desert. *The Bible* warns that God will "destroy them which destroy the earth."[2] In the eighth century AD, Mohammed predicted that in the final days "the heaven shall produce a visible smoke, which shall cover mankind; this will be a tormenting plague."[3]

In 1854, Chief Seattle replied to a United States government request to buy land: "Whatever befalls the earth befalls the sons of the earth. Man did not weave the web of life. He is merely a strand in it. Whatever he does to the web, he does to himself. Even the white man ... cannot be exempt from the common destiny." In 1845, American philosopher Henry David Thoreau wrote his classic *Walden* on the theme of preserving fragile nature.[4]

Human activity is directly responsible for the extinction of many thousands of life forms. The current rate of extinction due to destruction of tropical rainforest and related habitats is estimated at 1000 species per year, many of which are not even known to us.[5] If the environment is destroyed, neither the economy, the community nor the individual can endure. Has our ability to produce toxins and alter our surroundings overwhelmed our survival instinct—or can we find a happy medium between ecology and technology?

---

[1] Carter, V.G. & Dale, T. *Topsoil & Civilization*. U of OK Press. Norman OK. 1974
[2] John, St. 'Book of Revelation, 11:18.' in *The Holy Bible*. King James version
[3] Mohammed. *The Koran*. Chapter 44
[4] "I had not lived there a week before my feet wore a path from my door to the pondside; and though it is 5-6 years since I trod it, it is still quite distinct." Thoreau, Henry David. *Walden*. Peter Pauper Press. Mt. Vernon NY. 1966
[5] Ehrlich, Anne. of Stanford U Center for Conservation Biology, Dept. of Biological Sciences. also Rainforest Action Network. 301–A Broadway, San Francisco CA

Let's look at some major environmental problems to see how hemp can help solve them while sustaining progress.

Preserving Forests, Soil & Farms

Forests protect and nurture the diversity of life on the planet. Our forests also guard the sources of most of our clean drinking water, the watersheds. Deforestation is the road to desertification.

This was already a government concern in 1916, when the United States Department of Agriculture *Bulletin 404* reported that our forests were being cut down three times faster than they grew. It called for alternatives to the use of timber and recommended using hemp pulp for paper instead of tree pulp.[6] Hemp produces four times as much pulp per acre as forest land. This wood will serve for all the commercial uses of trees and save endangered forests.

Severe restrictions were placed on growing hemp in the southern states at the beginning of this century. Twenty years later, the region had become a "dust bowl." The wind and water were brown with the topsoil they carried away. The region's farm economy was destroyed and the environment has never fully recovered. Over two-thirds of our original topsoil was lost between the beginning of European colonization and the late 1980s.[7]

Current annual topsoil loss on agricultural land here is over five billion tons.[8] Some 85 percent of this is from croplands, pastures, rangeland and forest land directly used for raising livestock.[9] Farms need a profitable alternative. Overall, hemp is the ideal farm crop. It grows best in warm tropical zones or moderately cool, temperate climates, such as the United States. Hemp seedlings endure cold or light frost as well as oat seedlings or other spring crops. It even grows well on muck lands for purposes other than fiber.[10] Hemp leaves the soil in excellent condition for any succeeding crop, especially when weeds may otherwise be troublesome.[11]

Where the ground is loose enough to permit, hemp's fine roots go down for three feet or more. The taproot penetrates more than

[6]Dewey, Lyster H. & Merrill, Jason L. 'Hemp Hurds as Paper-Making Material.' *USDA Bulletin 404*. US Government Printing Office. Washington DC. 1916.

[7]Brune, William. of the Soil Conservation Service, Des Moines IA. Testimony before US Senate Committee on Agriculture & Forestry. July 6, 1976. also King, S. 'Iowa Rain & Wind Deplete Farmlands.' in *New York Times*. Dec. 5, 1976. p. 61. also in *Vegetarian Times*. March 1985. pp. 45-47

[8]USDA Soil Conservation Service, 'Summary Report, 1987 National Resources Inventory.' in *Statistical Bulletin 790*. December 1989

[9]Lappe, F.M. *Diet for a Small Planet*. Ballantine Books. New York NY. 1982. p. 80

[10]"The mighty hemp plant enters as savior of the moor lands. It grows quick and large & helps cultivate the land. ... It keeps the moor ground dark & healthy." *Die Lustige Hanffibel*. Reich's Nutritional Institute. Berlin, Germany. 1943

[11]Harvey, T. Weed. *USDA Extension Service Handbook on Agriculture & Home Economics*. Washington DC. October 1926. pp. 616-617

twice that distance. In fields long tilled, a hard pan tends to form at the depth of ordinary plowing. Clover roots, peas and rye often pierce this hard pan, and enable the hemp roots to go even further down.[12] Hemp anchors and protects soil from runoff. It builds and preserves topsoil and subsoil structures similar to those of forests. In newly cleared ground, where the subsoil was loosened deep down by tree roots, hemp taproots go down indefinitely, having been followed downward for seven feet.[13] During reforestation, tree roots will follow the path loosened by hemp roots, and thus grow more quickly and naturally.

Moreover, hemp does not wear out soil. Farmers have reported excellent hemp growth on land cultivated steadily for nearly 100 years.[14] This is especially important for rainforests, which are often cut down merely to clear more land for grazing and farming. When the soil retains its fertility, there is no need to clear more land.

Finally, hemp is capable of repairing depleted topsoil and reversing the effects of erosion. Hemp improves the physical condition of the soil, destroys weeds and, when cleaned on the same land where it has grown, returns most of the fertilizing elements used during the growing season. This self-fertilization by its own leafy matter, along with crop rotation, meets most of its fertilizer needs.

Additional nitrates, essential to plant growth, are easily supplied by clover, peas, soy, locust sprouts, etc. Such rotation has led to surprising growth of hemp on "old, jaded land which a few years before might have been considered worthless." Through the roots' loosening of the ground and their eventual decay, some nitrogen from the air may actually be trapped by the soil itself.[15]

Water: Ending Desertification & Pollution

The planetary water crisis is closely related to deforestation and soil loss. Ecological disasters from lost watersheds include desertification and loss of the aquifers, porous subterranean rock formations that hold most of our drinking water. Once crushed, there is no known way to restore an aquifer. Desalinization of ocean water and cloud seeding provide surface water, but not the underlying structure to maintain groundwater. The only solution found so far is forest preservation, discussed above, for watershed preservation.

---

[12]Moore, Brent. *The Hemp Industry In Kentucky: A Study of the Past, the Present & the Possibilities.* Press of James E. Hughes. Lexington KY. 1905. pp. 69-71
[13]*Ibid.* pp. 69-71
[14]*Ibid.* p. 68
[15]"A few years in clover will restore fertility to the most exhausted land. ... 17–ft. hemp followed timothy. ... Rye is a positive fertilizer, like clover." *Ibid.* p. 68

The next step is to reverse planetary desertification through reforestation. Again, hemp has a major role to play by restructuring the soil. When the forest goes, so does much of its inherent moisture. Certain strains of hemp grow well in the dryer conditions that follow the loss of forest canopy, keeping the land agriculturally productive. Drought can even have a good effect on hemp when fields have been well prepared and planted early, for a "remarkable yield of fiber of exceptionally good quality."[16]

When cannabis is sown loosely, it allows tree seedlings to be shaded, not suffocated, and gets them off to a protected start. The tall stalks and leaf canopy approximate a miniature forest that grows in a matter of months rather than years. The bushy, Christmas-tree shaped hemp plants provide shade and retain moisture, while falling leaves add rich humus to the topsoil. This organic matter holds water. Tighter hemp patches grown along the outer edges will hold weeds at bay while the forest recovers. Meanwhile, its nutritious seeds provide food for birds and other foraging wildlife.

Another crisis facing our water is chemical pollution. This has a catastrophic effect on people's health, and has been linked to numerous cancers and birth defects.[17] As raw material for paper, hemp will reduce pulp mills' use of sulfur-based acids, a major source of river contamination.[18] Tree-free hemp paper can be made without dioxin[19] producing chlorine bleach, another toxin.

In the United States, agricultural pollution such as soil, fertilizer and pesticide runoff accounts for more pollution than all municipal and industrial sources combined.[20] We can stop this problem at the source. Cotton, corn, sugar cane and tobacco are among the hardest crops on the soil, in terms of nutrient depletion. They all require heavy fertilization. About half the chemicals in American agriculture are used on cotton.[21] An acre of land will produce two or three times as much hemp fiber as cotton and serve the same industrial uses.[22] Livestock in the United States produces 230,000 pounds of excrement each and every second, much of which ends up as runoff

[16]The 1930 drought had a good effect on hemp grown in KY, IL & WI. in *The Official Record*. US Department of Agriculture. Dec. 25, 1930. p. 3

[17]Goldman, B. *The Truth About Where You Live*. Times Books. New York NY. 1991. also 'Warning: Unsafe for human life.' in *Longevity*. August 1991. p. 22+

[18]See chapter on paper for details.

[19]99% of dioxin emissions come from incineration of medical and municipal waste that contain chlorine. Washington Post News Service. "EPA study reinforces link between dioxin and cancer.' in *Buffalo News*. NY. Sept. 12, 1994

[20]Cross, Byers, et al. 'Current Issues in Food Production: A perspective on beef as a component in diets for Americans.' at Nat. Cattleman's Assn. April 1990. p. 526

[21]Cavender, Jim. Ohio U botany professor. in Phillips, Jim. 'Authorities Examine Pot Claims.' in *Athens News*. OH. vol 13:92. Nov. 16, 1989

[22]Moore, Brent. op. cit. p. 111

water pollution.[23] This is actually an abundant source of natural fertilizer for hemp, which digests the manure and simultaneously controls both erosion and chemical runoff. The best fertilizer for hemp
is manure applied to the preceding crop. Hemp is sown as "green
fertilizer" to prepare the ground for the next crop. It rarely needs
pesticides,[24] and has so few serious insect enemies that it has been
used to make organic pest repellents.[25]
    Thus hemp restoration will protect our clean water supply.

Diet & Destruction or Healthy Food & Hope

    Most people think that animal products today constitute two of
the four basic food groups in the diet. There were originally 12 official groups until the meat and dairy industries applied enormous
political pressure to change the groupings.[26] To exaggerate the importance of their products, ten of the other food groups were lumped
together as two. The American diet changed radically.[27] By 1985,
Americans ate only half as much grains and potatoes as they had in
1909, while their consumption of beef soared by almost half and
poultry consumption increased by over 280 percent.[28]
    This had an important effect on seemingly unrelated areas of the
economy and environment. It takes fuel to run the farm equipment
that produces our food. Livestock consume grain and other food
items, and need additional equipment and health care to raise them.
That's why the cumulative energy value expended to produce one
calorie of beef protein is 78 calories of fuel, while one calorie of
soybean protein takes only two calories of fuel.[29]
    The implications of even a modest change of diet are stagger-
ing. So is the extent of hunger. Some 75 percent of Central
American children under the age of five are undernourished.[30] A
child dies every 2.3 seconds as a result of malnutrition, according to
the UNICEF report, State of the World's Children. Some 38,000
children starve to death every day. Twenty million children die of

23Pimentel, D. 'Energy & land constraints in food protein production.' in Science.
Nov. 21, 1975. also: Robbins, J. Environmental Impact Resulting from Unconfined
Animal Production. Environmental Protection Technology Series. US EPA, Office of
R & D, Environmental Research Info. Ctr. Cincinnati OH. February 1978. p. 9
24Dewey, L.H. 'Hemp.' in US Dept. of Agriculture Yearbook, 1913. US GPO.
Washington DC. 1914. pp. 305-326
25Herer, Jack. Hemp & the Marijuana Conspiracy: The Emperor Wears No Clothes.
HEMP Publishing. Van Nuys CA. 1991
26Hausman, Patricia. Jack Sprat's Legacy: The science & politics of fat & cholesterol. Richard Marek Publishers. New York NY. 1981. pp. 16-17, 25-39
27EarthSave. Realities for the 90s. Santa Cruz CA 95062-2205. 408-423-4069. 1991
28National Research Council. Diet & Health: Implications for reducing chronic disease risk. National Academy Press. Washington DC. 1989. p. 57
29Pimentel, David & Marcia. Food, Energy & Society. 1979. p. 59
30Robbins, John. Diet for a New America. Stillpoint Pub. Walpole NH. 1987. p. 353

malnutrition every year, according to the Institute for Food and Development Policy. These numbers are growing. If Americans reduced their intake of meat by just 10 percent, 100 million people could be adequately nourished using the land, water and energy freed from growing livestock feed.[31]

There's an even better alternative than temporarily shipping grains from carnivorous lands: give people a permanent food crop they can grow themselves. Hempseed, a tasty, high-protein food, requires less attention than soy and, therefore, less fuel, and can be grown near the needy. Hempseed protein can feed those starving masses. It could also be used to feed poultry and livestock for a more ecologically sound base to the food chain. It can be processed to imitate meat—providing more nutrition without the cholesterol—for a healthier world, all around. Hemp provides more easily digested food than soybeans and provides extra nutrients. Even the "seed cake," left over from pressing the seed oil, is edible—a virtually free source of animal feed derived from a crop that was raised for an entirely different purpose.[32]

Nutritious hempseed oil serves both as cooking oil to prepare food and, if necessary, as fuel for the stove.[33] Properly processed, the hemp stalk also offers a plentiful source of dietary fiber.

Solid Waste: A Planet in Need of a Good Dump

The modern life style comes packaged in a throw-away wrapping. Previous societies did not face this problem because, until the past few generations, people recycled almost everything and wasted as little as possible. They made paper from worn-out hempen garments and from sails and rope sold by ship owners for this purpose. They used pottery, metal and glass, but most items were made with natural, organic materials that automatically recycled safely into the soil, providing mulch for new plant growth.

The solution to the garbage problem is well known: reduce our volume of waste (all too often merely excess packaging), return to using biodegradable raw materials that can be recycled or safely discarded, and reuse the wastes that we cannot help but generate. This answers two needs at once: waste disposal and energy demands. For example, two tons of waste packing materials can be profitably

---

[31]Lester Brown of Worldwatch Institute. 1974 estimates, adjusted using 1988 figures from USDA in 'Agricultural Statistics, 1989' tables 74 'High protein feeds,' & 75 'Feed concentrates fed to livestock & poultry.' also Resenberg, Boyce. 'Curb on US Waste Urged to Help the World's Hungry.' in *New York Times*. Oct. 25, 1974. also EarthSave. *Realities for the 90s*. Santa Cruz CA. 1991
[32]See chapter on seeds.
[33]This historical use that is not economical by modern standards because hempseed oil has other, more economically valuable uses today.

converted into a ton of heating oil.[34] In addition to environmental cleanup, cost-effective waste separation and recycling programs create new resources, jobs and business opportunities.

Using natural fiber instead of plastics will prevent the long-term build-up of effluence that threatens to bury our society. In a few situations, ultra-lightweight plastic rope may be preferable or even necessary. But a good, strong hemp rope will meet most cordage needs and then gently recycle into nature. Plastic bags can largely be replaced with reusable cloth or recyclable paper made of tree-free hemp cellulose. Hemp cardboard packaging can be designed to replace most styrofoam containers, and so on.

In short, the nontoxic refuse problem need not exist at all if we apply human intelligence and resourcefulness.

Energy & Atmospheric Contamination

Three aspects of air pollution deserve particular consideration: the buildup of carbon dioxide (CO_2) in the atmosphere, the phenomenon of acid rain, and the destruction of the ozone layer.

The alarming increase in this "greenhouse gas," CO_2, in the atmosphere is a direct result of burning, primarily of fossil fuels like petroleum and coal, which produce no clean air whatsoever. Many experts consider this to be the cause of global warming, another factor in desertification. Nature has an effective system for cleansing the air: rainfall, combined with the photosynthesis of the plant kingdom, which converts CO_2 to oxygen.

Biofuel technology converts plant matter into energy. Hemp produces a larger amount of dry vegetable matter than any other crop in temperate climates.[35] It is often possible to grow two crops in the same year. Each crop produces as much oxygen as it will later produce of CO_2 if every bit of it is burned as fuel, creating a balanced cycle. Furthermore, hemp deposits 10 percent of its mass in the soil as roots and up to 30 percent as leaves which drop during the growing season. This means that some 20 to 40 percent more oxygen can be produced each season than will later be consumed as fuel—a net gain in clean air.[36] Call it a "reverse greenhouse effect."

The acid rain problem occurs when certain contaminants wash out of the air each time it rains. When sulfur dioxide (SO_2) meets rain water (H_2O), the result is sulfurous acid (H_2SO_3). This common form of acid rain eats away at our cars, buildings and monuments. Trees and other plants, lakes and rivers are damaged by the

---

[34]Jabennberg Iberica s.a. (container manufacturer). Madrid Spain. 1991
[35]Dewey. 'Hemp.' op. cit.
[36]Exact proportions depend upon whether the harvesting method is designed to yield more oxygen or more fuel. See energy chapter.

acid itself and also by the soil-chemistry imbalances that result. There is strong evidence linking acid rain and snow to salamander deaths in the United States. Global climate changes may also play a role in the amphibian deaths plaguing the open woodlands of southeastern Australia, the mountain country of northern Colorado and the tropical forests of Costa Rica and Brazil. Why does this concern us? Because these mysterious deaths, which began 10 to 20 years ago, may be an ominous indicator of pollution problems. Amphibian skin readily absorbs chemicals present in soil and water, and many insects they eat harbor toxic compounds. Causes differ from region to region, but this is clearly a global problem.[37] The major culprit seems to be our fuel.

Fossil fuels contain sulfur. Lead and benzene are routinely added to gasoline to boost octane and improve engine performance. Biofuels, alternatively, do not contain sulfur or lead unless they are intentionally added, which is not necessary, thanks to the characteristics of biofuels like ethanol and methanol.[38] Hemp as an energy source will substantially reduce atmospheric contamination. Perhaps this will be a transitional use, as people evolve beyond use of the conventional automobile, and when even cleaner technologies, like photovoltaic cells and hydrogen fuel, are perfected.

Ozone depletion illustrates the importance of changing technologies to solve environmental problems. Unfortunately, hemp cannot be spun into a thread long enough to sew the hole in the ozone layer back together. Our best hope is to stop using chemicals that cause the problem, and let nature heal its wound. Du Pont is the world's largest producer of chemicals called chlorofluorocarbons, or CFCs, which destroy the atmosphere's shield against ultra-violet radiation.[39] Chlorine and its compounds are heavily implicated.

We have to change our consumption patterns to favor cleaner resources. A Florida firm makes a solvent for cleaning semiconductor boards from citrus fruits that is cheaper than comparable CFC solvents.[40] Hemp pulp lends itself to chlorine-free bleaching for making paper products. A refrigeration system without freon is now marketed in Germany under the name Green-Freeze.

In the meantime, hemp works as a buffer against the damage that is already being caused by this catastrophe of synthetic chemistry. While plants like the loblolly pine (for paper) and soybean (for food)

[37]Biologist Marc Hayes, U of Miami. Miami FL. & Henry Wilbur, Duke U. Durham NC. Reports at National Research Council conference. Irvine CA. 1990. in Cowen, R. 'Vanishing Amphibians.' in *Science News*. 1990
[38]These fuel sources have their own drawbacks. See energy chapter.
[39]'Toxic Ten.' in *Mother Jones*. CA. January 1993. p. 40
[40]Morris, David. 'Making Fossils of Fossil Fuels.' in *Utne Reader*. MN. May 1991

face a 30 to 50 percent drop in productivity from increased radiation due to ozone depletion, the reliable hemp plant remains unaffected. It merely increases its output of cannabinoids, which act as a shield, and keeps on growing.[41] To ensure survival, the adaptable hempseed increases the ratio of female to male plants produced when its seeds are exposed to higher levels of ultra-violet light.[42] Hemp thus will continue to offer a source of pulp products, food and other consumer goods, long after other sources begin to die off from radiation.

No Toxic & Nuclear Waste, or Oil Spills

The most hazardous of our toxic wastes result from two industries, petrochemicals and nuclear power.

Hemp and other biofuels can safely, cleanly and completely replace both. No petroleum means no oil wells, no oil well fires and no oil spills to destroy marine life, birds and beaches. A hemp spill is relatively harmless and easy to clean up. Although we will still need to store finished fuel for use, bombing a hemp field would be fairly pointless, as military targets go. Similarly, without nuclear reactors there will be no nuclear utility accidents and no radioactive waste generated by them or possible terrorist attacks. Hemp does not cause chain reactions, nuclear meltdowns or radiation leaks.

The argument that petroleum and uranium are cheaper does not hold up to scrutiny. Biofuels can already compete with the price of regular, non-leaded gas on a cost-per-mile basis. When we factor in all the massive subsidies, such as military costs of protecting oil fields, cleanup costs and the health costs borne by society, we find that only a small part of the costs of using fossil fuels is reflected at the gas pump. The rest is padded into tax, insurance and health care bills, and oil wars, such as in the Persian Gulf in 1991. We, the people, still pay all the costs. They are merely concealed from us.

One cannot put a price tag on the destruction of life forms, but it can be avoided by using life-supporting technologies. It's time to open up the market by allowing hemp to compete: our premier "biosustainable" industry. Hemp is the most profitable crop to grow and among the easiest agricultural feedstocks to use.[43]

In the case of nuclear power, there is more than a half century of accumulated damage to consider. Like ozone depletion, the damage

---

[41]Teramura, Alan. U of Maryland study. in *Discover*. September 1989
[42] Montemaruni, 1926. in Haney, Alan & Kutscheid, B.B. 'An Ecological study of naturalized hemp (cannabis sativa L.) in East-Central Illinois.' in *American Midland Naturalist*. vol. 93:1. U of Notre Dame Pub. Notre Dame IN. January 1975
[43]Lower, George A. 'Flax & hemp: From the seed to the loom.' in *Mechanical Engineering*. Feb. 26, 1937

will not simply go away when we stop making it worse. No one has an answer so far. The radiation produced by nuclear development is so scattered that it will be extremely difficult to locate, contain and eliminate. This will be an expensive process that no one wants to pay for. Yet, it is completely avoidable, since biomass can produce even more electricity without causing these toxic hazards.

We already have all the resources and expertise needed to combat pollution and punish those responsible for these crimes against nature. But on what are our government bureaucrats using our scientific and regulatory resources? The answer is sickening. The pork barrel of prohibition. They are testing urine seized from healthy, hardworking people and spying on our citizens to see if any birdseed in their flower box may have sprouted into a hemp plant. Well over $8 billion per year, nearly two-thirds of our police budgets, are spent enforcing "marihuana" prohibition.[44] America has its cocaine, heroin and alcohol problems, its nuclear problem, its petrochemical problems and so on, but there is a clear and simple distinction to be made. These problems are manufactured by people. Hemp grows from the Earth. It is a plant, a gift of nature. Anyone who can't tell the difference does not have enough common sense to make government policy decisions.

That money should be redirected to the legitimate needs of the community by reforming cannabis laws, as recommended by virtually every independent government study of drug law. Get rid of the political smoke screen and relegalize cannabis.[45] This will eliminate all the barriers to using hemp for everything outlined above.

We have laws on the books, as well as international treaties, legal precedents and simple bureaucratic practices that allow this to take place.[46] For the sake of the children, let's give hemp a chance. It did not create the problems, but hemp is an important part of the solution. It is time to come to grips with reality and utilize the cleaner technologies that are available for industry.

Aesthetic Pollution or a Beautiful New World

The aesthetics of our environment—how pleasant it is to live here and look around us—have sadly deteriorated. We deserve better. An honest, natural approach to life will go a long way toward solving pollution that offends both the eye and spirit.

---

[44]Sweet, Judge Robert, et al. See chapter on prohibition costs.
[45]'Raj' Commission, (UK) 1896. LaGuardia Commission, (NY) 1946. Wootton Report (UK) 1968. Shafer Commission (US) 1972. LeDain Commission (Canada) 1972. Alaska Commission (AK) 1988, 1989. Attorney General's Research Advisory Panel Report (CA) 1989. Et al.
[46]See chapter on restoration.

No other plant or practical combination of plants has ever been offered that can do as much for our environment while providing so amply for our people as can hemp.

There are many other examples of using hemp to solve human environmental and social problems: to replace whale oil and blubber and save the mammals of the sea; to increase our affordable housing stock without cutting trees; to give people back their jobs and dignity; to restore holistic herbal medicines instead of forcing people to rely on expensive and dangerous synthetic drugs; and so on. The many uses of hemp are limited only by our imaginations—and hemp could very well help with that, too. This does not mean that hemp is a panacea for all our earthly woes, by any means. It will take decades to resolve many of the problems created by pollution, and hemp is just part of that process. However, as we undertake the research and development and use hemp to solve whatever problems it can, this will free up our other resources to confront the barriers to peace, prosperity, justice and planetary survival which remain.

The restoration of hemp will allow future generations to breathe clean air, drink clean water and enjoy clean beaches to play on and healthy lakes, rivers and forests to walk among. This planet can still be the garden paradise we deserve—a beautiful, bountiful world.

We need our forests and quiet spaces, where people can enjoy nature and ponder life and the universe, where we can draw inspiration and strength. We must preserve our heritage and carry it forth to our children and future generations. By banning the most valuable natural resource on the planet, we also deprive ourselves of a beautiful and relaxing mellow that has been a pleasant part of the human experience since time immemorial: the sight of a glistening green panorama of vast hemp fields.

Picture yourself living next to a row of stinking, noisy oil wells on a barren, smoggy and eroded clear-cut zone which had only recently been a forest. Now imagine living by a tall field of lush green hemp plants waving luxuriantly, fragrantly, in the breeze as you gaze up through smog-free skies toward the glittering stars.

Which vision of the future do you prefer?

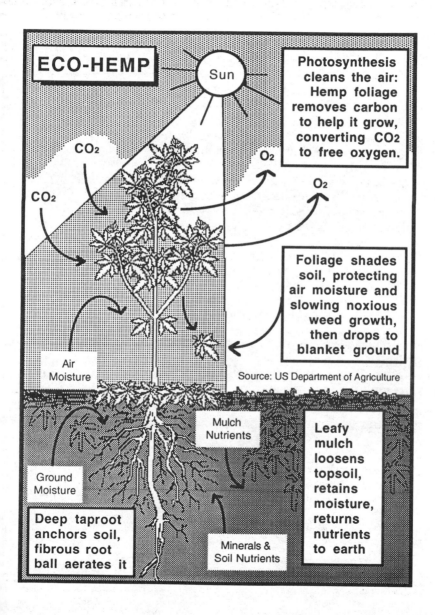

ECO-HEMP

Sun

Photosynthesis cleans the air: Hemp foliage removes carbon to help it grow, converting CO_2 to free oxygen.

CO_2

CO_2

O_2

O_2

Foliage shades soil, protecting air moisture and slowing noxious weed growth, then drops to blanket ground

Air Moisture

Source: US Department of Agriculture

Mulch Nutrients

Leafy mulch loosens topsoil, retains moisture, returns nutrients to earth

Ground Moisture

Deep taproot anchors soil, fibrous root ball aerates it

Minerals & Soil Nutrients

8

HEMPENOMICS: SUPER PROFITS

Economist Adam Smith once noted, "Capital employed in agriculture sets in motion more productive labor than that put in manufactures, and thus adds more real wealth to a country."[1] This statement applies to hemp more than any other commodity. It is not only a possibility but, for the sake of the environment, a necessity to restore hemp as a sustainable natural resource.

The consumers win when industries compete on a level playing field and are held accountable to pay for the environmental clean up and health-care costs they cause. Farmers gain by ending their dependence on monoculture and burn farming of sugar cane and grass: they are sure to profit, no matter which aspect of the hemp industry moves first. Taxpayers save by ending subsidies for tobacco, logging, sugar, nuclear and fossil fuel companies, etc., to allow prices to stabilize at a natural level. Politicians and police can again turn their attention to the real problems facing society. Governments will save taxes, reduce deficits, balance budgets and increase revenues in just a few years by allowing farms, families and industry to again utilize the full range of hemp products.

Give hemp a chance. Intangible life style benefits automatically accrue just by preserving forests, wilderness and natural biodiversity. We will leave a real legacy to our descendants if we can restore nature, and we all gain by restoring the ideals of personal responsibility, open competition, liberty and justice for all.

The sooner we make the change, the greater the benefits.

Dollars & Sense When Hemp Comes Home

The key to domestic hemp's potential is that the same crop can be harvested different ways to take advantage of market fluctuations, and one crop can produce up to three separate raw materials: textile fiber, pulp and seed. It will take a few years to develop the domestic crop from the research to the commercial level.

A research group[2] working with conservative estimates in 1990 projected that farmers can produce from two to five tons of raw,

---

[1]Smith, Adam. (l. 1723-1790) Scottish economist. in Moore, B. *The Hemp Industry in Kentucky.* Press of James E. Hughes. Lexington KY. 1905. p. 47

[2]Institute for Hemp. St. Paul MN. Estimates, market survey & projections based on 1987 estimates of National Agriculture Statistics Service, 1988 estimates of Dept. of Natural Resources & 1989 estimates of Energy Information Office. 1990

mature stalks per acre, used for fiberboard, etc., with a value from $150 to $400 per ton. Clean bast fiber prices range from $1000 to $3000 per ton, at around a ton per acre, including secondary fibers. Hemp hurd cellulose for paper, plastic, etc., has a value of $300 to $500 per clean ton, or $700 to $1200 per acre. Hemp pulp could be brought to market profitably by farmers for a price range of $350 to $500 per ton to successfully compete against tree pulp.[3]

Depending on conditions, 10 to 27 million acres of hemp will produce 54.1 million tons of pulp, and farms could eventually gross $18 to $30 billion per year for paper alone, with net savings up to 50 percent to the end consumer. Twelve to 38 million acres of hemp grown as biofuel could meet all transportation needs of the United States, giving farms a gross income boost of $5.7 to $34.3 billion dollars annually. At 10 dry tons per acre yielding 10-20 barrels of fuel brought to market at $15 to $30 per barrel, the grower earns $450 to $600 per acre with end user prices under $1 per gallon, and a low end return to the farmer of $400 per acre. Seed for vegetable oil and seed cake sells for $300 to $400 per ton, although the oil itself is considerably more expensive.

These data do not reflect the integration of hemp for housing and industrial fabrication, medicines, human consumption, etc., but do give an idea of market values. Higher output means higher profits; that's why the federal government authorized nearly a million acres during its *Hemp for Victory* program.

Furthermore, there will be spin-off jobs throughout the community, once our farmers grow the hemp to set things in motion. American technical information is out of date, and systems developed in other countries are often kept confidential; so the time is ripe for new technology and equipment. In 1948, the farm machinery giant International Harvester promoted a fully modern hemp machine designed for all bast crops and used primarily for kenaf, or *ambary*. Improved versions of this machine are still used internationally. John Deere planners said they could put all their laid-off employees back to work if they were making equipment for harvesting hemp.[4]

Companies like Ford, American Motors and General Motors could add whole new equipment lines and importers can already bring in hemp machinery. This is just the beginning, as vertical development opens up new opportunities from field to designer to factory to shipper—all the way from the commodities market to the retail market to the stock market.

---

[3] 1993 prices were $700 to $1000/ton. Prices are extremely volatile as of this writing, with the price of paper having gone up 40% during the year 1994 alone.
[4] McMahon, George. in letter. January, 1993

The Investment of the Coming Millennium

Truly outstanding investment opportunities occur only occasionally, and the better they are, the more rare they are. Such events are normally long-term in development and hence can be foreseen long before they come to the attention of most investors.

Analysts look for a series of indicators in the following categories of primary factors:

- Technical advances create new products and increase the demand for a particular raw material.
- New technology lowers the cost of producing goods.
- Market demand shows significant increases or elasticity.
- Market supply shows shortages or an increase in sources.
- There is a shift in political attitudes toward the market.

The highest profit potentials are said to occur when two or more of these indicators converge. All five factors apply to hemp today. The technical revolution that began in the 1930s has been revived in the 1990s, creating hundreds of valuable new uses for hemp, making it an exceptionally versatile and economical raw material for both new and existing products. Interest both in hemp supply and demand has expanded visibly around the world. The global and national political climates have shifted favorably for the industry.

We can meet many of our most pressing human needs with hemp and in a highly profitable way. Hemp is our finest resource, but not our only resource, and will be integrated with many other agricultural and mineral commodities for a mix that meets the needs of both local and global communities.

Myriads of Present & Potential Uses

Agricultural research will flourish with the restoration of hemp. Hemp fiber is used for thread, rope, paper, nets, lace, clothing, linens, canvas and other textile fabrics, caulking, fiberboard, dental floss, etc. Its pulp is used for paper, paints, sealants, construction materials, charcoal, biofuel, methanol, gasoline, auto bodies, plastics, industrial components, and so on. The seeds are used for oil products and nutrition. As the director of operations at one agricultural research firm said, "Hemp truly is an amazing plant. If you look at all the possible products that could be made from the hemp plant, it makes you wonder why we haven't pursued this."[5]

It is said that hemp has 50,000 commercial uses. We hold that to be a very conservative estimate, if not understatement. Anything made of cotton, timber or petroleum can also be made of hemp. The

[5]LeMaheiu, Patrick. Wisconsin-based Agrecol, W.T. Rogers Company. Leuders, Bill. 'An amazing plant.' in *Isthmus*. Madison WI. March 1991

Popular Mechanics estimate of 5000 textile products and 25,000 cellulose products was probably accurate for its time. It did not count the fiber paper industry, seed oil products, food and animal feed, medical and social uses, environmental and horticultural uses, etc., which account for an estimated 5000 more uses.

That gave a 35,000 total for 1938, back before the age of computers and fiber optics—before the big cellulose boom! New uses of cellulose burst onto the market—explosives, paper plates, plastic bags, synthetic fibers, fabricated products, fiberboard and resins, styrofoam, vinyl, magnetic tape and compact disc; pocket cassette players, console stereo and television systems. Stackable molded furniture, plexiglas, fashion sunglasses and accessories, digital watches—just go to a department store and look around you. Anything that is not glass or metal can probably be made with hemp. It might be an insult to the speed of technology to suggest that only 13,000 new cellulose products have appeared on the market since 1938; it is certainly no exaggeration. The number of products we make with hemp is limited only by our imaginations and ability to create new uses for it, which has been technologically compounded by the computer revolution.

Yet, how pure is the source of all the enterprise represented by those 50,000 products! An ancient reed; a stick that pops up out of the soil with little or no help from people; that patch of bright green foliage glistening in the sunlight as it lines the road ahead: Hemp is the plant that just refuses to say "no."

Fiber + Cellulose = The Amazing Hemp Stalk

If you hold a dried hemp stalk in your hands and crunch it up a bit, it breaks into two materials.

The stringy raw fiber holds together. That fiber can be made directly into items like yarn, twine, cordage, paper and so on. It can be combed one or more times, refined, dyed, spun and woven to whatever extent is required for cable, rope, string, thread, cloth, clothing, linen, etc. Fabrics can be made from hemp that are stronger, more insulative, more absorbent and more durable than cotton. With minor re-tooling, modern textile mills can spin and weave hemp fiber as coarse as burlap or as smooth as silk, as heavy as canvas or as intricate as lace.

The cream-colored core is a stick of pulp—a cellular mass that fractures into pieces and can be ground into a powder.[6] The pulp,

---

[6]Hemp stalk is hollow, & the space occupies at least half the diameter in the best fiber types. Cut crosswise, a layer of thin-walled tissue, or pith, is found next to the space. Outside is a layer of hard, thick-walled cells. This is the *hurd*. Hemp pulp is a very thin shell in the best fiber-producing varieties. It is filled-in in the better cellu-

also called *wood*, *hards* or *hurd*, includes the cellulose that can be processed into almost anything: paper, rayon, nylon, cellophane, fuel, industrial fabrication materials, food additives, etc. Hemp pulp is chemically related to petroleum but, as you see, it is not nearly as dirty. Simply blow its crumbs onto the ground and they revert back to soil. High technology extrusion processes can transform hemp cellulose into boards and beams for building furniture, houses and offices, or to make molds for casting concrete, etc., or into molded plastic goods and so on. Processing hemp into biodegradable plastics will free up vast amounts of petroleum for other uses and at the same time offer more environmentally sound products.

Beyond the stalk we find still more major uses of hemp.

Using the Seed for Food and Oil

Hempseed is a tasty and complete source of nutrition which contains eight essential proteins and rare essential fatty acids. Raw hempseed has traditionally been fed to poultry, livestock and other domesticated animals. It is typically prepared for human consumption by being pressed or ground up into a meal and cooked into soups, cereals, cakes and other foods. Globulin in the seed is an immune-boosting food additive with tremendous nutritional and medical potential. Quality vegetable oil extracted from the seeds is superior to petroleum for cooking, burning and precision lubrication, as well as cosmetic and medical uses, etc.

Herb for Medicine, Relaxation & Regulation

Industrial hemp and herbal cannabis are completely separate industries. Certain strains of cannabis, grown under the right conditions, produce compounds worth billions in savings to the health care and insurance industries, but cannabis is not just a drug. *Drug*[7] is a prejudicial catch-all term that includes manufactured chemicals and pharmaceutical medicines. The cannabis herb is used to treat many serious health conditions, and also provides valuable extracts. However, cannabis herbal uses include food seasoning, teas, perfume, incense fragrances and creating ambiance (as when planted in a garden to attract songbirds).

---

lose-producing ones. Behind the woody portion is soft, growing tissue, or cambium cells, which develop into pulp on the inside, or bast & bark on the outside. This is where fiber splits from the wood in the process of rotting & breaking. Outside the cambium is the green inner bark, or bast, made of short, thin-walled cells filled with chlorophyll, & thick-walled cells of bast fibers. These fibers are of two kinds, line & tow. Outside the bast fiber is a continuation of the thin-walled chlorophyll bearing cells, lacking fiber. Surrounding all is the epidermis. Dewey, L.H. 'Hemp.' in *Yearbook of the USDA, 1913*. 53C 2S No 989. Washington DC. 1914. p. 287

[7] Derived from the Dutch *droog*, meaning any dried substance, including herbs. *Webster's New 20th Century Dictionary*. Simon & Schuster. New York NY. 1988

This well-known mood elevating, anti-stress treatment is already used by millions of people for enjoyment and relaxation. Such strains of cannabis do not often yield sufficient fiber, pulp or bulk hempseed for other commercial usage. For herbalists, seed banks, gardeners and vendors, that means a great deal of money. These strains differ in appearance from industrial hemp and are easy to identify. Interest is growing simultaneously in reduced-THC industrial strains of hemp, in medical marijuana, and in social consumption, which is still a popular pastime.

Demand: A Sleeping Giant

People already buy billions of dollars worth of cannabis, as well as commercial products that are, or could be, made with hemp. New discoveries and products come onto the market almost every day, and hemp has demonstrated its potential to meet the expanding needs of a growing population and an economy in transition.

Consider the automobile industry's desperate condition, then consider a car. The body, chassis, upholstery, plastic parts, safety glass, lubrication, paint and fuel can all be made with hemp. Only a few metal parts cannot; and with emerging technology such as fiber optics wiring and improved characteristics in medium to high density fiberboard, that statement may not be true much longer.

Even the massive energy industry recognizes that it needs to find alternatives. Fossil fuels are just the dirty leftovers from an extinct era. It took nature tens of millions of years to "grow" a limited supply of petroleum oil deep inside the earth. But plant *biomass* is clean, domestic fuel that can be grown on farms right now to meet all our home and industrial energy needs.[8]

There is no inherent conflict between energy companies and biomass producers. Large firms which recognize this potential and support biomass research include Mobil Research Corporation and Diamond Shamrock Company. Hemp is the next logical investment step for the timber and synthetics industries. It can supply all timber and petroleum-based products: plastic, lubrication, paint, pharmaceutical drugs, food additives and so on.

At the same time that industrial hemp is making its rebound, cannabis and its derivatives continue to win respect for therapeutic applications. In 1991 the World Health Organization reduced its restrictions on the synthetic copy of THC, and local communities have begun to take additional measures to protect the rights of people who use cannabis as medicine. Once relegalized as a social lubricant, the flowers will be exceptionally valuable.

---

[8]See section on energy for details.

Supply: A Growing Trickle

Despite the plant's amazing productivity, world supply of hemp is very low and not performing up to its potential in the world economy. It is an underdeveloped, over-regulated resource that is relatively unknown and widely misunderstood. Many businesses are unaware that hemp can help solve their production problems. Few realize that, while illegal to cultivate in the United States, hemp is grown elsewhere and can be legally imported here. Still others are discouraged by the barriers that ever-meddlesome governments put in their way if they set out to use a raw material that is out of favor with the power brokers of the Western world.

However, all these factors are in a state of flux. Interest in producing hemp has been stated in all parts of the world and across the United States by farmers, investors and industry, indicating that the market is ripe for a dramatic turn-around. Meanwhile, consumers are demanding environmentally safer products at a greater volume than current levels of hemp output can meet. This indicates that a massive expansion in the market is fast approaching.

With interest growing in the research and development fields, as well as in genetic and environmental engineering, hemp teeters on the threshold of rediscovery. The millionaires of the next generation are likely to be hemp growers and brokers because, historically, demand for hemp has always greatly exceeded the supply.

You Can Do Business in Hemp — Today

Production, use and international commerce in hemp products is legally recognized by United Nations treaty which says:[9]

Article 28: Control of Cannabis
1. If a Party permits the cultivation of the cannabis plant for the production of cannabis or cannabis resin, it shall apply thereto the system of controls as provided in article 23 respecting the control of the opium poppy.
2. This Convention shall not apply to the cultivation of the cannabis plant exclusively for industrial purposes (fiber and seed) or horticultural purposes.
3. The Parties shall adopt such measures as may be necessary to prevent the misuse of, and illicit traffic in, the leaves of the cannabis plant.

Paperwork to Grow Hemp in the United States

The problem in the United States is that the regulation is designed to suppress hemp culture. Fertile hempseed is, therefore, a designated federally "controlled dangerous (sic.) substance."[10]

---

9 *Single Convention Treaty on Narcotic Drugs.* United Nations. New York NY. 1961
10 Meaning they are considered as dangerous as heroin & crack cocaine; more dangerous than handguns & automatic weapons.

Be prepared to show relevant public officials that hemp stalks and processing are legal here, but avoid telling too many people or stirring up opposition. Remember, these bureaucrats were able to reverse federal policy and encourage hemp farming in the Second World War, without Congress ever voting to repeal prohibition.

Now, to get the seed. With proper authorization, European companies can ship registered hempseed worldwide. To possess viable hempseed requires a federal registration number and permit. The United States Attorney General has responsibility for the registration of controlled substances.[11] He delegated it to the DEA.[12] Hempseed producers must therefore file DEA form 225 with an application fee, as must seed importers and distributors. To re-register, re-file the form along with a new application fee. This is laid out in federal law code 21 CFR 1301.32 (a, b).

Security requirements are stringent for handling any controlled substance, even the innocent hempseed. Federal code 21 CFR 1301.71-76 covers such requirements for the applicant. Filing diagrams of proposed storage and manufacturing facilities are required to apply. There is a section on employee screening.[13]

The following questions will become part of the employer's comprehensive employee screening program. *Question:* Within the last five years, have you been convicted of a felony, or in the last two years of a misdemeanor or are you presently formally charged with a criminal offense? If so, provide details. *Question:* In the past three years, have you knowingly used any narcotics, amphetamines or barbiturates other than those prescribed by your physician? If so provide details.

Further federal law code sections cover employee responsibility to report drug diversions and illicit activities by employees. The DEA recommends that inquiries be made into the criminal records of employees. So, get to know your local DEA and county agents, because they are unavoidable parts of the hemp farming process until prohibition has been ended.

Hemp Spans the Globe Today

Hemp, which once wrapped the globe with its generous bounty, is now limited to a few areas. As a protected industry under international law, Europe and Asia are both open to hemp enterprises.

Most significant in production and consumption is China, a self-contained market that exports some seed and fiber products, followed by India and Russia, who consume almost all of their product domestically. The European Community subsidizes hemp. Italy and

---

[11]Federal law Codes 21 USC 822 & 823
[12]Federal Code 21 CFR 1301
[13]Federal Code 21 CFR 1301.90, .91, .92, & .93

Germany both shut their industries down, but Spain, France, Hungary, Poland, the Netherlands and others are minor hemp exporters, mostly as cordage and specialty papers. Eastern Europe is a prime target, with its appetite for Western investment capital. Businesses there show great interest in producing and exporting raw, processed, semi-finished and finished hemp articles to the West and in upgrading their industries.

The illegal herbal market spans the globe in the Americas, Africa, Europe and Asia, and there is scarcely any place on Earth that cannabis or a resin derivative is not found.

Bringing New Hemp Products Home to America

In the United States, growing awareness of the global potential has increased political heat on elected officials to reconsider hemp. With new and established markets now been identified for thousands of hemp products and businesses, the first area to combine hemp farming with modern mass production technology stands to reap a windfall of profits rarely before seen in history.

Because hemp is an essential natural fiber, our bureaucrats had to allow for its use. The federal legal definition of *marihuana* does not include sterilized hempseed, seed cake or seed oil, the mature stalks of the hemp plant, fiber from such stalks, salt, compound, manufacture, mixture or preparation of the stalks, fiber, or any other hemp derivative except resin.[14]

In other words, almost any hemp item is legal here except the leaves and flowers, hashish resin or fertile seed.

Finished goods generally carry a heavier duty than do raw materials. Regulations change periodically, so check current regulations before you act. Customs can create needless problems for any importer, and more than one business has found it expedient to de-emphasize the hemp content of their goods. Be sure to comply with appropriate labeling requirements, however.[15] Importers need not list what paper is made of, other than hardwood content, and certain listed characteristics.[16] This means customs agents cannot single out hemp paper for harassment unless cannabis is voluntarily listed. After customs releases the shipment, the product should be tested to verify content and relabeled for promotion.

---

[14]Custom Regulations of the US, *Official US Custom House Guide, 1987*. Sec. 302.58–CR-360. (was *Controlled Substances Act*. USFDA. 1970. Chapt. 22, Sec. 802-15). Also see marijuana definition in California Health & Safety code 11018.
[15]*Importing into the US*. Dept. of the Treasury. US Customs Service. Govt. Printing Office. Washington DC. 1991. also *Tules & regulations under the textile fiber products identification Act*. FCC. USGPO. Washington DC. also *Questions & answers relating to the identification act and regulations*. FTC. USGPO. Washington DC
[16]*Customs Bulletin & Decisions*. vol. 23:1. Washington DC. Jan. 4, 1989. p. 38

American shippers set a weight limit of 45,000 pounds per container to conform with interstate trucking and rail requirements. A 40-foot shipping container for a dry bulk cargo of hemp hurd, fiber or finished goods needs only to be lined with aluminum instead of steel, which maximizes interior volume.[17] Overall dimensions of a truckload are 40 feet by 10 by eight, for 3200 cubic feet, or approximately 66 cubic meters.

Open for Business: European Community Today

In the late 1970s a young man was caught stealing a carload of hemp from a German farm, causing an uproar in the press. Despite the fact that the hemp was not an intoxicating strain, the government sought to ban hemp-growing. Germany then received the revelation in court that it did not have legal power to ban hemp growing, because that would contravene European Community (EC) rules.[18]

As far as EC[19] agricultural policy is concerned, hemp is a centuries-old industry and an accepted part of the modern business world. Hempseed is licensed for export, and economic support is available for growers. The commission headquarters in Brussels tightened controls in 1982 on types of hemp grown in the EC, to keep out "psychotropic substances."[20] Hemp was then mainly produced in Spain and France under strict national controls for use only in paper and textiles. The commission issued new regulations in 1986 that allow subsidized hemp cultivation in Greece and Denmark, where it had been curtailed.[21]

This means that European states can no longer ban cultivation, as this would be a breach of fair competition.[22] So, when the United Kingdom joined the EC, it began to issue commercial farming permits in February 1993 through the Home Office, in England, which had previously only granted them to researchers.[23]

In the early 1990s, two EC agricultural subsidies were in place on hemp. The first covers hemp fiber, at 340 ECU (European Community Units) per hectare.[24] The second, introduced in 1988, is

---

[17]Orgel, Steve. House of Hemp. Portland OR. 1991
[18]When the farmer concerned (the only major German producer) proved this fact, the government instead bought him out & stopped hemp production that way.
[19]Formerly European Economic Community, or EEC
[20]The subsidy was £150 per hectare for German hemp. A study showed that smoking 50 king-size cigarettes of farm hemp was needed for the same effect as one normal sized cannabis cigarette. 'Subsidizing Pot.' in *The Economist*. Feb. 27, 1982. p. 50
[21]As far as we know, hemp is not grown to any significant degree in these countries.
[22]'EC promotes hemp.' Reuters North European Service. March 6, 1986
[23]Fleming, J.H.B., Dept. of Agriculture & Fisheries. Pentland House, 47 Robb's Loan, Edinburgh EH14 1TW Scotland. in letter to L.M. Hendry. . Aug. 24 1990
[24]about £265, or $475 per hectare

250 ECU per ton for hempseed.[25] Hemp is being grown in The Netherlands for research,[26] and is sometimes grown by farmers as a wind break or pollen barrier between other crops. Resinous seed lines available in Holland[27] are not exported, however.

The Saga of *Cáñamo* in Spain

As one of the West's few remaining hemp exporters, Spain is letting a very valuable opportunity slip away. Under the Franco regime in the 1950s, cannabis was such a common crop that *cáñamo* was listed in the standard grammar school vocabulary lists of important farm products that all school students had to memorize.[28] Today we find Spain reducing its hemp production rather than taking advantage of the new opening in the global market. Spanish production peaked in 1986.[29] Since then, the government has shifted toward the general suppression of hemp to favor synthetics.[30]

Spain still produces hemp for domestic use in paper, ropes, etc., and some for export. Much of its hemp production comes from the Celesa Celulosa mill by Tortosa, an historical city in northeastern Spain. The site was selected for its water and the rice paddies at the mouth of the Ebro river offered a substantial source of straw for raw material.[31] In 1967 Celesa produced flax pulp with tow from Belgium, and started growing hemp. The capacity of the mill increased, and pulp was exported. Celesa developed its own technology for flax and hemp pulps and is on the leading edge of specialty-pulps technology. Celesa produces two grades of hemp pulp. Hempcell-A and Hempcell-B are both used for cigarette papers and Bibles. With high opacity and tensile strength, they are suited to a wide variety of papers. Celesa sells pulp all over the world, mainly to North America, Western Europe and Asia. It operates on a medium-term delivery forecast.[32] Danforth International Trade Associates sells the fiber in the United States.[33]

---

[25]about £195, or $350 per ton
[26]Wageningen University paper project. *Agrotech* Research Inst. Haagsteeg 6. PO Box 17, NL-6700-AA Wageningen. Holland. 31-8370-75000
[27]Sensi Seed. PO Box 1771, Rotterdam BT-3000 Holland. Fertile cannabis seed is legal throughout the EC. Only the US bans it.
[28]*Gramatico Primer Grado por Edelvivres*. Luis Vives. Zaragoza Spain. 1956. p. 87
[29]*Anuario Estatistico*. Barcelona & Madrid Spain. 1990. ISBN 84-260-2120-4.
[30]Spain banned public consumption of cannabis in late 1991, and Du Pont opened a new synthetic fiber plant there within a few months. 'Fibras Nuevas.' in *Muy Interesante*. Barcelona Spain. April, 1992
[31]Founded in 1952, Celesa's total paper production was rice straw pulp. Demand soon encouraged them to add other fibers to their lines, especially flax & hemp.
[32]Deliveries are made in lots of 20-30 tons of pulp, 90% air-dry, transported by truck, train, or ship. Cardoner, Marta. Correspondence sec., Celesa celulosa de levante, sa. Apartado 346, 08080 Barcelona Spain. in letter May 15, 1992
[33]Danforth Int. 3156 Rt. 88, Pt. Pleasant NJ 08742. West coast rep: Evanescent Press. 64200 Old Redwood Hwy., Leggett CA 95455. John Stahl. 707-925-6494

The French Have a Word for It: *Chanvre*

Hemp agricultural research in central France is done under the auspices of the *Federation Nationale de Producters de Chanvre,* National Federation for the Production of Hemp. Its research facilities are at Le Mans, under Director Jean Paul Mathieu. Their process for transforming stalks to paper fiber uses brushes to separate the fiber from the woody stem.[34]

One long-standing market for French hemp has been American cigarettes wrapped in cannabis-blend paper, and another is Bibles.[35] France exports hemp to England for use in paper making.[36] The Institute investigates the properties of many varieties of hemp, including Asian and Eastern European strains, and is exploring new markets, such as seed for animal fodder and oil. Another French company named Isochanvre built an entire subdivision of homes[37] using hemp as a primary building material.

Hungary for a *Kender* Trading Partner

Hungary recognizes hemp as a growing, environmentally sound resource for establishing trade with the West. It has a number of hemp products available and companies eager to find international investors and trading partners. The *Cellken* company uses hemp for upholstery, packing, interior decoration products, heat insulation, etc. The firm makes hemp into yarn, string, rope and felts for sound-proofing, as products "which do not have the effect of environmental pollution," as alternatives to wood and synthetics.[38]

Another manufacturer in Hungary, *Cél*, has been a cooperative venture since 1986. It specializes in hemp ropes in a diameter range of six to 120 mm, intended for use in the shipping and petroleum industries and freight load binding.[39] The company needs capital to update production equipment and improve its marketing. Its plant is in a covered building, five meters by 200 meters, with plans to start producing loops from hemp fiber for binding sausages. "We want to find a business partner who would contribute to the development of

---

[34]Leaves, woody hemp hurd & pulp are returned to the soil.
[35]Kimberly-Clark spokesperson. in the Prism. NC. 1991
[36]ESP, Middleway Workshop. MW Summertown, Oxford England OX27LG. 044-865-31151
[37]In Switzerland. Isochanvre. Le Verger, F-72260 Rene. France. 043-97-4518
[38]Founded in 1991, using new patent & manufacturing process for dry hemp stalk. Lajos, Váczi. Cellken Company. Termelö, Fejlesztö Kereskedelmi, Korlátolt Felelösségü Társaság, 4138 Komadi, Külsö iszap Hungary. in letter. June 2, 1992
[39]Est. 1991 sales, $f10$ million forints ($130,000 US.), from a 1989 high of $f35$ million. Assets are $f10$ million as non-capital contribution in the business. No debt burden. Stumpf, Erno. of Cél Könnyüipari Informatikai és Szolgátó BT. PF 39, H-3950 Sárospatak Hungary. in letter April 27, 1992

the plant and has the necessary market background for selling the products produced."

American Hemp Mercantile has arranged with Heavytex textile company to distribute their hemp products to the United States.[40]

Konoplya Grows in Former Soviet States

In the former East Bloc, many countries have produced hemp, including Hungary, Poland, Yugoslavia[41], the Czech Republic and Slovakia. These countries have not signed the Single Convention Treaty and so have more freedom in producing hemp.

Ukraine is one of several new republics which have massive amounts of hemp growing wild that could be harvested. A California firm, International Research Industries, has a joint development project in Kazakhstan to harvest 15,000 acres of wild hemp in 1994 and has permits to cultivate a farm crop in 1995.[42]

Russia, historically a prime producer of hemp and a processor of high-quality hemp products, is eager for new markets and economic ties with the West. The problems are backward technology and a weak economic structure. Multi-line phones, for instance, are almost nonexistent there. The Military Industrial Commission only devotes about 45 percent of its production to the military, down from 65 percent in the mid-1980s.[43] The figure is falling fast. By 1995 it may be only 20 percent.[44] The effort appears sincere, but the obstacles are great. "Unless the Soviet government succeeds at the monumental task of stabilizing a hyper-inflationary economy and making the ruble convertible, getting profits out of the country will be extremely difficult," the Wall Street Journal noted.[45]

Hemp could be their key to success. Nearly 155,000 hectares of hemp were grown in Russia to manufacture rope and products like CAF board.[46] With plans to develop the chipboard industry there, possible uses include shelving, furniture and building supplies. By expanding hemp agriculture and updating production methods, the

40American Hemp Mercantile. 506 Second Ave. # 1520, Seattle WA 98104

41The region is at war & under a trade embargo as we write this book. Yugoslav Hemp Institute. Belgrade Serbia. 011-646-242

42IRI. 1332 E. Ave. R-3, Palmdale, Ca 93550 USA. 805-947-4024

43Vladimir Koblov, Chair. Murray, A. 'Tough Sell: Soviet managers woo American investment against heavy odds.' in *Wall Street Journal*. Sept. 26, 1991. p. 1

44A large exhibit hall in Moscow displays the fruits of Soviet economic conversion: refrigerators made by an old cartridge factory; clocks & watches from a plant designed for mechanical bomb fuses; audiotape players from a former radio-fuse factory, sewing machines, exercise machines, disco lights, etc. Ibid.

45"Salaries here are low, even by Korean standards." Ibid.

46Compressed Agricultural Fiber. Konstantin Vysotsky, of the Soviet agency Agrovneshnauka. Meeting with Institute for Hemp. St. Paul MN. March 3, 1991

former Soviet States could stabilize a crumbling economy, add to their housing stock, increase productivity and fill store shelves.

An Ideal Item for International Exchange

United States investors want to get in on the ground floor of the newly opened Soviet market but are concerned about the weakness of the ruble. They want to put in the least amount of American money and recover the largest amount of Soviet profits back as dollars. One way to do this is to import hemp to America during the next decade, while the re-legalization of hemp and its resurgence as a commercial crop take place here. As in our colonial era, hemp can serve as a fair commodity of exchange. Old computers, PBX systems and multi-line phones considered garbage in the United States are desperately needed to help raise companies to a level of efficiency that helps investment pay off. Old American equipment can be shipped to the former Soviets to be cleaned, tested, repaired as needed and sold for rubles. Those rubles would purchase hemp, processed to an appropriate degree, to be shipped back to the United States and sold for dollars.[47] This process could be replicated throughout Eastern Europe and around the world.

Look, *Ma*, China Has Hemp

Almost 12 million tons of paper and paperboard are produced in China annually. China is the fourth largest paper producer in the world[48] and a leader in using non-tree fibers, like hemp. Some of this hemp blend paper is exported to America,[49] but most is still used for the nation's vast internal market.

The textile situation is better, however, as China still grows a lot of *tal ma*, or cannabis. More and more of its hemp fabrics are on the open market. After an absence of more than a half-century, hemp garments came home to America in 1989 as Stoned Wear® casual shirts and shorts made of a blended hemp/cotton fabric.[50] The National Textile Company has made great strides in blending cotton

[47]A real 'win-win' situation. US investors convert investment dollars into profit dollars. Soviets get new technology, jobs & production by processing the equipment for domestic markets. All get hemp for foreign exchange. US wins market for products we can't sell here anymore. US adds new products to process through its system, creating jobs & value here. Brokers make something at both ends & economic ties between US & Soviets enhances prospects for global peace. Linebarger, Richard, business consultant. CA. in letter. Oct. 1, 1991

[48]Behind the United States, Japan & Canada. 'Making the most of what's available.' in *Pulp & Paper Journal*. vol. 43:9. Nov. 2, 1990. p. 33

[49]Tree Free Ecopaper. 121 SW Salmon, # 1100. Portland OR. 97204. 503-295-6705

[50]55% hemp, 45% cotton blend garments marketed as Stoned Wear® & Hemp Colony lines. Joint Ventures Hempery. POB 15551 Main Station, Vancouver BC V5B 3B3 Canada. 604-879-2101

with hemp.[51] Now bolts of 100 percent hemp fabric are available in the United States,[52] as well as an assortment of blends.

China is renowned for its seed stock and bargain prices. Most sterilized hempseed sold here comes from China, just as the fertile seed has in years past, to fortify domestic seed lines.

Some Potential, But Avoidable, Pitfalls

Hemp is not a panacea to all the world's ills. It is a major part of many different solutions to many different problems; but mistakes can be made in any venture. Failure to identify markets properly can undermine your endeavor, as can overextension into too many projects. Have a clear concept of your strengths and limitations, and develop product lines that can be realistically marketed. Because it is so profitable and easy to grow, farms may come to rely on hemp monoculture, which should be discouraged. Although it does not seriously deplete the soil, hemp should still be rotated among other crops. Hemp is a natural, "environmentally friendly" industry, but bad farming practices and dangerous manufacturing techniques still need to be eliminated. Hemp is part of a larger, extended production cycle that must always be considered as a whole.

One problem is that some companies market the word hemp without using true cannabis in their manufacturing process. The most serious pitfall hemp faces, however, is government interference in the market, which amounts to industrial suppression. This practice should be relegated to the trash bin of history. Despite public support for clean, innovative industries, misguided or corrupt leaders give political favors to environmentally disastrous industries. This is why the recent shift of political discussion, both in the States and globally, is an important indicator of opportunities ahead.

Those who wait for the outcome of this debate will have missed out on the most important time to make a move.

Opportunities for Participation

A multitude of individuals and enterprises worldwide are involved in the legal hemp industry. It is important to research and develop new processes and uses for hemp, as well as to locate more sources of raw materials for existing industries. Entrepreneurs can readily identify sources of hemp products for consumer nations. They can also draw profits by helping develop commercial industries and markets within the producing nation.

51National Textile Company, Shanghai. in '100-year Textile Puzzle Solved.' Xinhua General Overseas News Service. Jinan China. Oct. 11, 1987
52House of Hemp. POB 14603, Portland OR 97204 USA. 503-232-1128

The herbal cannabis interests have made a serious initiative to gain legitimate recognition. When the medical and relaxational cannabis industries are allowed to move above ground, they will be blockbuster investments. Combined, they garnered a United States black market profit estimated by the government at $50 billion in 1989. Business groups have already filed trade names to sell cannabis. Offshoots in the health and service industries will blossom quickly, along with crafts and accessory items.

However, as the big money will be in the vast industrial hemp sector, investors should consider commercial start-ups worldwide. Most biosustainable technologies are compatible with the emerging hemp industries. Were it not for prohibition, any sane investor would jump at this prospectus, and there are things to do right now to position yourself to reap the benefits of restoration. Search for soundly managed companies involved in hemp production and utilization—particularly well-located and well-managed plantation development companies—and invest in such equities. Jump onto the hemp bandwagon and, when the time comes, swing stockholder support. The rewards promise to be enormous.

Recommendation: Get Started

Good ideas are hard to come by, but they still need to be marketed. People will never take advantage of hemp if they don't know about it. That's why there's so much talk about hemp today, but public awareness is just the beginning. People are promoting the industry, starting new businesses, retailing products, applying for farm permits, lobbying government for favorable legislation and environmental research, pressing the business community to support restoration, develop and market new products and so on.

You will often find such products for sale at most of the 500 or more hemp rallies held each year around the country.

This opening before full hemp restoration is a good time to identify farmers in the United States and elsewhere who are ready and willing to produce the crop and prepare the ground for a future economic harvest. Industries, factories and mill operators are advised to consider what modifications may be needed to use this "new" raw material, if they don't want to get left behind.

To ensure success, clearly define your goal and outline a realistic time frame for your activities. Choose an area of satisfying activity and make sure your rewards, monetary and otherwise, will be adequate to keep you motivated and also support your operation. Identify people with the right skills for the job to bring on board. Make sure the necessary resources are available, and maintain communications with others with whom you will be working. Be flexible but not scattered. The first step in this process is to learn enough about cannabis hemp to see how this aspiring industry is suited to the things you find most interesting and rewarding. The second step is to start doing business

Retail shops that specialize in hemp products are already open, such as *Hayward Hempery* near San Francisco,[53] *Legal Marijuana, The Hemp Store* in Houston.[54] Manufacturing, import, wholesale and mail order businesses are also operating, such as *Cannabest,*[55] *Ohio Hempery,*[56] *Hempstead,*[57] and *CHA,*[58] just to name a few. There are so many new business start ups now that it is difficult to keep them straight! In this book we have included other companies in the footnotes of appropriate chapters. On the international front there are *Hemp BC,*[59] *Still Eagle*[60] and *The Great Canadian Hemporium*[61] in Canada, *Cannabis in Amsterdam*[62] in Holland and *Hanfhaus* in Germany,[63] but again, there are many, many more.

An international organizing convention of over 40 hemp-related companies met in Arizona in November, 1994, to form a new trade association, with the name Hemp Industries Association, or HIA.[64] This Association, which represents legal commercial hemp fiber, pulp and seed-related interests, including food and oil, provides a directory of member companies who have agreed to abide by its bylaws and standards. HIA also offers a certificate of compliance and authenticity to be affixed to hemp products, and seeks to expand current uses and develop new markets and applications for hemp.

The Business Alliance for Commerce in Hemp, or BACH, is another organization available since 1989 for serious inquiry,[65] and offers a list of companies utilizing hemp. The BACH takes a more activist stance. In addition to industrial and environmental use of hemp, it promotes relegalizing regulated commercial production and sale of herbal cannabis and derivatives for both prescription medical use and adult social consumption.

[53]Hayward Hempery. 22544 Main St., Hayward CA 94544. 510-581-9581
[54]Legal Marijuana/The Hemp Store. 1304 W. Alabama, Houston TX. 713-521-1134
[55]Cannabest. 1536 Monterey St. SLO CA 93401. 805-543-4213
[56]Ohio Hempery. 14 N. Court St. #327, Athens OH 45701. 614-593-5826
[57]Hempstead Company. 2060 Placentia B-2, Costa Mesa CA 92627. 800-284-HEMP
[58]CHA. PO Box 9068, Chandler Hts. AZ 85227. 602-988-9355
[59]Hemp BC. 324 W. Hastings, Vancouver BC Canada V6B 1K6. 604-681-4620
[60]Still Eagle. 557 Ward St., Nelson BC V1L 1T1 Canada. 604-352-3844
[61]Great Canadian Hemporium, 183 King St., London Ontario. 519-433-5267
[62]CIA, #2 Drogbak 1e, 1013 GE Amsterdam, Netherlands. 020-627-1646
[63]Hanfhaus. Liegnitzerstr. 17, D-1000 Berlin 36 Germany. 030-618-2694
[64]At time of printing, details were still being worked out. Temporary contact location: HIA; PO Box 9068; Chandler Heights AZ 85227. 602-988-9355
[65]BACH; PO Box 71093; Los Angeles CA 90071-0093. 310-288-4152

A Proven Record: Centuries of Profits

We have seen that Herrodotus said the Thracians made beautiful linen from hemp; that in Europe linen labeled "all hemp" was a mark of excellence; that Washington and Jefferson both grew hemp; and that hemp helped defeat Hitler in the Second World War.

In 1865 *Facts for Farmers* called hemp "an exceedingly profitable branch of agriculture."[66] In 1906 Brent Moore reported that "The market will take almost any amount of hemp at the right price."[67] In 1937 *Popular Mechanics* predicted "a new cash crop with an annual value of several hundred million dollars. ... It is hemp." In 1943 the *Herald Tribune* announced that hemp had made "the largest annual increase of a major crop in American history."[68]

What has been done once can be done again. Modern technology has created the potential for an even more prosperous future.

---

[66]Calculated at 350% profit after expenses. *Facts for Farmers*; editor Solon Robinson. Johnson & Ward Pub. New York NY. 1865. p. 967

[67]Moore, Brent. *The Hemp Industry In Kentucky, A Study of the Past, the Present & the Possibilities.* Press of James E. Hughes. Lexington KY. 1905. p. 92

[68]'Hemp Cultivation in the United States.' in *Herald Tribune.* NY. May 30, 1943

9

FROM CELLS TO PLASTICS & BEYOND

The challenge of how to more fully and creatively use cellulose is the area in which the greatest potential for hemp industries has developed. We'll go from the relatively simple aspects of using hemp instead of trees, and explore cleaner high-technology replacements for petrochemical industrial fabrication. With modern processing equipment, amazing things are possible. Let's look at how to make virtually anything you want out of hemp.

Creating Homes & Offices From Plant Matter

In ancient times, people added handfuls of hemp fiber to their clay to strengthen the bricks they used for building. A problem still facing much of the world is the availability of decent, affordable housing. With the shortage of quality wood and the rising price of tree-dependent materials like wood molds used to cast concrete, hemp deserves serious consideration.

Fabricated boards and panels are superior to wood in many ways for construction of homes, offices and other buildings. The simplest way to make hemp into boards is to chop up or grind the stalk into chip, then bond it together using natural resins or glues and clamp it into molds under high pressure. To make it even stronger, just add heat. Compressed agricultural fiberboard (CAF) was invented in Sweden in 1935, using a combination of high pressure and temperature. Hundreds of millions of square feet have been installed in Europe, the United Kingdom, Canada and Australia. A new generation of hemp construction boards will soon be available in Oregon.[1]

Beams, boards and panels made of CAF possess many desirable properties in addition to low costs. High density CAF is used for heavy and structural work, while medium density CAF is commonly used in cabinetry, with a wood-grain veneer added for appearance.

One CAF line on the market (but not yet using hemp) is Envirocor® Paneling. It is made of agricultural fibers heated to 400°F (205°C), compressed under extremely high pressure in special machines and bonded with heavy kraft paper and a plastic adhesive.[2]

---

[1]Conde, Bill. Redwood Lumber. 23005 N. Coburg Rd., Harrisburg OR 97446. 503-995-6907. 800-728-9488
[2] The 4 standard sizes are 4.75 in (12 cm) thick by multiples of the panel width of 47.25 inches (120 cm) namely approx. 8, 12, 16 & 20 ft

These panels are strong enough to act as primary load-bearing structural materials. They have outstanding resistance to the type of shock forces encountered during earthquakes[3] and even a hurricane's high-velocity wind.[4] They have good insulating qualities with thermal performance that equals solid wood, in terms of conduction, mass and leakage. The panels also offer excellent sound absorption performance, but have only 40 percent of the density of wood, for a lighter structural weight. They are immune to termite infestation, more resistant to mold and decay than wood, and will not emit toxic fumes. Furthermore, they are highly flame resistant.[5]

Prefabrication: Aesthetics & Affordability

Now, let's lower the price farther. The secret of labor-saving construction is to use modular designs that combine pre-formed CAF panels with attractive and exceptionally strong designs. These include geodesic domes and pyramidal designs.[6]

Of course, traditional structures can also be designed and built, as can buildings that blend into their surroundings or stand out in a crowd. Standardized systems for water, electrical and climate control are easy to incorporate right into the floor plan. Working from blueprints, panels are cut with a diamond saw to finished dimensions, including window, door, skylight cutouts and so on. Assembling the pre-cut panels can be done quickly and inexpensively by relatively unskilled labor, creating more job opportunities from architect to laborer. No wooden framing is required. Panels fit together precisely, with just an adhesive to hold it and tape to seal the seams. The interior is painted or wallpapered, to beautify the structure. A number of finishes may be applied to the exterior, including non-toxic, seed-oil based paints or inexpensive fiberglass matting, saturated with a special acrylic latex compound which can be applied with a roller. The result is a comfortable, strong and aesthetic structure, built without cutting trees.

New Source of & Replacement for Plastics

Most of us know that chemistry has produced new products and improved existing ones. We are accustomed to beautiful chemical plastics, the durable lacquer finishes on automobile and refrigerator,

---

[3]Zone 4. The R value is 1.8/in. Specification sheets by Mansion Industries Inc. Box 2220, Industry CA 91746. (818) 968-9501
[4]Resistance: more than 130 mph
[5]Fire testing of 6 in (15 cm) thickness panels for safety indicated a 1 1/2+ hour fire rating, a level that requires special treatment for wood to equal. Pyramod report. Mansion Industries, Inc. PO Box 2220, Industry CA 91746
[6]Such as Pyramod.® Miller, Vincent H. 'A Grass House in Your Future?' in *Freedom Network News*. Libertarian Int. Pub. 9308 Farmington Dr., Richmond VA 23229. 804-740-6932. June/July 1989. p. 1

gleaming plastic wrapping materials, computer disks, holograms, the rainbow of artificial colors in cords and fabrics fashioned from rayon, nylon, polymers, acrylics and the like.

Plastics are made into the familiar toys, electrical appliances, costume jewelry, disposable lighters, unbreakable tableware, ash trays, disposable plates and cups, dental plates, shatter-proof glass, lighting equipment, buttons and buckles, scuffless shoe heels, mouthpieces for pipes, cigarette holders and telephones, airplane windows, motion picture film, cassette tapes and radio cabinets, automobile accessories and reflectors, fiber optics, PVC plumbing, beverage containers, packaging, cellophane tape, electrical tape, insulation and on and on. What is plastic, anyway?

The word *plastic* means moldable. In industry, however, plastic refers to a class of nonmetallic synthetic compounds which are molded into various forms and hardened for commercial use.

Where Does It Come From?

The primary constituent formed by plants through photosynthesis and mineral assimilation is the monosaccharide sugar, *glucose*, a fundamental building block and energy center of organic matter. Cellulose is a chain of glucose molecules, upon which all carbohydrate lignocellulose is based.[7]

People have taken this a step beyond the natural by using processes known as *cooking* and *extrusion*. The first plastics were made from cotton cellulose in the 1880s and named *celluloid*. Stronger plastics were formulated from wood.[8] Simple cellular compounds were transformed. The first synthetic fiber was not petroleum based nylon, but wood derived rayon. The first film plastic was *cellophane*, the thin, transparent material used as a moisture-proof wrapping. *Cellulose acetate*[9] is used for artificial silks, etc. *Cellulose nitrate* is used to manufacture rayon, varnishes, and so on. The British chemical giant ICI uses a bacteria that feeds on sugar to make high quality plastic for beverage containers.[10]

Another British firm, Harvest Polyol, produces a line of personal computers called Green Machines, with all the plastic parts made from vegetable oil. The company has a field manufacturing unit that fits into a 40-foot container to be trucked right to where the feedstock is grown. This unit produces polyol products from polyurethane to "foam rubber" to "polyconcrete" as moldable as

---

[7]Other constituents of lignocellulose are formed by more complex transmutations.
[8]Post World War I car radios were made from this material, called bakelite. Morris, David. "Making Fossils of Fossil Fuels." in *Utne Reader*. May/June 1991
[9]Made from acetic acid or acetic anhydride & cellulose with concentrated sulfuric acid
[10]in *Popular Science*. April 1990

plaster that hardens to be twice as strong as concrete but retains some flexibility.[11]

Both petroleum and organic matter are used to make the plastic objects we so commonly use. Once made into plastic, cellulose from plant carbohydrates has all the same characteristics as plastic made from fossil fuel hydrocarbons, which are simply putrefied residue of prehistoric plants that were compressed in heat below the Earth's surface. Most of the items described above are now made with petroleum. The difference is not in the product, because synthetic plastic and organic plastics have the same end uses. The difference lies in the choice of raw material, the processes used, and what we do with all that plastic.

Henry Ford and the Car He Grew From the Soil

"Here in America there's ... a revolution in materials that will affect every home," reported *Popular Mechanics* in 1941, citing Henry Ford's prediction that he would some day "grow automobiles from the soil." After 12 years of research, Ford Motor Company had completed an experimental car with a plastic body. Its tough panels were molded from a mixture of 70 percent cellulose fibers from hemp, wheat straw and sisal, plus 30 percent resin binder, under hydraulic pressure of 1500 pounds per square inch. The plastic withstood blows 10 times as great as steel could without denting.[12] While the streamlined car looked like its steel counterpart, its design took advantage of the properties of plastics. The total weight of his vehicle was about two-thirds that of a regular car.[13] This meant better gas mileage. Ford also planned to fuel his fleet of vehicles with plant power, but was thwarted first by alcohol prohibition, then by hemp prohibition,[14] and forced to use petroleum.

Yet, Ford's vision is once again within our reach. Using hemp cellulose for essential plastic products will reduce American dependence on imported petroleum and create jobs across the economic spectrum, without the risk of large-scale environmental disasters such as oil spills. Is hemp up to the task?

Hemp is the most abundant producer of cellulose on the planet.[15] At the same time, hemp pulp and fiber can also be used to make lots

[11]Lewis, S. 'Plastics from vegetables.' in *Earth Island Journal*. Winter 1991. p. 8. Environmental News Service. 3505 W. 15th Ave. Vancouver BC V6R 2Z3 Canada

[12]Weighed 2000 pounds, compared to 3000 pounds for the same size steel car. Even the windows & windshield were plastic. 'Auto body made of plastics resists denting under hard blows.' in *Popular Mechanics*. vol. 76:6. December 1941

[13]The only steel in the body was a tubular welded frame on which were mounted 14 plastic panels, each 3/16 in thick. Ibid.

[14]Morris, David. 'Pollution solutions; but Puritanism kills hemp, ethanol.' in *Mercury News*. Knight Ridder. San Jose CA. Dec. 5, 1990

[15]Merill & Dewey. 'Hemp hurd as paper making material.' *Bulletin 404*. USDA. 1916

of better, biodegradable and otherwise more environmentally sound replacements for many products now made of plastic.

Biodegradable Replacement for Petro-Plastic

Plastics are ubiquitous, surrounding us at every turn. They are not water permeable, digestible or biodegradable. They are related to fuels and solvents, and are difficult to recycle. Plastics overflow from our landfill dumps, which is a long-term waste disposal problem. Adding six to 12 percent starch makes plastic partially biodegradable.[16] But, by and large, the plastic we use is not biodegradable or recycled, whether made of hydrocarbons or cellulose. This creates environmental problems involving the mountain of waste that is not decomposing. The consequences must be considered carefully.

Let's stop and think about the planet and what technology is appropriate. After all, we're the ones who have to live here. Underlying all else is the suitability of materials to their usage. In some circumstances the light-weight character of nylon is essential. But there's no benefit in putting synthetic fibers to inappropriate uses. It only gives petrochemical industries more control over our money and lives. Agricultural commodities are cleaner. Hemp has natural advantages to offer, like less stretch, better traction and insulation, "breathability," more absorbency and so on.

We don't need to blight the Earth with all this unnecessary waste packaging, like plastic bags and containers. Hemp fiber and pulp can be made into tastefully designed carrying bags for re-use, or paper bags made of tree-free paper that can be recycled or used as fuel. Biodegradable "hempefoam" could replace chemical styrofoam.

The possibilities are almost limitless.

Hemp Can Be Extruded Into Almost Anything

Everything is a matter of degree, and processing hemp can go to the extremes. As usual, we start with the stalk and a system.

Varying the heat, pressure, chemistry, speed of mastication and retention time of raw biomass materials within a machine called an *extruder* produces fiber and cellular materials with different characteristics. The process generates a homogeneous mass with variable characteristics that range from lightly blended or kneaded foodstuffs to dense and impermeable plastics. This allows the development of an extremely wide range of new products.

To understand this better, we talked to George Tyson, president of Xylan Inc., a Wisconsin-based research and development firm.

---

[16]in *Popular Science*. April 1990

The company markets a system to convert various lignocellulosic materials like hemp into value added products. Tyson compares this patented process to putting whole eggs into a blender.[17] "When you run the blender, you end up with a mixture of egg shells and fluids. The extruder in the Xylan process is like a highly sophisticated blender. It uses high pressure, heat and chemicals to break down and dissolve the lignin that holds plant fibers together."

The combination of high pressure with the mixing and shearing action of the extruder forces the chemicals between the plant fibers and into the cells. When the material comes out of the extruder, the pressure is suddenly released and the liquid forced into the cells explodes the cell walls. Non-woody biomass is delignified through technology that uses hydrogen peroxide and an alkali agent to break down biomass and produce a broad range of alcohols or polymers from lignocellulose. Hemp cellulose can be pulped with this equipment. Available sugars can also be hydrolyzed and used in the fermentation of products like acetic acid, ethanol, lactic acid and other organic compounds. Lignin that is removed can be used as a glue.

The process is useful in forming a highly absorbent fiber material for use as a dietary fiber or an absorbent fiber. A material with about 89 percent total dietary fiber has been produced from lignocellulose for human consumption. It has fluffy consistency, a flour-like texture and increased water absorbency, and is extremely low in caloric content. It can be used in such foods as meats, cookies, cakes, muffins, sauces and pancakes. Dietary fiber plays a major role in cleaning the digestive tract for disease resistance, physiological metabolism and in preventive medicine.

The equipment prepares feeds for *ruminant* (cud chewing) animals like cattle. It greatly increases the availability of cell wall carbohydrates and allows digestion of these materials by cellulytic micro-organisms to nearly 90 percent of dry matter.

The system converts waste paper, such as old newspaper, cardboard and magazines, into an absorbent animal bedding and kitty litter.[18] Exceptional composite boards were obtained from the flax straw boards, which are the most similar to hemp. Fuel pellets for corn-burning stoves have been made from agricultural waste. Oat hulls and sunflower hulls have been converted into a soft, absorbent material for feminine hygiene products and baby diapers.

---

[17] Xylan products are derived from agricultural, industrial & other organic refuse, through their process under US patent no. 4,842,877. June 27, 1989. The firm licenses out its technology for fee & royalty. Xylan Industries. 555-A Science Dr., Madison WI 53711. 608-238-4600. September 1991

[18] Chopped up hemp stalk is used as an absorbent material for animal bedding, from horses down to gerbil & bird cages.

Due to the distinctive qualities of hemp at various stages of processing, its low lignin content and its exceptionally high proportion of cellulose, Tyson believes that hemp's possibilities greatly exceed those of any of the more readily available crops. He also remembers the Second World War *Hemp for Victory* program in his native Midwest and seeing hemp's huge output of raw material per acre. Tyson has already begun running tests on hemp.

Given the exceptional characteristics of the plant, extrusion technology may have met its perfect organic complement in hemp.

Earthquake Resistant, Fireproof Hemp Housing

As noted, processing hemp can go to the extremes. A company in France, Isochanvre, completes the circle from high tech back to the stone age to produce modern housing.[19] The company uses a patented, non-toxic process to literally petrify hemp into a stable mass as an organic replacement for concrete in construction. Isochanvre is light, weighing only one seventh as much as concrete. It is also more flexible and thus less likely to be damaged by earthquakes. However, it is also fireproof, wind-resistant, thermally insulative and seals out both noise and water seepage. Over 300 houses have been built in France using this material and a related loose-fill insulation the company makes from hemp stalk, and the cost is comparable to conventional building materials. And, like any good fossil, Isochanvre improves with age....

---

[19]Isochanvre. Le Verger, F-72260, René France. Phone: 43-97-4518

10

ENERGY INDEPENDENCE & SECURITY

Few things have as much impact on our daily lives as the choice of energy. No part of the economy can function without affordable energy. Energy affects the price of production and, therefore, the cost of everything produced: i.e., everything we buy.

The global society is addicted to petroleum, with disastrous health and financial consequences. It affects the quality of our air, of our water and of our lives. The federal Environmental Protection Agency estimated that up to one-half of all toxic-related cancer deaths are caused by auto emissions. Vehicles cause about 30 percent of the nation's total CO_2 emissions and are responsible for almost all carbon monoxide emissions.[1]

Department of Energy estimates suggest that renewable energy plus conservation could produce a return on investment of almost $100 for every dollar spent, through avoided oil imports and environmental damage.[2] Ideally, we want an energy resource that is abundant and efficient, wherein the source, money and jobs all stay in the nation and region in which it is produced and consumed. It should maintain low transportation costs and a minimum of damage to the environment. Society needs to find a sustainable resource to provide adequate liquid, solid and electrical energy.

A number of options under study have the potential of co-existing for the benefit of all. Resources like wind, sunlight, tidal and geothermal have regional applicability. However, they are unequally distributed and need more development, along with specialized, costly equipment. Cogeneration captures otherwise wasted energy to produce power and increase efficiency, but does not provide the initial fuel. Hydroelectric sources in America are already developed nearly to capacity. The human species must evolve beyond the automobile and adapt better systems of public and private transit and energy, perhaps powered by photovoltaics, hydrogen or some other clean energy system. We can return to the clean and efficient energy systems of the past to revive small scale windmill and hydro power technologies and add them to our inventory of energy resources.

---

[1] Strawn, Noni. 'Alcohol Fuels: Alternatives for today & the future.' in *Biologue*. September 1990. pp. 13-16
[2] Ibid

In the meantime, millions of internal combustion vehicles and burn generators are still in the world and will continue to be used for some time. Luckily, there is another option available to ease the transition. A University of Hawaii study found that biomass gasification could meet 90 percent of that state's energy needs.[3] Biomass is the term used to describe all biologically produced matter. Having the lowest cost-per-energy ratio and widest adaptability to existing technology, biomass methanol offers an immediate transitional energy source to put America back on its feet and give us energy independence. But methanol is just one part of the total energy we can produce here at home, thanks to advances in technology. Biomass can be converted into virtually every form of energy Americans use. No drilling or strip mining, and the best part is that the plants do almost all the work. Hemp actually adds oxygen to the atmosphere. Using water and minerals, photosynthesis transforms CO_2 into O_2 and carbohydrates that power plant growth. Fermentation transforms plant sugars into alcohol.

The hemp plant offers everyone who has access to a piece of land the opportunity of "growing oil wells," with an output equivalent to around 1000 gallons of methanol per acre year.[4] As such, hemp becomes an energy resource, but one of infinitely greater value and sustainability than fossil fuels.

Pyrolysis: From Plants to All Forms of Energy

World production of biomass is estimated at 146 billion metric tons a year, mostly wild plant growth. Some farm crops and trees can produce up to 20 metric tons of biomass per acre year, while some algaes and grasses may produce 50 metric tons per year. This biomass has a heating value of 5000-8000 BTU[5] per pound, with virtually no atmospheric ash or sulfur produced during combustion. About six percent of contiguous United States land area farmed for biomass could supply all current demands for oil and gas, without adding any net carbon dioxide to the atmosphere.[6]

The thermochemical process that converts organic materials into usable fuels is called pyrolysis. This consists of applying high heat to organic matter, in the absence of air or in reduced air. This can produce charcoal, non-condensable gasses, acetic acid, acetone, methanol and condensable organic liquids known as pyrolytic fuel

---

3Hurley, Timothy. 'Hemp ... advocate says crop too good to ignore.' in *Maui News*. HI. Nov. 10, 1991. p. D-1
410 tons biomass/acre, each yielding 100 gal. methanol/ton
5BTU=British thermal unit; a standard unit of heat equal to 252 calories, the quantity of heat required to raise one pound of water from 62° to 63°F
6Manahan, Stanley E. *Environmental Chemistry*. Willard Grant Press. 1984

oil. Pyrolysis can take two pathways to produce energy fuels with high fuel-to-feed ratios. It is the most efficient method of biomass conversion, capable of competing with, and eventually replacing, non-renewable fossil fuel resources while being refined using the same technology.

Biomass expert Lynn Osburn explained that "The process can be adjusted to favor charcoal, pyrolytic oil, gas or methanol production with a 95.5 percent fuel-to-feed efficiency." This process has been used since the dawn of civilization. If the off-gasses (collectively called smoke) are collected, the process is called wood distillation. The ancient Egyptians used wood distillation for embalming. Pyrolysis of wood for charcoal was a major industry in the 1800s, fueling the industrial revolution, until it was replaced by coal. Wood distillation was still profitable into the early 20th century for producing soluble tar, pitch, creosote oil, chemicals, and non-condensable gasses.[7] Pyrolysis can even produce gasoline, or provide fuel for electrical generation. Compressed biomass or pyrolytic off-gasses are then burned in boilers to produce steam, which turns turbines that generate electricity. In the mid-20th century, Henry Ford operated a biomass pyrolytic plant at Iron Mountain, Michigan.[8]

The modern process uses a pyrolytic reactor as a gasifier, adding air or oxygen to more completely burn the biomass to ash and release all the energy in the form of gasses. After purification, the syngas[9] is altered by catalysts under high pressure and heat to produce 100 gallons of methanol per ton of feed material.[10]

Biomass conversion has proven economically feasible both in laboratory tests and by continuous operation of pilot plants in field tests since 1973.[11] Emphasis has centered around using waste products: agricultural residues, forestry wastes of the timber and pulp industry, and municipal wastes. All of these combined cannot produce enough fuel to meet the needs of industry and the automobile, until we include the hemp that can be grown on farms around the world.

For the farmer to compete in the energy market, his crop must be woody in nature and high in lignocellulose. It must grow in all American climactic zones, but not compete with food crops for the

---

[7]The process was carried out in a fractionating column (a tall still) under high heat, sometimes as high as 1000°F. Charcoal was the main product with methanol as a byproduct at about 1% to 2% of volume or 6 gallons per ton. This natural process was replaced by a synthetic process developed in 1927
[8]Herer, Jack. *Hemp & the Marijuana Conspiracy: The Emperor Wears No Clothes.* HEMP Publishing. Van Nuys CA. 1991. p. 43
[9]Hydrogen & carbon monoxide in a two-to-one ratio
[10]Osburn, Lynn. *Energy Farming in America.* Access Unlimited. Frazier Park CA. 1989
[11]Ibid.

most productive land. Preferably, it should be grown in rotation
with food crops or on marginal land where food production is un-
profitable. One plant that meets all these requirements for an energy
crop is hemp. In this context, it is apparent that biomass crops like
hemp are the most appropriate source of energy, overall, on the
planet. The major obstacle to its development has been interference
by government bureaucrats.[12]

The Implications of Hemp Power

Biomass can meet most of our liquid, solid, gas and electrical
energy demand through a decentralized domestic industry in which
the fuel, money and jobs all stay right here at home. It will spread its
financial benefits throughout greater society and promote our economic independence. Everyone benefits from using a superior energy source processed using existing technology.

Hemp biomass is a sustainable, annual farm crop that is free of
sulfur and other contaminants, and therefore burns relatively
cleanly. Hemp is the single most productive, practical and profitable
biomass farm crop on Earth: 10 tons or more of raw product per
acre in temperate climates over approximately four months.[13] And
this kind of hemp does not produce any smokable "marijuana."[14]
Every year, throughout the growing season, hemp produces enough
oxygen to balance all the CO_2 it will later put into the atmosphere if
burned as an energy source. Hemp enriches and environmentally
benefits the community. A cleaner environment means fewer health
problems, which benefits the insurance and health care industries, as
well as the individual and society as a whole.

When all the peripheral costs are factored in, the cost of
petroleum in 1990 was about $89 per barrel. In spite of massive
taxpayer subsidies, military protection and exemption from paying
for the environmental damage that mining, drilling and petrochemicals cause, the United States Department of the Interior in May,
1991 projected that crude oil costs will average $40 per barrel by the
year 2000.

Hemp will not need massive subsidies or cleanup money from
taxpayers. Small, mid-size and large-scale farmers, truckers, com-

---

12The only sources of energy advanced by the policies of the oil & power companies
or the federal government in the 1980s & early 1990s were fossil fuels & nuclear.
Federal alternative energy spending peaked during the Carter years, the late 1970s.
13Dewey & Merrill. 'Hemp hurds as a source of papermaking material.' in *Bulletin
404*. USDA. Washington DC. 1916. Even in Holland they got yields of 6-7 tons per
acre. Meijer, E.P.M. de. 'Hemp variations as pulp source researched in the
Netherlands.' in *Pulp & Paper*. July 1993. pp. 41-42
14In addition to the low THC content of industrial seedlines & the THC-lowering effect of the planting pattern, the leaves & flowers are collected as biomass.

modities brokers, distributors, etc., can all share in the profits, along with the energy companies and utilities.[15] Using current crop statistics and technologies, this is equivalent to the mid-$30 per barrel range. By developing hemp, a practical energy crop for America's climate, we can potentially lower that price to compete with fossil fuel at under $30 per barrel and then bypass it, as petroleum becomes more expensive and technological and yield improvements continue to lower the real cost of using hemp.[16]

We can accomplish a long-term strategic goal of every American President since Nixon's oil crisis of 1974: to end the dependence on foreign oil. Using hemp as a secure energy supply will increase cost efficiency and spin off economic benefits throughout the economy. It will generate new jobs and bring new industries and revenues to all regions. Our first fuel crop can be in by next summer and on the market by the fall—as soon as the bureaucrats step aside to let our farmers do the job.

In America, the people have the power to make that happen.[17]

The Direct Approach to Using Hemp Power

In 1991, New South Wales, Australia, State Minerals and Energy Minister Neil Pickard told Parliament that he had asked the Electricity Commission to consider burning confiscated cannabis to generate electricity. "Marijuana burns at extremely high temperatures and gives off considerable heat energy," he said. "Burning marijuana would be cheaper than coal and produce about as much energy." The Commission was to look into modifications needed for power stations to handle the plant matter in addition to coal.[18]

This idea is not new and has been done before. Hemp has been used as a direct source of energy for a long time: in Asia for centuries past, during the Colonial Era of America and in 19th century Kentucky.[19] The "Hines & Bain's machines for cleaning hemp and flax," manufactured in Stillwater Village, New York around 1828, ran on steam power. "The *shives* (hurd) which are made in breaking hemp serve as fuel both for the engine and drying house, in all cases producing an excess of at least one half for other uses, thus saving an expense to the proprietors of two cords of wood per day."[20]

---

[15]Osburn. op. cit.
[16]In 1991, petroleum was held at an artificially low price range, $20 to $40/barrel.
[17]Provided for in the US Constitution
[18]AP. Sydney. 'Marijuana-fueled power suggested.' in *Los Angeles Times.* 1991
[19]"It is generally thought that the hurds will furnish sufficient power, by burning, to drive the machinery, & some machines carry the waste directly to the furnace." Moore, Brent. *The Hemp Industry in Kentucky, A Study of the Past, the Present & the Possibilities.* Press of James E. Hughes. Lexington KY. 1905. p. 97
[20]Letter to the manufacturer from E&E Cooke. Four Corners OH. June 20, 1828

During the Second World War, the head of the Hemp for Victory program explained that hemp was again powering its own mechanical processing and generating a 50 percent energy surplus. "Fiber is obtained from the stems of the plant, cannabis sativa. All of the factories use the hurd to fire the huge boilers which provide heat for drying and power to operate the machines. Fuel costs are eliminated through this ingenious procedure."[21] Imagine the potential now that better technology and cogeneration power are available.

Identifying Appropriate Sources of Biofuel

Biomass derived fuels are called biofuels. Numerous forms of organic waste are now recognized as local energy resources that vary from region to region. The raw materials depend on the circumstances of the community. For example, all farms produce agricultural waste. Urban areas generate large amounts of trash. Biofuel feedstocks include resources as diverse as these, plus annual and short-rotation woody crops, aquatic energy crops and recovered wood. Recent experiments in Holland using waste whey from cheese production yielded a 25 percent cost savings. A medium-sized whey-to-ethanol operation can earn $7.31 million per year.[22] Container manufacturing company Jagenberg Iberica, at Madrid, Spain, estimated that two tons of waste packing materials will yield a ton of commercial heating oil. It is conceivable for a company to be paid to remove solid waste, treat it and sell it back to consumers as liquid fuel.

Herbaceous energy crops like kenaf, elephant grass and bamboo are good biomass resources for tropical zones. Sugar cane also does well in the tropics, but it is the subject of "burn" agriculture, requires heavy fertilization and intensive watering, and has other economic and environmental drawbacks. Some grasses and reeds, like cat tails, perform well in marshlands. Most populated and agricultural regions in America and Europe are not underwater or in the tropics, however. They are in temperate zones that are best suited for hemp and tree farming; but cutting trees leads to topsoil erosion. Trees like poplar and eucalyptus deplete nutrients and change soil chemistry, and monoculture tree planting and harvesting cannot support the diversity of life found in natural forests. They require special equipment that is subject to a lot of wear and tear, cannot be ro-

---

21Only 20% of the hurd was used for fuel; disposing of the rest was a problem for the plant. Plans & descriptions of hemp-processing factories follow. Sackett & Hobbs. *Hemp; A war crop.* Mason & Hanger Co. New York NY. 1942
22Ahmed, Irshad. Whey-to-ethanol plants need no subsidies. Simply condense the whey & process. Transportation is an expense, otherwise, avoided disposal costs cover production costs & capital investment. in *Americans for Ethanol News.* vol. 3:4. Spring, 1991. p. 8

tated with other crops and produce less cellulose than hemp. Given the importance of forests in the overall biological organization of the planet, the question arises whether even fast-growing trees are an appropriate energy resource.

That leaves primarily one viable global option for farmers to combine energy sufficiency with planetary survival: hemp. Hemp yields the most energy per dollar of any crop, almost anywhere. We must combine these energy resources, especially organic waste materials and hemp, into a fuel mix suitable for any given region.

Biofuels: From the Field to the Refinery

Hemp pulp is 77 to 85 percent cellulose. As an energy crop, hemp can be harvested with available equipment. It can be "cubed" by modified hay cubing equipment to condense the bulk and reduce shipping costs from the field to the pyrolysis reactor. These biomass cubes are ready for conversion with no further treatment.[23]

According to Professor George T. Tsao, director of the laboratory of renewable resources at Purdue University, $30 per ton for biomass delivered to the conversion plant is adequate for the energy farmer. Hemp can meet or exceed those price demands, which have also been suggested by other studies.[24]

To keep prices down and profits up, energy farms should be located within 50 miles of the generators. Facilities will run three shifts a day, provide local jobs and restore life to our small towns. Sixty-eight percent of the energy of raw biomass will be converted to charcoal and fuel oils. This charcoal has nearly the same heating value as coal, with virtually no sulfur to pollute the air. The fuel oil has similar properties to No. 2 and No. 6 fuel oil.[25]

The charcoal and fuel oil produced will then be "exported" from small rural towns to large metropolitan areas to fuel the giant utility power plants in generating electricity. When these generators use sulfur-free charcoal instead of coal, the problems associated with acid rain will begin to disappear. Charcoal can be transported economically by rail to urban power plants and fuel oil by tanker or by truck, creating even more jobs.

Once this energy system is on line and producing a steady supply of fuel for electrical power plants, it will be feasible to build complex gasifying systems to produce methanol from cubed biomass, or to add a patented Mobil Oil processor (or equivalent system) to the gasifier and synthesize gasoline from the methanol.

---

[23] Osburn. op. cit.
[24] Ibid.
[25] Ibid.

Do We Even Need Gasoline?

The Department of Energy, or DOE, Office of Alternative Fuels is emphasizing production of liquid transportation fuels, particularly alcohol fuels. Ethanol and methanol fuels produced from biomass provide higher octane than gasoline with less carbon monoxide. Because they allow more complete combustion of hydrocarbons, ethanol and derivatives of methanol are used as fuel enhancers called "oxygenates." Residents of Arizona, Colorado, Nevada and other states often see the initials MTBE (methyl tertiary butyl ether) and the word ethanol posted on their gas station pumps.[26]

Oak Ridge National Laboratory and the Solar Energy Research Institute (SERI) are the lead laboratories for energy crop and biomass research and development, working with scientists in industry and academia.[27] Some hardwood trees are being genetically altered and tested.[28] Through genetic manipulation, average yields increased from two to six dry tons per acre year, and end-use costs decreased from $4.20 to $3.25 per million BTU. The goal is to increase short-rotation woody crop yields to 10 dry tons per acre year and reduce costs to $2 per million BTU. Hemp can already yield 10 tons or more per year and grows almost anywhere without federal subsidies or genetic engineering, but the DOE is forbidden from working with it and is focusing on non-traditional herbaceous crops that can only supplement and complement wood energy crops.[29]

Current emphasis is on thermochemical processes, biochemical conversion or a combination of both. High moisture herbaceous plants, manure and marine crops are feedstocks that are best suited to biochemical processes like fermentation and anaerobic digestion. Anaerobic digestion produces high- and intermediate-BTU gasses. High-BTU gas is methane. Intermediate-BTU is methane mixed with CO and CO_2.

On the Road to Better Transportation

Annual methanol consumption in the United States exceeded 1.5 billion gallons in 1990, about 20 to 25 percent of it as fuel. About 95 percent of fuel methanol is converted into MTBE. Methanol can also be used as 100 percent methanol, or as M85, a blend of 85 percent methanol and 15 percent gasoline.[30] Because of its low burning temperature, methanol emissions of hydrocarbons, nitrogen oxides

---

[26]Strawn. op. cit.
[27]Ibid.
[28]Some species, suited to various regions in the US, can be harvested every 2–8 years, rather than the 20- to 30-year rotation of conventional forestry.
[29]Sorghum, weeping lovegrass, reed canary grass & rapeseed, for example
[30]Strawn. op. cit.

and carbon monoxide are all lower than those of gasoline. While significant progress has been made to supply methanol at the gas pumps, it is important to realize that most methanol today is made from so-called natural gas, a fossil fuel. Far from being perfect, it produces a small amount of formaldehyde. The majority of such emissions occur while the engine is cold and can be substantially reduced by injecting air into the fuel feed during the first four minutes after start-up.[31]

Another option is to use ethanol. Larry Johnson, known as the "Ethanol Answer Man," cited ethanol's octane-boosting properties and natural anti-freeze action as two particular benefits. Ethanol holds condensation, eliminating oxidation and corrosion, and was designated the official fuel of pace cars at Brianerd International Raceway. American Coalition for Ethanol president Merle Anderson said ethanol reduces CO_2 emissions by more than 30 percent. Octane is increased by as much as three points in 10 percent ethanol blends, which improve overall automobile efficiency, further reducing the amount of carcinogens released into the air.[32] However, most of today's ethanol is distilled from corn. Even damaged grain is used. As demand rises, more grain is sold, which raises ethical questions. Should we take food from this hungry world to make fuel when we can turn garbage and energy crops into fuel?[33]

Direct use of natural gas is cleaner burning, and the needed pipelines for distribution are already in place. The extra equipment to run automobiles on natural gas and hydrogen are essentially the same, so adding some 15 percent hydrogen gas, or hythane, would promptly reduce CO emissions by about 89 percent. The Southern California Gas Company expressed interest in taking this first step toward phasing in pure hydrogen. Hydrogen is renewable, nontoxic and recyclable, since it is produced from water and its only waste product is steam. The process of converting water into clusters of H_2 and O_2 molecules is called electrolysis.[34] However, another energy production system needs to be in place to produce the electricity used. Systems to make the conversion are becoming more effective and economical. Another area of interest is the extraction of H_2 from hydrocarbons, or biomass, like hemp. The great fear of hydrogen is its explosive nature. However new alloys with iron titanium for solid storage are so effective that they actually hold more hydrogen per unit of volume than liquid hydrogen. The H_2 is re-

[31]'Clean air fuels for the 90s.' in *Popular Science*. Jan. 1990. p. 50
[32]'Declaration of Independence from Foreign Oil.' in *Americans for Ethanol News*. vol 3:4. Spring 1991. p. 1
[33]Blaska, D. 'Alcohol-fueled wheels.' in *Capital Times*. WI. June 29, 1981. p. 20
[34]Yes, it is the same word used for hair removal, but a different meaning.

leased slowly as it is heated, which solves the problem of potential explosions. Though it is beyond the scope of this book to fully explore such a plan, the research and technology exist to make such an environmentally and economically vital shift possible.

Road Map to Get There From Here

The USDA estimates that new non-food crops will be needed for about 150 million acres of existing farmland by 2010. Biomass feedstocks like hemp can be selected or genetically improved to increase yields, even on low-cost, marginal lands, to optimize their energy conversion qualities.

Cellulosic feedstocks are composed primarily of cellulose, hemicellulose and lignin.[35] Cellulose and hemicellulose are long chains of sugar molecules that are adaptable to alcohol fermentation.[36] The SERI "simultaneous saccharification and fermentation" process for converting woody crops to ethanol simplifies harvesting and feedstock preparation, increases overall yields and decreases waste. Recent research produced enzymes that convert xylose to xylulose, a fermentable sugar for ethanol production. Xylulose conversion increases ethanol yield up to 50 percent over glucose-to-ethanol processes alone. When a compound undergoes isomerization, it changes structure but not composition or molecular weight.[37]

Cellulosic biomass is substantially cheaper than food crops and has the potential to produce cheaper ethanol. Corn feedstock resulted in 1991 ethanol costs of about $1.25 per gallon. The estimated cost of ethanol from cellulosic biomass was $3.60 per gallon in 1979. Research and development reduced the 1990 figure to $1.35 per gallon. The DOE goal is to bring the cost down to $.60 per gallon, without tax subsidies.[38] And, apparently, without hemp.

By projecting conservative hemp crop yield estimates to that data, we achieve a price reduction of 40 percent, for a 1990 level of $.95 per gallon. Allowing for the DOE's anticipated rate of progress, we come to a potential price of $.36 per gallon for hemp fuel that is cleaner and superior in every way to fossil fuel.

---

[35]Lignin is basically a network of phenylpropane material, water-insoluble and impossible to ferment. It can, however, be used as an energy source in fuel production, or made into other fuels or materials.

[36]Cellulose is generally made up of 6-carbon sugars, or glucose. Hemicellulose consists of 5-carbon sugars called xylose. It makes up about 30% of sugars in hardwoods & up to 50% of sugars in herbaceous crops like hemp.

[37]The B-glucosidase enzyme breaks down the sugar, cellobiose, into single-glucose units that are then fermented by yeast to ethanol. This enzyme is the key to improved sugar yield, higher product concentration & conversion rate enhancement in the SSF process. B-glucosidase is being refined. Conversion activity increased from 33% to 47%. Xylose & xylulose have the same composition & molecular weight, but different structure. Strawn. op. cit.

[38]Strawn. op. cit.

Hemp Power: Hot Topic at Energy Conference

The development of hemp and other promising nonfood uses for fallow croplands was discussed at a 1991 conference organized by state agriculture officials in Middleton, Wisconsin. The Governor, the federal Small Business Administration head and representatives of agribusiness attended. One state agronomy expert called hemp "a very, very prime product for biomass."[39]

Tyson, now chairman of the board of the biomass research firm Xylan Inc., said that America could end its dependence on foreign oil simply by growing high-biomass crops like hemp on the acreage it now pays farmers to keep fallow. "It just seems silly for the government to be paying farmers $26 billion a year not to produce something that would replace what we are importing at a cost of about $100 billion a year," he said. "This is a national disgrace."[40]

Farmers Are Ready to Grow Hemp for Biomass

In his landmark 1989 report, *Energy Farming in America*, researcher Osburn said, "Farmers must be allowed to grow an energy crop capable of producing 10 tons per acre in 90-120 days." Hemp is the historic and appropriate worldwide crop that can meet this need. But are farmers ready to take on the task?

Chris Rosania, director of the Hawaii Agricultural Alliance, said when hemp is legal and money can be made, sugar cane farmers will "be the first ones out of the missile silo to cash in." She said farmers are already using "cane trash" biomass to fuel a power plant on Oahu, and are looking at ways to use cane to produce fiber board and paper.[41] "They would love an alternative crop."

Informal surveys and news reports show that farmers are in agreement in Kentucky, Wisconsin, New England, California, the South, the "Bread Basket," North Dakota, Nebraska and so on. In fact, in every state and region in which they are asked, farmers express interest in returning to hemp agriculture for energy and other uses. What will we do during the next fuel shortage? The stage is set for rapid change. The key to energy independence is to allow farmers to grow hemp along with other crops and select those that are most appropriate and productive for their land.

---

[39]Sholts, Erwin, WI State Department of Agriculture. in Leuters, Bill. 'An amazing plant.' in *Isthmus*. Madison WI. March 1991

[40]"We have the technology now to convert biomass to the fuel we're fighting for in the Persian Gulf," Tyson said during the 1991 "Gulf War." His company develops & licenses rights to biomass technologies. Tyson disagreed that the time for biomass fuels is still a long way off. "These people are 10 years behind. They don't know the current state of the art," he says. "We are much closer than that." Ibid.

[41]Hurley. op. cit.

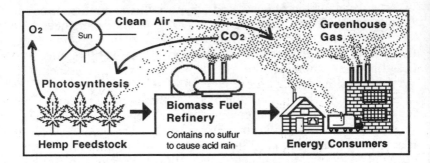

In the meantime, using a few modified 55 gallon drums, some sulfuric acid, yeast, water, sodium hydroxide and ingenuity, you can make your own backyard cellulose-to-fuel conversion process.[42] So long, oil spills! So long, oil imports! So long, oil wars!

[42]Brown, Michael. *Brown's Second Alcohol Fuel Cookbook*. Tab Books. Blue Ridge Summit PA. 17214. pp. 125-129

11

Hemp Blends & Tree-Free Papers

The best, most durable papers today, like rag and linen papers, are made of plant fiber, not pulp. The highest quality paper is often made with imported hemp fiber, although we could produce it domestically. Most of our paper is made from tree pulp.

The savvy investor of today wants to know how to expand our paper supply and keep the paper mills operating without destroying trees. The federal government found the answer to this problem in 1916, before the slaughter of over 70 percent of America's forests, much of which were used for paper: Use hemp pulp, which is high in cellulose for easy papermaking.[1]

In 1991, *Pulp and Paper* magazine repeated that suggestion and published an editorial that called for encouragement of domestic hemp production. It noted that "hemp can probably be pulped in existing kenaf-pulping equipment, but it will take more than imported stock to make it economically feasible."[2]

We shouldn't have to give up paper products—and we really don't need to. The United States Department of Agriculture has already proven that hemp can be made into every grade of paper we use and is easily recycled. From newsprint to index card to finished bond, corrugated cardboard and all kinds of packaging, parchment, tagboard and beyond: all classes of paper. The reason this is possible is that hemp produces three distinct materials in its stalk that can be used for paper: the long bark fibers, shorter secondary fibers, and the very short, woody core fiber.[3] The longer the fiber, the stronger the paper, so you can select the fiber portion that best suits the specific mechanical needs of the mill. The finish of the paper will determine how well the stock takes ink (which goes on liquid) and toner (which goes on dry), and for which purposes it is suited.

Hemp is easy to recycle and is often blended with other fibers to achieve proper weight, opacity and surface. Some typical paper uses for hemp are: cigarette paper, condenser, currency and securities, fine arts stock (for watercolors, printing, etc.)[4] and lightweight

[1]Dewey, Lyster H. & Merrill, Jason L. 'Hemp Hurds as Paper Making Material.' *Bulletin 404*. USDA. US Govt. Printing Office. Washington DC. 1916
[2]Young, Jim. 'It's time to reconsider hemp.' in *Pulp & Paper*. June 1991. p. 7
[3]Meijer, E.P.M. de. 'Hemp variations as pulp source researched in the Netherlands.' in *Pulp & Paper*. July 1993. pp. 41-42
[4]Stahl, John. Evanescent Press. PO Box 968, Laytonville CA 95454. 707-925-6494

printing and writing paper.[5] Bibles are often printed on hemp paper[6] because its lightness accommodates the large number of pages.

Leafing Through the Pages of History

The oldest documents written on paper are a mixture of bark and old rags, principally hemp. They are from the Western Han dynasty in Shensi province, China, dating back to at least 87 BC.[7] The first Western paper mill was built in Spain in 1150 AD by the Moslems, the second in Italy in 1276. The art of papermaking reached England in 1494.[8] Ian Wood of the Australian Commonwealth Scientific and Industrial Research Organization, confirmed that a lot of the world's paper was made from hemp until about 1850.[9] Old hempen clothes were used to make it, giving rise to the expression "rag" paper. After the American Civil War, sulfite tree pulping began to replace hemp paper fiber. This destructive process made tree pulp useable for many grades of paper, and by 1900 all newspapers and most books and magazines were printed on tree-pulp paper.[10] The new, cheap, throwaway paper seemed to fit the disposable economy.

The Department of Agriculture team of Lyster Dewey and Jason Merrill looked at the changes that were resulting, and gave a dire warning about the dangers of using tree pulp in *Bulletin 404.* "Our forests are being cut three times as fast as they grow. ... It is advisable to investigate the paper-making value of the more promising plant materials before a critical situation arises." They added that "The wholesale destruction of the supply by fire, as frequently happens in the case of wood, is precluded. ... (Hemp) is not endangered by the pernicious practice of overcropping."[11] The report noted that hemp produces a new crop every season, while trees took 20 years to be ready for cutting,[12] and hemp yielded more than four times as much pulp per acre as timber, making it a cheaper and more sustainable source for all grades of paper. It also declared that hemp

---

[5]50-100%, 20-60%, 60-80% & 20-80% hemp, respectively. Danforth International. 3156 Route 88, Pt. Pleasant NH 08742. Fiber balances of cigarette: wood, bagrasse, straw, kenaf; & lightweight, condenser & securities stock: wood, flax, cotton
[6]Kimberly-Clark (Paper) Corporation interview. Wallace, Steve. 'Hemp used in manufacture of Bibles.' in *Green Line.* Asheville NC. March 1991. p. 20
[7]Pan, Dr. Jixing. 'On the origin of papermaking in light of scientific research on recent archaeological discoveries.' in *Int. Paper Historian.* December 1986. also Inst. for History of Science, Chinese Academy of Science. 1 Gong-Yuan W. St. Beijing China.
[8]Frazier, Jack. *The Marijuana Farmers.* Solar Age Press. New Orleans LA. 1974
[9]Wood researches non-wood pulp production at Commonwealth Research Organization's division of tropical crops. Brisbane. DaSilva, W. 'Australians Want to Make Paper from Pot.' in *Sunday Punch.* Sydney Australia. March 24, 1991
[10]Frazier. op. cit.
[11]Dewey & Merrill. op. cit.
[12]Modern harvest cycles using faster growing trees average 7-12 years.

is easy to produce, treat and transport and is fully adequate to the task: "The permanency of the supply of hemp seems assured."

The *Paper Trade Journal* ran a survey of technical processes in 1930 that cited dozens of reports showing the structural advantages of using hemp over timber pulp.[13]

An engineering report warned in 1937 that "recent floods and dust storms have given warnings against the destruction of timber. Possibly, the hitherto waste products of flax and hemp may yet meet a good part of that need."[14] From 15 to 20 percent of the hemp stalk is fiber, four percent organic glue, called lignin, and 78 to 81 percent woody pulp at 77 to 85 percent cellulose. Tree pulp, by contrast, is 20 percent lignin and only 60 percent cellulose.

The process of breaking down the pulp to make paper is called *cooking*. It is the ability of these minute cellulose fibers to mesh together into a continuous sheet that results in paper. Furthermore, "the rapidly growing market for cellulose for plastics gives good reason to believe that this hitherto wasted material may be sufficiently profitable to pay for the crop, leaving the cost of the fiber low enough to compete against the inferior and cheaper hard fibers that are now imported."[15]

Instead of capitalizing on this important breakthrough, the government banned hemp cultivation. Prohibition has led to the unnecessary destruction of 70 percent of our forests, when hemp's use in building materials are considered. Canada, England and many other countries still use hemp fiber in their paper money.[16] It lasts three times longer than United States currency.

Virtually all stocks and bonds were printed on hemp fiber paper until the 1950s,[17] and most still are.[18]

As hemp prohibition spread around the globe, so did deforestation. In the 1980s, Tasmania's Emeritus Professor Bill Jackson warned that private forests would be stripped almost bare by the end of the century. Australia's Federal Bureau of Rural Resources assistant director Gordon Burch told the Resource Assessment Commission on June 14, 1990 that alternative plant fibers must be

---

[13]Schafer & Simmonds. 'Physical & chemical characteristics of hemp stalks & seed flax straw.' in *Paper Trade Journal*. TAPPI. May 15, 1930. pp. 67-70
[14]Lower, G. *Report to Agricultural Processing Meeting of the American Society of Mechanical Engineers*. New Brunswick, NJ. Feb. 26, 1937. Process Ind. Div.
[15]500,000 tons annually. Lower, George A. 'Flax & Hemp: From the Seed to the Loom.' in *Mechanical Engineering*. February 1938
[16]Most countries also vary the sizes of their paper currency denominations (eg., £2, £5, £10, etc.) to enable blind people to accurately keep track of their finances.
[17]Jeffries Bank Note Company. Los Angeles CA. 1990
[18]Celesa Cellulosa de Levante, s.a. Apartado 76, 43500, Tortosa Spain. 077-44-0795

promoted as an interim solution to diminishing timber supplies. In 1992, a hemp for paper project was undertaken in Tasmania.

Tree-Free Hemp Paper, Better in Every Respect

Paper is big business. The number of sulfite mills were surpassed by sulfate mills in the 1930s—one type used for non-tree pulping, along with mechanical pulping processes.[19] Yet today 93 percent of the world's paper is made from timber and only 29 percent of that is recycled. Seven percent is made from bamboo, grasses, bagasse, sugar residue and even wheat stalks. But 226 million tons of trees were pulped for paper in 1988 and, at current growth rates, the demand will triple by 2020.[20]

However, the cutting of trees is completely unnecessary for even large-scale paper manufacture. The main commercial value of quality timber will be most evident next century and is best maintained through selective cutting, not clearcutting and pulping. Tree wood is not needed for paper; any fiber high in cellulose can be used. One resource that best fits this description is hemp. Each ton of paper made from hemp will save 12 mature trees. Hemp farms can even be sited right next to existing paper mills, to save on shipping costs.

Using hemp for paper will protect the jobs of people in the information, trucking and paper industries while it creates new jobs for that endangered species, the loggers. The lumberjack is already as obsolete as the stage coach driver, due to forest destruction. But the labor-intensive sowing, harvesting, storing and transporting of hemp provide decent, respectable employment without prohibitive costs. This restores both workers' and communities' sense of self-worth—and their self-reliance.

Hemp fiber paper has many beneficial characteristics, including high tensile strength, opacity, tearing resistance, wet strength and folding endurance. It can be recycled seven times while maintaining a suitable substrate and surface for modern printing purposes, compared with three times for tree paper. Hemp has a low lignin content, so a non-Kraft, non-chlorine bleach mill is feasible.[21]

The paper industry has a responsibility to downstream communities to maintain an acceptable level of discharge into bodies of water, as measured by its biological oxygen demand (BOD) and anabolic oxygen exchange (AOX) rates. Powerful sulfur-based chemicals used to break down the organic glue in tree pulp, called

---

[19]In this process, hemp might often be used to augment tree pulp in a paper run, rather than totally replace it.
[20]DaSilva. op. cit.
[21]Harmsen, Patsy. 'Hemp for Paper Consortium Proposal.' in letter Feb. 5, 1991. 430 Tinderbox Rd, Tinderbox, Tasmania Australia, 7054. Ph: 002-29-2063

lignin, put off a horrible stench and kill fish. They add to the pollution of lakes, reservoirs and even oceans. This problem is so acute that the Kraft pulping process has now been banned by Dutch environmental laws. Hemp, on the other hand, can employ a soda process which lends itself to environmentally effective recovery processes[22] and other less harmful systems.[23]

The discharge into our waters of heavy metals and toxins like sulfuric acid and dioxin (from chlorine bleach) by the paper industry can be reduced 60 to 80 percent by changing over to hemp pulp.[24] Bleaching can be accomplished with the more environmentally sound systems using oxygen and hydrogen peroxide. This seems more expensive than chlorine until environmental costs are included. Dioxin residue was the cause of toxic shock syndrome, the physical reaction to chlorine in tampons which killed a number of women in the 1970s. Experts question if we should use white paper, anyway, since it is more reflective, and its glare harder on the eyes. This problem is especially severe for people with dyslexia, because it aggravates their reading disorder.

Advantages From Forest to Library

There are many problems involved in papermaking. We face ecological disaster from lost watersheds and oxygen resources caused by cutting trees, along with escalating tree pulp paper prices (40% for the year 1994!) and deteriorating books in libraries.

Using tree pulp results in short-lived, acidic paper that becomes brittle and yellow. As a result, we face a crisis of record keeping. A Library of Congress investigation came to the conclusion that "while the paper in volumes 300 or 400 years old is still strong ... 97 percent of the books of non-fiction printed between 1900 and 1939 will be useable for less than 50 years." It recommended , "To preserve man's recorded ideas for future generations, paper manufacturers, book publishers, librarians and archivists must not only understand the magnitude of the problem, but also its urgency and must join forces to stop it." Congress left out one critical group who must also "join forces" to solve the paper problem: the hemp farmers.[25]

Bulletin 404 noted that "hemp hurd (pulp) stock acts similarly to soda-poplar stock, but will produce a somewhat harsher and stronger sheet and one of higher folding endurance. ... In fact, the

---

[22]Ibid.
[23]Krotov & Lavrinenko. *Drip Percolation Pulping... in the Ukraine ... with particular application to alternative fibers.* Evanescent Pr. Leggett CA. 1994. 707-925-6494
[24]Herer, Jack. *Hemp & the Marijuana Conspiracy: The Emperor Wears No Clothes.* HEMP publishing, CA. 1991.
[25]Frazier. op. cit

hurd stock might very possibly meet with favor as a book-stock furnish." Paper made of hemp fiber has a lifespan of centuries, even millenia—compared to the 25 to 80 years of tree pulp paper—without hardening, cracking, yellowing, crumbling or otherwise deteriorating: It is known as the "archivist's perfect paper."[26]

Paper Production for the Modern Era

The Italian paper industry in the 1970s identified hemp as one of the main non-wood fibers for pulping and papermaking. It identified three main group headings: agricultural residues (from sugar, cereal or fiber crops); grasses and reeds; and bast and hemp plant fibers.[27] The problem of providing sufficient fibrous raw material supply for the Italian paper industry was widely discussed again in 1977.[28] Experts there suggested four steps to reduce consumption of raw materials: increased paper recycling; greater use of semi-chemical, chemi-mechanical and thermo-mechanical pulps; and more use of fibers like hemp and waste wood.

The 1970s was a decade of intensive study of cannabis papermaking, particularly in Italy, France, Spain and the Netherlands. Different cultivars of hemp have been developed for various applications, depending on the cooking process and end use of the pulp. Concurrent research and selective breeding have reduced THC levels. Studies were carried out on the use of hurd, as opposed to line fiber, to produce a pulp to replace hardwood. A dry process for separating the hurd from the bark long fibers was studied, as were mechanical or chemi-mechanical pulping of the hurds. They also investigated oxygen-alkali pulping of line fibers.[29]

In Portugal, studies were conducted in 1975 on hemp hurds' chemical composition and suitability to mechanical and thermo-mechanical pulping, and it again proved practical. Data from thermo-mechanical pulp production using hurd indicated that this material is still of commercial interest as a papermaking raw material. In

---

[26]Hemp books thousands of years old are in the British Museum, London. To preserve information printed on tree-pulp newsprint & counter the effect of acid chemicals involved in converting a living tree to a piece of paper, dissolve a milk-of-magnesia tablet in a quart of club soda & leave overnight. Pour into a pan large enough to accommodate the flattened clipping, soak for one hour, then remove & pat dry. Do not move until completely dry. Estimated life: 200 years. Try to do that to a whole book, or better still, a library full of books. Impossible.

[27]Statistical information presented on world non-wood pulping capacity in 1977. 'Non-wood plant fibers as a source of raw material for pulp industry.' FO: PAP/79/7. Ronze: UN Food & Agriculture Organization. (PM 5785) March 1979. 12 p.

[28]Nardi, F. 'Problems of raw materials: Short & medium term prospects of Italian paper industry.' in Ind. Carta (in Italian). vol. 15:7. July 1977. pp. 262-271

[29]Bosia A. & Nisi D. 'Complete utilization of hemp: Alkali-oxygen & chemi-mechanical processes.' in 17th EUCEPA Conference Preprints. *Recent developments in pulp & papermaking*. Vienna Austria. (PM 4132B) Oct. 1977. Book 1. pp. 77-86

durability tests, its breaking length ran as high as 3620 m. The GE brightness ran to 64.5 in bleached thermo-mechanical pulp.[30]

Over-regulation exists abroad, too. In France, farmers must inform the Ministries of Health and Agriculture of their intent, obtain low-THC hempseed directly from the National Hemp Producers Federation, and have a guaranteed purchaser of their crop. Low-THC registered hempseed is available throughout Europe.[31] French farmers formed a cooperative to finance a breaking mill, which in 1978 processed 2500 hectares of hemp. Their equipment is similar to that used in Australia for treating agricultural residues.[32]

Ten years of research at Wageningen Agricultural University, the Netherlands, integrated hemp growing to solve soil degradation problems with environmentally sound paper production processes.[33] The Dutch government forecast hemp paper production by 1994. Research there recommends growing an area of 15,000 hectares, 37,050 acres, of hemp for a minimum of 100,000 tons of pulp per year, to be economically viable.

One alternative to large scale pulping mills is available in the form of modular systems that can be scaled down for smaller operations. This would have the additional benefit of creating local jobs while reducing shipping costs, both from the farm to the mill and from the mill back to community paper outlets.

China: The World Leader in Non-tree Paper

There are about 5000 paper mills in China. About 75 percent of its production was non-tree fibers, for almost half of the world's total non-wood paper output. The most common pulping processes are sulfite, soda or sulfate, neutral sodium sulfate, neutral ammonium sulfate and lime. [34] Quick-cook technology has reduced the average cooking time for non-wood fibers from 12 hours to

[30]In studies at ENCC "The hardwood species, *paulownia fortunei*, is shown to be well suited to NSCC & bisulfite pulping." Bosia, A. 'New raw materials for paper: mechanical pulp from hemp hurds.' in *Papel.* (in Portuguese). vol. 36. Mar. 1975. pp. 43-47. Abstr. in *Bull. Inst. Pap. Chem.* vol. 46:3. Sept. 1975. p. 300

[31]Malyon, Tim. 'No marihuana, plenty of hemp.' in *New Scientist.* Nov. 13, 1980. pp. 433-434

[32]Maylon. pp. 434-435. in 'Hemp for Paper Consortium Proposal.' Feb. 5, 1991

[33]The study suggests a solution to agricultural problems in northern Holland. The potatoes/sugar-beet/potatoes/grain rotation pattern had a built-in disease factor, lowered organic humus & deteriorated the soil structure. Crops that helped remedy these problems include hemp, beans, peas, Brussels sprouts, leeks, grass & cooperative livestock breeding. Wageningen Agricultural U. Wageningen Holland. PO Box 17, NL-6700-AA Wageningen Holland. 1991

[34]They use kenaf to make standard cigarette papers, linerboard & printing & writing papers. As well, quality offset printing paper has been produced using 100% Mg-bisulfite reed pulp on a twin-wire fourdrinier at a speed of more than 350 m/min. 'Making the most of what's available.' in *Pulp & Paper Journal.* vol. 43:9. Nov. 2, 1990. p. 33

about two, while pulp quality has improved.[35] To reduce its imports, Chinese researchers stepped up efforts to develop more than 30 non-tree fiber sources, including bast fibers such as hemp, jute, flax and kenaf; crop residues such as rice and wheat straws; plants such as reed, amur silver grass and bamboo; and cotton fibers such as linters, rags and other textile scraps. Hu Shouzu, vice-president of the China Paper Industry Technology Association, noted that China's non-wood fiber papermaking sector has a long way to go to modernize. "Most mills are too small, and the equipment used in most of them is still outdated," he said. "But the paper industry as a whole has benefited a great deal from technological progress in non-tree fiber papermaking, and it will continue to do so in the future."

Of the 500 grades of paper and board made in China, about 350 are made almost entirely with non-tree pulps, says Shouzu. These include corrugating medium, printing and writing paper, banknote, tissue, stampbase, cigarette and photocopy papers.

Some Recent Technology for Processing Pulp

Discontinuous pulp cooking is an energy saving approach to carbohydrate processing. VAI Technology has developed a system for vapor cooking flax and hemp fibers to achieve cottonization.[36]

Digesting units can be tailor-made for any operational situation and all raw material, technological, material and design requirements. Digester components come in a variety of sizes for a modular design system. A variable transport screw allows precise adjustment of cooking time, in combination with temperature and chemical metering for perfect cooking. The proportional and homogeneous addition of chemicals ensures uniform cooking, generally in the vapor phase. The special impregnation method reduces primary steam consumption by about 70 percent. Plant capacity is greater, due to the short cooking cycle. The process gives homogeneous pulp quality, improved yield and a reduction in knots. Initial test results demonstrate that scraps and wood qualities that had been unsuitable for pulp production can be extremely well cooked.[37]

The VAI system has feeding screws in different sizes to regulate the feed of biomass against the digester pressure. It simultaneously provides aeration and de-watering to achieve an optimum ratio of raw material to liquid. The feed screws accommodate the specific physical characteristics of the raw material, such as hemp hurd,

---

35'Making the most of what's available.' in *Pulp & Paper Journal*. vol. 43:9. Nov. 2, 1990. Information Access Co. p. 33. Spanish hemp technology takes 8-9 hrs.
36VAI Technology promotional materials
37Using crown wood (up to 20% of total tree) & thin wood created by forest thinning.

short fiber, retted or unretted stalks, etc. Digester tubes can be arranged as required. Special discharge units provide problem-free cold or hot blowing of pulp into the blow tank. The sequence can be adjusted for a broad spectrum of raw materials, pulp types and final textural qualities—with or without using conventional chlorine bleaching. Chlorinated organic waste content is either totally or partially resistant to biological treatment plants. However, chlorine-free bleaching stages using oxygen, ozone, hydrogen peroxide, nitrogen dioxide can be used, generating waste water that can be recycled back into the process.

Hydrogen Peroxide for Bleaching & More

Hydrogen peroxide has been used for bleaching and in environmental applications for decades, although initially only for sulfide removal. One of the great beauties of peroxide is its compatibility with biological systems. In fact, one of its principal uses is to provide dissolved oxygen. Peroxide is an anti-bacterial agent that is not toxic at low dosage levels, creates no toxic byproducts and leaves only oxygen and water behind. In many cases, the application of peroxide can solve sulfide problems in sulfide contaminated pond water and sludges. In this situation, all that's required is to mix in peroxide until the odor goes away.[38]

One hazardous waste treatment facility in the Northeast often had to ship wastes off-site for commercial incineration. But by installing hydrogen peroxide treatment systems, they were able to treat the same industrial wastes enough to discharge it into the municipal sewer, thus saving the cost of incineration.[39]

Timber, Paper & Pulp Companies Need Hemp

High in the mountains of North Carolina is Pisgah Forest and the Ecusta paper mill, alongside the Davidson River. This American paper mill has adapted to using non-tree pulp and fiber for papermaking.[40] Flax straw is used there; but in just one growing

---

[38]In one pond closure, sludge to be removed contained sulfides at concentrations greater than 1000 mg/l, hydrogen peroxide created disposal sludge by virtually eliminating the sulfides. A Southwestern power utility used calcium hydroxide to scrub sulfur dioxide out of its atmospheric emissions, creating wastewater laden with calcium sulfite. By further oxidizing it with peroxide, they made calcium sulfate, gypsum, a profitable, marketable commodity.

[39]There are now ultraviolet (UV) catalyzed hydrogen peroxide systems. A West Coast food processor treated well water contaminated with trichloroethylene (TCE), reducing concentrations down from 5000 p.g/l to less than 1 p.g/l. Hydrogen peroxide is said to be over 10 times more effective than activated carbon in this application.

[40]Most mills used to make paper only from long-fibered raw material until relatively recently, so it is generally a matter of reconditioning the equipment already on hand or salvaging that of an earlier era. Ecusta Ind. NC. April 1989

season, with no major re-tooling, hemp, a crop even more bountiful and much more easily grown, could be pulped there.

Hemp also is preferable to kenaf for making paper and other products. But timber gets a few billion dollars of our tax money each year in access permits to cut down our forests. America needs to level the playing field by no longer subsidizing the cutting of trees. The key to economic sustainability lies in growing hemp for fiber and using the leftover pulp, in combination with recycled paper, for papermaking.

The high cost of imported stock and limited production currently restricts hemp to specialty use, such as European and Asian cigarette papers. The industry is well aware of this fact. "Hemp ... has more to offer the paper industry than we are taking advantage of (or more correctly, we are allowed to take advantage of)," commented Jim Young, technical editor of *Pulp & Paper* magazine, in 1991.[41]

"Interest in papermaking from hemp continues as our fiber, energy and environmental concerns increase," Young wrote. "Hemp-growing restrictions were set aside to meet material shortages during World War II. They should now at least be modified to meet pending shortages of fiber, energy and environmental quality."

Challenge for the Paper Industry

The paper industry will soon have to address the production and marketing issues of once again using hemp pulp and fiber. The cost of hurds is a barrier that will go down subject to crop availability, and the lack of environmentally benign processing systems must be rectified. The main technical problem to solve is that slightly more strings remain after pulping hemp than trees, which emphasizes the need for more research into the crucial areas of fiber length and fibrillation. That minor negative must be weighed against the numerous advantages of using hemp. These include superb sheet stability, opacity, one-dimensional and multi-dimensional folding, better tear strength, etc. Its burst strength is average, and varies with the straw content in the pulp mix.

From a marketing viewpoint, hemp paper can win widespread acceptance in application-specific papers that emphasize its strong points, especially products aimed at ecologically-aware purchasers and consumers. Hence, ESP Paper in Oxford, England has begun to offer a variety of blended hemp, straw and recycled paper stock.[42]

41Young, J. 'Time to reconsider hemp.' in *Pulp & Paper*. June 1991. p. 7
42ESP papers. Middleway Workshop, MW Summertown, Oxford England OX27LG. 44-865-31151

American Hemp Mercantile[43] and Ecolution are two firms that bring in hemp blend and hemp paper from Eastern Europe.[44]

Profit for Pennies: Papermaking at Home

"I make paper from cotton, hemp, flax, kozo bark, cattails, corn husks—you name it." P.J. Whitmarsh of Garden Valley, California, creates stationery, envelopes, blank books, art paper and more at her country home. She uses papermaking dyes and plant fibers to create delicate, colorful and unique paper of all textures, tints and colors.[45]

A good practice for the beginner is recycling old waste paper into brand-new, custom paper. "One sheet of newspaper can usually yield about five sheets of paper. I process the newspaper in my rehydrator, but it can be done in a regular kitchen blender." The more you process the pulp, the more the ink is washed away. It can be bleached in a washtub, using peroxide or household chlorine bleach. Divide the pulp into equal portions.

Next, gather the wet pulp, or *slurry*, onto the *mould*, a device which can be made with a framed piece of window screen. Gently spread and flatten the slurry out in a thin paste over the screen, with the edges either rough or straightened. Let it reconstitute for a while. The hard part of the process is called *couching*, where you remove the paper from the mould. The individual sheets are then stacked between pieces of felt and further smoothed or flattened down with an old book press, or under boards weighted down by heavy books, bricks or whatever. At this point, the paper is as fragile as tissue.

The paper is removed and laid onto drying screens that Whitmarsh sets on a wooden rack on her porch. "Drying the paper can take anywhere from a couple of hours to several days, depending on the weather." Finally the paper is peeled from the felt and flattened or run through the book press. "I use the press to create a smooth finish for writing. On paper to be used for art, I don't use the press."

The process for hand-made hemp paper is essentially the same, but using hemp fiber instead of old newsprint. There are many useful books on the topic of papermaking, and papermaking kits are available from environmental groups such as Friends of the Earth, Greenpeace, etc. Hand made papers can be further processed into artworks, origami and other crafts, and marketed.

---

[43]See title page insert. 70% Hemp/30% cotton. American Hemp Mercantile, 506 2nd Ave. #1520, Seattle WA 98104. 206-340-0124. 1-800-624-HEMP

[44]100% hemp. Ecolution, PO Box 2279 Merrifield VA 22116-2279. 703-207-9001 fax: 560-1175 800-769-HEMP.

[45]Pesses, Betsy. 'The papermaker.' in *Weekend* supplement, *Mountain Democrat*. CA. April 12, 1991. p. 10-11

12

THE BEST IS ALWAYS FASHIONABLE

Clothes: We all like to look good, but how often do we look past style and fashion to consider the consequences of our style choices? Jobs, business, environment, international trade: Many aspects of society are affected, one way or another, by what we wear.

The first use of hemp was for textile fiber and the latest word is that cannabis insignias and hemp clothes are the new fashion rage.[1]

America imports practically all its fibers except some cotton. The Whitney gin, along with improved spinning methods, brought cotton goods so far below the cost of flax and hemp that linen manufacture practically ceased here. By the late 1930s, America could not produce fibers at less cost than other farmers of the world, due to hemp prohibition at home and low wages elsewhere.

An acre of land will produce about 1000 pounds of primary hemp fiber, about two or three times more fiber than cotton or flax, and serves all the same industrial purposes.[2] Fiber comes right off the plant ready to comb and use. The hemp fiber of commerce consists of the primary bast fiber, or line, and some secondary bast fiber, or tow. The line consists of numerous overlapping, thick-walled cells with long, tapering ends.[3]

A current temporary problem is the lack of hemp thread for sewing. Traditionally, the value of hemp has been for its long fiber. It is recorded that the finest laces of olden days were always made of hemp in preference to flax, and that two and one-half pounds of hemp can be spun into 600 miles of lace threads.[4]

Make no mistake: for hemp to be its best, it must be treated with due respect. The fiber's characteristics result from the processing it receives. Unretted fiber is less strong than retted. *Cottonized* fiber is no stronger than cotton, and a poorly made fabric will not hold up. Many characteristics of comfort, softness, elasticity, texture, etc. are

---

[1]Zeman, N. & Foote, D. 'Turning over a New Old Leaf: An Unfashionable Icon Comes Back in Fashion.' in *Newsweek*. February 8, 1993. p. 60. Also Morris, B. 'Higher Ground.' in *Details*. February 1993. pp. 26-31+

[2]Moore, Brent. *The Hemp Industry in Kentucky, A Study of the Past, the Present & the Possibilities*. Press of James E. Hughes. Lexington KY. 1905. p. 111

[3]"Individual cells are .015-.05 mm (.003-.012 inch) in diameter, & 5-55 mm (.1875-2.125 in.) long." Some extend the length of the stalk, some are branched, & others terminate at each node. They are weaker at the nodes. Dewey, L.H. 'Hemp.' in *Yearbook of the USDA, 1913*. Washington DC. 1914. p. 287

[4]Boyce, S.S. *Hemp*. Orange & Judd. New York NY. 1900. p. 48-49

a result of the weave, not the fiber used. Due to the scarcity of hemp thread and fiber, many source countries stretch out the fiber beyond its normal length to make a larger piece of fabric. The problem is that when you later wash it, the fiber goes back to its natural length, so shrinkage can be a problem. Hence cloth should be washed or preshrunk before being made into garments.

However, if hemp items are properly manufactured, their quality and durability can be assured.

The New Fiber for Modern Textiles

Hemp has the casual fashion wear, athletic wear, work clothes and natural fibers markets open to it, along with the large environmental consumers market that has barely been tapped. It also has niches in the formal linens and heavy industrial textiles.

If prices are approximately equal, linens are always preferred to cotton goods, on account of their sheen, greater whiteness and far greater strength, absorbancy and durability. While cotton was once better for spinning, these problems have been solved. Hemp should regain many of the lines where it gives superior service.

Hemp has long been the primary fiber of industry because it has been steadily available and is extremely versatile and valuable. John Baxter astounded people in the 1840s, saying hemp would "bleach whiter than either flax or cotton, and make the finest fabric, from lace and cambric down to good shirting, and far cheaper than either."[5] Don't be surprised to learn it is still true today. Hemp has a number of advantages over other fibers, even synthetics.

The absolute market potential is enormously greater than it ever was before. One must not think that the whole fiber market is open to hemp, though there is probably no fibrous article which has not at some time been made of it, with a net gain in the quality of the goods. The natural level is for hemp to share the market with synthetics and other natural fibers. After all, wool has a warmth peculiar to itself and the softness and sheen of silk is difficult to imitate in a natural fiber.[6] Some synthetic fibers combine unusual strength with light weight, and with extrusion technology, hemp can be made into rayon and other continuous synthetic fibers.

Natural hemp has distinct advantages to offer. Organic hemp fiber "breathes" and is biodegradable. Like linen, however, hemp fabrics will crease easily. With its special characteristics, hemp will open up a whole new realm in the fashion industry, from designer to

[5]"Such is the competition to purchase hemp that it always brings the last cent that the manufacturer can afford to pay." in Moore, Brent. *The Hemp Industry in Kentucky.* Press of James E. Hughes. Lexington KY. 1905. p. 55-56
[6]*Ibid.* p. 94

boutique. As of this writing, hemp is one of the wold's rarest and most expensive fabrics, and deserves special care and attention, such as shaking out the wrinkles and hanging after each washing.

Cordage, Carpet, Caulk & Other Fiber Uses

Hemp line is used to manufacture tying twine, seine twine, sails, standing rigging and heaving lines for ships.[7] The English word *canvas* derives from the Latin word *cannabis*. Its combination of ruggedness and comfort as duck canvas were utilized in the first jeans by the Levi Strauss company in California.[8]

A carpet made of hemp is just as warm and durable as one made of wool. The fiber is especially adapted by strength and durability for carpet warp, hall rugs, aisle runners, tarpaulins, belt webbing, anchor cables, upholstery webbing, spring twine and all textile articles where strength, durability and flexibility are desired.[9]

The best marine cord came from Russian hemp harvested while still green, and kiln dried, thus fixing the essential oil in the fiber.[10] Softer grades of tow are used for lamp and candle wicks, matches and oakum, as well as gaskets and packing for pumps, engines and similar machinery. It endures heat, moisture and friction with less injury than other fiber used for these purposes, except flax.

Old & New Processes Team Up for Progress

Degumming of hemp is analogous to the treatment given flax.[11] The shards probably offer slightly more resistance to digestion, but they readily break down upon completion of the digestion process.

Cotton has historically lent itself more readily to machine spinning, but hemp's possibilities greatly exceed those of cotton. The Commissioner of Agriculture told Congress that boiling hemp in potash and washing it in soap yielded a fiber "stronger than cotton, took a better color, could be spun on cotton machinery with less waste than cotton, and was as white or whiter."[12] Such processes consisted essentially in breaking down the bast fiber bundles into

---

[7]Dew retted hemp was never used to make tarred cordage, because the fiber is held to the stalk by globules containing a resinous gluten. Dew retting loosens up those globules, which then adhere to the lint and keep the tar from doing so. Mr. Billings. in *US Patent Office Report, 1845*. in Moore. op. cit. p. 83

[8]Levi Strauss company historian Lynn Downey said all company records were destroyed in San Francisco's 1906 earthquake/fire. Remaining notes refer to duck, a hempen fabric. The name denim is for the blue dye, which came from Nim France.

[9]Dewey. op. cit. p. 341

[10]*Ibid.* p. 101

[11]"No essential morphological technological–mechanical or chemical differences exist between the ultimate fibers of flax & hemp. The similarity in spinning qualities is not surprising." Ibid.

[12]March 1, 1865. cited in Moore. op. cit. p. 62

single cells, removing the gums and rendering the fiber soft and pliable. In the 1920s, these chemical processes were revived[13] and very considerably improved.[14]

Putting Textile Workers Back on the Job

As in flax, hemp fibers end where leaf stems are on the stalks and are made up of laminated fibers that are held together by pectose gums. The fibers are so alike that they are hard to tell apart.[15]

Already more insulative and absorbent than cotton, a little extra combing can also render hemp softer than cotton, too. The extra absorbency of hemp fiber gives it a decided advantage for making things like sponges,[16] towels, tampons and diapers.

Industrial textiles and apparel, once major industries in the United States, now account for 59 percent of our imports. In 1989, textile imports accounted for 21 percent of the national merchandise trade deficit. Foreign governments often subsidize textile industries or exempt them from environmental and health regulations.[17] Hemp is environmentally safe. It uses much less irrigation, fertilizer and petrochemical pesticides than cotton. Returning hemp as a domestic fiber can put America back on top of the international textile market, without compromising our health standards.

Many states have grown hemp for fiber, a practice banned in 1937, in part to advance the synthetic fiber industry.[18] However, because of its unique characteristics, hemp has never been completely replaced by other fibers. We just have to import it now, along with cotton and other fibers. Shandong Province, China, is rich in hemp. A technician there saved an almost-bankrupt factory by finding a better way to spin hemp. He came up with a new process for degumming hemp in 1987, producing clean fiber 20 cm to 40 cm in length, to be spun with wool or cotton to produce textiles. Developed by Dongping Linen Textile Mill, the hemp chemical degumming and spinning technology makes hemp even more useful to industry.[19] Hemp is also produced in Russia, Yugoslavia, Ro-

---

[13]As early as 1859, attempts were made in England & Sweden to subject flax & hemp waste to chemical treatment & prepare a product to use in the textile industry for spinning, but the process was cumbersome, consisting of 10 separate processes, so that it had to be abandoned as too expensive & uneconomical. Boermann. op. cit.
[14]Ibid.
[15]Boermann, Professor Paul, of Staatliches Material Prufungsamt. 'Cottonized Flax & Hemp as a Substitute for Cotton.' in Manchester Guardian Commercial. 1924
[16]This was common in the US after 1950. *Encyclopaedia Brittanica.* 1957
[17]*The Washington Spectator.* vol. 17:4. Feb. 15, 1991
[18]DuPont patented nylon that same year.
[19]In the summer of 1982 Zhang Daochen "boiled hemp & added different chemicals at different temperatures. After 100 tries, they succeeded & won a gold medal at the 15th Zagreb International New Invention Fair." '100-year Textile Puzzle Solved.' Xinhua General Overseas News Service. Jinan, China. Oct. 11, 1987.

mania, Spain, France, Poland, etc., but little fiber is imported from these countries at the moment. Until recently, water-retted hemp was imported from Italy.

While hemp from the larger farms has been sold directly to the spinning mills, most hemp produced in the United States traditionally passed through the hands of local dealers in the farm region. Imported hemp was purchased either directly from foreign dealers by the mills, or through fiber brokers in New York and Boston.[20]

Along with cost savings from using domestic hemp instead of imported cotton, we can get those textile sales and jobs back—at a decent wage and without sacrificing our environment. By doing so, we can create a new export industry. The economic implications are clear. As the *Louisville Courier* said, "Manufacturing establishments will always spring up wherever the raw material can be obtained the cheapest, and there is no reason why the United States should not supply Europe with, not only hemp for all navy purposes, but also goods of various kinds fabricated from that material."[21]

A Matter of Manufacturing Machinery

The milling of retted hemp consists of four major processes: the drying, breaking, scutching and hackling. All this can be done by hand, but modern equipment now makes easy work of it. During the Second World War, the cost of the machinery was liquidated in just five years from rentals and profits from the hemp.[22]

Entering the mill, the hemp passed through long driers where hot air removed all moisture from the stalks. It then went through the break, consisting of fluted iron rollers which crushed the hurds into small pieces. Hurds were separated from the fibers in the scutchers, large drums in which beaters pummeled the broken stalks. In the final operation the hackles, giant combs, straightened the line and removed the tow. The strands were graded, twisted into hands and baled to be sent to the cordage mills. The hurds were burned as fuel to operate mill machinery and heat the driers.[23]

Since most textile mills today are tooled for either short cotton fiber or continuous, synthetic fibers such as nylon, one of three

[20]Moore. op. cit. p. 340
[21]"When we consider the various purposes to which every quality of hemp can be applied, whether it is the manufacture of cable, sail cloth & rigging, coarse & fine linens, table cloths, bagging, bale rope, twine, sewing thread & many other things of common use & necessity, no fear need be entertained of an overproduction." 1844. in Moore. op. cit. p. 52. also "Cotton bagging was scarcely ever made of cotton, almost always hemp, & was used to cover bales of cotton." *Ibid*. p. 39
[22]New types of reapers & binders were developed, & equipment manufacturers turned out 2400 of these machines. 'Hemp Cultivation in the United States.' in *Herald Tribune*. New York NY. May 30, 1943
[23]Ibid.

things can be done. The machinery can be adjusted for long fiber; hemp pulp can be extruded into a continuous fiber, such as rayon or nylon; or hemp can be treated to replicate cotton. When treated by a chemical process, hemp can be spun on cotton, wool and worsted machinery.[24] The result has all the absorbancy and wearing quality of linen made from flax.[25]

Cotton is prepared and spun on machines different from those used for preparing and spinning long fibers. It is the most common natural fiber, and suited to a wide range of textile products. A soft, pliable fiber that is white, lustrous and similar to cotton in every way is obtained by cottonizing hemp.[26] Coarse yarns[27] are spun from cottonized fiber alone. Finer yarns[28] are spun from this fiber mixed with cotton or cotton waste.

Cottonizing Hemp for Existing Textile Mills

Experience has shown that cottonized hemp is as good for spinning as that obtained from flax. The processes employ alkalis or alkaline earths, with or without pressure and high temperature, sulfite lye, alternating acid and alkali treatments, intensified retting and grassing, etc.

A process using free chlorine, devised at the Dresden Research Institute, proved very economical.[29] The raw material was not subjected to high temperature and pressures or to mechanical treatment, so damaged and broken fibers, one of the chief disadvantages of mechanical treatment, are avoided. A further advantage of the process was to allow all kinds of waste, even very weedy ground straw, to be cottonized successfully. In works employing this process, the strength of the fiber is not affected by cottonization, and corresponds to that of bleached flax yarn, at least. The decrease in strength of cottonized yarn is largely due to the smoother surface of the fibers, which causes them to slip and pull apart. This can be mitigated to a considerable degree by increasing the twist. The cost of the process is comparatively low. Woody constituents are so completely removed that a good, level-dyeing product is obtained. The yarns so obtained are quite suitable for the manufacture of woven and knitted goods. In this way, an amount of cottonized fiber

---

[24]Worsted is long hair wool that is tightly twisted.
[25]Lower, George A. 'Flax & Hemp: From the Seed to the Loom.' in *Mechanical Engineering*. February 1938
[26]For an end product very similar to cotton, the process used is termed "cottonization" & the treated fiber is known as "cottonized" flax or hemp.
[27]up to about 12s
[28]up to 20s
[29]But, in 1924, "the uneven staple of flax & hemp fibers makes it difficult to produce the finer counts of yarn." Ibid. This was solved by the Chinese in 1987.

could be obtained equal to the total amount of flax and hemp fiber waste produced in the world. Approximately half would derive from retting, hackling and spinning waste, and half from the seed straw.[30]

As always when using chemical processes, the fiber should be thoroughly washed out before being manufactured into garments.

A Comparison of Selected Fiber Resources

Hemp works well in blends with other fibers. When combining threads, it is important to maintain the compatibility of the fibers not only in the spin and weave, but also in the dying and handling. Smooth fibers such as silks and synthetics use different dyes than absorbent natural fibers like hemp. Be wary of dyes that keep washing out of the clothing, due to the pollution factor. While hemp prefers gentle handling in washing, it can also be quite rugged or it can be dry cleaned, depending on your preferences.

Pulling, retting, breaking, hackling, and scutching hemp produces by-products like ground straw, hackle and spinning waste. Its use as a valuable textile material to supplement the demand for cotton products was completely overlooked.[31] With effective waste recovery, the cost of cottonized hemp for spinning is potentially less than half the price of cotton.[32] Hemp can produce fabrics stronger and more durable than cotton or woolen fabrics of the same weight. Hemp would serve better for specific uses like carpet warp.

Synthetic fibers like nylon which are strong, lightweight and non-absorbent can be made of hemp cellulose, but synthetics have the problems of being non-biodegradable, causing allergic reactions in people and lacking surface traction, which causes slippage. Hemp is biodegradable, stretches less in heat, does not crack in cold, has better traction and does not require petrochemical processes.

Line fibers of flax and hemp are so similar they are hard to distinguish. But wetting a few strands of fiber and holding them suspended will definitely identify the two. Upon drying, flax will twist clockwise, and hemp counterclockwise. When chemically treated

---

[30]"Reckoning the world production of flax & hemp, including tow yarns, at about 1.5 million tons, & taking the average world cotton crop at about 6 million tons, it follows that the world's cotton production could be increased by about 25% by working up the flax & hemp waste with the cotton, an amount which should be of great value both to the industry & to the consumer." Ibid.
[31]"A small proportion of this waste was always employed in the tow-spinning industry for the manufacture of coarse yarns (for sacks, coarse canvas, sailcloths, twines, etc.), while the greater part was allowed to lie or was burnt with boiler fuel & occasionally utilized in the manufacture of paper, upholstering furniture or as caulking material." Ibid.
[32]Boermann, op. cit.

like flax, hemp yields a beautiful fiber so closely resembling flax that a high-power microscope is needed to tell the difference.[33]

While tropical hard fibers serve well enough in cordage, if stiffness and weight are no objection and exceptional strength is not required, hemp is two to three times as strong as any of the hard fibers. This means that much less weight is required to give the same length of thread or cord. For instance, sisal binder twine of 40-lb. tensile strength runs 450 feet per pound. A better twine made of hemp would run 1280 feet per pound. Hemp fiber is more rugged and pliable than hard fibers, hence more difficult to cut in the knotter as binder twine. Hemp is not subject to as many kinds of deterioration as hard fibers, and none of them lasts as long in either fresh or salt water.[34] Because hemp is unaffected by salt water, it is used for cordage, fish lines, nets and sail cloth and other items that are routinely exposed to weather or dampness.

Fresh jute fiber is about two-thirds as strong as hemp fiber of the same weight, but lacks its durability. It rapidly loses strength, even in dry air, and if exposed to moisture, jute quickly goes to pieces. It is not suitable for any purpose where strength or durability is required, but is extensively used for burlaps, gunny bags, sugar sacks, grain sacks, wool sacking and covering for cotton bales. Even in this field, hemp may regain some of its uses where jute does not give sufficient strength or durability. Jute could not compete with hemp were it not already used in established lines of goods and manufacturers could be certain about securing hemp.[35]

It is to the interest of the purchaser as well as to the producer of hemp and the manufacturer of true hemp goods that the line between hemp and jute be sharply drawn. Unfortunately, the difference in the appearance of the fibers is not as strongly marked as the differences between their strength and wearing qualities.[36]

---

[33]In hemp, some of the ends are split. Lower. op. cit.

[34]Lower, George A. 'Flax & Hemp: From the Seed to the Loom.' in *Mechanical Engineering*. February 1938

[35]Dewey, L.H. 'Hemp.' in *USDA Yearbook. 1913.* 1914. p. 345

[36]"The two fibers may be distinguished with certainty with a microscope & chemical reagents, as indicated by the differences in the table which follows:

	Hemp	Jute
Schweitzer's test:	clean fiber dissolved more or less distinct swelling	bluish color
Iodine & sulfuric acid:	greenish blue to pure blue	yellow to brown
Anilin sulfate:	Faint yellow	golden yellow to orange
Warming in weak solutions of nitric acid	uniform blue or yellow	prismatic colors.

& potassium chromate, then washing & warming in dilute solution of soda ash & washing again; place on microscopic slide & when dry add drop of glycerol. Use polariscope (dark field)" Dewey. op. cit. p. 342-345

Profit for Pennies: Cloth, Crochet, Bags, Etc.

Hemp twines, yarns, ropes and cloth[37] are readily available, although care must be taken to be sure that they are true cannabis. Hemp cords can always be used for tying and lashing things. Short, stout ropes tied off at the ends make dandy chew toys for dogs.

The cloth can be printed, dyed, tie-dyed or decorated with silk screen, embroidery, etc., and is easily sewn into simple items like durable shopping bags. The skillful and ambitious tailor can make clothing, upholstery and other finished items, from futons to hackey sacks. Fabric glued onto a hard surface works as a computer mouse pad that has traction and keeps the mechanism clean longer.

Some garment wholesalers have hemp products available for bulk purchase and resale.[38] These can be marketed on the retail level, or customized and marketed as specialty items.

Thin twines and cords have been died and made into a variety of braided and crocheted products, such as bags, hats and bracelets. They can be woven into tapestries and wall hangings and so on with a hand loom. Thicker cords can be used for macrame items, like plant hangers. Hemp twine is exceptionally strong, so thinner and lighter weights can be used, if the appearance would be enhanced.

Such items are marketable, but are also useful educational tactile and visual aids for promoting the use of hemp.

---

[37]House of Hemp. POB 14603, Portland OR 97204. 503-232-1128
[38]Joint Ventures Hempery. POB 15551 Main Stn., Vancouver BC V5B 3B3. Canada. 604-879-2101

13

MAKE THE MOST OF THE HEMP SEED

As far as the plant is concerned, the most important use of the hempseed is to make more hemp plants, which it does at a rate of about 55 million seeds per hectare. This is more than enough seed for next year's crop. However, we have numerous other uses for the nutritional hempseed and its valuable oil.[1]

The hempseed is technically a fruit. Half the weight of a mature, harvested seed-bearing hemp plant is the actual seed. It is a primary food source that aids digestion and does not contain detectable levels of the chemical THC.[2] It is eaten by song birds, both in the home and in the wild. The shell and solid parts of the seed are pressed into seed cakes as a year-round food source for livestock. The extracted vegetable oil can be used for culinary or fuel oil, as high-viscosity lubricating oil, in shampoos, hair creams and gels, skin creams, ointments, massage oils, moisturizers and so on. One gallon of hempseed oil weighs almost exactly eight pounds.

Sterilized hemp seeds are legally available in the United States, but the sterilization process and shipping costs make it expensive. Fertile seed is strictly controlled.[3] The method used to sterilize the seeds compromises their nutritional value. It is good to know how the seed was treated before using it. Viable seed is the most nutritional and oil-rich; steam-treated seed is almost as good,[4] and dry-heated or smoked is the worst.[5] As far as we know, no major seed importer currently irradiates hempseed, and the effects of radia-

---

[1]"The seed of hemp is produced in great abundance. ... A fixed oil, *oil of hempseed*, is obtained from it by expression, which is at first greenish yellow & afterwards yellow, & has an acrid odor, but a mild taste. This oil is used in Russia for burning in lamps, although the wick is apt to get clogged, also for making paints, varnish & a kind of soft soap. 'Agriculture: Hemp.' in *Encyclopaedia Britannica*. Belford Clarke/The Werner Company. London England. 1897

[2]Furr, Marion & Mahlberg, Paul G. 'Histochemical analyses of laticifers & glandular trichomes in cannabis sativa.' in *Journal of Natural Products*. vol 44:2. March 1981. pp. 153-159. also Hemphill, Turner & Mahlberg. 'Cannabinoid content of individual plant organs from different geographical strains of c. sativa L.' in *Journal of Natural Products*. vol 43:1. January 1980. pp. 112-122

[3]The official hempseed sample of the US is kept at the USDA Seed Bank in Colorado Springs CO. DEA form 225 & a permit are required to possess fertile seed here.

[4]Ohio Hempery. 14 N. Court St. # 327, Athens OH 45701. 614-593-5826

[5]The protein yield of seed devitalized by heat treatment "is reduced to less than 1/20 of that from untreated seed. ... Licensed importers are not enthusiastic about cooperation, since they think in terms of tons & are also fully alive to the penalties that are risked if unauthorized persons secure some of the seed." Vichery, Smith & Nolan. Connecticut Agricultural Experiment Station. 'A Substitute for Edestin.' in *Science*. Oct. 4, 1940

tion remain highly controversial. Imported seed is twice fumigated for pests and should be cleaned well before human consumption.

Seed Selection for Special Characteristics

Hemp is generally cultivated for three different products: fiber from the bast, oil from the seeds, and herbal resins from the flowers and leaves. As such, it has developed into three rather distinct types.[6] Hemp strains are so easy to cross-fertilize that it is more difficult to keep distinct types separate than in crops with self-pollinated flowers. Hence, it is often best to isolate the plants cultivated for seed for selection each season.[7]

Through careful selection of parent plants, one can develop the seedline traits most desired. This could mean longer or finer fiber, higher pulp or seed yields, specific medicinal properties, shorter growing season and different soil or climatic condition requirements, unusual leaves or appearance, etc.

There are scores of sativa lines best suited for fiber, a few more for pulp, and a few more for commercial seed. Most hybridization of herbal sativa and indica strains has been undertaken in secret since prohibition, so there is no count of such strains. Judging by the names now on the market, there appear to be quite a few.

Feed the Birds, the Fish & the Beasts

Whole hempseed can be fed raw to many creatures. Alternatively, pressed seed cake left over from oil extraction is used for roughage, protein, animal and livestock feed, birdfeed, green fertilizer, etc. Seeds are ground up and fed to aquarium fish.

"Fishes love this plant, and fly to it," wrote an Englishman in 1766.[8] In Switzerland, whole hempseed is still used for bait. Soak it overnight, and push the hook in through the split in the shell.[9]

Another traditional Swiss use of cannabis was as an attractive plant to dress up the garden and draw wild songbirds that love to eat its seed,[10] just as in England. "Notwithstanding the coarseness of its leaves, it is an elegant plant and is sometimes sown on this account in shrubberies and large flower borders."[11] Its flowers were used

---

[6]Dewey, Lyster H. 'Hemp.' in *Yearbook of the USDA, 1913*. US GPO. Washington DC. 1914. p. 295

[7]Selecting plants for length of internode, height, thin shell & well-fluted stems yielded an improved strain in 1909 called Minnesota no. 8. *Ibid.* pp. 304-305

[8]Marcandier, M. *A Treatise on Hemp*. Boston MA. 1766. pp. 8-9

[9]VS Hanf Freunden. Postfach 323, 9004 Gallen Switzerland. 1992

[10]'Eine Zierde für jeden Garten: Die hübschen Haschisch-Pflanzen.' in *Sonntags-Blick*. Switzerland. July 10, 1988

[11]"It is commonly sold as food for cage birds; & birds are so fond of it that not only the ripening fields, but the newly-sown fields must be carefully guarded against their depredations." *Encyclopaedia Britannica*. London England. 1897

for seed or medicine.[12] People without gardens may still want to attract birds. One expert recommended a wild bird seed mixture "from the Audubon Society or pet store" that combined hempseed with canary seed, cracked corn, Kafir corn, millet and sunflower seeds. "Hemp is a favorite because of its nourishing oily content." [13]

An industry representative told Congress hempseed needed to be protected because it contains an oil substance that is a valuable ingredient of pigeon feed, and "we have not been able to find any seed that will take its place. If you substitute anything for the hemp, it has a tendency to change the character of the squab. ... (Hempseed) has a tendency to bring back the feathers and improve the birds."[14]

The former head of the United States Signal Corps Pigeon Section, W. M. Levi, wrote that "In addition to the actual physical effect produced upon the bird's body, its feeding has a decided beneficial psychological effect upon the bird's happiness. Pigeons fed sparingly with a little hemp in the middle of the day during the moulting season take a new interest in life which is almost inconceivable." Among his citings were an 1895 report that "If a bird appear low-spirited, nothing will cheer it up more than a little good hempseed mixed with some dry raw rice," and a 1914 report calling it "a pick-me-up in the case of a bird that happens to be out of sorts."[15] The seed is mixed with crushed, dried nettles to add to chicken feed during the winter, to increase their egg production.[16] Hempseed is such an important source of food for wild and domestic songbirds that its ban has been said to be a key factor in the reduction of wild bird populations worldwide.[17]

Oil To Burn, Clean, Cook & Make Things

The hempseed ranges in oil content from 30 to 35 percent. Industry once used the oil for making paints, varnishes and soaps,[18] also for cooking oil and dressings, ointments, lotions, cosmetics,

[12]'Auch in der Schweiz alte Hanftradition.' in *AZ*. Zurich Switzerland. April 7, 1988
[13]Goldfinches are fond of hemp, millet & sunflower seeds. Catbirds take hempseed. The Junco, tree sparrow, song sparrow, goldfinch, fox sparrow, catbird, purple finch, pine siskin like mixed small seeds, hemp, millet & chick feed. McKenny, M. *Birds in the Garden & How to Attract Them*. Reynall & Hitchcock. New York NY. 1939. pp. 64-65
[14]"If we were deprived of the use of hempseed, it would affect all the pigeon producers in the US, of which there are upwards of 40,000." Scarlett, R.G. of W.G. Scarlett Corp. of Baltimore MD. *Transcript of the Hearing on HR 6385*. op. cit.
[15]Levi. W.M., Palmetto Pigeon Plant president, 1923-1956. *The Pigeon*. Levi Publishing Co. Sumter. 1957. p. 499
[16]'Cáñamo.' in *El Maravilloso Mundo de las Hierbas*. Jose Dalman Socias, director editorial. Ed. Dalmau Socias. Barcelona Spain. 1982, 1988
[17]Herer. op. cit. p. 42
[18]'Hemp' in *Encyclopaedia Britannica*. London England. 1957

creams, for fuel and heating oil, precision engine lubricants, varnish, lacquer, sealants, etc.

Hempseed oil is said to burn the brightest of all lamp oils and has been used since the days of Abraham.[19] Herodotus described Scythians purifying and cleansing themselves with hemp oil, which "makes their skin shining and clean."[20] The same words echo in King David's song of praise for "wine that maketh glad the heart of man and oil to make his face to shineth."[21]

In America, hemp was cultivated almost exclusively for fiber, which drew sharp criticism from botanist Luther Burbank. "The seed of [hemp] is prized in other countries for its oil, and its neglect here illustrates the same wasteful use of our agricultural resources."[22] Soon, its use was so widespread that the domestic crop did not meet the demand. The country imported 116 million pounds of hempseed in 1935 alone.[23] A lot of it went into paints. A 1937 engineering report stated that "Paint and lacquer manufacturers are interested in hempseed oil, which is a good drying agent."[24]

A confidential federal memorandum in 1936 noted that cannabis was used extensively by veterinarians and industry, which created a problem for prohibitionists.[25]

> We can satisfy them by importing their medical needs. We must also satisfy the canary bird seed trade, and the Sherwin Williams Paint Company, which uses hemp seed oil for drying purposes. We are now working with the Department of Commerce in finding substitutes for the legitimate trade, and after that is accomplished, the path will be cleared for the treaties and for federal (prohibition) law.

Ultimately, hempseed oil was excluded from the prohibition "because of the need for hempseed oil."[26] Growing hemp from which to obtain seed was banned, however. So was importing viable seeds. American businesses were cut out of the profits.

---

[19]Herer, Jack. *Hemp & the Marijuana Conspiracy: The Emperor Wears No Clothes.* HEMP Publishing. Van Nuys CA 1991. p. 8
[20]Herodotus. *Histories IV.* 450 BC. University Press. Cambridge MA. 1906. pp. 74-76
[21]"He causeth the grass to grow for the cattle & herb for the service of man; that he may bring forth food out of the earth; & ..." King David. 'Psalm 104:14-15' in *Holy Bible*
[22]Burbank, Luther. 'How Plants are Trained to Work for Man.' in *Useful Plants.* P.F. Collier & Son Co. New York NY. vol. 6. p. 48
[23]Loziers, Ralph. *Transcript of the Hearing on HR 6385.* Committee on Ways & Means, House of Representatives. 75c 1s. April 27-30, May 4, 1937
[24]Lower, George. 'Flax & Hemp.' in *Mechanical Engineering.* February 1938
[25]FBN Director Harry Anslinger to Asst. Sec. Treasury Stephen B. Gibbons. Feb. 1, 1936. in Musto, D.F., M.D. *The American Disease: Origins of narcotic control.* Colonial Press Inc. Clinton MA. 1973. p. 224
[26]'Hempseed oil out of marijuana bill.' in *Industrial Arts Index.* 131:3. May 3, 1937

Return of the Essential Fatty Acids

The promise of better health and the possibility of feeding the world "is at our fingertips," according to a 1991 statement released by Dr. R. Lee Hamilton, and fellow UCLA researcher William Eidelman, M.D. Hempseed oil is among the lowest in saturated fats, at eight percent of total oil volume. The oil ranges from 51 to 62 percent linoleic acid (LA, or omega six) and from 19 to 25 percent linolenic acid (LNA, or omega three). Only flax oil has more linolenic acid at 58 percent; but hemp oil is highest in total essential fatty acids, at 80 to 81 percent of total oil volume.[27]

As Hamilton says, "Essential fatty acids are responsible for our immune response. In the [European] old country, the peasants ate hemp butter. They were more resistant to disease than the nobility."[28] The aristocrats wouldn't eat hemp[29] because the poor ate "the oil of it in their soup."[30] Hamilton reports that these oils do not raise cholesterol levels but, in fact, help clear the arteries.

"What are essential fatty acids? The term 'essential' is the tip-off." These oils, linoleic and linolenic acids, support the immune system and guard against viral infection and other insults to the immune system. Studies by Joanna Budwig, M.D., nominated for the Nobel Prize every year since 1979, showed unparalleled results in their use in treating terminal cancer patients. Studies are in progress using these essential oils to support the immune systems of those with the HIV virus, connected to the disease AIDS. So far they have been extremely promising. "What is the richest source of the essential oils? Yes, you guessed it, the seeds from the cannabis hemp plant. What better proof of the life-giving values of the now-illegal seed. ... What the world needs now is intelligent re-legalization of cannabis hemp, especially for medical intervention."[31]

The Perfect Source of Protein for People, Too

Hempseed has long been a part of the human diet. Use of the seed for food has been important in history, especially where people have survived on marginal farmland. Ralph Loziers, of the National Institute of Oilseed Products, told the 1937 Congressional hearing on cannabis prohibition that hempseed "is used in all the Oriental

---

[27]Osburn, L. 'Hempseed: The most nutritionally complete food in the world. Part 2.' in *Hemp Line Journal.* Access Unlimited. Frazier Park CA. November 1992. p. 12. also Miller & Wirtshafter. op. cit.
[28]R. Lee Hamilton, Ed.D., Ph.D. medical researcher-biochemist emeritus. UCLA
[29]Erasmus, Udo. *Fats & Oils: The Complete Guide to Fats & Oils in Health & Nutrition.* Alive Books. 1986.
[30]Marcandier. op. cit. pp. 8-9
[31]Open letter from the researchers. Dec. 29, 1991

nations and also in a part of Russia as food. It is grown in their fields and used as oatmeal. Millions of people every day are using hemp seed in the Orient as food. They have been doing this for many generations, especially in periods of famine."[32]

Worldwide starvation has become a fact of life in the years since cannabis was banned. Widespread use of hempseed protein could feed and nourish much of the world's hungry again, thanks to the unique characteristics of hempseed nutrition. Since 25 percent of the seed is protein, a handful of it provides the minimum daily requirement for adults. While not particularly filling, a baggie full of hempseed would provide all the essential protein, oil and dietary fiber necessary for human survival for two weeks.[33] The protein in hemp is more digestible than soy protein.[34] Hempseed is used in traditional Asian medicine as a nourishing food for infants or the ill, and as an intestinal lubricant and coolant to the system.[35]

Recent research by Lynn Osburn reveals that "Hempseed is the highest in essential fatty acids of any plant. It contains all the essential amino acids and essential fatty acids needed to maintain healthy human life. No other single source provides complete protein in such an easily digestible form. No other plant has the oils essential to life in as perfect a ratio for human health and vitality."[36]

Why Hempseed Is So Good for Everybody

Hempseed is a complete vegetable protein. "There are eight amino acids essential to life that the human body cannot make, and two more the body cannot make in sufficient quantity. ... The complete protein in hempseed gives the human body all the essential amino acids required to maintain health."[37] It provides the necessary types and amounts of amino acids the body needs to make serum albumin and serum globulins, such as the immune-enhancing gamma globulin antibodies, the body's first line of self-defense.[38]

The body's ability to resist disease and recover from illness depends on how rapidly it can react with sufficient antibodies to fend off the initial attack. If the globulin protein starting-material is in short supply, the number of antibodies may not be enough to

---

[32]Loziers. op. cit.
[33]Miller, Carol & Wirtshafter, Don. *The Hemp Seed Cook Book.* The Ohio Hempery, Inc. Athens, OH. 1992. 21 p.
[34]Though soy provides slightly more protein per pound of seed
[35]Ibid.
[36]Osburn, L. 'Hempseed: The most nutritionally complete food in the world. Part 1.' in *Hemp Line Journal.* no. 1. Access Unlimited. Frazier Park CA. August 1992. p. 14
[37]Ibid.
[38]Ibid.

prevent the onset of symptoms.[39] Globulin is the third most abundant protein in the human body. Hempseed protein is 65 percent globular edestin, plus quantities of albumin (present in all seeds), so its easily digestible protein is readily available in a form quite similar to that found in blood plasma.[40]

Whatever Happened to the Elusive Edestin?

Today, edestin, the globulin of hempseed, is frequently not even listed in the dictionary. But until a half century ago, it was one of the most studied of all food sources. Edestin was regarded as the standard example of seed globulins for many years. It was also proven to be adequate as the sole source of protein in the diet of animals.[41] Edestin facilitates the digestion process; in fact the word "edible" has the same Greek root. This led to extensive use of edestin as a convenient protein, relatively free from phosphorous. Over the years, many amino-acid determinations were made upon edestin. Its composition was better known than any other globulin in its molecular weight class. Preparation of a sample of this protein was a long-time standard laboratory exercise in biochemistry courses.[42]

In 1941 *Science* magazine lamented the loss of this vital globulin: "Passage of the Marijuana Law of 1937 has placed restrictions upon trade in hempseed that, in effect, amount to prohibition. ... It seems clear that the long and important career of the protein is coming to a close in the United States."

Hempseed at Home: The Proof Is in the Tasting

According to some theories, sprouting any raw seed improves its nutritional value. Hemp seed can be used like any other seed sprout, in salads, stir-fry cooking, etc.

Like soybean, hempseed extracts can be made into vegetable milk or texturized and spiced to taste like chicken, beef or pork. It mixes well with soy milk nutritionally.[43] Hempseed can be used to make tofu-style curd. It can be ground into meal, cooked, then sweetened with milk, raisins, nuts and dried fruits added in a nutritional hot cereal, like oatmeal or cream of wheat. Or it can be

---

[39]Ibid.

[40]Osburn, L. & J. 'A Supplement & Answer to Dr. Walker's *Can Hemp Save Our Planet.*' presented at NORML 20th Anniv. Conf. Wash. DC. Reprint in *Hemp Line Journal* no. 2

[41]"Osborne subjected this protein to more detailed & extensive study than any other globulin, & his demonstration with Mendel of its (full nutritional) adequacy. ... In the cases of only a few other proteins are higher summations of amino-acids available." Vichery, Smith & Nolan. op. cit.

[42]Ibid.

[43]Coincidentally, the two crops provide a complete soil treatment in rotation; soybeans fixing nitrogen from the air & hemp re-mineralizing the topsoil from below.

salted or seasoned for those who avoid sweets. This porridge has a better flavor than name: "gruel."[44] Hempseed can be further ground into a paste similar to peanut butter but with a more delicate flavor. This margarine is common in Russia. "Hemp butter puts our peanut butter to shame for nutritional value," adds nutritionist Udo Erasmus, Ph.D.[45] The seeds are roasted, seasoned and eaten as a snack. Roasted and ground seeds can be baked into breads, cakes, pancakes and casseroles. Hempseed makes a hearty, crispy addition to granola or granola bars. The second-century physician Galen commented on the Roman citizens' appetite for sweets and pastries made with hempseed.

Now that you know how nutritious it is, see for yourself how delicious it can be.[46] Dr. Andrew Weil of the University of Arizona College of Medicine notes, "Hemp oil . . . actually tastes good. It is nutty. . . . I use it on salads, baked potatoes, and other foods and would not consider putting it in capsules. I like the idea of having one food oil that supplies both omega-3s and GLA, without the need to take . . . capsules."[47] These cooking tips and recipes are from Carol Miller and Don Wirtshafter, authors of the *Hemp Seed Cookbook.*[48] For more recipes and tips, this book is indispensable.

Hempseed Meal: The Basis of Hemp Cooking

To prepare hempseed meal, the seeds are first washed several times. Select only the seeds that float. Immediately dry roast in a heavy skillet on top of the stove, or at a low temperature (250-300°F) in the oven. Roasting will take five to 10 minutes. You will know they are done when they stop popping and begin to smell like roasted nuts. Avoid French roasting. Cool the seeds and grind. Any grain grinder, nut grinder or coffee mill will work. To reduce the coarse texture of the hulls, you may want to flash blend the toasted seeds briefly, then sift out the fragments. For a buttery texture, you may want to grind twice.

Hempseed Porridge (Gruel)

In a small pan, combine: 1 c. toasted, ground hemp seeds, 2 c. water, or more if you prefer. Heat to boiling, then turn heat down and cook 5-10 minutes. Remove from heat and let stand until it is the consistency you want. Sweeten with maple syrup or honey and serve with milk.

44Herer. op. cit. p 41
45interview with Lynn Osburn. 1991.
46Hempseed is available in bulk at many pet stores, or can be ordered through the Ohio Hempery (below) & various other hemp distributors.
47Weil, M.D., Andrew. Therapeutic Hemp Oil. Natural Health. March/April 1993.
48Miller, C. & Wirtshafter, D. *Hemp Seed Cookbook.* Ohio Hempery, Inc. 14 N. Court St. #327, Athens OH 45701. Phone: 614-593-5826. 1992. 21 p. $7 w/14 oz. hempseed

Nutty Hempseed & Walnut Loaf (Serves 12-16)

Saute, in 2 T. olive oil: 1 c. chopped herbs (oregano, cilantro, parsley, basil—any or all), 1 lb. chopped onions, 1 c. chopped mushrooms, 1 c. chopped carrots, 1 c. chopped cabbage (or chard, zucchini, or other seasonal vegetables), 1/2 c. chopped celery, 4 crushed garlic cloves

Add and mix together: 1 c. hempseed meal, 3 c. walnuts, 1 c. cooked rice (part wild rice is nice), 3 T. tamari or soy sauce, 1 lb. mashed tofu, 1/2 c. nutritional yeast

Press into 9" x 13" baking dish. Sprinkle with a thick layer of nutritional yeast. Bake for 35 minutes at 325°F, or at 300° in a glass baking dish. Cut into squares. Smother with mushroom gravy. Optional additions: 1 c. cheddar cheese, shredded; 4-6 eggs, beaten.

Chocolate-Almond Hempseed Torte (Serves 12-16)

Whip: 3/4 c. butter or margarine. Beat in: (one at a time) 6 egg yolks. Mix in: 1 c. melted chocolate chips, 1 3/4 c. ground almonds (about 1 lb.), 1/2-3/4 c. hemp seed meal. Beat until stiff: 6 egg whites. Fold in. Put in two 8" or 9" round cake pans. Bake at 375° for 10 minutes. Lower heat to 325° and bake for another 20 minutes. Cool before frosting.

14

THE NATURAL FLOWER OF HEALTH

Cannabis has proven in numerous studies to be valuable in a wide range of modern clinical applications. Cannabis is not a panacea, but it has the overall effect of relieving chronic pain as well as small aches, helping people to eat, sleep and see better, thereby creating a mental attitude conducive to healing. The herb is known to create temporary feelings of calmness and well-being, as well as to prevent nausea, reduce blood pressure, stimulate appetite, suppress convulsions, ease muscle spasms, and much more.[1]

Like any drug, cannabis is a tool without intrinsic moral value, negative or positive. There is a wide range of responses to it, from miracle drug to unpleasant experience, depending upon set, setting, personality and pharmacology. No drug is perfectly safe and harmless for all people at all dosage levels under all conditions of use.

Nonetheless, "It's probably true that (cannabis's) greatest danger is if a bale of it falls on you," David Friedman, deputy director of the National Institute on Drug Abuse (NIDA) pre-clinical research division in charge of cannabis research, noted in late 1990.[2]

An understated value of cannabis is as preventative medicine. People who consume cannabis regularly may never develop ailments such as glaucoma, migraines, insomnia or stress-related health problems that they otherwise might have without the herb's effect.

The herb is typically smoked in a pipe or a hand-rolled cigarette often called a joint. Its effect depends on the quantity and potency consumed. While an average joint weighs about a gram, one can feel the effect of top quality cannabis with just a single puff of smoke. The smallest amount of actual THC used to produce a "high" is estimated at a half milligram, but, since a lot of that will be destroyed in the burning process and still more is lost into the air as unconsumed smoke, the threshold dose is really about 2.5 mg.[3] Cannabis

[1]Grinspoon, Dr. Lester & Bakalar, J. *Marijuana the Forbidden Medicine*. Yale U Press. New Haven CT. 1993. also *Marihuana: Medical Papers, 1839-1972*. Mikuriya, Dr. Tod, ed. Medi-Comp Press. Berkeley CA. 1973. also Booth, W. 'Marijuana receptor exists in brain.' in *Washington Post*. DC. Aug. 9, 1990. also Cohen, Dr. Sidney. 'Therapeutic Potential of Marijuana's Components.' American Council on Marijuana & Other Psychoactive Drugs. 1982
[2]*Washington Post*. Washington DC. Sept. 19, 1990
[3]Abel, Ernest L. *Marihuana: The first 12,000 years*. Plenum Press. New York NY. 1980. pp. 260-262

has no proven long-term or permanent effect. When smoked, the peak effects come in about 15 minutes and last two to four hours.

Cannabis is also eaten, taken in a beverage, or made into a topical preparation, or *poultice*, for conditions such as abrasions, burns and infections. In some cases, tinctures and extracts may serve better. When eaten, the threshold level for hashish is from .25 to .5 grams, and for cannabis it is one to three grams. The peak effects occur in 2.5 to 3.5 hours and last six to eight hours.[4]

The restoration of hemp drugs to the pharmacopeia will benefit the national health, on many levels. The plant's therapeutic applications mean cost savings for insurance companies and hospitals, along with better lives and extended productivity for people with illnesses that respond to cannabis therapies.

We will examine various body systems and see how cannabis affects them, to better understand how it affects human health.

Immune System Support, Rest & AIDS Relief

An important and still legally available use of cannabis is eating hempseed to support the immune system. The complete protein in hempseed gives the body the combination of essential amino acids and essential fatty acids needed to maintain health. It provides the components necessary to make human serum albumin and serum globulins, including the immune enhancing gamma globulin antibodies.[5] No epidemiological data indicate a rise in infections from smoking cannabis, as had once been claimed.[6] The *Journal of Psychoactive Drugs* criticized the highly publicized reports of Dr. Gabriel Nahas and others for being conducted only in test tubes and lab cultures (in vitro), not on people, noting they were "seriously flawed" by using unrealistically large doses of cannabis. When researchers at UCLA directly challenged the immune systems of 22 regular cannabis smokers, they all maintained strong, vigorous immune reactions. "Since responses were normal in the chronic marijuana users we tested, it would appear that chronic marijuana smoking does not produce a gross cellular immune defect that can be detected by skin testing."[7]

---

[4]Cone, Johnson, Paul, Mell & Mitchell. at NIDA Addiction Research Center, Baltimore MD. 'Marijuana-laced brownies: Behavioral effects, physiologic effects & urinalysis.' in *Journal of Analytical Toxicology*. vol. 12:4. 1988. pp. 169-175
[5]See section on hempseed
[6]A Gabriel Nahas test tube study on T-lyphocyte cells, projecting that cannabis smokers would get cancer at 80 times the rate of the general population, is disproven statistically, & was clinically disproven by Silverstein & Lessin (see below), who also disproven the immune-suppression theory of Gupta, Sudhir, et al., at Roosevelt/St. Lukes Hospitals. New York NY. in *New England Journal of Medicine*. 1974
[7]Silverstein, M.J. & Lessin, P.J. 'Normal skin test responses in chronic marihuana users.' in *Science*. vol. 186. 1974. pp. 740-741

Repeated follow-up studies verified this.[8] Moreover, at least two studies indicate that cannabis use stimulated the immune system.[9]

Herbal cannabis controls nausea and improves the appetite, permitting adequate nutrition to support the immune system. Other drugs used to treat people with Acquired Immunity Deficiency Syndrome (AIDS), like AZT, damage the immune system.[10] Many HIV-positive people, considered at risk for AIDS, report from personal experience that cannabis helped them. They report that cannabis dramatically improves their quality of life and helps stabilize their weight, to combat the "wasting syndrome." The compound THC, considered the primary chemical in cannabis that causes the high, has been synthesized as dronabinol under the trade name Marinol. The pill is available by prescription, but persons with AIDS consistently report that it is far less effective than the natural herb. They often report feeling more optimistic and cheerful after smoking and regain their will to live.[11]

Cannabis also helps people to relax and sleep more soundly, to overcome insomnia and get the rest needed to recover strength.[12]

Saving Eyes & Helping Vision

A well-known effect of cannabis is to redden the eyes[13] as it lowers pressure inside the eyeball, or Inner Ocular Pressure (IOP). A common cause of blindness, called glaucoma, interferes with the eyes' normal pressure release mechanisms and raises IOP. Cannabis reduced IOP in lab animals as well as, or better than, pharmaceutical drugs, with fewer or no medical side effects.[14]

Cannabis is smoked or eaten for this benefit, and THC and other derivatives have been extracted into eye drops.[15] Cannabis is two to three times as effective as are currently legal medicines for reducing eye pressure, without toxic side effects or damage to liver and kid-

[8]Including: Petersen et al. 1975 & 1976; White et al. 1975; Cushman & Khurana. 1977; & McDonough et al. 1980

[9]Kaklamani, et al. 'Hashish smoking & T-lymphocytes.' 1978. also Kalofoutis, et al. 'The significance of lymphocyte lipid changes after smoking hashish.' 1978

[10]MARS. op. cit.

[11]Ibid.

[12]MARS, Marijuana AIDS Research Service. From Alliance for Cannabis Therapeutics & Richard Dennis. Box 21210 Kalorama Stn. Washington DC 20009. 202-328-6391

[13]This seems to suggest that people with conjunctivitis, or inflamed eyes, might be aggravated by smoking cannabis, but we found no data to support this.

[14]Lansky, Philip S., M.D. 'Marijuana as Medicine?' in Health World. February 1991 pp. 46-49. also Cohen, Dr. Sidney. 'Therapeutic Aspects.' in Marihuana. NIDA monograph. Washington DC. 1976. ch. 9. pp. 194-225

[15]Green, K. & McDonald, T.F. at Medical College of Georgia, Augusta. 'Ocular toxicology of marijuana: Update.' in Journal of Toxicology. vol. 6:4. 1987. pp. 239-382

neys associated with presently approved glaucoma drugs. Both human studies and practical experience bear this out.[16]

Another possible benefit may be improved night vision. M.E. West of the University of the West Indies in Kingston said Jamaican fishermen who smoke cannabis or drink an alcoholic beverage made from the stems and leaves of the plant "have an uncanny ability to see in the dark."[17]

Cardiovascular System & Migraine Headache

Cannabis' effect on the cardiovascular system is a variable that may be influenced by the emotional state of the consumer. Unlike tobacco which is a vasoconstrictor, cannabis is a vasodilator, meaning it opens up blood vessels. It dilates the arteries to lower blood pressure and inner eye pressure and creates a sense of well-being that reduces stress. Such benefits are temporary.

Cannabis also slightly elevates mean arterial blood pressure and stimulates the heartbeat.[18] This effect lessened in regular herb smokers over the course of a few weeks, showing that tolerance had developed.[19] Oral doses of clonidine, taken three hours before consuming cannabis, suppressed but did not eliminate that response without diminishing the herb's psychological effects.[20]

Since cannabinoids can inhibit platelet serotonin release induced by migraineur's plasma, regular smoking of the herb appears to prevent migraine attacks.[21]

Appetite, Eating & the Digestive Tract

Consuming cannabis stimulates the appetite, resulting in "the munchies." This helps people with debilitating diseases to eat and gain weight, giving them strength. Smoking cannabis has clinical utility in treating persons with anorexia nervosa, and the wasting syndrome associated with cancer, tuberculosis, and AIDS.[22]

---

[16]Young, Francis L. DEA Administrative Law Judge. *In the Matter of Marijuana Rescheduling Petition.* Docket no 86-22. Sept. 6, 1988

[17]He joined a night fishing crew & studied how they navigated without lights in treacherous waters. West, M.E. U of West Indies, Kingston. in *Nature.* July 1991. also 'Marijuana may aid night vision.' in *Los Angeles Times.* July 1, 1991. p. B-3

[18]Foltin, Capriotti, et al. 'Effects of marijuana, cocaine & task performance on cardiovascular responsivity.' in NIDA Monograph. June 16-18, 1986. pp. 259-265

[19]Chait, L.D. 'Delta-9 THC content & human marijuana self-administration.' Pritzker School of Medicine. U of Chicago. IL. 1989

[20]Cone, Welch & Lange. NIDA. Baltimore MD. 'Clonidine partially blocks the physiologic effects but not the subjective effects produced by smoking marijuana.' in *Pharmacology, Biochemistry & Behavior.* vol. 29:3. 1988. p 649-652

[21]El-Mallakh, R.S. 'Marijuana & Migraine.' UC Health Center, Dept. of Neurology. Farmington CT. 1987

[22]'Two drugs approved for AIDS.' in *Washington Post.* DC. Dec. 24, 1992. p. A-5

Hempseed is widely used in China as a gentle means of managing constipation.[23] Its oil "lubricates" the bowels, and the hulls provide roughage to flush the system. Its easily digestible edestin and proteins are critical in combatting problems such as pancreatic cancer, which block the body's ability to absorb nutrients.[24] The seed also contains nourishing gamma-linoleic acid, found only in human mothers' milk and two rare seed oils.[25] These are invaluable for treating cases of severe malnutrition and near starvation. Hempseed has also proven useful to treat nutritional deficiencies caused by tuberculosis.[26]

Reducing Nausea in Cancer & Chemotherapy

Studies on cancer patients legally permitted to smoke cannabis in New Mexico, California, Michigan, New York, Georgia and Tennessee reveal cannabis often reduces nausea and vomiting when all available prescription drugs fail to work.[27] A majority of cancer specialists from around the country surveyed in 1991 agreed that cannabis should be allowed to be prescribed for their patients.[28]

It is in fact a potent anti-emetic,[29] and many people with AIDS report improved appetite with a weight gain after they begin smoking cannabis. People with AIDS who use cannabis medically report that the drug allows a "more normal life" with relatively few side effects.[30] According to a survey of cancer patients, smoked cannabis is more effective than the Marinol pill in controlling nausea in cancer patients undergoing chemotherapy.[31] Smoked cannabis is less expensive and more practical, since it cannot be vomited up and is less likely to cause unpleasant side effects. The herb has also proven useful to settle the stomachs of people with motion sickness and for morning sickness in pregnant women.

Analgesic Pain Control

At least 3000 years ago in ancient China, cannabis was used for its pain lowering, or analgesic, properties. Mixed with wine, it was the sole means of pain management for surgical procedures. More

---

[23]Lansky. op. cit.
[24]Herer, Jack. *Hemp & the Marijuana Conspiracy: The Emperor Wears No Clothes.* HEMP Publishing. Van Nuys CA. 1991. p. 39
[25]Hamilton, Dr. Roberta. Professor Emeritus. UCLA. Los Angeles CA. 1991, 1992
[26]*Tubercular Nutritional Study.* Czechoslovakia. 1955
[27]MARS. op. cit.
[28]Ostrow, R. '48% of cancer specialists in study would prescribe pot.' in *Los Angeles Times.* CA. May 1, 1991. p. A-12
[29]Sallan, et al. 'Antiemetics in patients receiving chemotherapy for cancer.' in *New England Journal of Medicine.* vol. 302. 1980. p. 135
[30]MARS. op. cit.
[31]'Smoked marijuana called effective remedy.' in *Boston Globe.* June 28, 1991. p. 12

recently cannabis has proven to possess analgesic properties comparable to that of morphine, in experiments on both rats and dogs.[32]
It has proven especially useful for treating unilateral vascular headaches, or migraine. Cannabis completely alleviates most migraine headaches most of the time, and was the standard remedy for these and other headaches and neuralgia earlier this century.[33]

Many people with the genetic blood disorder sickle-cell anemia also report that cannabis often relieves the unpredictable and violent episodes of pain associated with that condition.[34]

It is not THC but another group of cannabinols that provide the most effective analgesic relief.[35] Doctors who used self-administered doses recorded this effect as a mental distancing from the pain.[36]

Antibiotic & Bacteriostatic Use

Ancient pharmacopeias refer to squeezing hemp flowers into a tonic for earache, and boiling the root for a salve to soothe burns. In the 1950s, Czechoslovak scientists discovered that the juicy resin, expressed from fiber hemp flower-tops with ripe seeds, is rich in cannabidiolic acid. This is remarkably effective as an analgesic for burns and as an antibiotic against bacterial infections that might invade the ear,[37] nose,[38] throat or wounds.[39]

This antibiotic was found to cure many cases of oral herpes and ulcerative gingivitis in Czechoslovakia. Bacteriostatic (stopping bacteria) and bactericidal (killing bacteria) properties have also been demonstrated in test tube studies on positive bacterial cultures.[40] Direct contact with THC killed herpes-virus lab cultures in 1990 studies in Florida.[41] There is anecdotal evidence that a tincture or poultice of cannabis helps clear up attacks of genital herpes.

Commercial antibiotics' effectiveness has declined rapidly,[42] in part due to the routine feeding of antibiotics to livestock in factory

---

[32]Lansky. op. cit. also Cohen. 'Therapeutic aspects" in *Marihuana.* op. cit.
[33]Osler, W. & McCrae, T. *Principles & Practice of Medicine.* Appleton & Co. New York NY. Eighth edition. 1916. p. 1089
[34]Kambui, Somayah. Editorial. in *Crescent Star News.* Crescent Alliance Sickle Cell Self Help Group. 824 W. 40th Place, Los Angeles CA 90037. 1992
[35]Loewe, S. Ph.D. 'The active principles of cannabis & the pharmacology of the cannabinols.' in *Arch. Exper. Path. u Pharmakol.* vol. 211. Germany. 1950. pp. 175-193. also in *Marihuana: Medical Papers.* op. cit
[36]Hare, Dr. H.A. in *Marijuana Medical Papers.* op. cit. p. 162
[37]Navrátil, J. 'Effectiveness of c. indica in chronic otitis media." (in Czech) *Acta Univ. Palack.* Olomuc. vol. 6. 1955. p. 87
[38]Jubácek, J. 'A study of the effect of c. indica in oto-rhinolaryngology.' in Czech. *Acta Univ. Palack.* Olomuc. 1955. p. 83. also Hubácek, J. 'A contribution to the treatment of sinusitis maxillaris.' in Czech. *Acta Univ. Palack.* Olomuc. 1961 p. 207
[39]Cohen, S. 'Marijuana as Medicine. in *Psychology Today.* April 1978. p. 60
[40]Lansky. op. cit.
[41]Lancz, Dr. Gerald. U of South Florida. Tampa FL. 1990
[42]In 1960, 13% of staphylococci infections were penicillin-resistant; in 1988, 91%.

farms.[43] Animals fed hempseed will be healthier and more disease resistant (see immunity, above), but since this is nutritional rather than antibiotic, bacteria can not become resistant to its effect.

Musculoskeletal System, MS & Epilepsy

A 1989 report in the *Journal of Neurology* by doctors in the Federal Republic of Germany quantified various neurological improvements in multiple sclerosis, or MS, symptoms after taking cannabis. The study demonstrated "powerful beneficial effects on both spasticity and ataxia."[44] No other antispasmodic drug decreases both. The study involved a patient whose neurological indices, such as tendon reflexes, ataxia and clonus,[45] were measured by sensitive equipment after a painful electro-muscular stimulus. It corroborated other clinical reports in recent medical literature showing that cannabis is a powerful aid to reducing spasticity in patients, including people with MS or who sustained spinal injury.[46] Benefits were achieved both by smoking and by eating cannabis.

Cannabis is also an anti-convulsant. Smoking some during pre-seizure symptoms can inhibit epileptic attacks and reduce the intensity of seizures that do occur.[47] Sixty percent of epileptics can benefit from using the herb, and it is held to be the best medication for many types of epilepsy, as well as for post-seizure trauma.[48]

Respiratory System & Asthma

Many cannabis smokers like to savor the flavor as well as enjoy the health and psychological benefits of the smoke. Yerba santa, coltsfoot, hoarhound and other herbs are traditionally smoked to sooth the lungs, and cannabis seems to fit in that same category.[49] Cannabis smoke is an expectorant that clears out air passages. Heavy concentrations of smoke cause coughing that helps break up and expel phlegm. The herb is an excellent dilator of the airways called the bronchi, opening them up to allow more oxygen into the blood, and of the bronchioles, small air tubes of the lungs.[50] It

[43]55% of antibiotics used in the US are fed routinely to livestock. US meat & pharmaceutical industries support this practice. The EC bans it. Molotosky, I. 'Animal antibiotics tied to illness in humans.' in *New York Times*. Feb. 22, 1987
[44]Ataxia is the loss of muscular coordination. Spasticity is characterized by uncontrollable muscular contractions. Meinck, Schonle & Conrad. 'Effect of cannabinoids on spasticity & ataxia in MS.' in *Journal of Neurology*. no 236. 1989. pp. 120-122
[45]A series of muscular spasms
[46]Lansky. op. cit. also Cohen. 'Therapeutic aspects.' in *Marihuana*. op. cit.
[47]Cohen, Dr. Sidney & Stillman, Richard, editors. *Therapeutic Potential of Marijuana*. Plenum Press. New York NY. 1976
[48]*Ibid.*
[49]Herer. op. cit. p. 81
[50]Cohen & Stillman. op. cit. also studies by Dr. Donald Tashkin. UCLA. 1969-1983

works as a bronchiodilator for asthmatics,[51] and sometimes helps with emphysema. Research into these oxygen transfer effects indicates that chest pains, shallowness of breath, headaches and other symptoms of heavy smog exposure can be alleviated by moderate cannabis smoking[52]

Cannabis and hashish are often mixed with tobacco, and studies in Jamaica found that "Users in our matched pair sample smoked marijuana in addition to as many tobacco cigarettes as did their partners. Yet their airways were, if anything, a bit healthier than their matches. We must tentatively conclude either that marijuana has no harmful effects on such passages or that it actually offers some slight protection against the harmful effects of tobacco smoke."[53]

Some people contend that cannabis smoke, while effective relief, is inappropriate for respiratory therapy because it causes irritation. So delta-9-THC was isolated and administered to asthma patients in an aerosol that relaxed the bronchiospasms. Unfortunately the aerosols also proved to be locally irritating.[54] Since the active alkaloids are not water soluble, using a water pipe can cool the smoke and remove irritants without reducing the herb's effectiveness.

The Lungs: Clearing the Air About Smoke

There is no suggestion whatsoever that THC harms the lungs. Cannabis smoke can, on rare occasion, cause bronchitis, as does air pollution. If this happens, the treatment is simple: Stop smoking.

Watch out for word games: Calling lesions associated with cannabis smoke "pre-cancerous" just means they are not cancer. Dr. Donald Tashkin, who has headed the nation's cannabis pulmonary research program at UCLA for many years, reports that cannabis definitely does not cause emphysema, and that any suggestion of a lung cancer risk is merely "hypothetical."[55]

Inhaled smoke is an irritant.[56] Some claim cannabis is four times as damaging to the lungs as tobacco smoke if they compare intake of particulates and absorption of carbon monoxide.[57] However, it is the smoking pattern for cannabis that causes a larger accumulation of

---

[51]Tashkin, Dr. Donald. et al. UCLA. 1974 & 1975
[52]Tashkin, Dr. Donald. 'Marijuana Pulmonary Research.' UCLA. 1969-1983
[53]Rubin, Dr. Vera & Comitas, Lambros. *Ganja in Jamaica: A medical anthropological study of chronic marijuana use.* Mouton & Co. Anchor Books. New York NY. 1975
[54]Lansky. op. cit. also Cohen, S. 'Therapeutic aspects" in *Marihuana.* op. cit.
[55]He mentioned 10 reported cases in Florida of espartic cancers in cannabis smokers under age 40 as deserving more study, but no causal link has been established to date. Where such clusters have occurred, the presence of contaminants may be a factor.
[56]Tashkin et al. 'Marijuana Pulmonary Research.' UCLA. 1980. also Leuchtenberger, Dr. C. (Swiss). also Tennant, Dr. Forest S.
[57]'Marijuana smoking worse for lungs.' in *Journal of the American Medical Association.* vol. 259:23. 1988. p. 3384

particulate matter.[58] Herb smokers evaluated at UCLA took 70 percent larger inhalations than tobacco smokers, and held them four times longer. In other words, they had 6.8 times as much exposure. This suggests that cannabis smoke actually only causes about 59 percent as much irritation as tobacco.[59] For safer consumption, inhale less deeply, take in more air and exhale sooner.

Cannabis smoke contains potentially harmful components,[60] but tobacco smoke frequently causes lung cancer, heart disease, birth defects, impotence and a variety of respiratory problems. A major factor in tobacco cancers may be its radioactivity, according to Dr. R.T. Ravenholt.[61] Cigarettes hold enough polonium-210 to account for most of the lung cancer reported in smokers, reports radio chemist Dr. Edward Martell with the National Center of Atmospheric Research.[62] The bottom line is that tobacco kills 400,000 Americans per year while not one person has ever died from smoking cannabis,[63] as far as scientists can document. It is quite obvious which smoke is worse.

The Jamaican and Costa Rican[64] studies of very heavy, regular cannabis smokers showed no significant difference in respiratory health from the non-smoking control group.

When cannabis is legal, people can afford more potent strains and take lighter and shorter inhalations—and use vaporizers, water pipes or other systems to minimize possible damage. However, all forms of safer smoking apparatus, or paraphernalia, are currently illegal to import, sell, use or even possess in some places. Hence, it is prohibition that causes this avoidable lung damage, not cannabis.

Furthermore, for many uses cannabis need not be smoked. Eating prepared blossoms as an ingredient of food or dessert may offer a better option. *Bhang* is a drink, as is cannabis flower tea. Various extracts and non-smoking preparations could soon be produced to further reduce the reasons to smoke.

---

[58]Tashkin, Wu, Djahed & Rose. UCLA School of Med. 'Marijuana & tobacco: comparative hazards.' in *Brown U. Digest of Addiction Theory & Appl.* 7:3. 1988. p. 29
[59]Calculation: 1.7 (volume) x 4 (duration) = 6.8 (gross difference); 4.012 (measured difference) ÷ 6.8 (gross difference) = 59% (difference as a percentage)
[60]Institute of Medicine. *Marijuana & Health*. National Academy Press. Washington DC. 1982. p. 17
[61]Former director of World Health Surveys at the Center for Disease Control. 'Would you still rather fight than switch?' in *Whole Life Times*. April-May, 1985
[62]Nat. Academy of Science. Biophysics & Biological Science proceedings. March 1983
[63]Young, Judge Francis. *In the Matter of Marijuana Rescheduling Petition*. 1988. et al. also see listing in *Marijuana: Medical Papers*. op. cit. p. 151. also World Health Organization statistical reports, 1991.
[64]Hernandez-Bolanos, et al. 1976

Metabolite Disposal, Fat Storage & Urine

The fact that THC is fat-soluble rather than water-soluble makes it impractical to take by intravenous injection and helps explain why it is virtually impossible to reach a toxic overdose level; it doesn't leave the system fast enough to cause withdrawal symptoms.[65]

Soon after smoking or eating cannabis, active THC converts into inert THC metabolites, which are sealed in other fats and stored with no further effect. They do not cause a high. Concentrations found in the testes and ovaries of cannabis smokers were the lowest in any body organs.[66] They collect in the system for several weeks, along with other fat-soluble compounds, and are eliminated in feces and urine. Because of this process, THC can be traced through urinalysis for a long time, but it does not indicate intoxication.[67]

Obstetric & Gynecological

As an herb, cannabis has been used for centuries to ease menstrual cramps, PMS and the pain of childbirth.[68] One physician wrote, "There is no medicine which has given such good results. ... The failures are so few that I venture to call it a specific in menorrhagia," or excessive menstrual bleeding.[69] No birthing or early childhood complications were reported among hundreds of such patients.

Two studies link a minor reduction in birthweight to cannabis use, although nutritional mechanisms were unaffected. The reduction was less significant for cannabis smokers than tobacco smokers.[70] Repeated clinical studies show that normal children are born to women who smoke cannabis, although a tendency to decrease consumption during pregnancy has also been noted. In follow-up studies, their children all developed normally.[71]

---

[65]Biernson, G. 'Data on storage of marijuana in the body.' in *Drug Awareness Information Newsletter*. March 1988

[66]Leger, C. & Nahas, G. 'Kinetics of cannabinoid distribution & storage with special reference to brain & testes.' in *Journal of Clinical Pharmacology*. August 1981

[67]Morgan, J.P. 'Marijuana metabolism in the context of urine testing.' in *Journal of Psychoactive Drugs*. vol. 20:1. 1988. pp. 107-115

[68]'Effects of cannabis ... during labour.' in *Journal of the AMA*. v. 94. 1930. p. 1165

[69]Brown. Dr John. 'Cannabis Indica: A valuable remedy in menorrhagia.' in *British Medical Journal*. May 26, 1883. p. 1002

[70]Frank, Cabral & Zuckerman. 'How does exposure to cocaine & marijuana in utero depress birthweight?' in *Pediatric Research*. vol. 25. 1989. p. 290 also Zuckerman, Frank, et al. 'Effects of maternal marijuana & cocaine use on fetal growth.' in *New England Journal of Medicine*. vol. 320:12. 1989. pp. 7652-768

[71]Tennes, Avitable, et al. 'Marijuana: Prenatal & postnatal exposure in the human.' NIDA Monograph Series. vol. 113. pp. 48-60. 1985. also Fried, P.A. 'Postnatal consequences of maternal marijuana use.' NIDA monograph series. vol. 113. pp. 61-72. 1985. also Scher, Richardson, et al. 'Effects of prenatal alcohol & marijuana exposure.' in *Pediatric Research*. vol. 24:1. pp. 101-105. 1988. also Richardson, Day & Taylor. 'Effect of prenatal alcohol, marijuana & tobacco exposure on neonatal behavior.' in *Infant Behavior & Development*. vol. 12:2. 1989. pp. 199-209. Etc.

Sex Life, Hormones & Reproduction

Some people smoke a cigarette after having sex, but many prefer to smoke cannabis beforehand. Cannabis enhances sex for most people. The Masters and Johnson sex research team studied 1000 cannabis users. Some 83 percent of the men and 81 percent of the women found that the herb enhanced their sexual experience. They generally agreed their orgasms were not more intense, but discovered more sensuality throughout the body.[72] Also reported by a few very heavy users was difficulty to maintain an erection. This is odd in light of the traditional use of cannabis as an aphrodisiac. However, since tobacco smoking has been linked to impotence,[73] it is possible that cigarettes were a mitigating factor in the study.

A 1974 study found mean plasma testosterone[74] was lower in heavy-smoking novices than in a control group, and a "swift return to normal" on abstention from cannabis or after stimulation.[75] Later studies have either found no reduction, or note that sperm count and testosterone levels return to normal after a brief initial phase. In one study, 27 young men, who smoked cannabis an average of 5.6 years each, refrained from smoking for two weeks and were tested, then admitted for a 31-day stay in a locked hospital ward.[76] No cannabis was permitted for six days. Testosterone levels registered in "the upper range of normal adult male levels." For the next 21 days they gradually increased consumption, some to very high levels. Their hormonal count remained stable. "High-dosage marijuana intake was not associated with suppression of testosterone levels."

Government experts have managed to cause similar chromosomal cell breakage in test tube and petri dish studies by using aspirin, caffeine and cannabis. Reports claiming sperm damage in the late 1970s were found to have been falsified.[77]

Thinking About the Brain Studies

The human brain has evolved special receptor sites for THC to attach to and effect their influence. The identified sites were most concentrated in the cortex and hippocampus areas of the brain,

---

[72]'El Correo del Sol' sup. in *Integral*. Barcelona Spain. December 1991. p. 89
[73]Rosen, Dr. Max. Boston U School of Medicine. in *Journal of Urology*. May 1991. also Elias, M. 'Study says cigarettes cut down on virility.' in *Courier News*. (Gannett News Service.) May 16, 1991. p. A-11
[74]High testosterone levels in males may lead to increased aggressive behavior.
[75]Kolodny, R.C. at Masters & Johnson sex research center, St. Louis. 'Depression of plasma testosterone levels after chronic intensive marijuana use.' NIDA Research Monograph series No. 2. Nov. 1974. pp. 30-31
[76]Mendelson, Dr. Jack H. Alcohol & Drug Abuse Research Center, Harvard Medical School/McLean Hospital. in *New England Journal of Medicine*. November 1974
[77]Another Nahas story. Spermazoa were damaged by 'researchers' who waited 16 hours to take pictures, knowing they would deteriorate & be pock-marked.

associated with memory, perception and cognition, and in the cerebellum and striatum, which are associated with movement.

Miles Herkenham of the National Institute of Mental Health suggested that the arrangement of binding sites indicate that THC analogs and antagonists might ease symptoms of movement disorders like Parkinson's disease and Huntington's chorea.[78] Discovery of a simpler molecule that binds to the cannabis receptor in 1992 was hailed as a major breakthrough for chemically triggering therapeutic activity within the brain.[79]

Despite elaborate attempts,[80] no cannabis link to brain damage has ever been discovered. The 1974 Tulane University "Heath Monkey" study, claiming such results, was exposed long ago as a textbook case of laboratory fraud.[81] Fixation, tissue preparation and photography were carried out without proper controls or safeguards against bias. The initial peer review warned that the claims "must be interpreted with caution. ... No definitive interpretation can be made at this time." The studies were not replicated.[82] On closer examination, it was revealed that the results were, in effect, fabricated. Researchers had suffocated monkeys with a dense cloud of smoke proportional to 90 joints a day for six months, pumped in through gas masks.[83] The predictable brain damage from oxygen deprivation and carbon monoxide was then blamed on cannabis. Even the

---

[78]Wallach, Leah. 'The Chemistry of Reefer Madness.' in Omni. August 1989. p. 18

[79]Maugh, Thomas Jr. 'Keys to body's pain control system found.' in Los Angeles Times. Dec. 18, 1992. p. 3-A

[80]E.g., "evidence" in Campbell, A.M.G. et al. 'Cerebral atrophy in young cannabis smokers.' in Lancet. December 1971. Dr. Robert Kolodny reviewed the study and noted, "8 of the 10 had used amphetamines. One subject had a previous history of convulsions. 4 had significant head injuries, & a number had used sedatives, barbiturates, heroin or morphine. On the basis of these facts, speculative connection between cannabis use & brain damage is highly suspect. Unfortunately, this type of report is typical of much of the research done in this field." in 'Marijuana: The health questions.' in Consumer Reports. March 1975. p. 147

[81]Heath, Robert G. of Tulane U. New Orleans LA. in Marijuana & the Brain. Amer. Council on Marijuana & Other Psychoactive Drugs. 1981. 21 p. Dr. Julius Axelrod, who won a 1970 Nobel Prize for 2 studies, one dealing with the effects of drugs on the brain, noted: "Doses he has given for the acute effect, for example, would be equivalent to smoking 100 marijuana cigarettes, a very heavy does of marijuana, & the amount he has given for the chronic effect represents smoking 30 marijuana cigarettes 3 times a day for a period of 6 months. ... The amounts are so large that one wonders whether it is due to the large toxic amounts Dr. Heath has given." Also Dr. Lester Grinspoon of Harvard Medical School noted that given the difference in lung size, doses could actually be 15 times greater than stated. Brecher. op. cit. p. 147

[82]"The stories were based principally on limited examinations of two brain area samples of only 3 rhesus monkeys. ... It is possible that unknown but systematic differences occurred between experimental & control animals in fixation & preparation fixation & preparation of tissue or in selection of samples. ... At least one of the changes noted, clumping of vesicles, is a normal variant ... & does not represent a pathological change." Institute of Medicine. 1975

[83]For 5 min. at a time with no air in between. Herer. op. cit. p. 78

puncture wounds, caused by stabbing needle-like probes deep into the brains, were blamed on the cannabis.

In an Indian Hemp Drugs Commission experiment, a rhesus monkey was given 181 inhalations of ganja smoke over about 8 1/3 months at a daily dosage level proportional to a heavy human smoker. After killing the animal, an autopsy found: "There is no evidence of any brain lesions being directly caused by hemp drugs. There is evidence that the coarse brain lesions produced by alcohol and dhatura are not produced by hemp drugs."[84]

Human studies have found no brain damage or atrophy at all.[85] Dr. Igor Grant matched pairs of 29 cannabis smokers to 29 non-smokers in the 1970s. "A battery of the most sensitive neuro-psychological tests now available could demonstrate essentially no differences between moderate users and non-users of marijuana."[86]

Stabilizing Psychological Effects

When cannabis is consumed orally, people almost invariably experience an elevated state of mind marked by heightened sensitivity, creative insights, relaxation, deeper awareness, either sociability or self-consciousness, time distortions (usually expansion), and a sense of contentment which sometimes ends in a pleasant state of sensuality or drowsiness. This is called getting high.

A Federal Bureau of Narcotics expert, psychiatrist Dr. Walter Bromberg, remarked in 1938 that "The patient who is developing a functional psychosis strives in the incipient stage to overcome the unconsciously perceived difficulties. In this sense (cannabis) usage represents a healthy reactive tendency, even though the mechanism may be unknown to the patient."[87] Social smokers often develop a sense of community and rapport among themselves that helps keep their spirits up, and this often has a stabilizing effect on their lives.

Cannabis is known to mitigate withdrawal pain from alcohol and heroin in human populations. Various studies have shown that the

84*Report of the Indian Hemp Drugs Commission. 1893-94.* British Government Central Printing House. Simla, India. 8 vols. 1894. vol. 1:251
85Co, Goodwin et al. 'Absence of cerebral atrophy in chronic cannabis users.' in *Journal of the AMA.* 1977. Kuehnle et al. 'Computed tomographic examination of heavy marijuana smokers.' in *Journal of the AMA.* 1977
86"These results agree with those of Mendelson & Meyer, who employed similar tests with 10 casual & 10 heavy users." Grant, Dr. Igor. U of PA. cited in Brecher. op. cit.
87Sloman, Larry. *The History of Marijuana in America: Reefer Madness.* Bobbs-Merrill Company, Inc. Indianapolis IN. 1979. pp. 152-158

herb is useful in drug abuse diversion,[88] including alcohol.[89] This effect has also been demonstrated in animal models.[90]

The herb can provide a pleasant distraction from situations that are beyond one's control. Some 65 percent of American soldiers in Vietnam used cannabis at least once, and a fairly high percentage were regular users. Dr. Lester Grinspoon noted that this may explain why the psychiatric incidence rate (e.g., for post traumatic stress disorder) among Army troops in Vietnam was much lower than for both the Korean War and World War II.[91] During World War II, 23 percent of all medical evacuation cases were psychiatric; the proportion for Vietnam was about six percent.[92]

Cannabis smokers generally remain aware of their pains and problems, but feel a sense of detachment.[93] This perspective, along with the herb's pain-relieving effects, has played a profound role in helping terminal patients face death with dignity, enabling the physician "to strew the path to the tomb with flowers."[94]

Some Potential Side Effects of Cannabis

Negative physical effects resulting from consuming cannabis may include sleepiness, reddened eyes, cool extremities, dry mouth, increased heartbeat and respiratory irritation including risk of bronchitis (from smoking only). People have smoked cannabis in high doses for 16 hours a day for up to 50 years with no apparent psychological or physical harm.[95] The only proven, truly serious negative consequences of cannabis consumption are the criminal penalties imposed by prohibition.

Many people enjoy being high, but not everyone. People in this state are cautioned to make careful, responsible judgements regarding safety. Never drive if feeling impaired. References to "panic attacks" and "freak outs" mean that a relatively few users, almost always beginners, have on occasion briefly felt anxious, paranoid or confused. Some people lose track of time, feel mentally scattered

---

[88]The Mayor's Committee on Marihuana. *The Marihuana Problem in the City of New York*. Jaques Cattell. Lancaster PA. 1944

[89]Mikuriya, Dr. Tod. 'Cannabis Substitution.' in *Medical Times*. 1970. vol. 98. p. 187. also Scher, J. 'Marihuana as an agent in rehabilitating alcoholics.' in *American Journal of Psychiatry*. 1971. vol. 127. p. 147

[90]Lansky. op. cit.

[91]Vietnam: 12/1000 troops/year, calendar years 1965 & 1966. Korea: 73/1000/yr, July 1950-December 1952. WWII: 28 to 101/1000/yr, September 1944-May 1945

[92]Grinspoon, Dr L. *Marihuana Reconsidered*. Harvard U Press. Cambridge MA. 1971

[93]*Marijuana: Medical Papers*. op. cit. p. 239

[94]O'Shaughnessy, Dr. William B. 'A case of hydrophobia' in 'On the Preparation of India Hemp Drugs. *Ibid*. p. 22

[95]Weiss, B.L., M.D. '(Ethiopian Zion Coptic Church) Coptic Study.' Florida. 1980. also 'Cognition & long term use of ganga.' in *Science*. no. 213. 1981. pp. 465-466

or experience some forgetfulness.[96] A few well-chosen words of comfort and support will usually take care of this.[97]

Depending on the circumstances, the individual, and the kind and amount of cannabis used, some people become so relaxed after smoking that they just want to sit back, enjoy their sensations, or go to sleep. Others feel motivated to get out and dance or to concentrate on work. Others may feel inhibited or incommunicative. The cannabis high tends to be an intensifier rather than an escape, because it focuses attention onto things. Fixating on problems can be a negative experience, or it may result in creative problem solving.

A great many people who are under stress or who suffer from asthma, MS, migraine, glaucoma, cancer or AIDS and have tried cannabis agree that the herb's few negative effects are more than off-set by its powerful therapeutic benefits.

Economic Aspects of Cannabis Restoration

When access to cannabis is restored, a major new branch of the health care and concessions industry will emerge, generating billions of dollars of new capital for the whole economy. The implications must be viewed on several levels: personal, social and economic.

People now incapacitated by certain debilitating health problems will again live as self-respecting, productive members of society, with less need of public health care dollars. Many will grow their own medicine, saving more billions of dollars. Benefits for society at large will be manifest in a wide range of social and economic gains when cannabis is relegalized. There will be a drop in destructive behaviors, like abuse of alcohol, tobacco and other hard drugs, and less social hostility and aggression. Insurance companies will reap huge savings when people self-medicate with hemp instead of paying doctors and pharmacists for costly synthetic drugs that may or may not work.

Where will all that money come from? The illegal and legal drug dealers (big pharmaceutical companies) will experience a short term financial adjustment, and less money will go to police. Instead, commercial growers will produce high quality herb, and manufactures of natural derivatives will recover prescription markets.

---

[96]For memory, 100-1000 mg/day of the amino acid Tyrosine, in two doses on an empty stomach may help. Start with small amounts & increase. If there is negative reaction, like headache, reduce the dosage. 'IQ Plus.' by Vitamin Research Products
[97]Young, Francis L. DEA Chief Administrative Law Judge. *in the Matter of Marijuana Rescheduling Petition*' Docket No 86-22. Washington DC. Sept. 6, 1988

Many of today's most expensive pharmaceuticals serve purposes that have been successfully treated by cannabis.[98] Cannabis was once included in all major drug company catalogs: Merck, Burroughs Wellcome, Eli Lilly and Parke Davis. It was found in various patent medicines like Piso's cough cure and Neurosine. Until 1937, virtually all fistulas, corns and fibrosis were treated with poultices made from the herb, or else treated with cannabis extracts.

It is estimated that cannabis and its derivatives will safely replace more than half of diazapam (Valium), Librium, Thorazine, Stellazine, etc., prescriptions.[99] Cannabis is the best way presently known to dry the mouth's saliva for dentistry. If legal, it would replace the highly toxic drug Probanthine, made by Searle & Co. Cannabis can also partially replace Halcion and Darvon. It has been successfully employed as a mood elevator/antidepressant, as a sedative/hypnotic for inducing sleep, and as a pre-anaesthetic agent for modern surgical procedures, again used similarly to Valium.[100]

In a series of studies in the 1970s, two active principles of cannabis were demonstrated to block experimentally induced seizures in animals comparable to diphenyl-hydantoin, or Dilantin. The only AIDS treatment said to be as effective as cannabis in controlling nausea is Zofran. It requires a hospital visit, costs $600 a day, and does not stimulate the appetite.

Why haven't the drug companies tried to get government approval for it? Dr. Lester Grinspoon explained it like this.[101] "They can't make any money. No way. You see, in our country, the way drugs come into being, a drug company gets hold of a chemical somebody discovered has some sort of effect. They review it, they decide is it worth trying to do it. They have to invest between $80 and $100 million to get it from chemical to drug on the shelf. But then they get an exclusive patent for 17 years, and they can earn a lot of money. How could they possibly do this with cannabis?"

Sure enough, when a binding agent to the brain's THC receptor site was found, drug companies expressed excitement about patenting synthetic drugs that attach to it.[102] President William Clinton's Surgeon General spoke in support of natural cannabis in 1992[103] and 1993, and pharmaceutical companies let out a howl. A few days

[98]Marijuana: Medical Papers. op. cit.
[99]Cohen & Stillman. op. cit.
[100]Lansky. op. cit.
[101]'Smoking to live.' CBS News. in 60 Minutes. vol. 24:11. Dec. 1, 1991
[102]Maugh, Thomas Jr. 'Keys to body's pain control system found.' in Los Angeles Times. Dec. 18, 1992. p. A-3
[103]AP. 'Surgeon general nominee backs use of marijuana as medicine.' in Los Angeles Times. Dec. 20, 1992. p. A-27. also Leveritt, M. 'Elders backs right to prescribe marijuana, ... labels ban "almost criminal".' in Arkansas Times. Dec. 17, 1992

later, plans were announced to make the synthetic THC pill, Marinol,[104] on the market since 1985, more readily available.

However, well into Clinton's term of office his agents have been no more compassionate or humane than their predecessors, and the drug companies have tightened their grip on our health system.

The Healing Herb & Some Medical Derivatives

The correlation between the herb's medical potency and its psychotropic effect makes it easy for a person to understand and regulate their intake at an effective and comfortable level. Since the benefit is almost instantaneous when smoked, this method of ingestion is often preferred to eating it, which takes longer to have effect and is less predictable in terms of its therapeutic effectiveness.

The titration (dosage adjustment) for smoking potent cannabis is quite simple: Take one puff and hold it; exhale; wait 15 minutes; if needed, take another puff and repeat the pattern until effective relief is obtained. Note how many puffs are required and how long the effect is felt. If you experience negative effects, reduce your intake accordingly. Now that you have established your dosage, take the medication as necessary.

Cannabis' potency is the result of a combination of factors, primarily seed line and growing conditions.[105] Seed lines range from the virtually THC-free industrial hemp to pungent indicas and sweet sativas. Some people prefer more potent strains, while others prefer milder ones. Many people get a special feeling of involvement and connection by growing their own herb. The national standard sample is kept at the Food and Drug Administration in Washington DC.

Adjusting the dose of cannabis for a given effect may require initial experimentation to determine the potency of a given crop. Doctors, pharmacists and researchers prefer a dependable dosage. Consistent makeup and potency of herb can be assured by using sinsemilla clones, or cuttings, grown in controlled hydroponic nutrients using precise artificial light systems and measurements.

Scientists can clinically isolate active ingredients from the plant, like THC,[106] or make synthetic analogs—like THC. Yes, it is the exact same chemical compound, the only difference is that nature makes an illegal version and corporations make the drug legally.

---

[104]Dronabinol, a synthetic THC dissolved in sesame oil is a schedule 2 drug requiring prescriptions in triplicate. Produced only by one company, Unimed of NJ, in fixed dosages of 2.5, 5 & 10 mg that sell for over $8/capsule: a price comparable to high-grade, black market sinsemilla cannabis.
[105]Bazzaz, Dusek, Seigler & Haney. 'Photosynthesis & cannabinoid content of temperate & tropical populations of cannabis.' U of IL. Urbana IL. October 1974
[106]Process by Cambridge Pharmaceutical Corp. 881 Mass Ave., Cambridge MA 02139

Another way of stabilizing dosage is to use extracts rather than plant matter. A potent "red oil" was first extracted with alcohol in the early 1940s. It takes about 25 kilograms of good cannabis or five kilos of good hashish[107] to make one kilo of high-quality oil.[108] It can be refined into a more potent product by removing most of the substances that give it taste, smell and color.[109] Oil samples analyzed in 1974 averaged more than 23 percent THC.[110] Fresh Afghani hash, by contrast, ranged from eight to 15 percent in Kabul. By the time it reached America, oxidation had reduced it to three to five percent THC, the same range found in medium quality herb.

Cannabis is often eaten. A cannabis sweet, *ma'joun*, is made with powdered blossoms, sugar, honey, cinnamon and almonds. It is baked to the consistency of moist fudge and eaten with the fingers. Bhang is a sweet, spicy beverage that is drunk like a milkshake.[111] The dried flower itself is a tasty and therapeutic seasoning cooked into sauces and baked goods. It is best to remove the stems, then grind up and saute the herb to improve the flavor and texture. Otherwise, the consistency may be more like chewing hay.

For a topical disinfectant and anaesthetic tincture, place 20 grams of potent cannabis flowers into 100 grams of 90 percent solution isopropyl alcohol. Soak for 15 days and filter. Use as drops.[112] For an herbal pack or plaster, soak large cannabis leaves in strong alcohol for two weeks. Remove and wrap around stiff, aching joints. Dried flowers soaked in alcohol for the same period can be mashed into a paste and applied to affected areas. This homeopathic process was published in 1842, based on an earlier German text.[113]

> We take the flowering tops of male and female plants and express the juice, and make the tincture with equal parts of alcohol; others advise only to use the flowering tops of the female plants, because these best exhale, during their flowering, a strong and intoxicating odor.

---

[107]Hash in North Africa takes at least 2 days to make, with many stages of cooking. This differs from in India, where resin is harvested by beating the blossoms on leather aprons. Mikuriya, Dr. Tod. 'Marijuana in Morocco.' in *Psychedelics*. Doubleday & Co. Garden City NY. 1970. pp. 115-128

[108]Boil finely powdered cannabis or hash in a solvent such as methyl or ethyl alcohol. Cannabidiol, THC & cannabinol dissolve in it, and the plant matter is removed by straining. The solvent evaporates, leaving a residue of basic hash oil.

[109]Adams, Roger. 'Marijuana.' in *Science*. vol. 92:2380. pp. 115-118

[110]Some were in the 45-65% bracket; some had less than 1%.

[111]Take 220 grains cannabis; 120 gr each of poppy seed, pepper, almonds & cucumber seed; 40 gr ginger; 10 gr each caraway seed, cloves, cardamom, cinnamon & nutmeg; 60 gr rosebuds, 4 oz sugar, 20 oz milk. Boil together & cool. Ball, M.V. 'Effects of haschisch not due to cannabis indica.' in *Therapeutic Gazette*. vol. 34. 1910. pp. 777-780

[112]'El Cáñamo.' in *El Mundo Marvilloso de las Hierbas*. Barcelona Spain.

[113]Jahr, G.H.G. *New Homeopathic Pharmacopoeia & Posology of the Preparation of Homeopathic Medicines*. J. Dobson. Philadelphia PA. 1842. p. 137

The root is boiled in water and applied in the form of a poultice to soothe joint pains and reduce inflammations. Crush fresh root and mix with butter as a topical cream for burns and abrasions.[114]

The Herb's Role in Holistic Healing

The holistic approach to health involves the whole person and their environment, rather than just the condition being treated. In this regard, too, cannabis has a great deal of value. From a holistic viewpoint, getting rid of pollution by restoring clean hemp technologies will be a good start on curbing many kinds of disease. For example, a major contributor to sterility and sperm count reduction is the presence of chlorinated hydrocarbons in industrial waste, such as chlorine dioxin, and pesticides like DDT.[115] Hemp industry and agriculture can reduce these contaminants, thus easing the problem.

Eating hempseed regularly fortifies the basic defense systems of the human body. Recent medical research has been directed toward the role of essential fatty acid deficiencies in the degenerative diseases such as cancer, arteriosclerosis and multiple sclerosis. In addition, the essential fatty acids clean out arterial cholesterol buildup from saturated fats, and reduce the risk of heart attack.[116]

In aromatherapy, just smelling the fragrance of cannabis flowers can bring psychological, even physiological, benefit.

Various Homeopathic Uses

The homeopathic therapeutic strategy uses a substance which produces certain effects at very high doses to treat a person with the same symptoms, much as a vaccine is used to protect people from disease. When administered to a patient in an ultra-dilute, energetically potent homeopathic form, it can cure similar symptoms.

For example, rather than use cannabis to stimulate creative vision, homeopathic therapy might use it to treat a patient with hallucinations or to comfort people on LSD. Tinnitus, a pathological ringing in the ears, has often yielded to treatment with cannabis.[117] Other problems which have been cured with homeopathic cannabis include urinary infections, muscle cramps, backache, dry mouth, dry vagina, tremors, pneumonia and palpitations of the heart.

There are significant differences in the effects of the two major cannabis types. In general, sativa is more useful in treating milder physical or mental problems, while indica is more effective in treat-

114Marcandier, M. *A Treatise on Hemp*. Boston MA. 1766
115Dougherty, Ralph. Florida State U. in Robbins, John. *Diet for a New America*. Stillpoint Pub. p. 330
116Hamilton, Dr. Roberta. Professor Emeritus. UCLA. Los Angeles CA. 1991, 1992
117Lansky. op. cit.

ing more serious physical maladies. However, sativa is indicated for swelling of the nose or prostate, indica is recommended for problems like sudden memory loss and ravenous overeating.

Promising Areas for Future Investigation

Three major areas of research deserve future exploration. The herb's psychophysical effect, the chemical structure activity of THC and related alkaloids, and long-term health studies.[118] The first area should involve the psychometric and neurometric functions, like cognition and motor performance, as well as looking further into the brain's electro-physical topology. The second involves clinical efficacy studies of natural and synthetic THCs as well as other cannabis alkaloids, including their antibiotic and topical anesthetic effects.

Long-term health studies will be required to determine the actual therapeutic efficacy in the broad range of applications and possibilities discussed above. Special consideration should be given to the herb's potential for healing in connection with its effects on the central, peripheral (post-injury pain, tic doloroux, uterine hypotonia) and autonomic (appetite stimulation, control of hyperreactivity) nervous systems, as well as in the prevention and treatment of vascular and auto immune diseases (glaucoma, Raynaud's disease, Nail Patellar disease) and conditions arising from HIV infection (anorexia and wasting syndrome).

Other studies will explore the herb's usefulness as an antidepressant, and in the control of premenstrual tension, bronchitis and tracheobronchial irritation. The herb's effects on creativity, productivity, academic and workplace performance, motor coordination and driving, emotions, social intercourse and involvement with other psychoactive chemicals will also be closely examined.

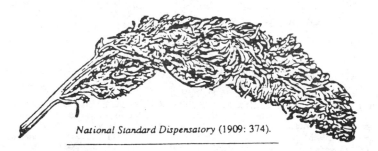

National Standard Dispensatory (1909: 374).

[118]Mikuriya, Tod. M.D. correspondence. December 1992

15

A Sustainable Cash Crop for Farms

We can restore health and prosperity to our heartland. There never has to be another farm foreclosure in America. "Hemp can be grown on any good land with profit and, as the supply never equals the demand, consider it a sure and profitable crop," advised the manual *How to Make the Farm Pay*.[1]

Most states have successfully grown hemp for fiber production.

Today, in addition to its traditional profitability, hemp offers environmental benefits and can solve a number of problems through cost effective, organic farming techniques. Its need for nitrogen can be met by a prior crop; and it does not exhaust soil fertility. Its leaves and roots, left to return to the soil after harvest, replace most fertilizing elements used in the growing season.[2]

Farming hemp is like raising a dense mass of pulp, fiber, grain and oil, all at once. An Ohio University botany professor recently noted, "At this latitude there probably wouldn't be anything to compete with it. ... It grows like a weed. It doesn't have too many enemies."[3] As one farmer put it more than 100 years ago, "At a time when the supply of the ordinary products of the farm exceeds the demand, and consequently the price is so low as almost to discourage agricultural enterprise, it deserves the consideration of farmers in different parts of the country, whether their interest does not require them to turn a part of their land and to apply a portion of their labor to the cultivation of hemp."[4]

The United States began as an agrarian society, and 200 years ago vegetable matter, rather than mined ores and fossil fuels, provided all our tools, houses, clothing, fertilizers, paints, dyes, machines and energy, and it did so relatively cleanly.[5] Technology has vastly expanded what we can do with nature's abundance.

---

[1]Dickerman, Charles W. *How to Make the Farm Pay, or the farmer's handbook.* Zeigler, McCurdy & Co. Philadelphia PA. 1855. p. 235

[2]Dewey, Lyster H. Bureau of Plant Industry. 'Hemp.' in *US Department of Agriculture Yearbook, 1913.* USDA. Washington DC. 1914

[3]Cavender, Jim. "Cotton is the worst, as far as effect on the soil is concerned. ... Someday we may have to get away from cotton, & hemp might be an alternative." Phillips, Jim. 'Authorities examine pot claims.' in *Athens News.* OH. Nov. 16, 1989

[4]Lathrop, Samuel. Letter in *New England Farmer.* March 16, 1829. in *Compilation of Articles Relating to the Culture & Manufacture of Hemp in the United States.* Fairbanks, E, ed. Jewett & Porter. St. Johnsbury, VT. 1829. pp. 9-15

[5]Gates, Paul W. 'The Farmer's Age, Agriculture 1815-1860.' in *Economic History of the US.* vol. 3. Holt, Rinehart & Winston. NY, NY. 1960. pp. 99-117

What Hemp Needs to Grow

Hemp needs remarkably little: some soil, water, sunlight and air. The crop needs little attention. It is even self-seeding, self-weeding and self-fertilizing. Like people, hemp successfully adapts to its circumstances. Different types have distinct characteristics. Some strains do better in a wet climate, while others flourish in a drier one. Almost any soil or climate condition can support hemp growth, from equatorial tropics right to the edge of the arctic circle. Of course, like any crop, hemp performs better in ideal conditions. It prefers great soil and weather; but a quality yield has also been realized in even the most harsh conditions. The soil can be worn, the water undependable, the sunlight patchy and the air dirty. For this reason, people often refer to cannabis as a "weed." In fact, hemp is an important domesticated crop that is suited for almost anyplace; and people have planted it almost everywhere.

Miscellaneous Horticultural Uses

Hemp has been grown as a windbreak or to protect and isolate certain crops for selective breeding, since a thick stand of hemp provides a pollen barrier. It can also be grown to rebuild and aerate the soil structure and to neutralize the pH level of acid soil. Hemp is sown on dung heaps to compost the manure and grown on hillsides to anchor soil and prevent erosion. Special environmental uses include growing hemp as an oxygen crop, for erosion control, manure digestion, reforestation and soil improvement through its deep taproot system. Some agricultural advantages of using hemp as a rotation crop include its ease of cultivation and absence of pests and diseases, hence almost no need for weed-killer or insecticides.

Acres of hemp have been sown just to destroy noxious weeds. Very few troublesome weeds can survive the dense shade of a good hemp crop. A thin, short or weak growth, from unsuitable soil or other causes, has little effect in checking weed growth. But a good, dense crop, six feet or more in height, will leave the ground practically free from weeds at harvest time. If hemp is grown primarily to kill perennial weeds, it may be grown repeatedly on the same land until the weeds are subdued. Canada thistle has been completely killed and quack-grass severely checked by only one crop of hemp.[6] Some vines, like wild morning-glory and bindweed,

---

[6]In Vernon County WI, where Canada thistles were very thick, "95% of thistles were killed where hemp attained a height of 5 feet or more; but on a dry, gravelly hillside where it grew only 2-3 ft high, thistles were checked no more than they would have been in a grain crop." Dewey. op cit.

climb up the hemp stalks and so secure enough light for growth, but low-growing weeds cannot live in a hemp field.

Next we will investigate the process of farming industrial hemp and gardening herbal cannabis.

Challenge & Potential of the Modern Farm

World population is expected to double its current six billion person level by 2030. Can we transfer farm resources to industrial applications without hurting our food supply? Farmers will again be in a position to increase production. Look at our 1985 farm production: 50 percent domestic food; 35 percent food for export; and 15 percent land kept out of production due to government farm programs. Advances in biotechnology and genetic engineering enable farmers to produce more per acre and per animal unit.

The projected change by the year 2000 looks more like this: 35 percent domestic food production,[7] 35 percent export food grains,[8] and 30 percent as fiber production for food, energy and industry.[9] In order to survive, farmers will need markets other than domestic or foreign food exports. Biological processing technologies and production technology have far outpaced marketing.

"Industrial commodities" are non-food crops. This blends sustainable resources produced by farms with the technologies of today and tomorrow. The problem has been finding crops versatile enough to meet a wide range of applications, hearty enough to grow anywhere and abundant enough to meet the demands of ever-expanding and ever-changing consumption patterns.[10]

Utilizing the special qualities of different crops that are easy to grow will create new wealth, add jobs and boost the whole economy. New processes will use vast amounts of agricultural fiber aided by genetic engineering and gene splicing.

Visualize Your Own Ideal Industrial Crop

Dean of North Dakota State University College of Agriculture H. Roald Lund called it *Next Century Agriculture*.[11] "Let your mind conjure up in a mind game as to what a maximum starch production plant would look like. Do the same for a fiber, oil or protein factory

---

[7]Due to farm productivity rising faster than population growth
[8]Rise in exports to equal increase in production
[9]New Uses Council. 1112 Sixth St. SW #400, Topeka KS 66603. 913-235-5886
[10]Especially one that is still legal to grow, since cannabis prohibition.
[11]"As we move from a commodity-driven approach to food, feed, fiber & fuel production, in which we produce foods which are good to eat as they come from the field, let's begin to think in terms of food, feed, fiber & fuel stocks." Lund, Dean H.R., College of Agriculture, NDSU. 'Next Century Agriculture.' in *Americans for Ethanol News*. vol. 3:4. Spring 1991. p. 3

with roots in the soil." Biologically sustainable agriculture will not need chemicals to control plant and animal diseases. "We will, within the next 50 years, have agricultural science 'in tune' with nature." Lund's vision has a new set of crops and a new "millstream" going from farm gate to factory.

"It is entirely possible that the maximum production of starch, protein, oil, fiber and sugar ... will not look like anything that we have ever seen growing in a field." That is a pretty good description of that great staple of world agriculture, cannabis hemp, which we have not seen growing in our fields for over half a century. With its versatility, the farmer can adjust the hemp crop to best take advantage of market conditions, and with its durability, it can be stored to take advantage of fluctuations in market price. With hemp as the logical and historical anchor, many other suitable crops with special qualities can be grown in appropriate regions and integrated into the economy. By systematically introducing such crops, we can phase out destructive technologies.

Overview of Hemp Farming Techniques

Few people have said it better than a farmer named Cooke.[12]

"In a national point of view, (cannabis hemp farming) will ultimately confer the most lasting and important benefits upon this country, and at no distant day be looked upon as constituting the brightest era in the history of American agriculture. ... No branch of agriculture will afford as great a profit, or contribute so vastly to advance the wealth and prosperity of the country, as that of the culture of hemp, aided by ... machine."

The most profitable way to grow hemp during our emerald era was said to harvest the crop when half the seed are mature, so the farmer could have a fair portion of the male hemp fiber, along with the nearly mature female. In addition, he got eight to 10 bushels of seed per acre, with line nearly as good as that cut later.[13]

Hemp grows well in a moderately cool, temperate climate. Hemp seedlings can endure cold and even some frost, just as well as seedling oats or other spring crops. Cannabis does not do as well in swampy or clay soils, but it even grows on muck lands for purposes other than fiber.[14] The best fertilizer for hemp is stable manure applied to the preceding crop. Hemp improves the physical condition of the soil, and when retted on the same ground where it grows, it returns most of the fertilizing elements. It prefers neutral or slightly alkaline soil pH. Plow the soil as early as possible, and

[12]Cooke, E. in *Compilation*. op. cit. p. 33
[13]Barnum, Gen. A.W. in *VT Aurora*. April 1829. in *Compilation*. op. cit. pp. 15-21
[14]Harvey, T. Weed. *Handbook on Agriculture & Home Economics*. USDA Extension Service. October 1926. pp. 616-617

the deeper the better. The subsoil plow is beneficial, as the plant has a long tap-root. As soon as the ground is warm, generally in late April, the ground is re-plowed with a lighter plow. It is then heavily harrowed and promptly smoothed with a light harrow or brush-drag, to leave the surface very mellow, even and as smooth as possible. That is a very important part of the whole art of growing hemp for an easier harvest.

Carefully selected and preserved seed is sown on this fresh soil. Most hemp is grown in tight, thick stands to inhibit side branches, since straight stalks produce better fiber and more pulp. If grown for seed or herb, it is sown loosely or in mounds to grow stalks full of branches on the females. To assure a supply of acclimated seed without dedicating a whole field to the crop, leave patches or narrow strips standing where seed will be allowed to ripen. Hemp males ripen earlier, and are usually removed first. For the small gardener, this is no problem and many enjoy tending to the personality of their crop, which will tell them a lot about soil conditions.[15]

However, for the large scale industrial grower, modern hermaphrodite, or monoecious, strains offer the advantage of a more homogeneous growth and harvest pattern. All the plants go to seed. They grow more evenly and mature at the same time. A machine can remove the seeding tops of the plants, to even off the stalk height for harvest while collecting seeds that might otherwise be lost.

It is generally ready for harvesting the first of August, south of 40° latitude. Then it is set up in shocks to stand until October, when the process of retting is begun. If an early harvest is made, a fall cereal crop may still follow on the same land.[16]

The best hemp, with stalks of even size and length, grown close together, offers the most fiber and is easiest dressed and easiest to separate from the pulp, because the wood is weak and brittle after retting.[17] If it is necessary to plow hemp land after harvest, sow a green crop, like corn, oats, rye or buckwheat, to shade the surface and enrich the soil. It can be fed down in autumn, plowed under, or dragged down to decay into humus.

Many hemp growers report that rotation is not necessary because the leaves of one crop produce sufficient fertilization for the next.

---

[15]Lathrop, S. in *New England Farmer*. Mar. 16, 1829. *Compilation*. op. cit. pp. 9-15
[16]Robinson, B.B. 'Hemp.' in *USDA Bulletin, 1935*. (rev.) 1952
[17]"Breaking usually commences about New Year's. ... Plantations we know averaged 1000 lbs (line)/acre. ... Upon some of the inexhaustibly rich bottom lands of MO, 1400 lbs/acre have often been made, & successive crops taken from the same land, without manure, ever since it was denuded of forest. ... A MO hemp grower averaged 800 lbs/acre 11 yrs in succession. The mode of estimating the yield per acre while the crop is growing is to calculate 100 lbs of lint for every foot." *Facts for Farmers*. Robinson, S., ed. Johnson & Ward Publishers. New York NY. 1865. p. 967

But hemp is great for rotation, for it destroys troublesome weeds and grass. Hemp should follow corn, clover or grass and pasture. Its stubble produces good conditions for wheat, corn or clover. It leaves the soil in excellent condition for any succeeding crop.[18] Hemp leaves and stubble afford a good supply of "green manure." An application of compost, one third barnyard to two thirds muck, peat or leaf mold, keeps the land in good condition for years.[19]

Harvesting Hemp Fiber & Pulp

Every kind of hempseed has a definite time to ripen. The same seed will ripen about the same time, whether sown in March or May. As a long period of growth is an advantage, the better seed lines ripen later. For female flowering, the critical point is when the ratio of day to night is 12 hours of darkness.

Timing the harvest is subject to interpretation. When fully grown, the ideal crop stands nine or 10 feet high and level as one looks over the field. It leans out eagerly for light and air around the edges. Stalks stand about 150 to the square yard, about half an inch thick, and with a fair-size hollow in each. Large-hollow stalks take the lobed shape something like four tangent circles, while the more woody ones (yielding more pulp) tend to grow round.

The rule some use is to harvest when a bundle of stalks rattle on being thrown, and some like to hear the stalks pop sharply in cutting. Some growers cut just four months after sowing. Some wait until the first ripe seeds appear. Some cut while the pollen is rising in clouds from the field. Some wait until the male stalks begin to drop their leaves and turn yellowish; others wait until these have bowed down and died, leaving the females still tall and growing. If cut earlier, the fiber will be finer and softer, but also weaker and lighter.[20] Fields harvested so late that the birds had picked off all the seed have made excellent yield and quality. Small patches of hemp left standing through the winter have yielded remarkably clean and strong lint. It seems there is no great hurry about cutting.[21] The leaves whither and dry up, and give little or no trouble, even when not beaten off before stacking.

A two-year test conducted in Italy on cultivars and hybrids of hemp in the 1970s studied the effects of two levels of nitrogen fertilization, two application methods, and two harvesting times. Better results for cellulose fiber yields were obtained when harvesting

---

[18]"It should not follow grain." Harvey. op. cit. pp. 616-617; but "Rotation with ... wheat ... is beneficial." Dickerman. op. cit. p. 235
[19]*Ibid.*
[20]In CA, hemp has been cut in late July or August. In KY, IN & WI, in September.
[21]Moore. op cit. pp. 78-79

plants with mature seeds.[22] Chemical analysis of hemp shows that cellulose content in both the bark and the woody core increases as the plant matures, while the extractives, ash and lignin contents decrease. This indicates that better pulping results can be obtained by delaying the harvest as long as the weather permits.[23]

Each farmer should see what works best in his or her own case. Plant a few acres. Harvest the first quarter when the pollen is flying, the second and third a week or ten days apart, and the last when the seed is fully matured. These four lots should be handled and processed separately to detect any difference in the quality and quantity of the fiber, pulp and seed produced.

It is important for the cut stalks to lie evenly without over-lapping, in order to attain an even cure throughout the crop.

Seed, Fiber, Tow & Pulp Yields

While fiber hemp is cut and waiting for the winter rains, the seed crop is ripening. Under normal conditions, the seed yield ranges from 12 to 25 bushels per acre. A good year can see 30 or more bushels per acre.[24] From 16 to 18 bushels are regarded as a fair average. An acre of land will produce two or three times more hemp fiber than flax or cotton. A very rough estimate of yield per acre is 100 pounds per foot in height of the standing hemp. According to USDA records, domestic hemp fiber yield ranged from 400 to 2500 pounds per acre, averaging about 1000.[25] Yields of the principal hemp-producers of Europe were: Russia, 358 pounds; Hungary, 504; Italy, 622; and France, 662.[26]

The average American yield per acre at different stages of preparation was approximately: green stalk, freshly cut, 15,000 pounds; dry stalk as cured in shock, 10,000 pounds; dry stalk after dew retting, 6000 pounds; long fiber, rough hemp, 750 pounds; tow fiber, 250 pounds. The 750 pounds of long fiber produce about 340 pounds of single-dressed hemp, 180 pounds shorts, 140 pounds fine tow and 90 pounds hurds and waste. Proportions vary

---

[22]Volturno river plain. 80 & 160 kg/ha, solid & liquid, at full bloom & mature seed. Basso & Ruggiero. 'Cellulose by Cultivars & Hybrids of Hemp.' *Cellulosa Carta.* vol. 27:3. March 1976. pp. 17-26. (in Italian). in *Bull. Inst. Pap. Chem.* vol. 47:5. November 1976. p. 518

[23]Becietti R. & Ciaralli, N. 'Variation in the Content of Cellulose During the Vegetative Period of Hemp.' *Cellulosa Carta.* vol. 27:3. March 1976. pp. 27-30 (in Italian). in *Bull. Inst. Pap. Chem.* vol. 47:5. November 1976. p. 518

[24]Hemp seeds average 55,000/kilogram for an average of 55 million seeds/hectare.

[25]Dewey said US hemp fiber yield was 3/4 line to 1/4 tow. Some other fiber yield estimates included Dodge (US 1890) 1850 kg/hectare, or 1650 lb/acre. Dempsey (1975) found a range from 1800 kg/ht in Italy down to 370 kg/ht in the Soviet Union. Letter from McPartland, John M., D.O., M.S.

[26]Dewey. op. cit. pp. 335-336

according to the strength of the hemp. A ton of good fiber yields roughly a half double-dressed long line, the rest yielding about equal parts midlength fiber and tow. The loss during handling is around two percent.[27] Beyond these, however, there is no certain loss, since every bit of the tow can be used for something.

As biomass feedstock, including both stalk and foliage, hemp can produce 10 dry tons per acre per season. Heavy fertilization can dramatically increase the yield, as long as the mix is not too acidic.

Equipment Farming

Seed hemp can be planted in rows like corn, using recalibrated seeders. Hemp planted for fiber is sown or drilled exactly like wheat or oats and with the same machinery.[28] Hemp harvesting equipment was manufactured by International Harvester, but due to the ban on cannabis in the United States, we are almost 50 years behind in hemp-specific machinery. France, Spain, Russia, China and East Bloc countries keep their separate technologies up to date. Some countries, like Russia, express interest in exporting equipment while others, like Spain, keep their trade secrets to themselves.

Several types of machine have been available in this country for harvesting hemp.[29] Growers of hemp in the Midwest rebuilt regular grain binders for it, which is not particularly expensive and reportedly gave satisfactory service.[30] Both specialized and modified equipment are used for cutting, rolling or baling stalks, threshing seeds, etc. Plantings often leave space for the wheels of equipment, based on the width of the harvester's cutting blades. One machine goes through to collect the seeding tops and move them to a drier and thresher, then a second harvester cuts down the stalk. A single machine might do this by offsetting the cutters to first take off and collect the tops, then have a second, lower set of blades come from behind to cut the stalks

The film *Hemp for Victory*, prepared by the USDA for the Second World War, offers these suggestions:[31]

> For fiber, hemp should be sewn five pecks to the acre, when drilled. The closer the rows the better. These rows are spaced about four inches. ... Thick enough to grow slender stalks that are easy to cut and process. ... For seed, hemp is planted in hills like corn, sometimes by hand. ... (For harvesting, use) the self-rake with its lateral stroke. A modified rice

[27]In processing, some dust & hurds, specks of mud & lint float off into the air.
[28]"It requires no further cultivation & a growing period of only 120 days." in 'Hemp Cultivation in the US.' in Herald Tribune. NY. May 30, 1943
[29]'Hemp Harvesting the rope crop.' in *Compton's Encyclopedia*. NY. 1930. p. 1631
[30]Lower, George A. 'Flax & Hemp: From the Seed to the Loom.' in *Mechanical Engineering*. February 1938
[31]*Hemp for Victory*. USDA film. Washington DC. 1943

binder has been used to some extent. This machine works well on average
hemp. ... The hemp harvester with automatic spreader is standard
equipment. Note how smoothly the rotating apron lays the swaths
preparatory to retting. Here it is a common and essential practice to leave
headlands around hemp fields. These strips may be planted with other
crops, preferably small grain. Thus the harvester has room to make its
first round without preparatory hand cutting. The other machine is
running over corn stubble. When the cutter bar is much shorter than the
hemp is tall, overlapping occurs: not so good for retting. The standard cut
is eight to nine feet. ... When conditions are favorable, the pickup binder
is commonly used. ... The picker won't work well in tangled hemp.
After binding, hemp is shucked as soon as possible.

Retting the Crop & Preserving the Fiber

Retting traditionally has been done on farms,[32] but today commercial vat-retting appears more practical.[33] The same systems used
for flax will work to ret and process hemp. Nonetheless, farmers
garner more profits by doing their own retting.

Dew retting consists of spreading and turning the hemp stalks
right in the fields for anywhere from one to five weeks, or until the
cured fiber easily pulls free of the stem. This process also restores
nutrients to the soil. For water retting, bundles of stalk are tied up at
both ends to avoid tangling, and submerged in vats or ponds for a
few days or longer.[34]

After retting, the crop is ready for breaking or to have the fiber
stripped off the stalk by hand. For hand stripping, it is easier to
work with stalk that has not dried out yet.

Fermentation is the first step to decay. The pyroligneous acid of
smoke unites with the gluten of hemp and helps preserve it from
decay in an antiseptic solution. Chloride of zinc was used to
preserve cords made of unretted hemp.[35] The color is close to the
rich yellow of Russian fiber.

Ropes were used on boats, wet daily for months, without decay.
Outdoor clotheslines and ropes on the ground in damp situations for
a year show no signs of decay. Pieces of rope and bagging placed in
dung heaps for weeks were unaffected.

---

[32]Stalks have often been only partially retted & the fibers removed by machinery.
The green stalks are spread on the stubble & left until sufficient decomposition has
taken place for bark to be removed. Under favorable conditions it may be in 2-3
weeks. In dry, cool weather retting may require many weeks. Retted straw is bound in
bundles & placed in shocks to cure. It can be stacked either in the field or at the mill.
[33]See textiles chapter.
[34]The ratio of water (15°C) to hemp is 40:1. Various chemicals can be added to speed
the process or clean the fiber. Dempsey, J. 'Hemp.' in *Fiber Crops*. U of FL Press.
Gainesville FL. 1975. p. 71
[35]Dissolve sufficient chloride of zinc in muriatic acid diluted with water in a large tub
to give a slight alum-like taste to the chloride when placed on the tongue. Yarns were
immersed for about 12 hours, drawn out with a heavy reel from the tub to drip for an
hour or two, then stretched out to dry. Leavitt, O.S. Maysville KY. in *Patent Office
Report*. 1861. Moore. op cit. pp. 103-104

Time Cures All Hemp

If the long fiber is injured by too long exposure or was not fully retted before being taken up, it can be stacked, stored and processed the next year, when it will have regained its strength.[36] It is said that quality and color are much improved in hemp that is stacked and held over until the next season.

The leaves disappear entirely, the fiber bleaches straw-color, it rets much more quickly and the ends will not be lost. Whether it actually gains strength and weight, hemp certainly improves in softness and general appearance by storage.[37]

After cutting, it is well to have the hemp rained upon before being taken up, as there is little danger from too much rain. If the rain should partially ret it, no harm is done. If there is no rain, it might as well be taken up after one day's sunning, or as soon as convenient. While it is often over-cured, hemp's molding from being stacked too soon is unheard of.

Some think that sunburning makes hemp hard to ret and lowers the yield and quality by reducing the oil in the lint. Stalks are roughly sorted before breaking, so the longer and better fibers are kept separate. The sorting can usually be done best at this point, keeping short stalks from one area separate from the longer stalks of another, and over-retted stalks from stalks with stronger fiber.

After curing, stacking the hemp is thought to expose less surface to the weather and bleach the hemp to some extent. Stacking retted hemp stalks for storage before breaking is not recommended in climates where there is danger of gathering moisture. Hemp stalks to be stacked are bound in bundles about 10 inches in diameter, with small hemp plants for bands, before being placed in shocks. They are allowed to stand in the shock for 10 to 15 days. A hemp stack must be built to shed water. A well-built stack may be kept four or five years without injury.[38]

Shocking is faster, easier and cheaper, but the outside stalks rot more quickly, and must be stripped from the shocks and spread apart from other stalks. Otherwise they injure the appearance of the good lint, and go largely into tow.

---

[36]from *American Farmer.* in *Compilation.* op. cit. pp. 24-25

[37]Moore, Brent. *The Hemp Industry In Kentucky, A Study of the Past, the Present & the Possibilities.* Press of James E. Hughes. Lexington KY. 1905. pp. 81, 82, 84

[38]Start around a shock, place bundles in tiers, butts sloping downward & outward. The stack is kept higher in the center & each succeeding outer tier projects slightly to a height of 5-6 feet. Another shock is built in the center, around which bundles are carefully placed to shed water. The peak is capped with an upright bundle.

Systematic Selective Breeding of Hybrids

Having the right seeds is critical to the outcome of the crop. Different seed grown on the same ground under the same conditions can have a dramatically different yield. Beyond that, hempseed can also be acclimated to conditions through selective breeding.

Seeds are selected for characteristics which are fine-tuned for a particular need. For example, three varieties of hemp developed by the Department of Agriculture were compared with hemp from unselected Kentucky seed in a field test in Wisconsin.[39] The three were called Michigan Early,[40] Chinamington[41] and Simple Leaf,[42] which began as a mutation with simple-lobed leaves, and was propagated because its peculiar leaves marked it as a distinct variety, and in the hope that it might yield a distinct fiber.

Owing to variation in the size of the seeds, the seeding was not uniform.[43] Germination was fairly good and uniform in all cases, though poorest in Simple Leaf.[44] Stalks averaged about 60 inches in height, except Simple Leaf, at only about 40 inches but with remarkably fine, uniform stalks. Chinamington yielded much more than did Kentucky. Michigan Early compared well in yield, and was ripe 19 days early.[45] This shows the value of systematic selection.

Programs for developing monoecious strains have been going on for more than 100 years. The period 1940-1960 saw major advances in producing lines that are simultaneous-maturing, with more uniform fiber quality and higher yields of pulp, fiber and seed.[46] French farmers now use a line of low-THC hermaphrodites.

Chinese hempseed has long been used to fortify domestic lines. It first came back with missionaries, then in commercial enterprises.

---

[39]They were grown under very uniform conditions. The retted straw of each was scutched in the mill at Juneau. USDA Bureau of Plant Industry. 'Simple Leaf & Other Hemp Hybrids' in *Official Record*. Feb. 27, 1930. p. 5

[40]Originated as a single selected plant in MI, with individual plants selected for earliness & vigor. The variety sown in the field test resulted from 10 consecutive years of selection from a hybrid of Italian X Kymington, first grown in VA in 1918.

[41]Chinamington was a cross of China seed & 2nd generation MN # 8 selected for height, length of internodes & seed production. Seed used was the product of 14 generations selected at Arlington Farm from Chington & Kymington. 1914

[42]Second generation cross of Ferrara (Italian) & Kymington at Arlington Farm in 1918. Selected for height & length of internodes.

[43]Common KY, 69 lbs. MI Early, 44 lbs. Chinamington, 64 lbs. Simple Leaf, 32 lbs. MI Early was harvested Aug. 3, the others Aug. 19.

[44]Simple Leaf gave a poor yield, owing to thin seeding, short straw, & a yield of only 10% fiber form the retted straw, compared to about 15% for others.

[45]Fiber yields per acre, line & tow combined: Chinamington, 1054 lbs; MI Early, 694; KY, 680; Simple Leaf, 360

[46]Dempsey. op. cit. pp. 58-60

Around 1865, *Facts for Farmers* praised a new line introduced to the Western States under the name of Chinese hemp.[47]

> So striking was the contrast between the Chinese hemp growing on land so washed and worn that it would no longer produce the common hemp, it required only to be seen to convince the most skeptical as to its value.

There was more pulp in the stalks, making it harder to break but easier to clean, the hurds falling out freely in long pieces. The seed was somewhat smaller, requiring less to be sown per acre. For rope purposes it equaled other varieties, though not for bagging and twine. The greatest benefit was in the largely increased yield per acre: ". . . double and even treble the amount of the old variety— making it a more profitable crop than 'King Cotton' itself."[48]

Crossbreeding ruderalis with sativa or indica will produce a seed line that combines the desired characteristics of another species with the early maturity and rugged adaptability of ruderalis.

The Agriculture of Herbal Cannabis

Due to its legal definition, it is equally illegal in the United States today to grow hemp as a fiber crop or as an herb.[49] From a medical point of view, there may come a time when growing cannabis is essential to relieve suffering or health conditions. From a social point of view, herbal cannabis is clearly a market that will be hugely profitable for years to come. No comprehensive study of the value of hemp can overlook these controversial markets.

Cultivation of herbal cannabis is allowed in a precious few places around the world today,[50] and the best sources of information — the growers — have mostly been driven underground. Prohibition agents illegally seize and destroy agricultural and horticultural notes and data. The multi-billion dollar black market economy of cannabis cultivation and marketing has been seeking to come above ground for more than 20 years and has made some headway in recent years, especially for medical users.[51]

---

[47] *Facts for Farmers.* op. cit. p. 966
[48] Ibid.
[49] Actually moreso; the 1994 federal crime bill included the death penalty for growing 50,000 plants or more — just 1/10 of an acre of fiber hemp.
[50] Including Holland, Eastern Europe, Russia, China, Transkei (South Africa), Wakeshada (Brazil), & a few others.
[51] WARNING: As of this writing, it is strictly prohibited to grow hemp in the US, whether for fiber, pulp, seed or herb. Thus, growing cannabis can be hazardous to your liberty, & may result in imprisonment & property seizure. Such penalties are clearly unconstitutional under the 1st, 4th, 9th, 10th and 14th amendments, internationally recognized human rights law, etc. Prohibitionists hold such rights in contempt. Anyone who grows cannabis should protect their anonymity.

A discussion of technique highlights the differences between an industrial feedstock and a pharmaceutical herb. While industrial stalks stand 150 to the square yard, each herbal plant wants at least a square yard for full growth. Males flower first and are removed. The female plant is more desirable, since it is more potent than the male, more robust and often has twice as much foliage. These differences make it clear that those who claim it is difficult to distinguish between the crops are most likely speaking out of ignorance.

This is not a textbook on cannabis farming. There is much more in-depth information in other sources.[52] Rather, we consider the topic from the post-prohibition viewpoint of both commercial farmer and hobbyist. We will first look at herbal cannabis as it will be grown outdoors when legal. Next we consider indoor and finally greenhouse growing, which may diminish somewhat after prohibition has ended, although it will continue to be important for cities, in certain climactic zones and for clinical needs, where more precise control over the chemical compounds must be ensured.

Choosing an Outdoor Garden Site

Cannabis should have as much sun as possible and a moist but well-drained soil. Flat open areas are best. In the northern hemisphere, avoid north facing slopes, since they are coldest and receive the least light. Eastern slopes are shaded in the afternoon and western slopes are shaded in the morning. Southern slopes receive the most light and are generally warmest. The steeper the slope, the more pronounced the shading. Orient rows along a north-south axis, perpendicular to the course of the sun, especially on steep slopes.[53] The exception is where plants receive sunlight only at midday, in which case rows should run east-west. A square plot angled diamond-style with its corners pointing in the cardinal directions will gain about 10 percent more sunlight.[54]

Since the herbal crop does not return as much leafy matter to the soil as industrial crops, it is more important to rotate it with other farm crops, especially legumes and other nitrate-producing crops. Test and adjust soil chemistry at least two months before planting. It should be high in nitrogen and potassium, but medium in phos-

[52]Frank, Mel. *Marijuana Growers' Insider's Guide*. Red Eye Press. Los Angeles CA. 1988. Rosenthal, Ed. *Marijuana Grower's Tips*. Quick American Printing. San Francisco CA. 1986. Frank & Rosenthal. *Marijuana Grower's Guide*. Red Eye Press. Los Angeles CA. 1978, revised 1990
[53]This advantage is a factor at all US latitudes but less significant farther north
[54]Aldrich, M., et al. *High Times Encyclopedia of Recreational Drugs*. Trans High/Stonehill Publishng. New York NY. 1978. pp. 145-158

phorus.[55] Turn and loosen the soil, break up large clods of earth and mix in fertilizers. If no rain is expected, water the area to dissolve the fertilizer. It is beneficial to continue testing the soil for its pH level. It should be at least 5.5 and preferably between 6.5 and 7.5. It can be raised by adding ground limestone, dolomite limestone, hydrated lime, marl or ground sea shells.

Indoor Cultivation: The Urban Farmer

Cannabis adapts well to indoor conditions, whether in sunny rooms or under artificial light. It grows into a fully formed bush with a minimum of five hours of sunlight a day. However, you can grow small, but potent, plants with only two hours of direct sunlight each day. Indoor gardens are simple to build using materials that are readily available from nurseries, garden shops and hardware or lighting stores. Water, nutrients and air are fairly easy to supply, so the determining factor indoors is often the amount of light.

Windows are the easiest, cheapest and most conspicuous light sources. Keep glass clean for better light. If privacy is an issue, use diffused glass rather than clear. Paint window sills and sides white or line them with white or reflective sheets to increase light. Keep seedlings raised at sill level.[56]

Using natural light, the best time to plant is in March or April. At that time of year, both the sun's intensity and the length of daylight are increasing. Windows facing south usually get the most light, followed by windows facing east and west. Never use north windows; they don't get direct sun.

An alcove or corner with windows facing in two or more directions is often the brightest spot. A greenhouse, sun porch, particularly sunny room or skylight can support larger plants than most artificial lighting systems can. A sunny porch enclosed in sheet plastic makes a simple, inexpensive greenhouse.

A final note; house plants are said to enjoy being talked to. One report claimed cannabis grows better in the presence of rock music, but it has also been suggested that plants actually respond not to the music, but to the enjoyment of the listener. Hence jazz, country, classical, pop, new age or whatever music you prefer will work equally well.[57]

---

[55]For best results, add fertilizer a month before planting so nutrients will dissolve & become available to the plants without burning the roots.
[56]*High Times Encyclopedia.* op. cit.
[57]Whitman, J. *Psychic Power of Plants.* W.H. Allen . London England. 1975. p. 64

Greenhouse Growing

Greenhouse horticulture combines aspects of both outdoor and indoor growing. Combining artificial lamps with light shields, the greenhouse can at any time simulate the day pattern desired, 18 hours of light for maximum growth or 12 hours for maximum flowering. Roots are not restricted by being enclosed in a container, but the crop is protected from weather, to offer early plantings and late harvests. Since cannabis should grow for a couple of months before it is ready to consume, using cuttings saves a substantial amount of time. This means more than one harvest per season.

Due to height constraints, greenhouses and indoor systems lend themselves to a "sea of green" planting pattern, using cuttings planted close together and brought to flower early so they flower while still small and go straight to bud without wasting light on height. Since there are more plants per area and the upper foliage normally shades out lower branches on hemp, this does not diminish the overall yield to the extent one might otherwise expect.

Artificial Lighting & the Electric Sun

Cannabis grows fast under artificial light, averaging three to six feet in three months. Hang fixtures by a rope or chain from the walls or ceiling, or from the top of a frame at least six feet high and constructed of a two-by-two inch wood stud. To minimize light loss, use industrial fixtures with built-in reflectors. Otherwise mount lamps on a sheet of plywood painted white, or add reflectors of white posterboard. Standard lengths of fluorescent tubes are four and eight feet long, at about 10 watts per foot.[58] Surround the garden with reflective surfaces to help hold moisture for a healthy degree of humidity. Reflective floor surfaces help spread the light to the bottom of the plants. As you raise the fixtures, attach aluminum foil or reflective sheets to their sides to recycle the light.

Plants primarily respond to red and blue light, so for healthy growth, a combination must be provided.[59] Incandescent lamps are only a third as efficient as fluorescent, with a much shorter life, and their extra heat can also dry or burn plants. The size of the garden corresponds to the light system, so if the garden is one by-four feet, use two four-foot tubes (80 watts) or up to 60 watts per square foot. More light means more growth. Ten watts per square foot of growing area is adequate for healthy growth, but for a fast-growing, lush crop, use at least 20 watts per square foot, or switch to halide

---

[58]Incandescent & 'Natural White' tubes provide strong reds 'Gro-Lux' standard or wide-spectrum & 'Plant-Gro' favor blue. Evenly distribute at a one-to-one ratio.
[59]White light is not really white, but a combination of red, blue & green lights.

or other sophisticated lighting system. Tubes standing along the sides of the garden can bring light to lower parts of the plant that are otherwise blocked by the upper leaves. Rotating halide lamps, high pressure sodium lamps, irrigation systems, ventilation systems, and other high-technology units are available for the serious high-volume indoor grower.

Reaping the Rewards of the Indoor Harvest

There are two basic systems of indoor cannabis harvesting: continuous growth collection and periodic harvests.

Continuous growth emphasizes heavy growth and a continuous supply of foliage. Using a timer, the grower keeps the photoperiod set at a constant 18 hours or more of light per day. This also keeps "mother plants" for clones growing indefinitely without flowering. These can be used for cross-generational breeding to reinforce special characteristics. By changing the light schedule, or photoperiod, the grower can trigger female flowering. Cut down to 12 hours of light at six to eight weeks before you plan to harvest. Within two weeks, females respond to the longer "night" and begin to flower.

Allow the flowers to grow another four to six weeks to develop into large, thick clusters which are by far the most potent part of the plant. Pick them just above the point where they connect to the main stalk. New flowers grown from there give a higher yield. This produces a crop of buds every four to nine months. Flowers can be harvested two or three times before the plant loses vigor.

A happy medium in terms of potency and yield is to harvest about every six months for a minimum of one ounce of flower per square foot of growing area.

Resin Enhancement Techniques

Certain kinds of stress increase the female plant's resin output and, thereby, its potency. A common method is to withhold water during the last week or so before the harvest. The most popular system is to prune the main stalk, causing more branches. Other processes entail removing branches on the lower third of a two and a half or three feet high plant, or pruning back branches on the lowest 12 to 18 inches of plant, leaving leafless stubs about six inches long to promote easy healing. Another approach is less drastic pruning of lower branches, leaving about six leafy inches of each branch, and removal of the top six to 12 inches of the central stalk.[60]

---

[60]Drake, William Daniel Jr. *The International Cultivator's Handbook.* Wingbow Press. Berkeley CA. 1974. p. 30

Another technique is to bend the tops more or less horizontally so they continue to draw some liquids from the base of the plant, but not enough to stop them from wilting within 10 days.[61]

Manicuring plants using a scissors (to reduce loss of resin) and cutting out leaves among the calyx of the bud allows more light to reach lower parts of the plant and increases bud size and thickness. This also improves the visual and tactile quality of any herbal cannabis, increasing its market value.

The name sinsemilla comes from a Spanish phrase, *sin semilla*, or "without seed." The crop is also referred to as *sensi*. This very potent and exceptionally fragrant form of female cannabis flowers produces unfertilized flowers and resin rather than seeds.[62] This can be achieved by the timely elimination of males, but pollen can travel over great distances and it is impossible to know if everyone has gotten rid of all other males within range. A more dependable alternative is to loosely cover the branch with a loose transparent plastic bag that lets light in and keeps the unwanted pollen out.[63]

Other techniques disturb the growth cycle at the polar opposite of the top flowers. One way is to grab the lower stalk of a nearly mature female plant and twist until vertical cracks appear in the bark, but not so great as to open the plant to infection. Or jam a sharp object into the lower stem near the ground to open a wound. This is left in the plant, which is sometimes bound back together and continues to mature, but produces more resin than seed.[64]

An unusual method is from the Himalayas. A loosely-woven wicker basket, about three feet in diameter with a narrow mouth, is inverted over a six-week old plant, hopefully female. Stakes are driven into the ground, on which the basket rests and to which it is lashed, to avoid crushing the plant or being pushed off by it. Trapped inside the basket, which lets in air and faint rays of sunlight, the plant grows to full size wrapped around itself. When the basket is cut away at season's end, the plant looks like a pale green brain or a giant, stringy cabbage connected to the earth by a limp cord of stalk. This process "vastly increases resin secretion."[65]

---

[61]*High Times Encyclopedia*. op. cit.
[62]Seedless cannabis is not a genetic freak, like seedless oranges & watermelons. If male pollen is kept away, the female produces more sticky THC-resin to catch pollen.
[63]Take care not to stifle the plant or to allow mold to grow.
[64]Drake. op. cit. pp. 29-33
[65]*Ibid*. pp. 32-33

Curing: Preparing the Crop for Market

The farmer has several options to dry and prepare the crop's foliage to prevent molding and enhance herbal flavor, aroma and effect.[66] These parallel tobacco in many respects.

• Flue curing, whereby plants are hung upside down in a space with dehydrators or where heat is regulated and artificial.

• Air curing, in which the plants are placed similarly, but in larger airy rooms to age in a slower and more natural manner.

• Smoke curing, i.e., heating the leaf in a small area with fires to flavor the herb, or

• Sun curing, which allows the plant to mellow in the sunlight for a golden color. To avoid dew, plants should be spread on dry ground during the day and turned so the whole plant is exposed to similar amounts of sunlight, then gathered inside at night.

At this point the farmer cleans his crop by stripping the leaves from the stalk by hand, being careful not to injure their appearance by crushing them or breaking the leaves too severely. Large, robust, well-cured leaves and buds will bring a higher grade to the crop and result in a higher selling price. During this cleaning process the farmer also removes seeds from the herb, either to utilize in next years crop or to sell. Buds are tied to sticks, shaped or wrapped up in their own leaves to protect them during later handling.

Dealing With Assorted Pests

One difference between industrial and herbal hemp that becomes immediately obvious is that of pest control. The dense growth of tall sticks with thin clusters of leaves that typifies industrial crops is much less attractive to pests than the fragrant, thick, luxuriant foliage of the herbal crop. Also, the loss of a dozen plants out of tens of thousands is not significant, but that might well be an herb gardener's entire crop. Lastly, if the foliage of an industrial crop is damaged, it doesn't matter, whereas for the herb, it is everything.

A number of insects like to eat or suck on cannabis, and there are several good methods to discourage them. Companion planting of thyme, chives, savory, onions, garlic or marigolds keeps some insects away and protects the garden. Predatory insects, like ladybugs, praying mantises and lacewings eat troublesome insects but not the plant. They can be purchased from commercial hatcheries or hardware stores. Be careful not to spray the plants with insecticides while these predators are present. For aphids, simply spraying the plant with soapy water is usually sufficient to get rid of an

[66]Galbraith, Gatewood, et al. *The plan for taxing & controlling hemp in Kentucky.* KY Marijuana Feasibility Study. POB 1438, Lexington KY 40501. 1977, 1988.

infestation. For more persistent critters, botanical repellents are concentrated, naturally occurring insecticides,[67] sold in spray form. They do not build up in living plant tissue, but the grower should wash the plant afterwards. Never spray during the flowering cycle; harvest early if necessary. If any kind of pesticide is used, wash off the plant as early as possible, so as not to disturb the surface resin that occurs in the mature female flower.

Weeding the patch is only important until the plants get a good head start on their competitors. Cannabis will effectively fight off weeds to acquire limited resources. More developed plants are apt to be attacked by foraging animals. Sprouts are delicacies for rabbits and snails, and when larger they can serve as the main course for deer, cows and groundhogs. Blood meal placed on the ground near the garden will keep deer away. Chimes, bells and scarecrows also help. An old plastic shopping bag tied to a branch and blowing in the breeze is an alternative that draws less attention. On a farm, fences serve to keep hungry animals from the crop. In other locations, a more natural looking barrier is aesthetically preferable.

Some people claim that the smell of human urine discourages wild animals, which generally avoid populated places. If so, it is certainly an inexpensive and readily available product, and applying it may offer a believable excuse for being at the garden if unwanted company arrives. Do not urinate directly onto roots, however, because it throws off the pH and causes root rot.

The most dangerous pests, of course, are the anti-Eden policing agents parading as civic protectors. The first Cheech and Chong film, *Up In Smoke*, comes to mind wherein Cheech Marin wastes the DEA agent played by Stacy Keach with his urinary waste—a high point of hilarity for all those well aware of the lives put to waste by those who would kidnap growers and other givers.

Thieves (governmental and otherwise) are best kept at bay by silence. Growing through these times requires utter discretion—a secret shared only among the fewest and most loyal. Bringing to fruition something so precious as flowering hemp puts into perspective the nature of the human pests who would be enemies.

The World's Most Valuable Crop

Depending on cultivation methods and environmental factors, a grower can harvest from 1000 to 5000 pounds of cured foliage per acre.[68] Planting an acre (208 x 208 feet) with a four foot outer rim and plants clustered in mounds spaced 10 feet apart for maximum

---

[67]Pyrethrum & Rotenone are common varieties
[68]43,560 square feet. *High Times Encyclopedia*. op. cit.

light results in 20 rows each way, or 400 cannabis clusters. Rounding that up to 500 plants to allow for multiple plants in some mounds, and using the figure of a pound of bud per plant,[69] we calculate 500 pounds of cured bud per acre season.

Allowing for an expected drop in price of 90 percent after prohibition is abolished and using the figure of $200 per legal pound, we arrive at a gross income estimate of $100,000 per acre for the grower. That is bud only. By including leaf and following closer planting patterns, we get an average yield of about 1600 manicured pounds, with a lower open market value of $100 per pound, or $160,000 per acre.[70]

No other crop can even begin to approach this profit level to the farmer. Berber tribes in the Rif Mountains of northern Africa raise cannabis for the partially Westernized coastal plains. Local farmers estimate the average yield of their marginal rocky land, on which little else can be grown, at two kilograms per square meter of dried tops and stems, leaves not included.[71]

Just Do It — Plant Now

So now you are in on the major economic discovery of the era: Hemp is the most important part of the market to keep an eye on, as it will shape our progress for centuries to come—and it is ripe for ground-level investment now, before the market takes off. Whether you have billions to invest, or only pennies, hemp offers an opportunity to make money.

Revival of the hemp industry will create jobs and business opportunities from the smallest cottage industry level to multinational corporations. It will send ripples throughout society, creating many new spin-off businesses. As research into this remarkable plant continues, and we discover more about what it can do, there will be even more industries and products developed which use hemp. But even today with research in its infancy, we are astounded by the dazzling array of uses to which hemp has already been put.

[69]US Drug Enforcement Administration estimate

[70]Other estimates: Stockberger (US), 400-500 lbs/acre dried flowers. Small, et al. (Canada), nearly 1800 lbs/acre manicured leaves & tops. Cherian (India), 246 to 820 lbs/acre pressed flowers. letter from McPartland, J.M. 1991

[71]Harvested in August & early September, when blossoms are ripe but not yet in seed. Mikuriya, Dr. Tod. 'Marijuana in Morocco.' in Aaronson, B. & Osmond, H. *Psychedelics*. Anchor Books/Doubleday. Garden City NY. 1970. pp. 115-128

Part III

—

Beyond the Marijuana Smoke Screen

HEMP
Lifeline to the Future

16

A WORLD OF CANNABIS CULTURES

This herb should be treated with respect. The hemp plant is holy to the Hindu — a guardian lives in the leaf. Hemp is holy to Sufi Muslims and Coptic Christians, as well. Literally scores of religions hold cannabis in special reverence. Producing quality herb and resin has always been a fine and noble art. Selecting and providing the best herb is an honorable and often a well paid position.

These talents and responsibilities have a long tradition of being highly valued, and yet racists and prohibitionists harbor special animosity towards this healing herb which is a sacrament to many. Moralistical objections and political intrusion caused its suppression. In recent years, antagonism towards cannabis' social and religious use has overshadowed even its medical potential. It was removed from the British Pharmacopoeia in 1932, the United States Pharmacopoeia in 1941, and even the Indian Pharmacopoeia in 1966.[1]

Let's take another look at this venerable gift to humanity.

The Hindu & the Holy Herb

One of the fundamental texts of Hinduism, the *Rig Veda*, from 1500 BC, says, "Drug plants preceded even the gods by three ages." Cannabis was a gift from the gods, who spilled a drop of nectar onto the Earth. Where it touched the ground, the hemp plant sprouted.[2] Hindus believe that Lord Shiva brought the plant down from the Himalayas for human use and enjoyment. One day, Shiva went off by himself in the fields. The shade of a tall cannabis plant brought him comfort and refuge from the blazing sun. He tasted its leaves and felt so refreshed that he adopted it as his favorite food, hence his title: "Lord of Bhang."[3] Cannabis is also called *Indricana*, the food of the god Indra. The Supreme Lord Krishna at one point in the *Bhagavad-gita* declares, "I am the Healing Herb."[4]

In late Vedic India, cannabis was used in fire ceremonies for good fortune as well as for healing. The fourth book of the *Vedas*, the last accepted into the orthodox religion, written around 1400 BC, calls it one of the "five kingdoms of herbs ... which release

---

[1] Evans, Fred J. 'Separation of Central from Peripheral Effects on a Structural Basis.' in *Planta Medica*. 57. Sup. Issue 1. London England. 1991. p. S-60
[2] Schultes, Richard & Hofmann, Albert. *Over de Planten der Goden*. Spectrum Boek. Utrecht Holland. 1983. p. 92
[3] Abel, E. *Marihuana: The first 12,000 years*. Plenum Press. NY NY. 1980. p. 17
[4] *Bhagavad-gita*. Ch 9:16

anxiety."[5] Sadhu priests have wandered through India for millennia sharing chillum pipes full of cannabis and the blessing *"Bom shankar."* In 1894, the British Raj Commission made a study of hemp drugs in Indian belief systems, and reported that:[6]

> Yogis ... take deep draughts of bhang that they may center their thoughts on the Eternal. ... By the help of bhang, ascetics pass days without food or drink. The supporting power of bhang has brought many a Hindu family safe through the miseries of famine. To forbid or even seriously restrict use of so holy and gracious a herb as hemp would cause widespread suffering and annoyance and to the large bands of worshipped ascetics, deep-seated anger. ...
>
> These beliefs the Musalman devotee shares to the full. Like his Hindu brother, the Musalman fakir reveres bhang as the lengthener of life; the freer from the bonds of self. Bhang brings union with the Divine Spirit.

When Hindus came to Jamaica and the Americas, they brought *ganja* and their ancient growing techniques with them.

Some of the World's Other Cannabis Religions

Cannabis is named in Assyrian sacred texts from the seventh century BC, although wine was more important in religious life there. The Essenes of ancient Israel and the Theraputea of Egypt both used it as medicine.[7] Tradition holds that the name Coptic is a derivation of the name Kuftaim, a grandchild of Noah. He settled in the Nile Valley, in the neighborhood of the ancient capital of Egypt, Thebes, where cannabis beverages were drunk.[8]

Zoroaster, the Persian founder of one of the world's first monotheistic (one god) religions, may have been a cannabis user.[9] The *Zend-Avesta,* said to have been written by Zoroaster himself around the seventh century BC, called it the "revealer of the highest mysteries."[10] Hemp is favorably mentioned in myths of the fire-worshipers, known as *Magi* in The Bible. Zoroaster's wife Hvovi made offerings to the lower gods so they would ask the Supreme Being to "give her his good narcotic, *bangha* ... that she might think ac-

---

[5]*Atharvaveda* 12:6.15

[6]"To meet someone carrying bhang is a sure omen of success. To see in a dream the leaves, plant or water of bhang is lucky; it brings the goddess of wealth into the dreamer's power.... A longing for bhang foretells happiness; to see bhang drunk increases riches. No good thing can come to the man who treads under foot the holy bhang leaf." Campbell, J.M. 'Note on the Religion of Hemp.' in *Report of the Indian Hemp Drugs Commission.* vol. 3. Simla India. 1894. pp. 250-252

[7]Herer, Jack. *Hemp & the Marijuana Conspiracy: The Emperor Wears No Clothes.* HEMP Publishing. Van Nuys CA. 1991. p. 50

[8]Schultes, Richard. 'Man & Marijuana.' in *Natural History.* 1973. vol. 82. pp. 59-65

[9]Eliade, Mircea. *Shamanism.* Pantheon Books. New York NY. 1964. pp. 399-400

[10]*The Zend-Avesta.* Oxford U Press. London England. 1882. pp. 267-268,

cording to the law, speak according to the law and do according to the law."[11]

Buddhism permeates Korea, Japan, China, Tibet and Southeast Asia. In one legend, Gautama Buddha in the sixth century BC subsisted on a ration of one cannabis seed per day, nothing else, during his six years of asceticism that led to his revealing the Four Noble Truths and the Eightfold Path to knowledge.[12]

By the first century AD, Taoists in Japan used cannabis seeds in their incense burners.[13] A fifth century Japanese booklet stated that "Hemp and mulberry ... have long been used in worshipping the gods."[14] According to Japanese Shinto beliefs, purity and evil cannot exist side by side. Waving the *gohei* (a short stick with undyed hemp fibers—for purity—attached to one end) above someone's head will drive evil spirits from inside him.[15]

The most cannabis-oriented Moslems are probably the Sufi sect. It draws its devotees largely from the lower and middle classes to become ascetics with a mystical approach toward Islam. An important Sufi tradition encourages the attainment of spiritual insights through the arousal of ecstatic states, including intoxication by hashish, to stimulate mystical consciousness and appreciation of the nature of Allah. To the Sufi, eating hashish is "an act of worship."[16]

Further south in Africa, Chief Kalamba-Moukenge of the Balubas, a Bantu tribe in the Congo, sought to unify diverse tribes he had conquered. He burned their ancient fetishes and instituted a religion using cannabis as the central sacrament.[17]

Various cults were carried with slaves from the Gold Coast of Africa to Jamaica. In the 1930s, inspired by Marcus Garvey's "Back to Africa" movement, Jamaicans looked to Ethiopia for guidance.

The Ethiopian Zion Coptic Church, headquartered in Jamaica,[18] traces its origins back 6000 years to Ethiopia, whose civilization preceded ancient Egypt.[19] The Bible is its holy book and cannabis is its sacrament. Its theology perceives the use of cannabis throughout

---

[11]In the *Avesta,* Gustasp & Ardu Viraf were "transported in soul to the heavens & had the higher mysteries revealed to them" by drinking bhang. Aldrich, et al. *High Times Encyclopedia.* Trans High Publishing. New York NY. 1978. p. 119

[12]Beal, S. *Fo-Sho-Hing-Tsan-King.* Clarrendon Press. Oxford England. 1882. p. 143

[13]Needham, J. *Science & Civilization in China.* Cambridge Press. Boston MA. 1974

[14]Chohoki, K. *A Handy Guide to Papermaking.* UC Press. Berkeley CA. 1948. p. 2

[15]Joya, M. *Things Japanese.* Tokyo News Service. Tokyo Japan. 1963. pp. 23-24

[16]Abel. op. cit. p. 39

[17]von Wissmann, Hermann. in *High Times Encyclopedia.* op. cit. p. 126

[18]The church is not directly connected to Egyptian Coptics. It was revived in Jamaica, in response to Garvey's teachings.

[19]Tradition holds that the Copts were Christianized by St. Mark in Alexandria, Egypt, in 45 AD. Members adhere to traditions set forth in the Old Testament regarding diet, dress, grooming, sexual conduct & so forth.

the Bible, in numerous passages regarding incense, herbs, smoke, fire and clouds.[20] The Church teaches that "Only through the sacramental use of marijuana, combined with prayer and spiritual reasoning among the brethren, can members of the Church come to know God within themselves and within others."[21]

A man named Ras Tafari was crowned Haile Selassie, the 225th in a line of Ethiopian kings stretching in unbroken succession from the time of King Solomon and the Queen of Sheba. A new religion based on the Bible took his name for their title, and cannabis for their sacrament.[22] Rastafaris were composed originally of freedom fighters, they began wearing their hair in dreadlocks and chanting the praises of God, or *Jah*. They trace ganja smoking back to the Genesis command to use "every seed bearing herb," and their hair style to various admonitions against cutting the hair.[23] Smoke is used for visions, cleansing, healing and refreshment; those who don't know how to use the smoke are told to "use the tea."

European Cannabis Cultures

The Western world knew something of the cannabis activities going on in Asia and Africa. Islam had a firm foothold in Spain from the eighth to the 15th centuries. Nearly all of the early herbalists and botanical writers of Europe mention hemp.[24] References are made to Avicenna and other Arab druggists in the miller's tale of Chaucer's *Canterbury Tales*. Nynauld's 1615 work *Lycanthropy, Transformation and Ecstasy of Sorcerers* listed hashish as a major ingredient in some ointments and brews.[25] Portuguese slave traders exchanged tobacco for East African tribes people to be used as slaves. These tribes were long accustomed to cannabis smoking.

The Dutch were soon trading other products for cannabis in South Africa. Since imported tobacco and cannabis were expensive, the thrifty, resourceful farmers of Holland began to chop up domestic hemp tops to add to the long-stem pipes they carried.[26] It has been suggested that cannabis smoking came to the Netherlands from the East Indies. Dutch artist Adriaen Brouwer and others painted

---

[20]*Marijuana & the Bible.* EZCC. PO Box 1161, Minneda FL 34755-1161

[21]Mazur, Cynthia S. 'Marijuana as a "Holy Sacrament" ' in *Notre Dame Journal of Law*, Ethics & Public Policy. vol. 5:3. 1991. pp. 696-701 (pp. 693-727)

[22]Selassie's death in 1975 was not an impediment to faith, since he was always seen to have human limitations, while the spiritual base of Rastafari is universal & timeless. Nicholas, T. *Rastafari: A way of life.* Anchor/Doubleday. Garden City NY. 1979

[23]Leviticus 19:27; Leviticus 21:5; Numbers 6:5

[24]Dewey, Lyster H. 'Hemp.' in *Yearbook of the USDA, 1913.* US GPO. Washington DC. 1914. pp. 288-291

[25]*High Times Encyclopedia.* op. cit. pp. 13, 124-127

[26]van't Hoff, Ron. *Het goede leven: Pijpen en pijptabak.* Het Spectrum. Utrecht Holland. 1980. p. 8

farmers with broad smiles on their faces, pipes in hand, in smoking poses. He depicted the distinctive inhalation pattern of cannabis, deep puffs and held breath, as well as states of intoxication.[27]

In 1798 Napoleon led his troops and a contingent of academics to Egypt where they discovered hash.[28] Queen Donia Carlota Joaquina of Portugal, threatened by Napoleon's advances, fled to Brazil in 1808. Her royal court discovered potent Amazon cannabis and brought it home to Lisbon after the wars. Back in France, young painters like Gros, Géricault and Delacroix painted images of sexy harem courtesans, with hookahs, on canvas made of hemp. A year or two in Algeria or Egypt was *de rigueur* for students of every profession, and exotic customs like hash eating caught on.

In 1840 a French doctor reported on the use of hashish in treating plague and typhoid fever in North Africa. This inspired a young psychologist, Jacques-Joseph Moreau de Tours, who had traveled in the Orient. He researched hashish as a treatment for mental illness and thereby invented modern psycho-pharmacology. His work "On Hashish and Mental Alienation" won honorable mention at an 1850s Academy of Sciences competition.

Soon, however, hashish was adopted by tragic-poet types with Gothic sensibilities, who mentioned the resin in melodramatic literary plots. Hashish soon became an exotic, macabre, sensational plot device. The Parisian literati formed the *Club des Haschischins*.[29]

Charles Baudelaire warned against holding too wild expectations in his 1860 "Poem of Hashish."

> Let it be well understood by worldly and ignorant folk, curious of acquaintance with exceptional joys, that they will find in hashish nothing miraculous, absolutely nothing but the natural in a super-abundant degree. The brain and the organism on which hash operates will only give their ordinary and individual phenomena, magnified, it is true, both in quantity and quality.

Cannabis Comes to the Americas

Both tobacco and the pipe originated in America. A fifth-century relief of a smoker at the Palenque Mayan ruins of southern Mexico is among the oldest such renderings known.[30] Indigenous peoples shared peace pipes of various blended herbs, tobacco and hallucinogenic mushrooms. "Before talking of holy things, we prepare our-

---

27Roessingh. *History of the Dutch Tobacco Industry*. in Schama, S. *The Embarrassment of Riches: An interpretation of Dutch culture in the Golden Age*. Knopf. New York NY. 1987
28*High Times Encyclopedia*. op. cit. pp. 21, 128, 24
29Moreau, Théophile Gautier, Boissard, Charles Baudelaire, Victor Hugo, Alexandre Dumas, H. Balzac, Flaubert & others. *Ibid*. pp. 122-123
30*Ibid*. p. 50

selves by offerings. ... One will fill his pipe and hand it to the other, who will light it and offer it to the sky and earth ... they will smoke together ... then they will be ready to talk."[31] Pipes and cannabis textiles have been unearthed dating from 400 BC in the Hopewell Mound Builders' funerary mounds in modern day Ohio.

Africans brought euphoriant varieties of cannabis to Brazil by 1549,[32] when the Portuguese allowed them to plant cannabis indica in between the rows of sugar cane, finding it helped them work better.[33] The King of Spain ordered in 1564 that cannabis must be grown throughout his dominions, which included all of the Americas except Brazil, which was controlled by Portugal.

"There is a kind of wild hempe groweing plentifully all over the country," came the report from Massachusetts.[34] The Virginia General Assembly in 1619 specified that "both English and Indian" hemp, meaning the resin bearing cannabis indica, had to be grown by settlers at the very beginning of colonization.[35]

Merry Mount was a New England trading settlement whose free spirited leader, Thomas Morton, grew Indian hemp and smoked the peace pipe with the native peoples, staging bonfires and wild Maypole parties. The outpost was burned down by angry Puritans who sent Morton back to an English prison, where he later wrote a book about his experience entitled *New Canaan*—a name with a Biblical reference to cannabis.

With sprawling, vigorous river and coastal trade routes, commerce spread throughout the Americas and the Caribbean and up the Mississippi River. The native peoples of the Americas smoked from pipes ceremonially and were experts at discovering the medicinal and other properties of herbs. They mingled with slaves and had an excellent communications network from South America to Canada. On both sides of the Atlantic, African men farmed the cannabis plant familiar by so many names in their ancestral homelands, but in America simply called hemp.

How many secretly retained the cannabis custom is not recorded—slaves were not allowed to write. But African-Americans

[31]Chased by Bears, Sioux nation. quoted in visitors station, Pipestone National Monument. Pipestone MN

[32]The Angolan names *maconha, diamba & riamba* still survive. in *Cannabis & Culture*. Rubin, Vera, ed. Mouton. The Hague, Netherlands. 1975

[33]*High Times Encyclopedia*. op. cit. pp. 126, 127

[34]*Records of the Colony of Massachusetts Bay*. June 2, 1641. Shurtleff Court Records 1628-1641. p. 322

[35]*High Times Encyclopedia*. op. cit. p. 127

were known to communicate among themselves and eventually became "thoroughly organized and one in spirit under slavery."[36]

Starting in the 1840s, British plantation owners brought thousands of Hindu indentured laborers from India to Trinidad and Jamaica as sugar cane workers, and smoking ganja for energy was soon adopted. Hindus were treated like slaves, and the two groups naturally mixed. This is why cannabis is still called *ganja* in Jamaica, and good class herb is called "Kali Ganja."[37]

From the balmy Caribbean it was a short sail over to Mexico, where peasants were farming herbal cannabis at least by 1886.

American High Society

The extent of cannabis smoking during the Colonial era is still subject to debate. President George Washington wrote a letter that contained an oblique reference to what may have been hashish. "The artificial preparation of hemp, from Silesia, is really a curiosity."[38] Washington made specific written references to Indian hemp, or cannabis indica, and hoped to "have disseminated the seed to others."[39] His August 7, 1765 diary entry, "began to separate the male from the female (hemp) plants," describes a harvesting technique favored to enhance the potency of smoking cannabis, among other reasons.[40] Hemp farmer Thomas Jefferson and paper maker Ben Franklin were ambassadors to France during the initial surge of the hashish vogue. Their celebrity status and progressive revolutionary image afforded them ample opportunities to try new experiences. Jefferson smuggled Chinese hemp seeds to America and is credited with the phrase in the *Declaration of Independence*, "Life, liberty and the pursuit of happiness."

Did the Founding Fathers of the United States of America smoke cannabis? Some researchers think so. Dr. Burke, president of the American Historical Reference Society and a consultant for the Smithsonian Institute, counted seven early presidents as cannabis smokers: George Washington, Thomas Jefferson, James Madison, James Monroe, Andrew Jackson, Zachary Taylor and Franklin Pierce.[41] "Early letters from our founding fathers refer to the plea-

---

[36]Moore, Brent. *The Hemp Industry In Kentucky, A Study of the Past, the Present & the Possibilities.* Press of James E. Hughes. Lexington KY. 1905. p. 94
[37]Aldrich, Michael, Ph.D. 'On the arrival of Indian indentures servants mixing with black slaves.' in *Best of High Times.* vol 10. 1991. p. 61
[38]A region now shared by Germany & Poland. Letter to Dr. James Anderson, May 26, 1794. in *Writings of George Washington.* Washington DC. vol. 33. p. 384
[39]*Ibid.* vol. 35. p. 72
[40]Such as creating more space for females to flower for seed production, or to take advantage of the male fiber before it overmatures in the field.
[41]Burke asserted that Washington & Jefferson were said to exchange smoking blends as personal gifts. Washington reportedly preferred a pipe full of "the leaves of hemp"

sures of hemp smoking," said Burke. Pierce, Taylor and Jackson, all military men, smoked it with their troops. Cannabis was twice as popular among American soldiers in the Mexican War as in Vietnam: Pierce wrote to his family that it was "about the only good thing" about that war.

Central and Western African natives were farming and harvesting cannabis sativa in North America as slaves. If they did smoke on the plantations, that would be kept secret.[42] By the time of the Louisiana purchase in 1803, New Orleans had a mixed Spanish, French, Creole, Cajun, Mexican and Black population. The city teemed with adventurers and sailors, wise to the ways of cannabis. It was mixed with tobacco or smoked alone, used to season food,[43] to treat insomnia and impotence, and so on.

Cannabis was mentioned as a medicinal agent in a formal American medical text as early as 1843.[44]

A Puff of Melodrama & Moralizing

The public image of cannabis in America was shaped by writers of adventure tales and melodrama, as a plot device to engender a sense of exotic and sinister forces at work.

American adventurer Bayard Taylor wrote an 1854 essay on "Visions of Hashish" he had in Damascus. He described an "exquisite lightness and airiness," the "wonderfully keen perception of the ludicrous," and "fine sensations which spread throughout the whole tissue of my nervous fiber, each thrill helping to divest my frame of its earthly and natural nature."[45]

American curiosity was piqued. Transcendentalists like John Greenleaf Whittier and Thomas Bailey Aldrich waxed poetic about the herb. Fitz Hugh Ludlow's 1857 *The Hasheesh Eater* was read from New York literary salons to California gold camps. Like many such accounts of hashish, Whittier and Ludlow described powerful hallucinations and painful withdrawal symptoms inconsistent with modern scientific knowledge. Small wonder. The *Boston Medical*

---

to alcohol, & wrote in his diaries that he enjoyed the fragrance of hemp flowers. Madison once remarked that hemp gave him insight to create a new & democratic nation. Monroe, creator of the Monroe Doctrine, began smoking it as Ambassador to France & continued to the age of 73. Burke. 'Pot & Presidents.' in *Green Egg*. CA. June 21, 1975

[42]"That might explain some cultural differences." Aldrich, Michael, Ph.D. 'On use of marijuana by slaves in colonial times.' in *Best of High Times*. vol. 10. 1991. p. 61

[43]Hakluyt, *Divers voyages touching the discoverie of America*. London 1582

[44]Pereira, J. *Elements of Materia Medica & Therapeutics*. Lea & Blanchard. Philadelphia PA. 1843

[45]Taylor, Bayard. *A Journey to Central Africa*. G.P. Putnam. New York NY. 1854

and Surgical Journal published a report in 1857 that specimens of hashish tested from Damascus contained about 25 percent opium.[46]

Hashish was soon adopted by trendy socialites reaching for the outrageous. Mordecai Cooke, who inspired the hookah-smoking caterpillar in *Alice in Wonderland,* noted that chewing bhang mixed with red betel was the latest vogue.[47] Frederick Hollick's *Marriage Guide* recommended the consumption of hashish for marriages in trouble, as a sexual stimulant "of extraordinary power."[48]

Next it was seized upon by the moralizing Puritanical literati as a device to symbolize all vice and abandon, which had to be punished. The author of *Little Women,* Louisa May Alcott, wrote a play in which a character cries out, "I am mad, for I, too, have taken hashish!"[49] Thomas Bailey Aldrich's short poem, "Hascheesh," first describes beautiful dreams under its influence, but soon ugly creatures appear from a black hole and crawl toward him. "Away, vile drug! I will avoid thy spell. ... Honey of paradise; black dew of hell!"[50] One can only wonder what these people were really taking, and which experiences were purely the fantasy of the writer.

In one Hearst magazine's lurid drug-horror story, fire breaks out in the hold of a ship. Smoke overwhelms and intoxicates the passengers, who become excited and talkative. Soon they are in a stupefying frenzy. The crew is senseless and unable to function. Most on board perish, but a few are rescued from the "soporific fumes of hashish" from the "burning jute." The author's mistake was due to the jute fiber's recently adopted nickname, "New Zealand hemp."[51]

Back in the real world, in 1860, the Ohio Medical Society was the first modern official commission to catalogue conditions in which cannabis had been successfully used.[52] Among those men-

---

[46]Bell, Dr John. 'On the Haschish or Cannabis Indica.' in *Boston Medical & Surgical Journal.* 1857. vol. 56. pp. 209-216

[47]"Young America is beginning to use the 'bhang,' so popular among the Hindoos, though in rather a different manner ... a mixture of bruised hemp tops & toe powder of the betel, rolled up like a quid of tobacco." Cook, Mordecai C. *The Seven Sisters of Sleep.* London England. 1860

[48]Abel. *op. cit.* also "Women of Atala capture men & induce them to drink an intoxicating beverage made with cannabis indica. This potion endows the men with great sexual prowess, of which the women take advantage for enjoyment. A woman will enchant him with attractive glances, intimate words, smiles of love & then embraces. In this way she induces him to enjoy sex with her to her full satisfaction. Because of his increased sexual power, the man thinks himself stronger than 10,000 elephants & considers himself almost perfect." Hindu *Bhagavat-purana.* Canto 5, ch. 24:16

[49]Alcott, L.M. 'Perilous Play.' 1869. in *Tales of Hashish.* Kimmens, A.C., ed. Wm. Morrow. New York NY. 1977. p. 228

[50]Aldrich, T. B. *The Poems of Thomas Bailey Aldrich.* Houghton, Mifflin & Co. New York NY. 1882. p. 36

[51]Robertson, Morgan. 'The Poison Ship.' in *Harper's New Monthly.* 1915

[52]Ohio State Medical Society. *Transcripts of 15th annual meeting.* White Sulphur Springs OH. June 12-14, 1860

tioned were neuralgia, nervous rheumatism, mania, whooping cough, asthma, muscular spasms, tetanus, epilepsy, infantile convulsions, palsy, uterine hemorrhage, dysmenorrhea, hysteria, alcohol withdrawal and loss of appetite.

Indian hemp use was a major medical breakthrough. Virtually every president from the mid-19th century, right up until prohibition, routinely used cannabis medicines.[53] Abraham Lincoln's wife was prescribed it for her nervous breakdown after his assassination.

From Soda Parlors to Jazz Clubs

In Baltimore, a pleasant and popular hashish candy was sold over the counter at soda parlors and drugstores in the city's business district.[54] "Tilden's C. indica Extract" was sold for six cents. Popular "Gunjah Wallah Co. Hasheesh Candy" was described in newspapers as "a most pleasurable and harmless stimulant." *Scientific American* recognized in 1869 that "The cannabis indica of the United States Pharmacopoeia, the resinous product of hemp, grown in the East Indies and other parts of Asia, is used in those countries to a large extent for its intoxicating properties, and is doubtless used in this country for the same purpose to a limited extent."[55]

The Turkish bazaar at the 1876 American Centennial Exposition in Philadelphia proudly featured hashish smoking. Some pharmacists in the city stocked 10 pounds or more of hashish, in case people wanted to take home a souvenir of the festivities.[56]

The Exposition sparked a lively interest in privately operated—and profitable—smoking parlors. H.H. Kane's review of a New York hash parlor in 1883 described swirling gold dragon chandeliers casting a light show across men and women in diaphanous gowns eating cannabis treats, smoking ganja and drinking coca-leaf tea as they recline on plush divans surrounded by rich Oriental carpets and tapestries. "There is a large community of hashish smokers.... All visitors, both male and female, are of the better classes and absolute secrecy is the rule. The house has been open about two years."[57] Such parlors could be found in New Orleans, Philadelphia, Boston and Chicago, "but none so elegant as this."

American agronomists planted Indian hemp everywhere to try to produce as good a product as from Bengal. The grand experiment

---

[53]Herer. op. cit. p. 55
[54]Grover, G.W. 'Shadows Lifted or Sunshine Restored in the Horizon of Human Lives.' in Kupferbert, T., ed. *The Birth Book*
[55]*Scientific American*. 1869. no 21. p. 183
[56]True, R.H. & Klugh, G.F. 'American Grown Cannabis Indica.' in *Proceedings of the American Pharmaceutical Association*. 1883. no 67. pp. 944-949
[57]'A Hashish House in NY: Curious adventures of an individual who indulged in a few pipefuls of ... hemp.' in *Harper's New Monthly*. 1883. v. 67. pp. 944-949

moved into the 20th century. Victor Robinson's 1912 "Essay on Hasheesh" couched the sensory experience in terms of space travel.

After the Civil War, hard-working African-Americans continued to be gainfully employèd in the labor of farming, harvesting and breaking hemp. Despite the deteriorating situation of the hemp fiber market, many of them were still employed in manufacturing cordage and rough bagging for the southern market.[58]

In the early 20th century, hemp farmers still depended on "the labor of Negroes."[59] The decline, however, continued. Eventually, more and more African-Americans moved to the cities, looking for new opportunities in households and factories. They used their musical talent to create a thriving circuit of clubs, where cannabis smoking was just another part of the scene.

During alcohol prohibition, as liquor became more expensive and legal penalties more harsh, legal cannabis became an attractive alternative. Hash was cheap and readily available in New York City, which had a thriving network of 1200 hash parlors by the late 1920s.[60] A musical number by the Flying Colors called "Smokin' Reefers" opened in a review on Broadway in 1932 starring "Mr. Belvedere," Clifton Webb. The lyrics called it "the stuff that dreams are made of, ... the thing that white folks are afraid of."[61] In the 1930s, "reefer" songs were the rage of the jazz world. Among them were Louis Armstrong's "Muggles" and "Song of the Vipers,"[62] Cab Calloway's "That Funny Reefer Man," Fats Waller's "Viper's Drag," and many more by lesser known artists recorded by studios like Columbia, Victor and Bruhnswick—songs with titles like "Viper's Moan," "Texas Tea Party," "Mary Jane," and the "Mary Jane Polka." Even Benny Goodman had "Sweet Marihuana Brown," also recorded by the Barney Bigard Quartet.

By now, Hearst's propaganda machine was running smoothly. *Literary Digest* contrasted lurid headlines with known facts and reported that the *reefer* craze led to parties where spontaneous music broke out without "any of the yelling, dashing about, playing of crude jokes or physical violence that often accompany alcoholic parties; under the effects of marihuana, one has a dread of all these things. Sensuous pleasure is the beginning and the end."[63]

---

[58]Moore. op. cit. p. 110
[59]Ibid. pp. 81, 94
[60]Brecher, Edward M. & the editors of Consumer Reports. *Licit & Illicit Drugs*. The Consumers Union Report. Little Brown & Co. 1972
[61]Abel. op. cit. p. 220
[62]Armstrong "smoked pot daily." Giddins, Gary. *Satchmo*. Dolphin Books/Doubleday. New York NY. 1986, 1988. pp. 42, 118-120, 128, 189+
[63]'Facts & Fancies About Marihuana, It's non-habit-forming & gives users delusions of grandeur.' in *Literary Digest*. NY. Oct. 24, 1936. pp. 7-8

The cannabis scene merged with the jazz scene, and both were forced more or less underground when prohibition hit in 1937. All that was necessary to see cannabis as evil was to label it "narcotic."

The Short History of Cannabis Prohibitions

For the first 9200 years of human consumption and use of the hemp plant, cannabis prohibition did not exist.

Then, in the late Dark Ages, the medieval Inquisition prohibited cannabis ingestion in Spain in the late 12th century, then in France in the 13th. While embracing wine as a Sacrament and tolerating alcohol (forbidden to Moslems), the church hierarchy systematically banned most other natural remedies. Anyone using hashish, to heal or otherwise, was branded a *witch*. Those accused of witchcraft were often tortured until they either confessed or died. In either case, their property was taken and divided among the Inquisitors.[64]

Over in Egypt, a favorite gathering place for hashish connoisseurs was the Garden of Cafour in Cairo. "The green plants which grow in the garden of Cafour replaces in our hearts the effects of old and noble wine," said a poetic tribute to the renowned spot. Suddenly, in 1253 the army closed the garden and all cannabis plants were chopped down and hurled into a massive bonfire seen for miles around.[65] Farmers on the outskirts of the city saw their market opening, and promptly began sowing cannabis seeds. In 1324 and 1378, governors of Cairo sent troops to destroy crops in the outlying areas. Also in the year 1378, the brutal Emir Soudon Sheikhouni of Joneima decided to end the consumption of cannabis by the poor and had all the plants destroyed, and all hashish eaters imprisoned. He also ordered that all those convicted of eating the herb should have their teeth pulled out, and many were subjected to this punishment. By 1393 its use in both Arabia and Egypt had increased.[66]

A few centuries later, Britain colonized India. In 1800 manufacture and sale of resin was banned, but in 1824 the restriction was rescinded.[67] A British government study reported that use of *charas* "was found on examination to be not more prejudicial to health than ganja or other intoxicating drugs."[68]

In the 18th century Sultan Morat IV banned alcohol, cannabis and tobacco in Turkey, and used the prohibition to persecute his

---

[64]Herer. op. cit. p. 50
[65]Abel. op. cit. p. 44
[66]Lewin, Louis. in *High Times Encyclopedia*. op. cit.
[67]In 1790 duties were first levied on alcohol & other intoxicants by the British upon landlords in India. Regulation to license the manufacturer & vender of cannabis preparations was added in 1793.
[68]*Report of the Indian Hemp Drugs Commission, 1893-94*. op. cit. vol. 3:16

political enemies. Napoleon prohibited its use by his men in Egypt in 1800, with little noticeable effect.[69] Decades later, yet another attempt to suppress hashish was made when the Egyptian emir handed down a law in 1868 making mere possession a capital offense. However, in 1874, hashish importation was again allowed with a set duty, but possession was still prohibited. In 1877, the sultan of Turkey ordered a new campaign to seize and destroy all the hash in Egypt, followed by another law in 1879 making importation illegal.

In 1884, growing cannabis became a criminal offense, but customs officers could sell the confiscated hashish outside the borders. The profit was divided among informers and officials responsible for the seizures. These laws had little effect on the use of hashish in Egypt, yet they were reissued in 1891 and 1894. In 1898, over 10,000 kilos of hashish were seized and over 500 businesses closed because proprietors allowed hashish to be used on site. There were almost 2000 such closures in 1908.[70] South Africa took up the cause, prohibiting cannabis there in 1910. Eventually, the fall of the Ottomans during the First World War brought the Turkish war on cannabis to a halt in Egypt. However, the prohibition potentates kept their power, and in 1944 the Egyptian Government's annual report on narcotics declared, "Cannabis is a thoroughly vicious drug, deserving the odium of civilized people."

Hashish has since risen and fallen in popularity several times. European governments did not understand why American prohibitionists insisted on banning cannabis along with other drugs. However, its social use was not widespread enough there to bring about any serious opposition by the time that international prohibition laws were adopted, and there were supposed to be guarantees for its medical availability, so they went along with the plan.

The Prohibition Mentality

Thomas Jefferson warned America about prohibition. He said that if people let government decide what foods they eat and what medicines they take, their bodies will soon be in as sorry a state as are the souls of those who live under tyranny. American political philosopher Ogden Livingston Mills wrote that freedom of mind is the basis for all other freedoms.[71]

> Human liberty comprises, first, the inward domain of consciousness in the most comprehensive sense: liberty of thought and feeling, ... scientific, moral or theological, ... liberty of tastes and pursuits.

---

[69]Abel. op. cit. pp. 148-149
[70]*Ibid*. pp. 133-134
[71]Mills, Ogden Livingston (1884-1937). 'On Liberty.' in *Addresses & Essays*. [S.1. s.n., 1935-1936]

When the tentacles of the anti-alcohol "temperance" movement began spreading across the United States, a young politician named Abraham Lincoln was outraged. "Prohibition," he said in December 1840, "makes a crime out of things that are not crimes. ... A prohibition law strikes a blow at the very principles upon which our government was founded."

Prohibition, or temperance, got its boost to legitimacy in the late 19th century, when investigative reporters called "muckrakers" began to uncover all sorts of social problems in America, like child labor and poverty. They focused their rage on alcoholism, tobacco and "snake oil" scams—worthless patent medicines. In their zeal not to miss anything, they also caught up in their nets medicines like cannabis, which worked in many cases. While the muckrakers were busy going after the flimflam medicine road shows, they missed the real slight-of-hand production going on in the prohibitionist arena.

The medical profession was left to fight alone for access to the herb. And fight they did. They held off nearly a half-century of attacks. In the early 1900s, prohibition fanatics like Dr. Harvey Wiley of the Agricultural Department's Bureau of Chemistry even wanted to ban caffeine-containing drinks such as Coca-Cola.[72] The Pure Food and Drug Act of 1906 required the listing of cannabis and narcotics on the labels of patent medicines for interstate commerce.[73]

Congress rarely heard any witness defend opiates or cocaine, but during the January 1911 Foster Anti-Narcotic Bill hearings, Dr. Charles West of the National Wholesale Druggists Association attacked the bill for including cannabis and its derivatives. West pointed out that cannabis was not a habit-forming drug. The AMA and the Drug Trade Section of the New York Board of Trade also came out in opposition to the Foster bill.[74] Albert Plaut, representing the New York pharmaceutical firm of Lehn and Fink, objected to the inclusion of the herb with opium, morphine and cocaine.[75] *The American Druggist Pharmaceutical Record* editorialized against the prohibitionists' zeal, in "The Dangers of Enthusiasm."[76] The editors called for a bill like the 1906 District of Columbia Pharmacy Act, with no mention of cannabis. This was roughly what Congress enacted in 1914.[77] The news media continued to crusade, and every-

---

[72]Musto, David F., MD. *The American Disease: Origins of Narcotic Control.* The Colonial Press Inc. Clinton MA. 1973. p. 12. In a compromise, the company agreed to take out the coca but keep the cafeine.
[73]Within a few years of implementing this simple device, it was estimated that patent medicines containing such drugs dropped in sale by about a third. *Ibid.* p. 22
[74]*Ibid.* p. 45
[75]*Ibid.* p. 217
[76]Vol. 58, no. 2
[77]Musto. op. cit. p. 269:89

one got into the act. *The New York Times* misreported that cannabis
had "practically the same effect as morphine and cocaine."[78]

Prohibitionists had their biggest victory when they got the 18th
Amendment to the *United States Constitution* passed in 1919, banning alcohol. Gang warfare erupted from coast to coast, centered in
Al Capone's Chicago. By 1933, the country had had enough of it
and passed the 21st Amendment, repealing the policy of prohibition.

In retrospect, the Assistant Director of prohibition enforcement,
Harry J. Anslinger, admitted,[79]

> Prohibition, conceived as a moral attempt to improve the American way
> of life, would ultimately cast the nation into a turmoil. One cannot help
> but think in retrospect that prohibition, by depriving Americans of their
> "vices," only created the avenues through which organized crime got its
> firm foothold.

But Why Pick on Cannabis?

What is it that prohibitionists find so terrible about people getting
high, especially with cannabis? Reasons have varied. Some people
just don't like the idea of other people having fun. Charles Towns,
representing the interests of a commercial drug and alcohol hospital
in New York, explained this position in 1911.[80]

> To my mind it is inexcusable for a man to say that there is no habit
> from the use of that drug. There is no drug in the *Pharmacopoeia* today
> that would produce the pleasurable sensations you would get from
> cannabis, no, not one. ...
> Of all the drugs on earth I would certainly put that on the list.

An American stunned the delegates to the international Hague
Conference by declaring that Californians were frightened by the
large influx of Hindus "demanding cannabis indica" and dragging
"the whites into their habit." He wanted the plant outlawed.[81]

While most spokespersons for the drug trades testified against
federal regulation of cannabis, one said that, while it was "used only
to a slight extent in this country," he heard there was a demand for it
"in the Syrian colony" in New York. He concluded that the evil was
small, but cannabis should still be included in the bill.[82]

As early as 1919, federal officials blamed cannabis for violence
among Mexican prisoners in the Southwest. Although employers
welcomed them in the 1920s, Mexicans were also feared as a source

---

[78]*New York Times*. July 30, 1914
[79]Anslinger, Harry Jacob. *The Protectors: The heroic story of the narcotics agents*.
Farrar, Straus. New York NY. 1964
[80]Musto, D. *The American Disease*. Colonial Press. Clinton MA. 1973. pp. 47, 217
[81]Henry Finger. 1911. in Bonnie, Richard & Whitebread, Charles. 'Forbidden Fruit.'
in *Virginia Law Review*. vol. 56:6. p. 971
[82]Dr. William Jay Schieffelin of NY. in Musto. op. cit. pp. 217-218

of crime and deviant social behavior. Coincidentally, they also often smoked cured cannabis herbs to relax. By the mid-twenties, horrible crimes were routinely attributed to "marihuana-crazed" Mexicans. Legal and medical officers in New Orleans published articles claiming many crimes could be traced to marijuana, which they said was a sexual stimulant that removed civilized inhibitions.[83] Real surveys of crime and delinquency clearly demonstrated that Mexicans exhibited "delinquent tendencies less than their proportion of the population would entitle them to show." When the records of one officer who adamantly denounced the "Mexican crime wave" were examined, it was discovered that he had overestimated the proportion of Mexican arrests by 60 percent.[84]

Propagandist and key Anslinger ally Courtney Cooper wrote,[85]

> There is only one end for the confirmed marihuana smoker, and that is insanity. Therefore, it might be of interest to know that one of the main selling places ... is in the vicinity of high schools. ... Apartments are run by ghoul-minded women; in such apartments high school students gather. A girl wanted to dance. Immediately, everyone wanted to dance. ... Girls began to pull off their clothes. Men weaved naked over them; soon the entire room was one of the wildest sexuality.

Music and new dance crazes were another target. Accused of encouraging sex on the dance floor, the tango, hesitation waltz, turkey trot, black bottom and the Charleston were all denounced as licentious. The Kansas City, Missouri school superintendent mused, "This nation has been fighting booze for a long time. I am just wondering whether jazz isn't gong to be legislated against as well."[86]

Spearheaded by authoritarian movements like the Fascists in Italy,[87] the drive for total drug criminalization moved to the international level. Even there, the medical profession was able to mitigate their impact. The Second Geneva Conference, sponsored by the League of Nations in 1925, allowed social use of the herb, but limited international trade to "medicinal and scientific" consumption and use. The United States, however, refused to sign the treaty because it was not strict enough.[88]

Near the end of alcohol prohibition, one tactic for getting alcohol legalized again was to blame other substances and ethnic groups for the problems which had previously been blamed on alcohol, and to

---

[83]*Ibid.* p. 219

[84]Helmer, J. *Drugs & Minority Oppression*. Seabury Pr. New York NY. 1975. p. 59

[85]Cooper, C.R. *Here's to Crime*. Little Brown. Boston MA. 1937. pp. 333-338

[86]Abel. op. cit. p. 198

[87]Black, Winifred. 'Mussolini Leads Way in Crushing Dope Evil: Italy jails smugglers & peddlers for life with no hope of pardon; US acting at last.' in Hearst newspapers. March 9, 1928.

[88]Musto. op. cit. p. 202

tie alcohol to theories of racial purity. A classic example was written by Dr. A.E. Fossier in 1931.[89]

> The debasing and baneful influence of hashish and opium is not restricted to individuals, but has manifested itself in nations and races as well. The dominant race and most enlightened countries are alcoholic, whilst the races and nations addicted [sic.] to hemp and opium, some of which once attained to heights of culture and civilization, have deteriorated both mentally and physically.

The American Coalition was a racist group whose stated goal was to "keep America American." Prominent member C.M. Goethe of California, claimed that marijuana and the problem of Mexican immigrants taking jobs from whites were clearly linked.[90]

> Marijuana, perhaps now the most insidious of our narcotics [sic.], is a direct by-product of unrestricted Mexican immigration. Easily grown, it has been asserted that it has recently been planted between rows in a California penitentiary garden. Mexican peddlers have been caught distributing sample marijuana cigarettes to school children. Bills for our quota against Mexico have been blocked mysteriously in every Congress since the 1924 Quota Act. Our nation has more than enough laborers.

And so a combination of racism, vested financial interests, scapegoating, fear of differences, and power-hungry meddling came into play against cannabis. Held in check at every bend, the prohibitionists in 1937 made a surprise attack by having the Treasury Department introduce a routine tax revenue bill under the name "Marijuana Tax Act" before a small Congressional committee. The deck was solidly stacked in their favor.

---

[89]Bonnie & Whitebread. 'The Marijuana Conviction, Part One. The Birth of Prohibition.' in *Common Sense for America*. Washington DC. Spring, 1987. p. 15
[90]in *New York Times*. Sept. 15, 1935. in Musto. op. cit. p. 220

17

QUESTIONS OF SOCIAL USE ARISE

To dispel any possible misunderstandings, we will state up front that we remain unconvinced that anything people do "just to have fun" is inherently evil. Quite the contrary, we hold that some of our most satisfying and important creative experiences are achieved amid playful diversion, to the betterment of both the individual and society at large. To be objective about this very subjective matter, we have set aside the pseudo-moralistic stigma attached to cannabis use and accept that being human is meant to be somewhat fun. Amid all this serious research, let's not take ourselves too seriously. That tendency is part of the problem we face today.

Like anything else, cannabis is inherently good,[1] but subject to misuse. The herb is used to raise the spirits, improve the mood, elevate the consciousness—in other words, to primarily enhance the life experience, not avoid it. For most of history, a person's use of cannabis was as accepted as having a dog or eating broccoli: Not everyone did it, but no one thought much about those who did.

However, in response to some ugly rumors, a question was raised in the British House of Commons on March 2, 1893, as to the effects of hemp drugs. This led to an in-depth two-year study on the subject and an eight volume report well over 3,280 pages. *The Report of the Indian Hemp Drugs Commission* confined its attention to effects of a "physical, mental or moral nature. ... They now unhesitatingly give their verdict against such a violent measure as total prohibition in respect of any of the hemp drugs."[2]

The Commission found that "It has been clearly established that the occasional use of hemp in moderate doses may be beneficial; but this use may be regarded as medicinal in character." The risk of bronchitis was noted, but "moderate use of hemp ... appears to cause no appreciable physical injury of any kind, ... no injurious effects on the mind ... (and) no moral injury whatever."

In sum, it stated:

Total prohibition of the cultivation of the hemp plant for narcotics, and of the manufacture, sale or use of the drugs derived from it is neither nec-

---

[1] *Bible*. '...and God saw that it was good.' Genesis 1:12. 'Every creature of God is good, and nothing to be refused if it be received with thanksgiving.' 1 Timothy 4:4
[2] *Report of the Indian Hemp Drugs Commission, 1893-94*. Johnson Reprint Corp. New York NY. 1971. 9 vols., map. originally: British Government Central Printing House. Simla/Calcutta, India. 1894. 8 vols.

essary nor expedient in consideration of their ascertained effects, of the prevalence of the habit of using them, of the social and religious feeling on the subject and of the possibility of its driving the consumers to have recourse to other stimulants or narcotics which may be more deleterious ... There are well known cases in which intoxication from alcohol has led to crimes.

It discussed various charges against the herb, and noted that when "subjected to careful examination, the grounds on which the allegations are founded prove to be in the highest degree defective."

Further Behavioral & Scientific Studies

A series of studies by the United States government in Panama from 1925 to 1930 came to essentially the same conclusions. The department surgeon in charge of the inquiry reported in 1929 that "use of the drug is not widespread and ... its effects upon military efficiency and upon discipline are not great. There appears to be no reason for renewing the penalties formerly exacted."[3] In 1931, a third and final Canal Zone investigation was begun. Once again the committee found no evidence to link cannabis with problems of morale or delinquency.[4]

The physician Colonel J.M. Pholen later reviewed the record:[5]

There is no hesitancy in saying that the reputation of marijuana as a troublemaker in the Panama department was due to its association with alcohol, which, upon investigation, was always found the prime agent. ... The legislation in relation to marihuana was ill-advised, that it branded as a menace and a crime a matter of trivial importance. It is understood that this legislation is furthermore a serious detriment to the development of a hemp fiber industry in this country. Finally, it is hoped that no witch hunt will be instituted in the military services over a problem that does not exist.

Dr. Walter L. Treadway, head of the United States Public Health Service Division of Mental Hygiene, examining these and other reports in 1937, noted,[6]

Cannabis indica does not produce dependence as in opium. ... There is no dependence or increased tolerance.... As with alcohol, it may be taken a relatively long time without social or emotional breakdown.

Marijuana is habit forming, although not addicting in the same sense as alcohol might be with some people, or sugar or coffee.

3Abel, E. *Marihuana: The First 12,000 Years*. Plenum Press. NY NY. p. 206-207
4Siler Commission. *Canal Zone Papers*. US GPO. Washington DC. 1931. p. 106
5in Military Surgeon. 1943. Sloman, Larry. *The History of Marijuana in America: Reefer Madness*. Bobbs-Merrill Company. Indianapolis IN. 1979. p. 161-163
6Treadway was not called on by Congress to testify at the Marijuana Tax hearings. Musto, David F., MD. *The American Disease: Origins of Narcotic Control*. Colonial Press. Clinton MA. 1973. p. 226

Nonetheless, prohibitionists banned hemp in 1937. But that was not the end of the matter. Within a few years, the medical community made an appeal to reason. Scientific work by the New York La Guardia Committee in 1944 and 1945 made "a substantial contribution to existing clinical and pharmacological knowledge of the subject."[7] Previous medical conclusions were supported by the studies. Cannabis smoking, as commonly practiced in America, "does not lead directly to mental or physical deterioration, does not develop addiction or tolerance as is characteristic of opiates, and is not a direct causal factor in sexual or criminal misconduct."[8] Using modern methods of standardization and control, as afforded by the clinical laboratory at New York's Welfare Hospital, the medical team systematically conducted blood chemistry tests, roentgenograms, electrocardiograms, electroencephalograms, psychological tests, Rorschach interpretations, etc.[9] It noted increased feelings of relaxation, disinhibition and a sense of self-confidence, expressed primarily through oral rather than physical activity. The basic personality structure was not changed. The panel's conclusion was "Marijuana is not a drug of addiction. ... Those who have been consuming marijuana for a period of years showed no mental or physical deterioration which may be attributed to the drug. ... Publicity concerning the catastrophic effects of marijuana smoking in New York City is unfounded."

Ganja in Jamaica,[10] a seven year study of moderate and heavy consumers in that country, found no medical symptoms to differentiate cannabis smokers from nonsmokers. "Despite its illegality, ganja use is pervasive, and duration and frequency (of use) are very high. It is smoked over a longer period in heavier quantities with greater THC potency than in the United States without deleterious social or psychological consequences."[11] As part of this study, sponsored by the United States National Institute of Mental Health, researcher Marilyn Bowman conducted intensive psychological

---

[7]Walton, R.P., Dept of Pharmacology, Medical College of SC. 'The Marihuana Problem: Review of NY mayor's committee report.' in Science. vol 101:2680. May 25, 1945. p. 538-539

[8]New York Mayor's Committee Report. *The Marihuana Problem in the City of New York*. State of NY. 1946. reprinted by Scarecrow Reprint. Metuchen NJ. 1973.

[9]72 subjects. 48 with a history of cannabis smoking. All drawn from the social level in which use was most likely to appear.

[10]"An objective study which not only exposes but demolishes many emotional & *fright symbollic*" myths about cannabis, per Raymond P. Shafer, who headed the 1972 US Commission on Drugs. in Sullivan, W. 'Marijuana study finds no serious harm." in *NY Times*. July 9 1975. p. C-2

[11]Rubin, Dr. Vera & Comitas, Lambros. *Ganja in Jamaica: A medical anthropological study of chronic marijuana use*. Mouton & Co. Anchor Books. New York NY. 1975 also available as *Jamaican Studies, 1968-1974*. Institute for the Study of Man. 3401 Science Center, Philadelphia PA.

evaluations of regular heavy consumers there in 1972, and reported there was "No impairment of physiological, sensory and perceptual-motor performance, concept formation, abstracting ability and cognitive style and tests of memory."

Another series of tests was made on an indigenous and accepted herb consuming population, this time in Costa Rica in 1980. The thorough and comprehensive study found once again that there was no distinguishable harm that could be attributed to cannabis usage.[12]

Despite decades of research, the worst known social and psychological effect of cannabis appears to be its effect on prohibitionists who do not use it. Their problem is not one of consumption, but a mental block that limits them to thinking of this therapeutic herb as a "dangerous drug." Let us look at some of the scientific data and the major findings of these many studies.

Effects on Personality & Motivation

In this age when both the President and Vice President are former cannabis smokers, with others that sit in Congress; and when top athletes and corporate heads are punished for failing urine tests—it seems ludicrous to question their motivation.

Nor is there substantial proof that their climbs to power were motivated by the herb. Most people use cannabis to relax, not for work. It might inspire one to engage in creative pursuits rather than the mundane, so they may feel less driven but more satisfied with life. Linking cannabis to an *amotivation syndrome* is difficult, at best. While the overwhelming majority of herb consumers are highly motivated, well-assimilated and productive members of society, amotivation is spread throughout society and, in the words of the National Academy of Science, occurs "in the absence of marijuana."[13] Reports are vague and often focus on anecdotal stories of an acquaintance who is said to be lazy, but is motivated enough to consume herb. It is easier to blame cannabis for their shortcomings than to face responsibility for their actions or inactivity.

Animal studies seem to indicate a temporary drop in motivation among adolescent monkeys.[14] Two survey studies published in the early 1970s used the California Psychological Inventory test to try to establish a connection in humans.

12Carter, William, editor. *Cannabis in Costa Rica: A study in chronic marijuana use.* Institute for the Study of Man. Philadelphia PA. 1980
13Institute of Medicine. *Marijuana & Health.* National Academy Press. Washington DC. 1982
14Leveritt, M. 'Reefer Madness; While courts send users to prison, scientists ... find little to support dangers of pot.' in *Arkansas Times.* Sept. 16, 1993. p. 11

In one of these, non-smokers scored a little higher on some motivational scales, like socialization, responsibility, communality, and achievement via conformity. Users scored a little higher on other scales, like empathy and achievement via independence. This scoring ratio lead researchers to conclude that herb users have all the "achievement motivation necessary for success in graduate school." Users also rated as more socially perceptive and more sensitive to the needs and feelings of others. Non-users' results were interpreted as meaning that they were "perhaps too deferential to external authority, narrow in their interests and over-controlled."[15] In other words, cannabis users tended toward the rugged individualist ideal aspired to by previous generations than do non-smokers.

In the second, no differences were found in Grade Point Averages or other indices of motivation. In interviews, heavy users revealed that they felt "bitter about society's attitude toward marijuana" and that "being defined as a deviant and law breaker, for something they could not accept as criminal, had driven them into increasingly negative attitudes toward the larger society."[16]

Another study followed 101 subjects over 15 years, from age three to age 18, and found that experimentation and moderate drug use — primarily cannabis — actually correlated with psychological health. The American Psychologist, a scientific peer review journal, reported on the longitudinal study of children by University of California at Berkeley researchers. They found that adolescents who occasionally used drugs were healthier than both drug abusers and drug abstainers. Moreover, years before their drug use began, distinct behavioral problems identified those who abused drugs as teenagers. Drug use is a symptom, not a cause. The report concluded that "current efforts at drug 'education' seem flawed on two counts. First, they are alarmist, pathologizing normative adolescent experimentation … and perhaps frightening parents and educators unnecessarily. Second, and of far greater concern, they trivialize the factors underlying drug abuse, implicitly denying their depth and pervasiveness." Said Jonathan Shedler, "The most effective drug prevention programs might not deal with drugs at all."[17]

A UCLA study of 1380 undergraduates beginning in 1970 categorized the participants into six categories of cannabis use (including no use) for three years, and followed up on those who left college.

---

[15]Hogan, Mankin, et al. 'Personality correlates of undergraduate marijuana use.'

[16]Zinberg, Norman & Weil, A.T. 'A comparison of marijuana users & non-users' in Nature. vol 226:119. 1970.

[17]Shedler, Jonathan & Block, Jack. 'Adolescent Drug Use & Psychological Health: A longitudinal study.' in American Psychologist. May 1990

Neither grades nor any other factor checked by the scientists reflected negative mental or motivational effects from the herb.[18]

In rural Jamaica, anthropologists reported that "rather than hindering, (cannabis) permits its users to face, start and carry through the most difficult and distasteful manual labor. ... Workers are motivated to carry out difficult tasks with no decrease in heavy physical exertion, and their perception of increased output is a significant factor in bolstering their motivation to work."[19] Overall, the study concluded, heavy use "does not diminish work drive or the work ethic." Dr. Joseph Schaeffer found that field laborers generally performed more motions and used more energy after smoking than before, although their overall output did not rise. The cannabis use tended to increase social cohesiveness among the workers in group labor situations. It appeared to make the prospect of long hours in the field more palatable and to increase the laborers' willingness to work: an effect he called the *motivational syndrome*.[20]

The Heaviest Smokers: Coptic Studies

Ethiopian Zion Coptic Church is a 6000 year old religion with cannabis smoking as its central sacrament. A group of members underwent intensive study in 1980. Some participants had smoked at least two to four large cigarettes (each containing 1/4 to 1/2 ounce of cannabis) over 16 hours a day for periods of up to 50 years.[21] After a "complete intensive neurological examination on 31 members" of the Church, the "most impressive thing ... is the true paucity of neurological abnormalities."[22] Heavy cannabis consumers suffered no apparent psychological or physical harm; tolerance appeared to have developed with no acute or chronic side effects.[23]

Prolonged and heavy use of ganja had not resulted in any systematic decrements in mental abilities to suggest impairment of brain or cerebral function. Cognition I.Q. scores were high, and individuals appeared healthy and highly functional.[24] One member underwent further evaluation. Despite measurable amounts of cannabinoids in his body and a history of very long-term use of the herb, he demonstrated no impairment of cognitive, cerebral intellectual or learning abilities. There was no suggestion of damage

[18]1380 undergrads in 1970, 901 in 1972. Brill, Dr. Norman W. UCLA School of Medicine. CA
[19]Rubin & Comitas. op. cit.
[20]Schaeffer, Dr. Joseph H. Ph.D. in *Ibid.*
[21]Lange, R.F. 'Does the IQ go to pot with heavy marijuana smoking?' in *Internal Medicine Alert.* Aug. 17, 1981
[22]Fischer, Kenneth C., M.D. 'Coptic Study.' Florida. 1980
[23]Weiss, Brian L. M.D., P.A. 'Coptic Study.' Florida. 1980
[24]'Cognition & Long-Term Use of Ganga.' in *Science*, No. 213. 1981. p. 465-466

to the central nervous system or to long- and short-term memory ability. Moreover, his ability to adapt to change was very high .25

Performance, Automobiles & Heavy Machinery

A major scientific study on this subject reported back to the Department of Transportation's National Highway Traffic Safety Administration in November 1993. It identified a dose related, "moderate degree of driving impairment which is related to the consumed THC dose. The impairment manifests itself mainly in the ability to maintain a steady lateral position on the road, but its magnitude is not exceptional in comparison with changes produced by many medicinal drugs and alcohol. Drivers under the influence of marijuana retain insight in their performance and will compensate where they can, for example, by slowing down or increasing effort. As a consequence, THC's adverse effects on driving performance appear relatively small."26

A 'driving simulator' is a portable form of impairment testing equipment that measures some impairment from alcohol, cannabis, antihistamines, tranquilizers, stress, etc. The term *tracking* describes the act of following a moving stimulus. With alcohol drinking tracking is significantly impaired for 36 to 48 hours, as are coordination, motor control and reaction time. With cannabis smoking there is only a minor effect on tracking lasting four to eight hours.27 A key difference is that while alcohol brings out risk-taking behavior and aggression, cannabis makes drivers more careful. This is important in drug substitution issues (below).

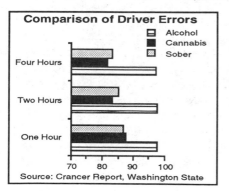

Comparison of Driver Errors

Alcohol / Cannabis / Sober

Four Hours / Two Hours / One Hour

70   80   90   100

Source: Crancer Report, Washington State

A study by the State of Washington Department of Motor Vehicles also revealed that cannabis had very little effect on actual driving ability.28 The Crancer study matched 36 smokers and nonsmokers to measure performance on a driving simulator under the influence of cannabis, of alcohol and sober.

25Shaeffer, J. 'Neuro-psychological Evaluation of Carl Eric Olsen.' CA. 1981
26Robbe, H. & O'Hanlon, J. *HS 808 078: Marijuana & Actual Driving Performance.* US DOT. Nat. Technical Info Svc. Springfield VA. 1993. p. 1
27'Science & the Citizen' in *Scientific American.* 1990
28Crancer, Alfred, et al. 'Comparison of the Effect of Marihuana & Alcohol on Simulated Driving Performance.' in *Science.* vol 164. 1969. pp. 851-854

There was almost no difference in performance between those who consumed cannabis and the sober drivers. Alcohol intoxicated drivers made many more errors than both these categories. Other studies support these results; none have disputed them. While the performance of novice users deteriorated slightly in tests of physical and mental dexterity, experienced smokers sometimes even improved their performance in these tests.[29] Statistics do not show how many accidents are caused by drivers in too big a hurry, or in angry, depressed or distracted moods. In those circumstances, some say that they drive better after smoking cannabis, because they focus on their driving and become more patient, friendly and relaxed.

Safe driving is still a legitimate concern, and there is a way to protect it. Since cannabis is not a major contributor to accidents, urine testing is useless as a safety measure. There remains the point that many accidents are caused by factors such as stress, tiredness and legal, over-the-counter medications that cause drowsiness. Impairment testing would create safer roadways and plug the gaps in enforcement by identifying people impaired by physical and mental factors that do not show up in their urine, breath or blood. Perhaps other policies are also in order. While heavy drinking is accepted in Japan, it has only 20 percent of the United States accident rate, largely due to government policies that get drunks safely home, such as free taxi service for inebriates.

Relationship Between Cannabis & Drug Use

Culturally, cannabis smoking has been historically connected to the use of coffee or tobacco. Cigarettes, not cannabis, comprise the 'gateway drug' that leads to polydrug use.[30] Alcohol and cocaine cause other problems, and cannabis gets the blame.

The National Institute on Drug Abuse pointed out that "The role of these nominally legal drugs as 'gateway' substances to later illicit drugs has led to a reappraisal."[31] Alcohol and tobacco users are far more likely to start using the herb earlier and to use more of it.

At the 1937 Senate hearings on the Marijuana Tax Act, the Federal Bureau of Narcotics admitted there was no connection between cannabis and hard drugs. "In Egypt particularly, where a great deal of hasheesh is used, they tried to show that the marihuana user went

---

29Weil, AT, Zinberg, Norman & Nelson J.M. 'Clinical & Psychological Effects of Marijuana in Man.' in *Science*. vol 162. 1968. p. 1234
30Beach, R., M.D. 'Health.' in *NEA Today*. Nat. Education Assn. November 1990
31Petersen, Robert. *Correlates & Consequences of Marijuana Use*. in Research Issues vol 34. NIDA. Washington DC. 1984. p. 4

to heroin, and when heroin got short he jumped back to hasheesh, but that is not true. This is an entirely different class."[32]

At the meeting of the UN Commission on Narcotic Drugs in 1946, the representative for Mexico suggested that too strict restrictions on the use of this plant might result in its replacement by alcohol, "which might have worse results."[33] This has proven true in Mexico, and also here in the United States.[34] All alcohols, even those intended for drinking, are toxic. Ethanol is the only one that our systems can handle at all, and only in small amounts. Cannabis and THC are non-toxic. Studies show herb users were actually less inclined to use other drugs, including alcohol.[35]

When cannabis is substituted for a less safe substance, there can be beneficial effects. Two surveys in 1992 found that states with decriminalized cannabis have proportionally lower overall rates of drug- and alcohol-related emergencies, and suffer fewer traffic fatalities than states with criminal penalties for marijuana use.[36]

The Costa Rica study showed that regular cannabis users had almost no alcoholism, and preferred to buy the herb instead of rum.[37] The Jamaican study of openly accepted cannabis users found that "No one in the study had ever taken any narcotics, stimulants, hallucinogens, barbiturates or sleeping pills."[38] Recent increases in American cocaine use indicate that many did not turn to the powder until the herb supply was cut, first by federal interdiction of foreign supplies, then by the domestic crackdown.

In Holland, where personal cultivation and possession of less than 30 grams is no longer prosecuted, cannabis use declined over the past decade while heroin use dropped by 33 percent.[39]

President Richard Nixon appointed the "Shafer Commission" to study the "marijuana problem." It reported back in 1972:[40]

---

[32]Anslinger, H. in transcript. *Hearing before a subcommittee of the Committee on Finance*. US Senate doc. 75c 2s. HR 6906. GPO. Washington DC. July 12, 1937

[33]Bruun, Pan & Rexed. *The Gentlemen's Club*. University of Chicago Press. Chicago IL. 1975. p. 195

[34]Passell, Peter. 'Economic Scene: Less marijuana, more alcohol?' in *New York Times*. New York NY. June 17, 1992. p. C2

[35]Zinberg, Norman & Weil, A.T. 'A comparison of marihuana users & non-users.' in *Nature*. vol 226. 1970. p. 119

[36]Passell. op. cit.

[37]Carter, William, editor. op. cit.

[38]Rubin, Dr. Vera. *Jamaican Studies*. Institute for the Study of Man. Philadelphia PA. 1968-1974

[39]Morris, D. 'Collective Conscience Breeds Dutch Tolerance.' in *Oregonian*. Oct. 19, 1989

[40]'Drug Use in America: Problem in Perspective.' *Report of the National Commission on Marijuana & Drug Abuse*. Commissioned by President Richard M. Nixon. US Federal Printing Office. 1973

Nothing uncovered in the current survey supported the long-held notion of many that use of marijuana leads to the use of heroin. ...

The typical behavior pattern is to try marijuana a few times and then to lose interest in it. Alcohol, the most commonly used drug, is strongly associated with violent crime and with reckless and negligent operation of motor vehicles.

Eighteen years later, the 20th annual California State Attorney General's report noted:[41]

Insofar as damage to the individual and society is concerned, the quantitatively most important drugs are alcohol and nicotine, in the form of cigarettes. ... An objective consideration shows that (cannabis) is responsible for less damage to the individual and to society than are alcohol and cigarettes. ... Use of marijuana has reached a plateau at this time, and that usage over foreseeable circumstances will remain about at its present level, as is the case with alcohol.

Moderate herb users show evidence of tolerance to its effect, but no tendency has been demonstrated for personal consumption to increase beyond an individual's preferred level of enjoyment.[42] In fact, many smokers find that as they become more experienced they consume less cannabis, either as an adjustment to meet personal taste or a greater sensitivity to the herb's effect.[43]

In an experiment, a pair of monkeys[44] were fed cannabis resin in milk at a daily dose proportional to a chronic user. They took the mixture, with only minimal to no negative effects. When the portion was then increased to six times that rate, the monkeys simply refused to indulge in it, which ended the study—and saved their lives. They were to have been killed and autopsied.

Relationship Between Cannabis & Crime

Florida State University conducted a study for the State legislature of 45,096 people arrested in 1987 for drug possession, often herbal cannabis. Eighty-eight percent had never been arrested for any property crimes, such as burglary.[45]

The 1972 President's National Commission took a survey of the nation's judges and found that very few of the respondents ap-

41*The Report of the CA State Research Advisory Panel, 20th Annual Report.* 1989. Commissioned by the State of CA Attorney General. Sections suppressed. 1990

42Lex, B.W., Mendelson, J.H. & Mello, N.K. 'Marijuana affect & tolerance: Study of subchronic self-administration in women.' NIDA Monograph Series. no. 49. June 12-15, 1983. pp. 199-204

43Zinberg, Norman & Weil, A.T. 'Cannabis: The first controlled experiment.' in *New Society.* vol 13:329. 1969. pp. 84-86

44Cynomolgus. in *Indian Hemp Drugs Commission.* op. cit. vol 3:192-196

45Morris, David. 'Drug Stories: Studies of users uncover some surprising statistics.' in *Anchorage Daily News.* May 12, 1991. p. J-1

proved of imprisonment to punish marijuana users.[46] The Commission reported back that,[47]

> Marijuana use, in and of itself, is neither causative of, or directly associated with crime, either violent or non-violent. In fact, marijuana users tend to be underrepresented among assaultive offenders, especially when compared with users of alcohol, amphetamines and barbiturates.

At a 1938 conference chaired by Federal Bureau of Narcotics director Harry Anslinger, Dr. Walter Bromberg reported that,[48]

> In considering all the marihuana cases in both General Sessions and Special Sessions courts ... no murders were found among this group of 67, not one murder committed in these six or seven years by a marihuana user. There were no sex cases among these 67. We have, however, 700 odd sex cases from first-degree rape down to exhibitionism, and in the course of the six or seven years, not one of them was a marihuana user, according to history or physical examination. ... In other words, the newspaper accounts must be discounted.

At the same hearing, Dr. Lawrence Kolb, head of the Division of Mental Hygiene in the Public Health Service, noted that "from the standpoint of rehabilitation, it was a rather harmful matter to put a man in prison for four years. He is liable to learn a lot of things in prison and then go out and hate society and use them against society." Asked "What percentage of these people would have been in jail if they had not smoked marihuana?" he replied, "Well, very few of them. ... That applies to a great many users of drugs."

In the September 1942 *American Journal of Psychiatry*, two practicing psychiatrists reported:

> (Cannabis) will not produce a psychosis *de novo* in a well-integrated, stable person. ... Marihuana does not of itself give rise to antisocial behavior. There is no evidence to suggest that the continued use of marihuana is a stepping stone to the use of opiates. Prolonged use of the drug does not lead to physical, mental or moral degeneration, nor have we observed any permanent deleterious effect from its continued use. Quite the contrary, marihuana and its derivatives and allied synthetics have potentially valuable therapeutic applications which merit future investigation.

Raising the Potency Question

There is an often stated claim that the herb has, as a result of prohibition, become more potent and, according to anti-cannabis

---

[46]*Marijuana: A Signal of Misunderstanding*. Technical papers. USGPO. Washington DC. 1973. Append. vol II. p. 845
[47]'Drug Use in America: Problem in Perspective.' *Report of the National Commission on Marijuana & Drug Abuse*. US Federal Printing Office. 1973
[48]Dec. 5, 1938. Sloman, Larry. *The History of Marijuana in America: Reefer Madness*. Bobbs-Merrill Company, Inc. Indianapolis IN. 1979. pp. 152-158

theorists, become even more of a potential but unproven risk. This claim is false on two counts:[49]

First off, strong cannabis has always been available. Hindus and Moslems prided themselves on the potency of their crop for centuries on end. More recently, independent assays of herbal potency revealed in 1973 and 1974 that seeded varieties of the herb averaged from 2.2 percent THC in Mexican to 4.9 percent in Panamanian, while sinsemilla averaged 2.8 percent from California to over six percent in Maui (Hawaii) and Thai.[50] In an open market, this is merely a matter of personal preference. People who use more potent cannabis simply consume less, just as people who drink scotch consume less liquid than beer drinkers. If the market has been skewed toward the high end, it is the result of prohibition pressure.

Secondly, on an open market, potent cannabis is normally viewed as a benefit, not a detriment, since smaller portions are required. American experience with very potent forms goes back over 150 years. Uniform extracts of 10 mg dose levels were listed in the 1930 Parke Davis product catalogue.[51] Furthermore, even massive amounts of cannabis have not been shown to have any ill effect, as shown by the Jamaican and Costa Rican studies above.

One study reported that Americans enjoyed smoking cannabis up to around 22.5 mg THC content, but found amounts of 40 mg and above to be "unpleasant." Smokers in Greece, on the other hand, reported that portions under 60 mg were "poor" and smoked up to 180 mg per session, two or three times per day. Many conventional measures of brain function were used to test the group, and in none was there evidence of damage. These men did not exhibit memory loss, confabulation, disorientation or confusion.[52]

The Pattern of Recent Medical Research

Since the National Institute on Drug Abuse, or NIDA, and all other groups who can fund, sponsor or even get permits for cannabis research have come under the firm control of prohibitionists, a distinct pattern of research has emerged.[53]

In every case, the studies have been structured to find something wrong with cannabis that could be used to rationalize prohibition.

[49]Mikuriya, T. & Aldrich, M. 'Cannabis 1988: Old drug, new dangers — the potency question.' in *Journal of Psychoactive Drugs*. vol 20:1. January 1988. pp. 47-55
[50]Ibid. also Morgan, J. 'American Marijuana Potency: Data versus conventional wisdom.' in *Neuroscience Behavior Review*. 1991.
[51]Ibid.
[52]Fink, Max M.D. 'Study of long-term hashish users in Greece.' in *Hashish: Studies of Long-Term Use*. Raven Press. New York NY. 1977. pp. 153-154
[53]Brecher, Edward 'Marijuana: The Health Questions.' in *Consumer Reports*. March 1975. p. 149

No studies are permitted which might show a beneficial health effect. Reports of health risks are released whenever public attitude shifts toward accepting cannabis and/or when there is a critical vote on cannabis policy. If a procedure is simple and can be readily checked by repeating the experiment or devising a better one, the allegation of adverse effects is relatively short-lived. No damage is proved, and eventually the report is dropped from scientific reference and only cited by prohibitionists. If verification procedures are complex, costly or difficult to undertake, independent studies are not run and the allegations continue to be cited in scientific literature and in the lay press. In these cases, it takes longer for it to happen, but eventually the allegations are either disproven or shown to be grossly exaggerated.[54]

Nonetheless, the police, prohibitionists, schools and news media continue to cite outdated and flawed reports even after they are publicly challenged and exposed. Discredited studies are usually not mentioned by name, although they eventually either resurface under the label "new findings" or are replaced with a new negative study which has yet to be disproven.

Even academic surveys, like the 1982 National Academy of Science and 1987 Harvard Medical Report, are flawed by treating theoretical conjecture and legal fiction as "conventional wisdom" rather than insisting upon conclusive scientific evidence. As a result, they mix legitimate research with spurious claims about implied risks, which biases their conclusions.

The scientific community must break this fraudulent pattern, not only for its own credibility, but also for the practical reason that misleading studies interfere with real scientific investigation.

The Other Side Presents "New" Dangers

We asked NIDA in 1991 to document its "new evidence" that serious health risks give prohibition agencies compelling interest for enforcing an absolute ban on cannabis that override the Constitution, the Bill of Rights and other federal and state laws.

The government responded with a 72-page report containing 61 abstracts under the title, "Harmful Effects of Marijuana." The reports covered: immunology, four; respiratory system, seven; cardiovascular, four; reproduction, 13; behavioral, nine; medical benefits, three; irrelevant, 11; and fraudulent, at least one. Nine were not studies at all, but unsubstantiated or duplicative press reports.

---

[54]Ibid.

Immunology: Four reports.[55] Two found no harmful effect from even "large doses" of cannabis. One of these showed definite immunological damage from tobacco. One was inconclusive but "suggests" possible cannabis risk; however, problems "were significantly more prominent in tobacco smokers" than combination smokers, cannabis-alone smokers or non-smokers. The only report of harm from cannabis was done on *in vitro* lab cultures and was never corroborated by life studies.

Analysis: Tobacco damages human immune response. Lab cultures should not smoke cannabis.

Respiratory: Seven reports.[56] Five of these revealed a link to bronchitis, as had been recorded in 1894 by the Raj Commission. A UCLA study showed that the way cannabis is smoked causes respiratory irritation. Cannabis smokers typically took 70 percent deeper inhalations than tobacco smokers did and held the smoke in four times as long, as discussed in the lung section.

Analysis: Criminalization and the high price of herb encourage an unhealthy smoking pattern. Cannabis irritates the bronchi but is not carcinogenic, and does not cause any serious or permanent lung damage. The abstracts point out that cannabis contains compounds that are not in tobacco but fail to mention that tobacco contains many compounds that are not in cannabis, such as radioactive isotopes.

Cardiovascular: Four reports.[57] All mention that cannabis elevates the heart rate and stimulates the cardiovascular system. One noted that Clonidine mitigated this effect without affecting the "high." When they combined cannabis with exercise, the effect was compound. In one study cannabis smokers were given intravenous injections of cocaine and researchers found that the heart rate went up again. Another said cannabis occasionally caused heart palpitations, but may reduce the frequency of these in cocaine users.

Analysis: Cannabis stimulates the cardiovascular system, as do sex, exercise, salt, adrenaline and numerous other things.

Reproduction: 13 reports.[58] Of these, three dealt with the same study, bringing it down to 11. Four showed normal development. One made a non-specific statement that there are differences between the pregnant cannabis smoker's child and the cocaine or alcohol user's. Two correlated cannabis use to a minor reduction in birthweight and size, while one challenged whether this was significant in scope. One asserted that the initial cry of a cannabis smoker's

---

[55]Records no. 2876, 2492, 2495 & 1701.
[56]No. 2467, 2497, 1412, 6665, 2731, 5119 & 2705
[57]No. 2056, 710, 3886 & 8698
[58]No. 836, 837, 1337, 2618, 3108, 8198, 8448, 8467, 8778, 9463, 9567, 11253 & 15152

baby is likely to be shorter and more variable, but did not establish whether this was harmful or not. Another showed that some pregnant animals should not smoke cannabis, and extrapolated that the same is true for people, although no human studies were presented to support that theory. One dealt with neonatal development, reporting "lower scores in verbal skills and memory which remained prevalent at 48 months" among offspring of cannabis smokers, but admitted it was "not conclusive," and found these same problems (along with lower cognitive scores) for children of cigarette smokers. It was not clear if the cannabis smokers also smoked tobacco. The final one claimed a lowered testosterone in cannabis smoking males, along with a "swift return to normal testosterone levels upon abstention or stimulation."

Analysis of data: Caution is advisable, as regards smoking cannabis while pregnant. Bear in mind that alcohol and tobacco are both known to cause far worse negative effects on reproduction than those alleged of cannabis. Studies found no significant problems among children of cannabis smokers. Smoking cannabis should not be used as a form of birth control.

Behavioral: Nine reports.[59] One demonstrated that smokers tend to finish a whole cannabis cigarette, whether it was potent or mild. Another found "no tendency for consumption to increase" except to relax during "days when anger or depression increased." One suggested that unstable personalities "may" have negative reactions to cannabis, while another showed that more experience with cannabis makes one more comfortable with its effects. Another noted a small correlation (not a causal link) between adolescent use of PCP and cannabis, and suggested that teens should "be cautioned about the danger of planned and/or inadvertent use of PCP."

One showed mixed results regarding cannabis' effect on memory, but noted that just over half the studies done found "short-term memory impairment." Another found only "minimal performance impairment" on only one measure, digit-symbol substitution. Still another study of a group of extremely heavy cannabis smokers were tested and demonstrated a "superior or very superior range of intellectual function" and normal to good "attention, concentration (and) visual-motor coordination." Lastly, a report stated that a mother who occasionally smokes cannabis "probably will not result in ill effects," but judged that, "Perhaps the most serious consequences to be considered in this case are her actions as a poor role model to her children."

Analysis: Cannabis is not for everybody. With all their strengths and weaknesses, cannabis smokers are still normal people. It affects people differently. Smoking cannabis rather than tobacco can be a seen as a positive role model or a negative one. It may affect short-term memory, and it may help with concentration.

Benefits: Three reports.[60] One demonstrated suppression of migraine headaches by cannabis smoking. One showed that either smoking cannabis or use of THC eyedrops helped relieve glaucoma. Another gave a whole list of therapeutic uses, including as an antiemetic in cancer patients, anti-glaucoma, anti-epilepsy, etc.

Analysis: Rather than being harmful, cannabis has some medicinal benefits and can relieve chronic and painful conditions.

Irrelevant: Eleven reports,[61] including six reports on drug testing.[62] One study compared three cigarettes according to "physical appearance, weight, burn rate and deliveries." One discussed prospects for synthetic cannabinoids. Two reports on blood chemistry made no reference to harm or benefits. One said some drug abusers tend to deteriorate physically, but did not distinguish between alcohol and cannabis, so the data was worthless for valid comparative purposes. It stated that this affected appearance and hygiene only, with no detrimental effect on growth or nutritional development.

Drug test reports: five were on urine testing. The sixth noted that testing for cannabinoids in the blood was a better indicator of intoxication. Another reported that eaten cannabis is detectable.

What is the harmful effect of all this? One report called drug testing "a costly testing procedure (that) ... says nothing about the individual's work ability, competence or impairment. ... Drug testing is concluded to be a method for surveillance, not a tool for safety."

Analysis: Cannabis can often be detected by testing body fluids.

Fraudulent Studies: At least one was included as if it had validity.[63] The Heath "Monkey Brain" study, is discussed in the health section. A number of other reports were questionable, at best.

Analysis: This report has no credibility whatsoever.

Press Reports: Nine reports,[64] 15 percent of the total, were simply press releases issued by prohibitionists themselves. They often proposed theories without offering any data to support them. Some referred to discredited studies. One was a review of a 1979

---

[60]No. 2251, 1595 & 2603
[61]No. 748, 7640, 2840, 2460 & 1528
[62]No. 2452, 3634, 2615, 2719, 2900 & 2622.
[63]No. 2616
[64]No. 6599, 2899, 1515, 8063, 2902, 2558, 5371, 4059 & 8057

book written by former CIA propagandist[65] Gabriel Nahas, out of "personal concern that (cannabis) might be legalized,"[66] which included statements Nahas later retracted.

Analysis: These reports have no credibility whatsoever.

Summary Review of the Prohibition Data

On analysis, the most striking characteristic of the federal report, prominently labelled in all capital letters, "HARMFUL EFFECTS OF MARIJUANA (MNM, UTL 63)" is its lack of truly harmful effects.

Often, spurious and unsupported comments were injected into the abstracts for the sole apparent purpose of creating an anti-cannabis bias. Anything that indicated an interest in gathering more research was automatically labelled harmful. Good effects were reported in a slanted way, so as to make them appear bad.[67]

Propaganda was disguised as science, reports were duplicated and even medical benefits were listed as harm. Labelling and filing were downright misleading. One report on how cannabinoids prevent migraine headaches was listed under "Dependence and withdrawal syndrome; Migraine case studies."[68]

Conjecture and hypothesis using "might," "maybe" or "may," are the realm of theory, not the world of science. Not a single study proved that cannabis has caused any social problem. If simple forgetfulness (which was not clearly linked to cannabis) is a crime, then surely arch-prohibitionist Ronald Reagan is the greatest criminal on the planet. The combination of false data and confusing double-talk was, for all intents and purposes, designed to confound honest interpretation of the data and to discourage careful reading. It looked like a desperate attempt to make the report appear thick.

The actual negative effects of cannabis were in every comparison much less than those of tobacco and those of alcohol. The federal government does not claim an "overriding interest" in criminalizing either of these. The inevitable conclusion is that there is no substantial data in existence that can justify or even reasonably support the policy of cannabis criminalization.

---

[65]See chapter 18 on hypocrisy
[66]The blurb continues "...might be legalized without proper scientific investigation into its effects." However, since Nahas had headed up the UN agency in charge of such studies, he was aware of the hundreds of legitimate reports on this topic at the time.
[67]No. 8058. Coptic studies found normal to superior mental & physical functioning in very heavy cannabis users. Listed as 'Brain Damage' & 'Memory Loss,' the back handed description was "absence of any deficit." Lange, R.F. 'Does the IQ go to pot with heavy marijuana smoking?' in *Internal Medicine Alert.* Aug. 17, 1981
[68]No. 1595. El-Mallakh, R.S. 'Marijuana & Migraine.' U of CT Health Center, Dept. of Neurology. Farmington CT. 1987

The questions left unanswered is: How does this information justify putting anyone in prison for using cannabis? And how does sending a person to prison help them?

The real question we need to address is this: What will we find when we have science look for new ways to use hemp's positive benefits for the good of society?

18

RISE OF THE MARIJUANA HYPOCRISY

International law guarantees everyone "the right to freedom of thought, conscience and religion."[1] America is called the "Land of Liberty." The pledge to the flag promises "liberty and justice for all." The Bill of Rights ensures individual freedom.

During the 1980s, America saw these ideals and guarantees sacrificed to the golden calf of the "drug war." Meanwhile, prohibitionists fight a war against reason over the hemp plant. As self-appointed guardians of public morality, their attack on cannabis has dragged on for more than half a century. It is a very real war—with enemies, offensives, front lines and huge military budgets. Truth was its first casualty and justice soon after.

The United Nations' Single Convention Treaty,[2] Article 23, requires governments to "maintain one or more" agencies to regulate compliance—entitlement programs for bureaucrats to meddle in our lives and business. Any treaty that equates cannabis with coca, and discusses making heroin from hemp, ensures irrational enforcement. In early 1992, world leaders publicly drank an alcoholic beverage toast to end drug use. Plans now include concentration camps for thousands of peaceful cannabis consumers. In the words of conservative commentator William F. Buckley:[3]

> Narcotics police are an enormous, corrupt international bureaucracy ... and now fund a coterie of researchers who provide them with 'scientific support' ... fanatics who distort the legitimate research of others. ... The anti-marijuana campaign is a cancerous tissue of lies, undermining law enforcement, aggravating the drug problem, depriving the sick of needed help, and suckering well-intentioned conservatives and countless frightened parents.

"Those who think that this is simply a do-the-crime, do-the-time issue, and nothing more, are fooling themselves. We have crreated a true industry of jails and prisons, as institutionalized and ingrained into the fabric of our society as the automotive and computer industries," wrote Sheriff Michael Hennessey. "...The only

---

[1]"... Includes freedom to change his religion or belief, & freedom, either alone or in community with others & in public or private, to manifest his religion or belief in teaching, practice, worship & observance." *Universal Declaration on Human Rights.* United Nations. New York NY. 1980. Article 18
[2]*Single Convention Treaty on Narcotic Drugs.* United Nations. NY. 1961, 1968
[3]Buckley, William. F. 'Commentary.' in *National Review.* April 29, 1983. p. 495

reasoned answer to this debacle is decriminalization of our nation's drug use laws. ... but who in government will lead the way?"[4]

Rejecting such anti-democratic themes and accepting cannabis use will be more consistent with international human rights law.[5]

Which Ones Are Drugs Anyway?

What do people mean by *drugs*, anyway? Some medicines, surely, including cannabis; but "a pill for every ill" is the theme of synthetic drug industry ads for over-the-counter medications. Maybe dangerous chemicals, but prohibitionists don't seem concerned about real poisons, like toxic industrial waste or household cleaners. Mind-altering chemicals? The body produces these naturally, such as hormones, endorphines, adrenaline and possibly something like THC.[6] Sugar, caffeine and even chocolate alter consciousness, none of which politicians wage war on—at the moment.

Abused drugs? If misuse is the issue, compare the 1985 emergency room admissions: 13,501 for cocaine-related problems, 14,696 for morphine and heroin, combined, and 18,492 admitted for bensodiazepines, a tranquilizer best known by its trade name Valium.[7] Not one person was treated for cannabis overdose.

Health and safety at risk? Mortality statistics speak for themselves. Tobacco kills more than 400,000 people per year. Alcohol kills 150,000—one Texas student died of toxic overdose after just a half-hour tequila drinking contest.[8] Illegal drugs kill 4000 or so. Aspirin kills up to 1000 per year. Cannabis, not one person—not ever, as far as scientists can document.

Habit-forming drugs? Former Surgeon General C. Everett Koop reported that nicotine is as addictive as cocaine or heroin.[9] *The National Review* looked over several studies and found drug use increased in groups under stress, but "Most people can walk away

[4]Hennessey, M. 'Our National Jail Scandal.' in American Jails. July-Aug. 1993

[5]*Universal Declaration on Human Rights.* op. cit. Article 12. "No one shall be subjected to arbitrary interference with his privacy, family, home or correspondence, nor to attacks upon his honor & reputation. Everyone has the right to the protection of the law against such interference or attacks." also Art. 27.1. "Everyone has the right freely to participate in the cultural life of the community, to enjoy the arts & to share in scientific advancement & its benefits."

[6]Hilts, P. 'Scientists learn how marijuana works in brain.' in New York Times. July 21, 1990. pp. 1, 9

[7]23 million of a total 81 million prescriptions filled for this type of sedative in 1985. 'Diazepines (Valium): #1 in Abuse.' Public Citizen Health Research Group. 2000 P St. NW, Washington DC 20036. 1989

[8]'£300,000 tequila girl.' in Daily Mail. London England. Oct. 1, 1992

[9]"Pharmacologic & behavioral processes that determine tobacco addiction are similar to those that determine addiction to drugs such as heroin & cocaine." Koop, C.E. 'Health Consequences of Smoking.' in Surgeon General's Report. Government Printing Office. Washington DC. 1988. p. 9

from high drug use if their lives become more normal."[10] The British *New Scientist* reported that the majority of those who become dependent on cocaine return to moderate use or total abstinence without any treatment at all.[11]

"The worst (drug) problem we face here in Iowa, by far, is alcohol abuse. Yet ... every time I start talking about it, all the television people turn off those cameras and the good quotations I give them never get used," State drug policy director F.H. Mike Forrest complained to the *Washington Post*.

Actually, prohibitionists use the word drugs to mean whatever suits the propaganda mill. In the past it has included alcohol, tobacco and even coffee. Right now it means *illicit*, or illegal, drugs, an arbitrary term based on bureaucratic juggling of lists.

Crimes of Prohibition

The most severely forbidden of all drugs are plants and natural derivatives that bring people pleasure or medical relief.

One federal district attorney declared it is "time to go after the user, and we are doing that," then publicly accused his own predecessor of smoking cannabis, saying he recognized the smell because he himself had recently smoked some.[12]

For policymakers to blame drugs for the crime problem is dysfunctional denial. Prohibition causes crime. Not only does it increase the sheer volume of offenses by making crimes of things that are not really criminal,[13] it also creates opportunities for police brutality, bribery and corruption.[14] Similar gang violence seen in the 1980s and 1990s also came with the ban on alcohol in the 1920s.[15] The murder rate began to rise at the start of Prohibition, increased throughout the ban, then declined for 11 years in a row after it ended. Assaults with firearms rose during Prohibition, then declined for 10 years straight after it ended.[16]

Prohibition increases the frequency and violence of crime—up 4.3 percent in just one year. After five years of the Reagan/Bush war on casual users, violent crime in the United States reached a new high in 1991, according to the federal *Unified Crime Reports*

[10]Thomson, Andrew W. Jr., professor of psychiatry at Dartmouth Medical School
[11]Morris, David. 'Drug Stories: Studies of users uncover some surprising statistics.' in *Anchorage Daily News*. AK. May 12, 1991. p. J-1
[12]Dershowitz, A. 'Drug-user witch hunt exposes hunters, unmasks hypocrisy.' in *LA Times*. CA. Nov. 27, 1988. p. V-5
[13]Lincoln, Abraham. December 1840
[14]Scruggs, K. 'Sheriff among 24 arrested after probe.' in *Atlanta Constitution*. July 15, 1992. p. D2
[15]18th Amendment, effective 1919, repealed by 21st Amend., effective 1933
[16]Ostrowski, James. 'Thinking About Drug Legalization.' *Policy Analysis No. 121*. Cato Institute. Washington DC. 1989. pp. 1-2

compiled from 16,000 local police agencies across the country. Washington DC, the "showpiece" of prohibition, had the highest murder rate of any large city in the world.[17]

Is crime a problem? Government agents commit many of the illegal activities they are supposed to fight, even making and selling crack cocaine.[18] It is well recognized that it is not drug use, but the high black market profit caused by prohibition that is directly responsible for crimes.[19] When Congressman Terry Bruce commented that tobacco "smokers are not breaking into liquor stores late at night to get money to buy a pack of cigarettes," Koop predicted that that would change if tobacco is banned.[20] "That's the difference between a licit and an illicit drug. Tobacco is perfectly legal. You can get it whenever you want to satisfy the craving."[21]

Prohibition enforcement runs on heartless brutality. On August 3, 1989, Bruce Lavoie lay peacefully sleeping in the room he shared with his young son in the village of Hudson, New Hampshire. At five in the morning he was awakened by a loud noise as his whole home was shaken violently. A battering ram had smashed his front door, and a dark band of armed and angry men rushed into his small apartment. Rising to defend his son, Lavoie was shot to death as his little boy watched helplessly. It was the "good guys," a small army of prohibition police agents who found what they were after: one cannabis cigarette butt.[22] Yes, Lavoie was a smoker; but no one is safe from a police state that is mad with greed.

Under state and federal forfeiture laws,[23] police keep much of the cash, cars and real estate taken from drug suspects.[24] People who were never arrested, much less convicted, have had property taken. Bullets pocked the doorway to his bedroom when millionaire Don Scott was shot to death inside his own living room as he pulled

17Reuters News Service. 'Violent crime in US reaches record high.' in *Turkish Daily News*. Aug. 31, 1992. p. 7
18Johnson & Romney. 'LA Police Department may manufacture cocaine for bait in stings.' in LA Times. Oct. 23, 1994. p. B10
19NYPD Deputy Chief Raymond Kelly noted in 1987, "When we say drug-related, we're essentially talking about territorial disputes or disputes over possession. ... We're not talking about where somebody is deranged because they're on a drug."
20Tobacco was banned in VT prisons for 5 months. Cigarettes went for $40/pack at Northwest Correctional Facility, St. Albans. Inmates began to smoke coffee. Guards smuggled tobacco to sell. AP. 'Prison smoking ban eased due to bizarre side effects.' in *Marin Independent Journal*. CA. Nov. 26, 1992. p. A-6
21During Koop's presentation of 'Health Consequences of Smoking.'
22Mauro, T. 'Some worry police out of control.' in USA Today. Nov. 5, 1989
23There, Ben. *Spectre of Forfeiture*. Access Unlimited. PO Box 1900, Frazier Park CA 93225. 1990. also Moore & Hood. 'The challenge to states posed by the federal adoptive drug forfeitures.' in *Civil Remedies in Drug Enforcement Report*. Nat. Assn. of Attorneys General. 444 N. Capitol St. Washington DC. June 1992
24"Beware the scribes ... which devour widows' houses, and for a show make long prayers: They shall receive greater damnation." *Bible*. Luke 20:46-47

a gun to defend his wife and home[25] from armed assailants. They turned out to be a drug task force planning to seize his prime California real estate on charges of growing cannabis.[26] Not only was Scott innocent of growing herb, he didn't even smoke.[27]

Gary Shepherd was a veteran who valued the liberty he had fought for. He smoked marijuana to treat his lingering Vietnam war-related problems and kept a small herb patch growing behind his house. On August 8, 1993, a peaceful Sunday morning, the air was torn by the loud throbbing of propellor blades as an armed helicopter hovered over his back yard and landed. They saw his plants. "We're going to cut them down." Shepherd replied, "You will have to kill me first."[28] He got a gun and told them to leave his land. Police sent in a swat team and blew his brains out, blood spraying across the porch and spattering his horrified lifetime companion and their four year old son, Jake.[29] They proceeded to cut his plants.

Enforcement agencies in Arizona routinely violated a law requiring them to report the value of private property they seized.[30] "We're talking about millions and millions of dollars not being reported," said spokesperson David Bartlett. "This is law enforcement failing to comply with the law. It is a mess."

Corruption and brutality are rampant throughout the system.[31] Police now steal other people's property for personal benefit. Even as he faced rape charges himself, a California police chief cruised around in a silver Mercedes seized from a drug suspect.[32]

A "revolving door" of jobs connects government bureaucracies that draft bills to companies that profit from them. New rules for government contractors require a "good faith effort" to ensure a "drug-free workplace," and withhold contracts from those who do not agree to the policy, which includes urine testing. Carlton Turner, chief prohibition agent under Reagan, initiated laws to force government agencies and private businesses to pay for employee drug

[25]Newton, J. 'Seizure of assets leaves casualties in war on drugs.' in *LA Times*. CA. Oct. 14, 1992. p. A-1. also Mauro. op. cit.

[26]Briggs, Jack. 'Forfeiture!' in *LA Reader*. CA. Dec. 18, 1992. pp. 10-17

[27]in Ventura, CA. Sobel, Ron. 'Violent confrontation ends man's colorful life.' in *LA Times*. CA. Oct. 12, 1992. p. A-1. also 'DA widens inquiry into raid killing.' in *LA Times*. Nov. 15, 1992. p. A-3. et al.

[28]Shepherd-Jones family statement. Brodhead, Kentucky. August 1993

[29]AP. 'KY troopers kill man defending his pot plants.' in *Arizona Daily Sun*. Aug. 10, 1993

[30]Which took effect in 1991. 'Police fail to report asset seizures' in *Arizona Republic*. reprinted in *Homegrown Update*. Phoenix AZ. March-April 1992. p. 4

[31]Pizzo, Fricker & Hogan. 'Shredded Justice: 12 years of criminal misconduct at the Justice Dept.' in *Mother Jones*. Jan. 1993. CA. pp. 17-23

[32]In Newport Beach CA. Wride & Weikel. 'Police chief battles for his career.' in *LA Times*. Nov. 8, 1992. p. A-3

tests, and also worked for a company that sells these tests.[33] Some companies hire secret investigators who pretend to be employees while they finger real workers who use or sell and develop evidence against them.[34]

Many police officers see the "War on Drugs" as a sham.[35] Something is "just not right" in the words of one police newsletter that warned officers to beware of "blind faith," and bluntly stated that prohibition is not a public policy, but a police action.[36]

Who Takes Drugs?

And who uses drugs? You. Me. Everybody uses aspirin, cold tablets and so on. Cartoon characters, athletes and rugged individualist types appear in billboards, cigarette in hand. Sugar and coffee come free with breakfast specials at the corner diner. Look in your medicine and liquor cabinets, your kitchen cupboard, your vitamins, food seasonings and additives. Read package labels.

Certain political bureaucrats get to decide which drugs we can use, and they are not doctors. And only certain people are punished for using forbidden drugs. These same bureaucrats pick and choose whom to prosecute. For example, arch-conservative, anti-communist and prohibitionist Senator Joe McCarthy was a morphine addict. Federal Bureau of Narcotics chief Harry Anslinger admitted he gave morphine to McCarthy illegally for many years, a felony offense.[37]

Before the 1972 Presidential Commission on Drugs report was released, Richard Nixon said, "I am against legalizing marijuana. Even if this commission does recommend that it be legalized, I will not follow that recommendation."[38] His commission did recommend that cannabis be decriminalized, stating among other reasons that alcohol, amphetamines and tranquilizers were more dangerous. During his final days as President and facing criminal charges for his corruption, the disgraced Nixon himself abused all three of these classes of substances, right in the Oval Office.[39]

---

[33]Turner illegally ordered cannabis sprayed with deadly paraquat, then sold phoney paraquat test kits to consumers. Herer, J. *Hemp & the Marijuana Conspiracy: The Emperor Wears No Clothes.* HEMP Publishing. Van Nuys CA. 1991. pp. 82-83
[34]'Security Wrap-up, Drug Use.' in *Security.* June 1989
[35]Levine, Michael. *Deep Cover: The inside story of how DEA infighting, incompetence & subterfuge lost us the biggest battle of the drug war.* Delacourte Press. 1990
[36]Editorial. 'It's time to end the killing of officers in phoney war on drugs.' in *Aid & Abet.* Phoenix AZ. vol 2:2. pp. 1-5
[37]Anslinger, H. & Oursler, F. *The Murderers.* Farrar, Strauss & Cudahy. New York NY. 1961
[38]King, R. *The Drug Hangup.* C.C. Thomas. Springfield IL. 1974. p. 101
[39]Stein, Benjamin J., NY Times columnist. 'Bush's Halcion days.' in *New York Times.* 1991. also Woodward, Bob. *The Final Days.* 1984

Nearly 20 years later in the White House, George Bush, already implicated in cocaine trafficking,[40] was using the powerful sedative Halcion, and the Secretary of State used it when he went overseas. Halcion was described by its maker, Upjohn Co., as an *anxiolytic* drug which literally cuts out anxiety.[41] The drug has been subject to major litigation around the world.[42] Bush finally stopped taking Halcion, not for moral or legal reasons, but "due to the controversy over its use."[43] Cannabis has similar benefit without the bad side effects. In 1992 Bush was a textbook case of someone who could have gained from cannabis. He could have used it for his glaucoma, for his travel sickness, to prevent nausea and vomiting on Japanese officials and to ease the stress of being thrown out of office by angry voters. Bush probably did not smoke cannabis. A former director and major stockholder in Eli Lilly drugs, which sells synthetic THC, Bush would do anything to help his investments.[44]

Yet, amid the fervor, the media have missed one truly sensational drug kingpin report.[45] The CIA has repeatedly been exposed for trafficking heroin and cocaine. A number of federal agents, including Iran-Contra figures John Hull, Oliver North, Admiral Poindexter, General Secord, Lewis Tambs, etc., were indicted in Costa Rica for smuggling and selling cocaine and arms.[46] The State Department refuses to extradite them to stand trial. Ronald Reagan[47] and Dan Quayle,[48] on the other hand, have both smoked cannabis.

---

[40]Snepp, Frank & King, Jonathan. 'The vice president & the contras.' in *LA Weekly*. CA. Oct. 14, 1988. pp. 16-18, 26-38. also Conason, Joe & Kelly, John. 'Bush & the secret Noriega report.' in *Village Voice*. NY. Oct. 11, 1988. pp. 1, 29-32, 115, 116

[41]It makes users alternately supremely confident & then panicky with an unnameable dread. It causes intense, terrifying forgetfulness with a serene bliss about that forgetfulness. Stein, B.J. 'Bush's Halcion days.' in *New York Times*. 1991

[42]Ibid.

[43]The most popular sleeping pill prescribed in the US, it is banned or restricted in 11 countries due to side effects including confusion, amnesia, anxiety, hyper-excitability, paranoia & dizziness. 'Bush said to be off Halcion.' Reuters. 1991.

[44]His 1981 financial disclosure statement & qualified blind trust agreement showed that when Bush assumed office as Vice President, he had been a director of Eli Lilly & Co. from 1977-79 & owned $145,000 worth of stock in the drug company. In 1982, he asked the Treasury Department to change its policies to save Lilly from paying $50 million in back taxes from 1971-75. Bush lied on April 14, 1982 that he had sold his 1500 shares in 1978. It was, in fact, still his single most valuable stock holding. Gerth, J. 'Bush tried to sway a tax rule change & then withdrew.' *New York Times*. May 19 1982. p. A-1

[45]General Electric, world's 2nd largest nuclear & military contractor, owns NBC-TV. Capitol Cities Corp., one of whose major stockholders was former CIA chief William Casey, owns ABC. Other CIA connected people heavily influence the networks & other news media, working as correspondents & editors.

[46]'Cocaine shipped by contra network.' in *The Guardian*. Manchester England. July 22, 1989. also Cockburn, L. *Out of Control*. Atlantic Monthly Pr. NY NY. 1987

[47]Kelly, K. *Nancy Reagan, Unauthorized biography*. Doubleday. NY NY. 1991

[48]'Smoke Screen, inmate sues Justice Dept. over Quayle-pot cover-up.' in Dallas Observer. Aug. 23, 1990. p. 1. also Labaton, S. 'Evidence links '88 Bush campaign to effort to silence accuser of Quayle.' in *New York Times*. May 3, 1992. p. 30

President Bill Clinton[49] and Vice President Al Gore both admit having tried it. None of them were penalized or rejected by voters for having done so. Defending admitted marijuana smoker Douglas Ginsberg as his choice of Supreme Court nominee, Reagan said previous use of cannabis should not be held against anyone; the unanswered criteria is this: *how recent*?

Distortion of Scientific Research

In the long history of cannabis research, almost all the negative reports came out in one brief cluster in the late 1970s and 1980s,[50] long enough to reverse worldwide momentum to relegalize cannabis. The tale begins amid the murky corridors of international spy networks. Lyndon LaRouche and Gabriel Nahas[51] worked in different departments of the OSS, now the CIA.[52] They met after the Second World War in Washington DC, then went to Columbia University to work on their common interests.

Both participated in the cover-up of the Nazi war crimes of Austrian politician Kurt Waldheim. They and others derived political leverage from it during Waldheim's rise to United Nations Secretary General. Despite a professional scandal[53] and lack of qualifications, anesthesiologist Nahas was put in charge of all United Nations grant money for cannabis research, at the suggestion of Waldheim's daughter. His 1971 appointment to its Narcotic Control Board staff entrenched him in the narcotic control bureaucracy for a decade.[54]

Cannabis relegalization appeared imminent during the Ford and Carter administrations. So, at the international level, Nahas, as money-man, handed out grants to special colleagues for "new studies" suggesting any possibility cannabis can be harmful. The first test run with their disinformation was to parade a group of pseudo experts, primarily drawn from the CIA,[55] before the 1974 Senate Internal Security Subcommittee hearings.[56] The fruits of their efforts were again trumpeted as "proving" marijuana harm at a May 1978 symposium, held in Rheims, France. These included Heath's

---

[49]Ifill, Gwen. 'Clinton admits experiment with pot in the 60s.' in *New York Times*. March 30, 1992. p. A-15
[50]Antique & medieval reports of negative side effects, like dysentery, have all been disproven by modern scientific research (except bronchitis)
[51]Pronounced like 'nazi' without the final '-i'
[52]LaRouche in Washington DC, Nahas in Burma (1943) & later in Southern Europe
[53]For his fraudulent report of a cannabis death in Belgium. 1971
[54]Beal, Dana. 'Behind the Cocaine Glut.' *The Realist*. CA. 1990
[55]Hatch, Richard. 'Drugs, Politics & Disinformation.' in *Covert Action*. no. 28. Washington DC. Summer 1987. pp. 23-32
[56]Chaired by Sen. John Eastland. Donner, Frank. *The Age of Surveillance*. Knopf. New York NY. 1980

"Monkey Brain" study,[57] exaggerated lung damage reports, along with a photo of damaged spermatozoa which was deliberately faked. These spectacular claims did not stand up to peer reviews, but the Nixon-appointed head of the National Institute on Drug Abuse, Robert Dupont, declared he was "convinced" by this "new evidence" that marijuana was dangerous.

Reputable experts like Harvard's Lester Grinspoon were lobbying Waldheim to get rid of Nahas for being an embarrassment to science. Robert Gungk[58] eventually exposed Waldheim for his Nazi involvement, with documents declassified in the late 1970s. Then, in July 1978, Dr. Peter Bourne, Carter's drug policy advisor, whose stated goal was to decriminalize marijuana and "make cocaine expensive and hard to get," was exposed in the national media for his own cocaine use by the director of NORML, the National Organization to Reform Marijuana Laws. Criminalization hardliner and DEA head Peter Bensinger took over as policy director.

Nahas staged another press conference at New York University in June 1979, packed with neo-conservative journalists and LaRouche followers preaching a pro-nuclear, anti-cannabis line.

A medical journal reviewed a book devised by Nahas:[59]

To support his essentially moralistic viewpoint ... biased selection and interpretation of studies and omissions of facts abound in every chapter. ... So much of the volume is distorted that one must know the marijuana literature in order to judge the accuracy of each statement.

When former CIA agent Thomas Pauken became head of the government agency ACTION in 1981, he took money away from community self-help programs and put it into anti-cannabis groups.[60] These groups provided logistical support when the same discredited studies were compiled into a manual by the infamous Peggy Mann for organizing against cannabis relegalization in 1985 and trumpeted once again as "new evidence."[61]

Her book became the *Mein Kampf* of cannabis prohibition. To this day, Nahas' work is touted by prohibitionists to imply that cannabis is a danger. In 1992, he launched a similar prohibition assault against Europe, with a group called EurAD.[62]

---

[57]See chapter 14, Brain Studies section.
[58]An OSS agent who had worked on the de-Nazification project after the war.
[59]Review. in *Journal of the American Medical Assn.* April 30, 1973. p. 631
[60]Primarily, Families in Action, American Council for Drug Education, & Parents' Resource Institute for Drug Education (PRIDE). Hatch. op. cit.
[61]Mann, Peggy. *Marijuana Alert.* McGraw Hill. New York NY. 1985
[62]Europe Against Drugs

Playing With Numbers, Playing With Lives

In 1988 the director of the Division of Applied Research and the Office of Workplace Initiatives at the National Institute on Drug Abuse, J. Michael Walsh, testified under oath in federal court that, according to "conservative estimates," the "cost of drug abuse to United States industry" was nearly $50 billion a year. In 1989, George Bush pushed the figure up to "from $60 billion to $100 billion."[63] This staple of prohibition rhetoric is often quoted or enlarged upon by the media without qualification.

Where did that number come from? In 1982 NIDA surveyed 3700 households around the country. A contractor processed the data and found that the overall incomes of households where an adult admitted to ever having smoked cannabis "daily," or at least 20 days out of 30 in any single month in their entire lives, were 28 percent lower than those who did not admit ever having done so.[64] They labelled this difference "reduced productivity due to daily marijuana use," and extrapolated a total "loss" to the general population of $26 billion. Next they threw in estimated costs for all potentially drug-related crimes, accidents and medical care for a grand total of $47 billion in "costs to society of drug abuse."

There are several problems with this, beginning with their gross assumption that cannabis use directly determines income levels. That extra $21 billion was simply a made-up number. The "costs" to *society* were rounded up and shifted to *industry* by Walsh, and NIDA later admitted the figure is "based upon assumptions which need additional validation;" but both NIDA and the media still use it.

Why did data processors resort to the awkward variable of *almost-daily-marijuana-use-for-one-month-ever* as their key to drug use? Researchers had long-term information, right up to the last 30 days, on cannabis use—but there was no decrease in income, and in some cases drug users showed higher incomes than average.

If NIDA accepts that a single month-long cannabis binge reduced productivity, it should also conclude that ongoing use maintained normal productivity. Especially in light of its other findings. The federal agency reported that Utah Power and Light spent $215 less per employee year in health insurance benefits for its illicit drug users than on the control group. Employees who tested positive for drugs at Georgia Power had a higher promotion rate than the company average. Workers testing positive for cannabis only were absent some 30 percent less than average.[65]

63Horgan, J. 'Your Analysis Is Faulty.' in *New Republic*. April 2, 1990. pp. 22-24
64Research Triangle Institute. NC. Ibid.
65Morris, D. 'Drug Stories.' in *Anchorage Daily News*. May 12, 1991. p. J-1

Urine Testing Takes a Retreat from Reality

After exhaustive research, *Scientific American* found that studies usually cited to "prove" the dangers of drug use in the workplace were either shoddy or misinterpreted. The magazine found only one study on workplace drug use that had passed through the standard peer review process for scientific evaluation. That one, published in the *Journal of General Internal Medicine*, studied 180 hospital employees, 22 of whom tested positive after being hired. It found "no difference between drug-positive and drug-negative employees" in performance or supervisor evaluations. Except on one point. Eleven of the negatives were fired during their first year on the job, but none of the positives.[66]

Instead of running to Congress with the good news, NIDA published a 340-page report called *Drugs in the Workplace*. When *Scientific American* asked Walsh about the research, he pointed out three studies in particular.[67]

In a 1985 Navy study, 500 recruits tested positive for cannabis but were admitted anyway. Two-and-a-half years later, the Navy had discharged 43 percent of them, but only 19 percent of those who tested negative during the same period. Mitigating factors invalidate this study, however. The positives were given more frequent tests, thus were more likely to be caught. They had been given false senses of security, since they already "passed" one test. Sure enough, fully a third of them were discharged for failing a later drug test.[68] Correcting the statistics by discounting those cases, the difference between positives and negatives drops to just 10 percent. Surveillance or harassment could easily account for this difference. Conformity is a high priority in the Navy, but cannabis smokers tend to be non-conformist. The positives were constantly monitored by officers eager to get rid of them. They documented no loss of productivity or other misbehavior. But a common headache pill gives positive results for cannabis,[69] and 20 percent of NIDA-surveyed labs falsely identified drugs in clean urine.

The second study was by Utah Power and Light Company. Walsh claimed "a significant difference between drug users and non-users in terms of being involved in accidents, being absent from work and over-utilization of health benefits." Two flaws pop out

---

[66]Ibid.
[67]Ibid.
[68]The only rational conclusion is that people who have used drugs are more likely to do so again, not that they are any more likely to be deficient workers, the only conclusion that might be used to try to justify workplace testing.
[69]Advil. 'Drug Testing in the Workplace.' in *Briefing Paper No. 5.* ACLU. NY. 1990

here. It was an inconclusively small sample, only 12 positives,[70] and the control group was never tested for drugs. The data was worthless on this basis alone. But, to further distort things, eight were tested after they had accidents, and some needed time off to recuperate. Two were tested over performance-related problems. The other two had voluntarily enrolled in a substance-abuse program. High absenteeism almost always precedes, and often leads to, both employee testing and submission to such a program. Moreover, all tested employees were suspended until the results came back, usually three or four days. Researchers contrived the results by adding in both the accidents and the absenteeism due to testing.[71] The claim of "over-utilization of health benefits" was simply a lie. The positives consumed almost 50 percent less in health benefits than did the so-called control group.

The third study, by Georgia Power Company, admitted that it used a biased database, "the problem employee." It compared 116 people who tested positive with 713 people who did not. It found that positives had missed about five more days of work per year than negatives. But no one was tested for alcohol, the most damaging and commonly abused drug. Again, worthless results.

Walsh stressed the confidentiality and "high laboratory standards" for these tests that don't work. But his real job was to sell a concept. "Every company must assume that its employees will eventually be faced with a substance abuse problem."

He told Scientific American, "I think drug abuse has gone down because of these workplace programs." But NIDA's data show the decline beginning in 1979, long before testing caught on. "We have reached the point where the involvement of marijuana in accidents exceeds that of alcohol," he said. Asked for proof, Walsh admitted there is none. "It's one of the things in my research program we're trying to do right now." This is reminiscent of when Harry Anslinger told St. Francis College graduates, "There is considerable slaughter on the highways today due to the driver's being under the influence of marijuana or other drugs. These murders remain undetected. We are engaged in research to determine whether the driver was using drugs."[72] Studies eventually disproved his statement

---

[70]11 for cannabis, 1 for cocaine

[71]This could tie any trait to any problem. Take workers who have been in an accident or missed work, pick out the blondes & send them home for a few days. Then compare them to a 'control' group with no record of accidents or absenteeism, & assume they are not blonde. Result: Blondes have more accidents & miss more work.

[72]Loretto Pennsylvania. June 5, 1966. Sloman, L. The History of Marijuana in America: Reefer Madness. Bobbs-Merrill Company. Indianapolis IN. 1979. pp. 226-227

about cannabis,[73] yet the dangerous driver myth is another staple of prohibition propaganda.

This is their version of scientific procedure: make a conclusion first, then bill the taxpayers for expensive commercial analysts to play with numbers and studies until they can fabricate "proof." When there is no data, simply pretend there is. Mix skewed results with outright lies and never give a thought to the personal harm that others suffer from the results—the lives prohibition has destroyed.

Viewed as propagandist rather than scientist, Walsh did his job well. A decade ago virtually no company had testing programs. Now a majority test their employees, job applicants or both. "Drug testing," Walsh said with pride, "is here to stay."[74] If so, an employer's best approach is to test only when required to, then hire the cannabis positives. After all, they tend to earn higher wages and be promoted more throughout their employment careers.[75]

How DARE They Teach That in School

The United Nations set this goal: "Education shall be directed to the full development of the human personality and to the strengthening of respect for humans rights and fundamental freedoms. It shall promote understanding, tolerance and friendship."[76]

However, drug programs in schools are now used to infiltrate and subvert the family home. A costly program called DARE was invented by Los Angeles police chief Daryl Gates,[77] who testified before the Senate that casual cannabis smokers ought to be "taken out and shot."[78] Police officers, often armed, go into classrooms and encourage children to think about not taking drugs and act out drug deals that don't work, etc. A DARE officer receives about $90,600 per year in wages and benefits, compared to less than $30,000 per year for a real teacher.[79] "DARE is a sacred cow," noted Gary Peterson of Fort Collins, Colorado, founder of Parents Against DARE. Scientific follow-up has proven the program

[73]Crancer, A. et al. 'Comparison of the effect of marihuana & alcohol on simulated driving performance.' in *Science*. vol. 164. 1969. pp. 851-854. See chapter 17, section on performance for additional scientific data on this.

[74]Horgan, J. 'Your Analysis Is Faulty.' op. cit.

[75]Kaestner, Robert. 'The effect of illicit drug use on the wages of young adults.' in *Journal of Labor Economics*. vol. 9:4. October 1991. pp. 381-412

[76]Art. 26.2. Also 26.3. "Parents have a prior right to choose the kind of education that shall be given to their children." *Universal Dec. of Human Rights*. UN. 1980

[77]Drug Abuse Resistance Education. Gates is an Anslinger cronie who helped write the 1961 *Single Convention Treaty*, according to his resumé.

[78]Gates formed DARE Sept. 12, 1983. Senate testimony on Sept. 5, 1990. Gates' own son was a drug addict who would be a victim of his insane suggestion.

[79]Pope, Lisa. 'DARE-ing program at risk.' in *Daily News*. CA. Sept. 20, 1992

worthless to deter drug use,[80] and a Congressional study found that similar programs actually increased drug misuse.[81] DARE is also plagued with theft.[82]

Hate-mongering is routine. Disinformation is standard. A crime or violent incident is described and a hand-rolled cigarette or picture of a cannabis leaf is shown. A platitude is tossed out: *drugs* are bad, *abusers* are sick. Rather than tell facts about the herb, it is lumped in with hard drugs.[83] They sometimes ask kids to spy on their parents,[84] friends and family members, acting as informants within the family to turn in any pipes, herb, plants or even magazines with pictures of cannabis.[85] Children are told that people who smoke herb need "help." Turn your parents in, for their own sakes.

Which hurts a family more: Daddy smoking cannabis in his study, or Daddy in prison for cannabis? A Colorado fifth-grader did exactly what he was trained to do, said police officer Tim Mitchell, who taught the DARE class. Police locked up little Joaquin's mother and father when their 10-year-old son dialed 911 and reported marijuana in the house. The youngster then asked, "Can I come live at the police station?"[86] Children are not told that prisons and prohibition harm society. They are indoctrinated to wear red ribbons to show they are "drug free": a symbol borrowed directly out of George Orwell's prophetic book, *1984*. Big Brother's mind control system gave youth red belts and scarves to wear.[87]

Corporal punishment was illegal in schools in Missouri and Kansas, but humiliating strip searches of high school students elicited little protest, even when no drugs were found.[88] Schools send pledge letters of a "drug free home" home to parents;[89] and lists made available as to who returned them signed, unsigned or not at

---

[80]Cauchon, D. 'Cover Story: Studies find drug program not effective.' in *USA Today*. Oct. 11, 1993. p. 1A-2A. Ringwalt, Ennett & Holdt. 'An outcome evaluation of Project DARE.' in *Health Education Research*. Vol 6:3. 1991. pp. 327-337.

[81]*Review of International Narcotics Control Strategy Report: Mid Year Update*. Hearings Before the Commission on Foreign Affairs. House of Representatives. Second Session. Washington DC. Spring, 1988. p. 37

[82]Murphy, S. 'Misuse of DARE funds probed.' in *Boston Globe*. Sept. 18, 1994. p. 1

[83]"The leader of genius must have the ability to make different opponents appear to belong in one category." Hitler, Adolf. *Mein Kampf*. Berlin Germany. 1924

[84]Art 16.3. "The family is the natural & fundamental group unit of society & is entitled to protection by society & the state." Ibid.

[85]Specifically, *High Times* magazine.

[86]Ensslin, John C. 'Boy spots marijuana in house, turns in his parents.' in *Rocky Mountain News*. CO. Sept. 24, 1991

[87]Orwell, G. *1984*. Signet Classics. New York NY. 1961. Red sash: "young ones, ... the most bigoted adherents of the Party" p. 12. Red scarf: for *Spies*, students trained to spy on their families, "shouting 'Traitor!' & 'Thought criminal!' " p. 22-23

[88]Morris, D. 'Drug Stories.' in *Anchorage Daily News*. AK. May 12, 1991. p. J-1

[89]Another Nazi parallel: Germans had to sign letters that they had no Jewish blood.

all. This discriminates against people who oppose such an invasion of the sanctity of home and family.

Free Advertising for Drugs & Prohibition

Illegal drugs get millions of dollars of free publicity every day through news media exposure and "anti-drug" promotions and images designed to excite and entice the viewer. How better to interest rebellious youth to something than to forbid it?!

Television watching is, itself, probably the most mind-crippling and addictive behavior pattern in modern society.[90] Its intentional and unnecessary[91] glorification of violence directly coincides with the increase in violent crime in America.[92] At any hour, the day or night, it seems one can turn on television and see a simulated multi-million dollar drug deal in process. Glorified dealers drive big cars, live in mansions and have sexy girls hanging onto them. As P.T. Barnum once said, there is no such thing as bad publicity. In the case of hard drugs, the publicity is free and untaxed.

Both the print and electronic media are saturated with prohibition public service announcements, or PSAs.[93] The news media rarely correct the record when their hysterical "marijuana" scare stories prove false. Rarely do media produce factual reports on either the herb or industrial hemp but often carry rumors and speculation about imaginary hazards.

Nothing is free, and publicity is particularly expensive. The government adds up the dollar value of free publicity received by candidates and political groups, and applies the tax laws accordingly. It should do the same for the prohibition publicity supporters receive free of charge, courtesy of its corporate sponsors, DARE, police shows on television, etc. These political lobbyists for the police industry and organized crime deserve to be legally recognized and to pay their taxes. Let's follow the money trail that supports this advertising giveaway. Overall, the top 100 United States advertisers spent $33.9 billion in 1989.[94]

---

[90]A National Foundation for Educational Research survey of 1,000 English children linked excess television viewing to poor reading & writing skills. Experts warn that the 'lonely viewer' phenomenon could create a generation of solitary, passive children who do not know or care about how to behave socially. Massey, R. 'Pupils whose lessons interrupt TV.' in *Daily Mail*. London England. Oct. 1, 1992. p. 19
[91]Bash, Alan. 'Violence doesn't win ratings.' in *USA Today*. Oct. 4, 1994. p. 3D
[92] Easton, Nina. 'The meaning of America.' in *LA Times Magazine*. Feb. 7, 1993. pp. 16-20, 43-44. also Mander, Jerry. *Four Arguments for the Elimination of Television*. Morrow Quill. New York NY. 1978.
[93]Public Service Announcement. Corruption is built-in here, because this publicity profits both large-scale black market drug distributors & prohibition agencies.
[94]Up 6.4 percent, from $32.2 billion in 1988

Advertising Age reported that the alcohol, food and tobacco giant Philip Morris Co. was the heaviest advertiser for the third consecutive year. The manufacturer of Marlboro cigarettes, Miller beer, Maxwell House coffee, etc., spent $2.07 billion that year.[95] The Ad Council is a corporate-sponsored public relations consortium that produces a third of all television PSAs. It took in more than $1 billion in free airtime and ad space in 1989, making it one of the country's largest advertisers.[96] The Council does some "anti-drug" and responsible-alcohol spots, like "Drinking and driving can kill a friendship," but doesn't address smoking because, according to Eleanor Hangley, plenty of organizations do anti-tobacco ads.[97]

'Facts Are Not Important'

The Partnership for a Drug Free America, PDFA, is another well-financed, corporate-backed campaign, which received $362 million in free advertising in 1990, nearly reaching its goal of $1 million a day. Its campaign was one of the three biggest in advertising. These ads are not a public service but are designed to serve private interests, scattered as they are among paid ads for cigarettes, alcohol and assorted prescription and over-the-counter synthetic drugs made by big pharmaceutical corporations.[98]

PDFA has often been exposed for its lies about cannabis.[99] One ad went so far as to claim that the brainwaves of someone on cannabis were identical to being in a coma, which was promptly disproven by the scientific community.[100] Rather than risk factual embarrassment, the group relies on innuendo, among other things implying that marijuana leads to poverty, sterility, suicide, train accidents and is as dangerous as playing Russian Roulette. The Federal Communications Commission received complaints about the PDFA, yet it has been silent about the prohibitionists' deception.

95Proctor & Gamble was 2nd, $1.79 billion. GM slipped to 4th at $1.35 billion. in *Advertising Age*. 'Philip Morris has most ads.' in *Californian*. CA. May 1990

96The Ad Council calls itself "America's Catalyst for Change." It turned Bush's 1988 campaign slogan, "a thousand points of light," into a campaign for volunteerism. But innovative spots by Direct Effect, a progressive small-budget PSA project led by creative artists, were rejected by the 3 major networks & numerous cable channels.

97Rhodes, Steve. 'Public Service, Private Ideologies,' ['Free of Which Drugs?'] in *Extra!* NY. July/August 1991 pp. 15-16

98One ad agency simultaneously worked on a joint Ad Council/PDFA campaign, "Cocaine: the big lie," while putting up a 2000 pound, 16-foot bottle of Crown Royal whiskey on a billboard with the message, "Ready for another Chicago winter?"*New York Times*. Nov. 16, 1990

99Blow, Richard. 'This is the truth ... This is what the PDFA does to the truth.' in *Washington City Paper*. DC. Dec. 6-12, 1991

100Grant admitted to the media-watch publication *Extra!* "We kind of got left standing bare naked on the ice with that one." Rhodes, S. op. cit.

During our research for this book, PDFA spokesperson Theresa Grant was asked for factual data to back up its claims. She was curt with us, stating, "We don't need facts. We're shaping attitudes. Facts are not important here. Changing public opinion is what is important," and refused to continue the discussion.[101]

The PDFA enjoys a tax exemption that prohibits it from doing political activities. However, during the 1990 campaign to recriminalize cannabis in Alaska, its misleading anti-cannabis spots continued to run and influence voters. The agency was not penalized. The same thing happened during campaigns for medical cannabis in San Francisco, Santa Cruz, etc. The PDFA got a start-up grant from Johnson & Johnson drugs and receives steady funding from Philip Morris, which sells beer and cigarettes, drugs the PDFA doesn't try to free America from. Hearing that Philip Morris and RJR Nabisco expected to sell some 34 billion tobacco cigarettes in the former Soviet Union by the end of 1991, Alexander Cockburn said, "So much for the crusade against 'drugs.' ... All America is actually doing is consolidating its position as the biggest dealer in addictive and lethal substances on the planet, waging war on all rivals."[102] An ominous sign of what lies ahead is a 1992 PDFA slogan "They call it hemp but it's really marijuana."[103] This swipe at the hemp industries benefits the wide spectrum of petrochemical and timber interests who, coincidentally, pay for the anti-hemp ads.[104]

Prohibition promotion pays. The advantage—to media,[105] legal pharmaceutical,[106] tobacco[107] and alcohol[108] drug companies who sponsor anti-cannabis ads—is three-fold. First, cannabis users tend not to use other drugs, including alcohol and tobacco.[109] Of course, many still enjoy a drink or an occasional cigarette, but it's no secret they would rather have some herb. The drop in sales might be small, but advertising is war; and winner takes all. Second, by sponsoring these ads companies purchase a "community involved" image, an

---

[101]Telephone interview. Monday, September 16, 1991
[102]in *Wall Street Journal*. New York NY. "We're eroding our Constitution to pursue this war on drugs. The issue is not whether we buy drugs, but whom we buy them from. They want us buying from them." Kesey, Ken. in *Willamette Week*. Portland OR. Cited in 'Overheard at the Front' in *Sinsemilla Tips*. January 1991. p. 12
[103]This is an outright lie, as there is a legally defined difference between the two.
[104]Air Products & Chemicals, Amoco, BP, Bechtel Group, Chevron, Dow Chemical, E.I. DuPont, Eastman Kodak, General Dynamics, General Electric, General Motors, J.P. Morgan & Co., Kimberly-Clark, Mobil, Monsanto, Rockwell International, Shell Oil, Rockefeller Foundation, Waste Management Inc., etc.
[105]Capital Cities/ABC, Hearst Corporation, *Reader's Digest*, Time Warner, etc.
[106]Johnson & Johnson, Hoechst-Celanese Pharmaceuticals, Pfizer Inc., etc.
[107]RJR Nabisco, Philip Morris, etc.
[108]Anheuser-Busch, RJR Nabisco, Philip Morris, etc.
[109]There are exceptions. In some countries, cannabis is mixed with tobacco to smoke it. But even there, cannabis smokers frequently do not smoke tobacco alone.

invaluable public relations gimmick. Third, they get large tax write-offs, as their private interests can masquerade as a public service.

So we see that prohibition translates directly into cash in the bank for these companies. And yet there are persistent rumors that some of them have already patented brand names to market cannabis cigarettes ... for when the herb is finally relegalized.

Tobacco Use: One Drug's Cost to Business

While cannabis has little or no negative effect on the workings of a business, and a possible advantage, how does tobacco compare?

Tobacco is a legal, federally subsidized,[110] addictive drug which companies do not test for—at least not yet. However, the federal government characterized tobacco's properties as "similar to those that determine addiction to drugs such as heroin and cocaine."[111]

A government report estimated that health care expenses and productivity losses from tobacco smoking-related disease cost the nation more than $52 billion every year. It estimated that illness caused by tobacco imposed an average economic burden of more than $1 billion per state.[112] The cost of tobacco-related disease averaged $221 for every man, woman and child in the nation, from a low of $56 per person in Utah to $284 in Rhode Island, the report said.[113] "Each and every American, including those who don't even smoke, is paying a hidden tax" for the consequences of tobacco, as Health and Human Services Secretary Louis Sullivan told a Senate committee. "My view is simple and straightforward: No smoking." He said tobacco is responsible for more than one out of every six deaths in the nation.[114] It does this legally, with price supports, international tracking, retail distribution and both corporate and government protection.[115]

And somehow society survives. If society can tolerate tobacco, cannabis is no extra burden; it will be an improvement.

110In 1989, Bush said he would exempt new drug 'czar' William Bennett from "irrelevant" cabinet meetings on things "like agricultural subsidies," which tobacco growers receive. The conflict with hemp policy is obvious.
111'The Health Consequences of Smoking.' in *US Surgeon General's Report*. 1988. p. 9. Bennett was recovering from a 40-dose-per-day chronic nicotine drug dependence (in other words, 2 packs of cigarettes per day).
112Dept of Health & Human Services. *National Status Report*. February 1990. in Cimons, M. 'US smoking toll put at $52 billion.' in *LA Times*. Feb. 21, 1990
113Some states ran much higher tabs. CA, the most populous state, had the highest cost, $5.8 billion,/yr, followed by NY, TX, PA, IL, OH & MI. At the time AK had the cleanest air, the only legal cannabis, & the lowest tobacco bill, $82 million/yr.
114In 1965, 40% of US adults were cigarette smokers, compared to 29% in 1987, said Dr. Ronald Davis, HHS Office on Smoking & Health director. "It takes a good 20-25 years after the smoking rates go down before we begin to see a decrease in smoking-related deaths & costs." Cimons. op. cit.
115Taylor, Peter. *The Smoke Ring: Tobacco, money & multi-national politics*. Pantheon Books. New York NY. 1984

Relative Risks, Personal Responsibility

This brings us to the real point of any such comparison: Let people decide these matters for themselves. Adults should be treated as adults, given honest evaluations of the relative hazards posed by various activities and allowed to make their own choices.

They can then take personal responsibility for the consequences, instead of blaming drugs or being subject to arbitrary and irrational government and industry meddling in their lives and urine.

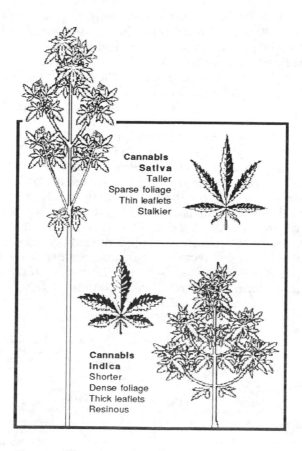

Cannabis
Sativa
Taller
Sparse foliage
Thin leaflets
Stalkier

Cannabis
Indica
Shorter
Dense foliage
Thick leaflets
Resinous

19

PORK BARREL POLITICS OF PROHIBITION

Americans heard a lot about the ever-escalating *War on Drugs* in the 1980s and 1990s. There was a lot of media hype about the cost of *drugs* to society, but little discussion of the social or economic costs of *prohibition*. Also ignored was how much the ban on cannabis itself costs us. The federal war on hemp began in 1937 and has lasted more than three times as long as the Vietnam War. Taxpayers and society foot an enormous bill for this political albatross. An estimated $10 billion nationally went for prohibition in 1988.[1] The 1992 federal prohibition budget surpassed $15 billion. What did we get for our money? Where is this approach taking us?

The National Commission on Marijuana and Drug Abuse noted a drastic surge in the amount of government resources spent to battle *illicit drug use*. Prohibition spending increased by more than 1000 percent from 1969–1973. "Yet, as federal spending approaches the one-billion dollar mark, establishing an entirely new 'drug abuse industrial complex,'[2] no one has systematically analyzed either the problem to be solved or the solutions to be employed."[3]

Enforcement practices and priorities gave mobile hard drug labs an advantage over cannabis gardens, which need to stay in one place for a whole season. During the most heavily funded years of prohibition of the 1980s, cannabis became extremely expensive while the price of street cocaine dropped by 80 percent and its purity rose from 12 to 60 percent.[4] Super-potent, smokable *crack* cocaine and *ice* amphetamine were invented. Estimated worldwide cocaine production rose by half from 1985–89, to 225 tons, opium production by 47 percent during 1988–89 alone.[5] The International Narcotics

---

[1] Ostrowski, James. 'Thinking About Drug Legalization.' *Policy Analysis No. 121.* Cato Institute. Washington DC. 1989. p. 2

[2] "The appointment of more judges to fill newly constructed courtrooms is big business. The building of new prisons is big business. The feeding, clothing & maintaining of inmates is big business. The exploding number of new employees hired by the Department of Corrections is big business. These factors & more contribute to an already large armada of private & public agencies whose primary goals include keeping drugs illegal to preserve profits, ensure job security & promotional opportunities." Cieslikowski, C. 'Bankrupting a Society.' in *Perspectives.* American Probation & Parole Assn. Fall 1992. pp. 18-20

[3] The annual 'drug war' budget was almost $800 million. *Report of the National Commission on Marijuana & Drug Abuse.* US Govt. Printing Office. Washington DC. 1973. a.k.a. Shafer Commission or President Nixon's Blue Ribbon Panel on Drugs

[4] "There is only one drug for which you can say with certainty that demand has gone up, & that is cocaine," Reuter, Peter. RAND Corporation analyst. 1988

[5] US DEA estimates. 1990

Control Board reported that cocaine users rose from 1.6 million in 1990 to 1.9 million in 1991, and abuse of crack, which had been declining, became level.[6] Prison guards can't even keep illegal drugs out of prisons,[7] periodically shoot prisoners;[8] and hire professional lobbyists to make some of the largest contributions to political election campaigns.[9]

Then came property seizure. Non-jury government confiscation of private property from drug *suspects* (not just convicts) rose into the multi-billions of dollars per year. Most of this stolen wealth was turned over to police agencies for more enforcement. This has corrupted our police at the cost of citizen rights. Fabrication of evidence leads to false convictions.[10] Brutality and violence on the part of police is epidemic.[11] Informants receive up to 25 percent of assets seized in police raids. Billboards advertise, "Need cash? Turn in a drug dealer."[12] The government engages in piracy on the high seas.[13] Prisons are run on a private, for-profit basis.[14] Innocent people's properties are taken by police.[15] Raiding savings accounts is a routine procedure.[16] The DEA runs amok.[17]

The human cost of the war exceeds any damage from drug use. Prohibition kills. Some 80 percent of "overdose" deaths were caused by black market factors, with 2400 killed by street drug impurities.[18] Prohibition took some 1600 lives through murders related to hard drug trafficking, along with scores of suspects killed by the police. Government-licensed methadone centers operate at a 1000

[6]INCB statistical reports. Vienna, Austria. also AP 'Drug abuse falls in US.' in *Marin Independent Journal*. CA. Feb. 15, 1993. p. A-1

[7]Or rape & sexual abuse, for that matter. Harrison, E. 'Female inmates locked up in a 13-year nightmare.' in *Los Angeles Times*. Dec. 30, 1992. p. E-2

[8]Morain & Hurst. 'Guard slayings of prisoners in state are high.' in *LA Times*. Sept. 17, 1994. p. A-1, 26. "For an inmate, what's he worth to me?" asked a guard.

[9]Morain, D. 'The Price of Punishment: California's profusion of prisons.' One in a series in *LA Times*. Oct. 16, 1994. p. A-1, 16-18

[10]Paddock, R. 'S.F. Police lab worker accused of drug testing fraud.' in *LA Times*. Sept. 20, 1994. p. A-3, 20

[11]Briggs, Jack. 'Forfeiture! When law enforcement plays cops & robbers.' in *LA Reader*. Dec. 18, 1992. vol. 15:10. pp. 10-17

[12]Anderson County, SC, etc.

[13]US Coast Guard 'zero tolerance' campaign seized a $2.5 million yacht in international waters off Mexico in May 1988 after finding 1/10 oz of herb on board. It was used to extort a fine from the owner. Morris, D. 'Drug Stories: Studies of users uncover some surprising statistics.' in *Anchorage Daily News*. May 12, 1991. p. J-1

[14]*Private Prisons: Cost savings & BoP's statutory authority need to be resolved*. Report no. GAO/GGD 91-21. US GPO. Washington DC. Feb. 21, 1991

[15]Mauro, Tony. 'Some worry police out of control.' in *USA Today*. Nov. 5, 1989

[16]*Money Laundering: Treasury's financial crimes enforcement network*. Report no. GAO GGD 91-10. US GPO. Washington DC. March 18, 1991

[17]Levine, Michael. *Deep Cover: The inside story of how DEA infighting, incompetence & subterfuge lost us the biggest battle of the drug war*. Delacourte Press. 1990

[18]Szalavitz, Maria. 'Costs of the War on Drugs.' in *High Times*. New York NY. September 1990. pp. 35-45, 56

percent mark-up for profit (the same level as street heroin), but methadone is far more addictive and much more physically damaging than the heroin for which it is substituted.

The knee-jerk drug warrior response is to plunge into the quagmire with more war and less thought. Candidates recite their oath: We've been "too soft;" it's time to "get tough." Historian Edward Gibbon described the collapse of the Roman Empire in similar terms: "The greatest part of the nation was gradually reduced into a state of servitude ... either by the real weight of fetters or by the no less cruel and forcible restraints of the laws."[19]

Summary of Prohibition's Direct Expenses

How much does this boondoggle cost us each year? Start with the conservative estimate of $500 billion or so that society loses in commercial hemp industries, exports, shipping and related jobs involving pulp, paper, textiles, construction, energy, farms, equipment, retail, commodities, the stock market, etc. They would have generated about $100 billion in tax revenue. Another $50 billion is spent by consumers on herbal cannabis, funnelled into the black market instead of the legal economy, with lost tax revenues of $10 billion. On the regulated market, the cost of that cannabis would be around $10 billion, freeing $40 billion for other consumer goods.

Some $14 billion was paid outright by taxpayers for prohibition enforcement in 1990, including related court costs, jail construction, and maintenance. Of that, state and local taxes paid $5 billion[20] and federal law enforcement $4.2 billion. Prison construction took $2.5 billion, interdiction $1.8 billion, international enforcement $512 million. Every American family paid out around $200 for that piece of the War on Drugs.[21] Yet, the real costs went far beyond the smoke and mirrors. There are hidden and secondary allocations, and secret CIA/NSA budgets.[22] The artificially high prices paid for illegal drugs[23] creates theft. This led hard drug addicts to steal an estimated $7.5 billion worth of property in 1990 alone. Prohibition and the resulting use of dirty, shared needles is implicated in 10,500 cases of AIDS annually. Each case cost about $100,000 in medical

---

[19]Gibbon, Edward. *Decline & Fall of the Roman Empire*. Moses Hadas, ed. Fawcett Crest Books/Random House. New York NY. 1962. pp. 95-96
[20]*The War on Drugs: Arrests burdening local criminal justice systems.* Report no. GAO/GGD 91-40. US GPO. Washington DC. April 3, 1991
[21]Szalavitz. op. cit. p. 35
[22]Cockburn, L. *Out of Control.* Atlantic Monthly Press. NY. 1987. also US Senate Subcommittee on Terrorism & Narcotics hearings, 1988, 1989. Senator John Kerry (MA), chair. also Levine, M., retired DEA agent. 'Going Bad.' in *Spin.* June 1991.
[23]Pharmaceutical cocaine cost $30/ounce, compared to $1000/oz for street cocaine.

expenses, for a total of $1 billion. These two factors added another $121 to each family's tax bill.[24]

Money diverted from the legal economy to the black market was around $125 billion per year. Lost salaries of prohibition prisoners hit $2 billion. Locking up drug offenders converted 135,000 citizens from being an economic asset to a loss—from being wage earners averaging $20,000 per year to being prison inmates costing $17,000 to $22,000 each per year to keep locked up.[25] These factors brought the one-year cost of prohibition to around $150 billion level, or $2136 per family. Including the $550 billion loss from suppressing hemp and cannabis commerce, we calculate $9993 per family sucked out of the United States economy each year.

Property seizures are based on stereotyped "drug dealer profiles" and flimsy evidence. Property and cash are kept, even if suspects are found innocent.[26] Meanwhile, the illegal drug industry ranked at the top of the Fortune 500 and was growing fast. The *Economist* reported, "A small group of drug criminals now probably launders tax-free sums of over $100 billion a year,[27] more than the gross national products of 150 of the 170 nations of the world."[28]

As Al Capone said during the Roaring 20s, "I like Prohibition."

The Military & Other Areas of the Economy

Programs for low-income families and children, which had effectively reduced both crime rates and health care costs, were starved off. From 1980 to 1988, tax outlays for low-income programs were cut by $58.43 per person, or nine percent,[29] and military spending bloated by $346.84, or 30 percent.[30] Offering $500 million in Job Corps' work training to an additional 160,000 disadvantaged youths[31] in 1987 would have saved $9 billion in costs to society for crime, use of public welfare programs and other ex-

---

[24]In Hong Kong needles are legal, methadone is widely available & there have been no reported cases of AIDS spread by intravenous drug use. In the US, cities which ban over-the-counter needle sales have an AIDS rate 6 times higher than ones which permit them. Szalavitz. op. cit. pp. 35-45, 56

[25]Dept. of Justice estimates. Costs vary from state to state.

[26]Schneider, A. & Flaherty, M.P. 'Presumed Guilty.' in *Pittsburgh Press*. PA. Series of reports. Aug. 11-16, 1991. p. 1

[27]Officials said Americans spent over $40 billion in 1990 on cocaine, heroin, marijuana & other illegal drugs. Johnston, D. 'Illegal drug sales.' in *New York Times*. June 20, 1991. p. A-20. This is highly suspect, since the DEA figure for cannabis alone had been $55 billion for 1989.

[28]in *The Economist*. April 2, 1988

[29]From $524.88 to $466.45. FY 1987 US dollars

[30]From 811.34 to $1158.18. FY 1987 US dollars

[31]$3100/enrollee year for 250,000 rather than the 90,000 actually served .

penses.[32] Investing $3100 per year in vocational training can save $15,000 per year for prison.

Analysts concluded that we would have to call up the National Guard into paid, active duty, pulling hundreds of thousands of people from their civilian jobs and disrupting the entire economy, to fully pursue the drug war.[33] Federal military troops were used to assault domestic cannabis farms for the first time in 1991. An ever-growing amount of military spending is earmarked for "drug interdiction"[34] and assistance to foreign prohibition activities. House Government Operations Committee Chairman, John Conyers, suggested that the government was giving foreign armies involved with drug running prohibition law enforcement money that is then diverted to fight political insurgencies. The panel called for a move away from law enforcement toward developing an alternative crop program for peasant farmers who now grow coca for a living.[35] Not mentioned in the report was the fact that the logical crop for the region is hemp.

The DARE school program sucked more than $10 million out of the Department of Education budget and $5.25 from the Bureau of Justice Assistance over four years. It took in about $1.3 million in tax-deductible donations in 1990, and $6 million in 1992. That money would otherwise have gone to charity. DARE officers are paid almost three times as much as school teachers.[36]

Ending prohibition means a massive influx of revenue for schools, roads, environmental clean-up, health care, payment on the national debt, etc.

What Has Criminalizing Cannabis Done?

Prohibition means arresting and embittering thousands of citizens, sending them to prison where they harden and learn how to commit serious crimes of theft and violence. To understand the effect of cannabis prohibition, we must first consider the magnitude of the "marijuana problem" it set out to address.

In 1937, an estimated 60,000 Americans smoked cannabis.[37] The street price of the herb averaged $1 per ounce.[38] Ever more

---

[32]in *Annual Report*. Children's Defense Fund. Washington DC. 1988

[33]Miranda, Joseph. 'Winning the War on Drugs.' in *Liberty*. November 1989. p. 25

[34]*Drug Interdiction: Funding continues to increase but effectiveness is uncertain.* Report no. GAO GGD 91-10. US GPO. Washington DC. Dec. 11, 1991

[35]UPI News Wire. 'Bush drug war called ineffective, dangerous.' in *US Naval Base News*. Guantanamo Bay Cuba. Dec. 21, 1990

[36]Pope, L. 'DARE-ing program at risk.' in *Daily News*. CA. Sept. 20, 1992

[37]Herer, Jack. *Hemp & the Marijuana Conspiracy: The Emperor Wears No Clothes.* HEMP Publishing. Van Nuys CA. 1991. p. 69

[38]Clinton Hester, Treasury Dep. Asst. Gen. counsel. *Hearing Transcripts.* Committee on Ways & Means, House of Representatives. April 27-30, May 4, 1937

Draconian measures have been routinely enacted ever since. *Time* magazine described the cannabis scene in 1943.[39]

> Known to the pharmacopoeia as cannabis sativa, it is a source of important paint ingredients and rope fiber. … It can be grown easily almost anywhere, hence tends to be inexpensive as drugs go. Its recent prices [10 to 50 cents a cigarette] have placed it beneath the dignity of big-time racketeers.
> But its furtive preparation and sale provide a modest living to thousands.

Nonetheless, by 1945, a reported 100,000 Americans were regular cannabis consumers.[40] By 1988, an estimated 60 million Americans reportedly had tried cannabis at least once.

The ban on hemp farming is strictly enforced, and cannabis grew as a weed throughout the country. The typical cost for surveillance of each targeted cannabis patch is a minimum of six police officers for 32 hours each, or 192 hours total. The minimum expense is around $3840.[41] If they do arrest anyone, things really get expensive. They don't usually, because the plants are usually wild. The State of Wisconsin, for example, captured and destroyed 849,324 hemp plants in 1990; 97 percent were wild.[42]

After Milwaukee County, Wisconsin, spent $2.2 million in 1991 on 78 cannabis gardening contacts and arrests, the Northwest Area Crime Unit ran out of money. Officer Mark Kelsey, who coordinated the task force, asked the State to inject another $40,000 into the program to finish the year. The State refused; Kelsey said his officers were "frustrated" with the decision.[43] Taxpayers, on the other hand, were relieved. In California four ballot measures to authorize billions of dollars for prisons and prohibition enforcement were all soundly defeated by voters in 1990. Prohibitionists then slipped marijuana use into a crime bill dealing with murder and rape, labeled it a panacea for "violent crime" and tricked state voters into passing the "Three Strikes"[44] initiative of 1994.[45]

Summarizing the results of its decades-long, multi-billion dollar, military-style attack on outdoor gardens, federal DEA coordinator

---

[39]'The weed.' in *Time*. July 19, 1943. p. 56
[40]'Army study of marihuana smokers.' in *Newsweek*. Jan. 15, 1945
[41]Three rotating 8 hour shifts of 2 officers on site for 4 days. $10/hour pay, with $10 in benefits & expenses, for $20 per hour. Does not include cost of overtime, bonuses or hazardous duty pay, helicopter time, backup, office support, donuts, etc.
[42]'An Amazing Plant.' in *Isthmus*. Madison WI. March 1991
[43]The unit later seized a cultivated crop of 1050 cannabis plants on a farm outside Webster. Two men were charged. Ryan, P. 'Drug unit out of money as marijuana harvest nears.' in *Capital Times*. Madison WI. August 1991
[44]Colvin, R. '3 Strikes found hobbled by enormous prison costs.' in *LA Times*. Sept. 22, 1994. p. A-1, 23
[45]Election results. Prop. 184. in Los Angeles Times. Nov. 9, 1994

246   HEMP, LIFELINE TO THE FUTURE

Charles Stowell said, "We have created this monster called *the indoor grow*."[46] Federal deputy director for drug supply reduction Stanley Morris likes that. "The best news is the number of indoor operations seized in California and Hawaii." Both states are prime areas for outdoor hemp growing, he enthused, and indoor growing is much more expensive; so law enforcement was taking money "out of the hands of mom and pop, casual entrepreneurs," and giving it to organized crime.[47]

Brutal violence is perpetrated by the prohibitionists against plants, suspects and innocent bystanders. Confronting attack helicopters, battering rams and heavy weapons, a few guerilla growers resorted to crude booby traps, like nail-studded boards.[48] Most don't fight back; they retreat indoors. Los Angeles County sheriffs found a massive underground grow operation near Lancaster, California in November, 1990.[49] Prohibition agencies enlisted public utility companies to spy on home energy use. If you use too much electricity, they send in the police.

While on the one hand claiming victory in their war on cannabis, DEA officials on the other hand devour ever more money,[50] saying it is still far from over, citing increased use of indoor cultivation and "amazing horticulture."

Agents pointed optimistically to trends of reduced supply, rising prices and self-proclaimed "victories." Said Stowell, "In California in 1989 we found 126 indoor operations. Last year we found 263. I think they could double again this year."[51]

This pattern of escalated enforcement and irrational claims of victory in the face of failure is similar to the final years of Alcohol Prohibition. Stills seized rose from 32,000 in 1920 to 282,000 in 1930. The enforcement budget rose from $7 million in 1921 to $15 million in 1930. Convictions rose from 18,000 in 1921 to 61,000 in 1932. In 1933, Prohibition was dead.[52]

46'Overheard at the Front.' in *Sinsemilla Tips*. January 1991. p. 12

47Morris said, "As the little guy gets out, the opportunity to build a hardened public attitude grows. The more organized grower makes for less sympathetic jury cases. You can really hammer them." Ostrow, R. 'Pot supply, demand dropping, US reports.' in *Los Angeles Times*. CA. Jan. 1 1991

48Lipkin, R. 'Kentucky's other grass.' in *Insight on the News*. Washington DC. July 1, 1991. p. 16. An amazing look into prohibition fascism in action.

496000 cannabis plants, just inches tall, in a 7000-square-foot basement. With 4 harvests possible, it might net up to $75 million a year. Ostrow. op. cit.

50"This seizure came as the result of an anonymous phone call . . . Are they trying to tell us that if we spend another billion dollars, we'll get more anonymous phone calls?" Levine, M. 'Ex-DEA agent calls drug war a fraud.' in *Extra!* July 1990. p. 3

51Lipkin. op. cit. p. 16

52Prison terms grew longer & were meted out with greater frequency in the last years of alcohol prohibition. Ostrowski. op. cit. p. 6

Contemporary American Cannabis Farming

Prohibition has led to some novel farming methods. It is surely one of the strangest eras in the history of agriculture. Why do people grow cannabis, despite plant prohibition?

One reason is financial. Growing a personal supply of cannabis increases both the medical and casual user's self-sufficiency. It provides a buffer from the risks of buying herb on the black market, and also from escalating street prices. Growing a marketable amount earns a decent income for the farmer, and for the hobbyist often means the difference between paying the bills and going into debt.

Also cannabis is a beautiful plant, and many growers become personally involved with their gardens. There is a sense of pride and special accomplishment that comes from growing a tall, lush herb patch from a few tiny seeds. They like to show off their plants and boast of their achievements, but must resist the urge so as not to give themselves away to secret police and undercover informers.

Finally, growing cannabis is a political statement against big government. Freedom-loving people refuse to bow to arbitrary oppression, and thus resist tyranny.[53] In the tradition of the "moonshiners" of alcohol prohibition, many thousands of farmers and hobbyists continue to grow cannabis despite the ban.

An economic survey rated the harvest value of cannabis cultivated in 1990 above that of the top crops grown in 37 states.[54] In four states, the value of cannabis harvested was more than the value of all other agriculture combined. First was Alaska, at 655 percent of all other farm output combined, followed by West Virginia at 335 percent, Hawaii at 237 percent, and New Hampshire at 236 percent. In 10 states cannabis generated from 50 to 99 percent as much income as total agriculture. Oregon and Massachusetts were at 90 percent or over each, followed by Vermont, South Carolina, Kentucky, Tennessee, Connecticut, Montana, Utah and down to 55 percent in Maine. The estimated value of herb harvested in Vermont, $370 million, was 118 percent of the value of the state's leading commodity.[55] Cannabis rated from 49 to 20 percent in 18 states.

Top farm states are not generally the top cannabis-producing states, except for California. Cannabis does not outrank the value of corn or soybeans in the Midwest corn belt, nor does it outrank cotton in Texas or citrus products in Florida—at least not yet.

---

[53] Rum & tea smuggling American Revolution hero John Hancock reputedly said of the Declaration of Independence, "I'll sign my name so old King George can read it without putting on his glasses."
[54] Excluding non-crop agricultural commodities such as livestock & dairy. 'Where Marijuana is the Top Crop,' in *EIR*. Washington DC. Feb. 8, 1991. pp. 30-31
[55] Dairy products generated $314 million.

The two centers of cannabis production are 1) the Pacific states of Hawaii, California, Oregon and Washington, and 2) the eastern and central states of Arkansas, Missouri, Tennessee, Kentucky, Georgia and North Carolina. Adjacent counties of southwest Virginia and remote parts of adjoining states, like West Virginia, could be included.

An Underground Multinational

In many ways, the cannabis trade is just like any other business.[56] In fact, thanks to prohibition's effect on prices, profits in this field are so vast that it is virtually impossible to eliminate the supply. Cannabis production is easy, since it requires no refining and very little handling prior to use. However, its bulk and strong aroma make the risks greater for cannabis dealing than for cocaine or heroin. Hence, Jamaican traffickers have moved from cannabis to cocaine, despite the continuing demand for the herb.[57]

The impediments to cannabis imports apply less to hashish, which continues to be supplied mainly by overseas producers. Despite its civil war, Lebanon remains the world's leading hashish producer.[58] Most of its 700 metric ton annual output goes to Western Europe. Pakistan and Afghanistan produce 200 to 400 metric tons of hashish each, for export mainly to Europe. Morocco is another region whose product is largely consumed in Europe.[59]

Overall cannabis production in Latin America was somewhere between 500 and 1000 metric tons in 1987, according to State Department estimates. Southeast Asian producers, led by Thailand, Laos and the Philippines, harvested a similar amount. Two foreign countries, Mexico and Colombia, divided equally about 60 percent of the United States market, the National Narcotics Intelligence Consumers Committee estimated. Mexicans harvested about 9000 hectares of cannabis in 1987.[60] Mexican growers sometimes have large agribusiness operations.[61]

---

[56]Warner, Roger. *Invisible Hand; the marijuana business.* Beech Tree/Morrow Books. New York NY. 1986
[57]Cooper, Mary H. 'The Business of Illicit Drugs.' in *Congressional Quarterly.* Editorial Research Reports. Washington DC. May 20, 1988
[58]However, the Syrian government, heavily tied to the heroin traffic, has begun to systematically destroy the cannabis crop. Weinberg, B. 'Burning the Bekka Valley.' in *High Times.* March 1993. pp. 45-49, 54-56
[59]Cooper. op. cit.
[60]For 1988, the DEA estimated the Mexican herbal harvest at 4750 metric tons, but revised its estimate up to 47,500 tons for 1989. Jehl, D. 'Mexico pot estimate up tenfold.' in *Los Angeles Times.* Feb. 25, 1990. pp. A-1, 12
[61]They met aggressive eradication campaigns by planting smaller crops in remote areas, & by harvesting & washing some plants that had been sprayed with herbicides.

Prohibition enforcement authorities said the United States cannabis supply rose from about 8300 metric tons in 1985 to as much as 12,585 metric tons in 1987. In 1988 about a fourth of that market was met by domestic growers across the country. The DEA estimated that 8300 metric tons of cannabis were produced here, though it also claimed to have destroyed more than seven million plants in 46 states, lowering the herb available for sale to 3000 tons.

Peter Reuter, an analyst for the RAND Corporation, said, "The United States has at last managed, rather expensively, to provide effective tariff protection for one industry: marijuana." Almost half the domestic crop is said to be sinsemilla. Distribution costs are low, since exchanges are generally between friends, and it may change hands as few as one to three times from garden to consumer.[62]

A Taxpayer-Financed Economic Disaster

In Hawaii, farmers and researchers have long sought an alternative crop to sugar cane. The success some residents achieved with cannabis drew a military response. Cannabis growing grew from a back-yard hobby in the 1970s into a sprawling, diversified, multi-million dollar market based on the legendary *Maui wowie* buds grown in forests and sugar cane fields. A federally financed six-month blitz called Operation Wipeout—spraying deadly herbicides on the state's fragile tropical ecosystems—claimed to destroy 80 percent of the 1990 outdoor crop, already small due to heavy rain.[63] Air Force reconnaissance jets methodically photo-mapped the entire State to spot cannabis patches. The State then paid sightseeing helicopters to crisscross the islands and shoot each one with *glyphosate*, a deadly toxin.

A Pahoa resident reported that she and her family suffered headaches and stomach problems. "We were poisoned. ... They would spray and then we'd get sick. Who wants to breathe this stuff in?"[64] Nearly 800,000 cannabis plants were destroyed, representing more than $1 billion in personal income. If the economic damage had been caused by a hurricane or volcano, Hawaii would qualify for federal disaster relief. But this disaster was deliberate. Roger Christie, a spokesman for the Marijuana Political Action Committee, said, "Some growing operations have been put out of business. It's devastating to the local economy." On the street, a pound of top-

[62]Reuter, Crawford & Cave. *Sealing the Borders: Effects of increased military participation in drug interdiction.* 1988. p. 127
[63]Essoyan, S. 'Hawaii drive destroys most of outdoor marijuana crop.' in *Los Angeles Times.* Jan. 1, 1991.
[64]Residents of the Big Island's Puna district called a state hot line to complain about helicopter noise & to express concern about herbicide drift & contamination of water.

grade cannabis, which went for $1600 three years earlier, jumped to $5000. State Attorney General Warren Price boasted, "Our objective was to break the back of the industry, and I think we've done that." The offensive made cocaine cheaper and more readily available than herb. This scenario, poisoning communities to deprive locals of income and drive marijuana smokers to use cocaine, is being repeated in California, Oregon, Kentucky and across the country.[65]

A Cannabis Policy That Saved Tax Money

There are at least two uncontroversial principles to follow in judging a law: laws should conform with Constitutional requirements, and laws with a large fiscal impact should only be passed after full and careful study of that impact. Under both criteria, cannabis re-legalization comes out looking very good, indeed. While the Constitutionality of prohibition and its enforcement are highly suspect,[66] the legitimacy of allowing cannabis is quite clear.[67] Cannabis reform offers major savings to taxpayers, with no demonstrable financial cost attached.

According to a detailed study of the entire State justice system budget from 1976 to 1985, California saved $958,305,499 in direct expenses by decriminalizing personal possession of up to an ounce of cannabis in the popular Moscone bill. Savings on each case may include the cost of grand juries, public defenders, prosecutors, judges, bailiffs, juries, hearings, trials, appeals, county jails, state prisons and/or probation and parole systems, depending on how each case proceeds.[68] That included only the costs of arrests, courts, state prisons and parole. It did not count the savings of reducing expenditures for county jails, prosecutors, public defenders and probation departments, or the revenue raised by the $100 fine for cannabis use.[69] Taking all this into account, California saved well over one billion dollars in a 10-year period—more than one hundred million dollars per year.[70]

After Ohio decriminalized cannabis, researchers studied the disposition of cases in Columbus and Cleveland. Before this, about 80 percent of possession cases had proceeded beyond arraignment, re-

---

[65]Lipkin, R. 'Kentucky's other grass.' *Insight on the News*. July 1, 1991. p. 16

[66]The US Supreme Court consistently ruled prohibition unconstitutional until well into the 20th century. This is why the phony tax scheme was adopted.

[67]Under Article 6 of the US Constitution, the Senate can abrogate the *Single Convention Treaty of 1961* or set up a federal agency to direct cannabis distribution.

[68]Aldrich, Mikuriya & Brownell. 1986. Calof 1968

[69]If all of the 40,671 people cited for simple possession of cannabis in 1985 paid a $100 fine, that amounts to more than $4 million/year.

[70]Aldrich, Michael R, Ph.d & Mikuriya, Tod, MD. 'Savings in California marijuana law enforcement costs attributable to the Moscone Act of 1976.' in *Journal of Psychoactive Drugs*. vol. 20:1. January 1988. pp. 75-81

quiring many police hours in court. Afterwards, only 10 percent went beyond arraignment. Police court hours dropped 91 percent in Columbus and 90 percent in Cleveland.[71]

Decriminalization did not substantially reduce the number of cannabis possession arrests in Maine, but police and court costs went down by factors of five to 13 times throughout the state. "Not-guilty" pleas fell 87 percent. "Guilty" pleas went up by 263 percent and the number of evidence suppression hearings plummeted from 148 per year to two. While the average fine decreased, total fine revenues increased, due to all the "guilty" pleas.[72] As a result, cannabis law enforcement went from being a substantial drain on Maine revenues to being a net revenue raiser.

This can be increased even more by taking the next logical step. Relegalize cannabis and tax it like alcohol and coffee.

Appropriate Use of Rehabilitation Programs

Another reform approach is to allow people caught with cannabis to take drug rehabilitation programs in lieu of prison time. The drug treatment option may reduce actual prison costs but will probably not substantially reduce trial and other pre-sentence costs.[73] Funding for drug treatment is severely limited. Cannabis users do not need treatment, nor are they the most appropriate recipients of those public health care dollars. According to the United States Surgeon General, cannabis is not addictive and significantly less habit forming than heroin, cocaine, alcohol and nicotine. It is even less habit forming than caffeine or sugar. People who break the cannabis laws are neither physically dependent nor psychologically sick. They simply refuse to conform to a dictum which they consider unjust.

Those who wish to stop using cannabis generally need only will power, not medical help.[74] Forcing cannabis offenders into such programs means the system will waste resources trying to "cure" persons who have no need or desire to be cured, and probably resent the whole ordeal. At the same time, overcrowding will force them to turn away cocaine or heroin addicts and alcoholics who desperately crave and truly need help. Such a policy not only makes drug treatment expenditures less efficient, it may well increase crime committed by hard drug addicts who cannot get treatment.

---

[71]Kopel, D. 'Marijuana Jail Terms.' in *Independence Issue Paper*. Independence Inst. Golden CO. no 5-91. April 24, 1991. pp. 1-8

[72]Ibid.

[73]Ibid.

[74]A very small percentage of people have addictive personalities & may need professional help to stop smoking cannabis, or for that matter to stop watching TV.

Business & Workers: Victims of Prohibition

Many companies routinely reject job applicants based on chemical analysis of urine. Around 20 percent of the time, these tests implicate innocent people.[75] When they do happen by chance to be correct, companies may well be purging the payrolls of some of their best employees, if information from the National Institute on Drug Abuse (NIDA) is correct.

Urine tests are body searches—unprecedented invasions of privacy that undermine the most basic Fourth Amendment safeguards, and Fifth Amendment guarantees against self-incrimination. In addition to being morally offensive, such programs violate international human rights standards.[76] The standard practice in administering such tests is to require employees to urinate in the presence of a witness who gazes intently at their genitalia to prevent "specimen tampering." Anyone who does this in a public restroom will likely be arrested for perversion. Yet, prohibitionists actually require it as a routine, even mandatory, procedure in the workplace.

One judge characterized urine sampling as "an experience which, even if courteously supervised can be humiliating and degrading."

A federal judge studying a random drug testing plan for government employees called it "a wholesale deprivation of the most fundamental privacy rights of thousands upon thousands of loyal, law abiding citizens."[77]

Business Community Pays Price of Urine Tests

A study of urine testing by City University of New York's Medical School concluded that it is "a costly testing procedure ... that says nothing about the individual's work ability, competence or impairment. Therefore, drug testing is concluded to be a method for surveillance, not a tool for safety."[78] In the case of cannabis, it does not even indicate how recently it may have been used. The most commonly abused drugs, alcohol and tobacco, are ignored completely.

Meanwhile, wide-scale urine testing of employees for cannabis continues at a cost of millions of dollars per year, and employees are less than happy about it. These tests do not prove much, since alco-

---

75'Drug Testing in the Workplace.' in *Briefing Paper No. 5*. ACLU. New York NY. 1990
76UN Universal Dec. of Human Rights. Art 23.1. "Everyone has the right to work, to free choice of employment, to just & favorable conditions of work & to protection against unemployment."
77'Drug Testing in the Workplace.' op. cit.
78Morgan, J.P. 'Marijuana metabolism in the context or urine testing for cannabinoid metabolite.' in Journal of Psychoactive Drugs. vol. 20:1. 1988. pp. 107-115

hol is only detectable in body fluids for six hours or so and cocaine for two or three days, but cannabis for over a month.

Proponents of testing, especially urinalysis, claim the costs of illicit drug use to industry are high but fail to produce real figures; and many who make such claims are drug test manufacturers who profiteer on industry-wide urinalysis. The urine-drug test industry recommends that, when a drug test comes up positive, it should be confirmed by a second analysis. This is a good idea, since poppy seeds and cold pills trigger false alarms for heroin and amphetamines, respectively, and ibuprofen for cannabis. It also means double the money for drug test companies.

The next problem is that urine tests insult workers without even measuring drug use.[79] They only identify chemical trace elements and are specifically designed to target cannabis users rather than hard drugs. An employee who smoked cannabis on a Saturday may test positive the following Wednesday, long after the herb has ceased to have any effect. What the employee did on Saturday night has nothing to do with his or her work on Wednesday morning. But a worker can snort cocaine on the way to work and test negative that same morning. That is because the cocaine has not yet been metabolized and will, therefore, not show up in the person's urine.

Cannabis tests are among the most expensive. How accurate are the results? When 120 forensic scientists—including some who worked for drug test manufacturers—were asked, "Who would submit urine for drug testing if his career, reputation, freedom or livelihood depended on it," not a single hand was raised.[80]

A 1989 Gallup Poll for the Institute for a Drug-Free Workplace[81] revealed that only 26 percent of respondents gave unqualified support for testing in the workplace, while 82 percent held that "Drug Awareness Education Programs" were the most appropriate employer action.[82] A whopping 94 percent agreed that "If employees are tested for drug use, top management also should be tested." Despite heavy indoctrination to support tests, less than one out of three[83] would agree that "Drug testing is very effective in the workplace."

So we find a rousing lack of support for these programs, which are also costly and unjustified; three good reasons to abandon them.

---

[79]Confirmed positives are not evidence of intoxication or impairment; they merely indicate that someone may have taken or simply been exposed to a drug at some time in the past month, or the results may be wrong again.
[80]in 1990. 'Drug Testing in the Workplace.' op. cit.
[81]Includes one of the nation's largest drug test companies, LaRoche Laboratories
[82]National Organization to Reform Marijuana Laws press release. Dec. 14, 1989
[83]32%

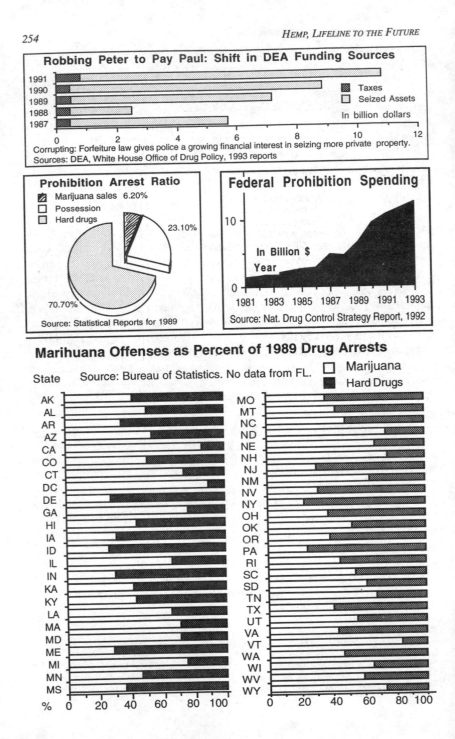

Robbing Peter to Pay Paul: Shift in DEA Funding Sources

Taxes
Seized Assets
In billion dollars

Corrupting: Forfeiture law gives police a growing financial interest in seizing more private property.
Sources: DEA, White House Office of Drug Policy, 1993 reports

Prohibition Arrest Ratio

Marijuana sales 6.20%
Possession
Hard drugs
23.10%
70.70%

Source: Statistical Reports for 1989

Federal Prohibition Spending

In Billion $
Year

Source: Nat. Drug Control Strategy Report, 1992

Marihuana Offenses as Percent of 1989 Drug Arrests

State   Source: Bureau of Statistics. No data from FL.   Marijuana   Hard Drugs

Primary Economic Losses from Hemp Prohibition

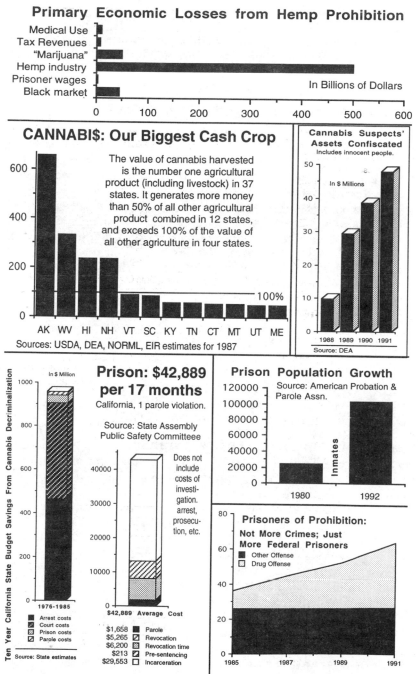

Medical Use
Tax Revenues
"Marijuana"
Hemp industry
Prisoner wages
Black market

In Billions of Dollars

0   100   200   300   400   500   600

CANNABI$: Our Biggest Cash Crop

600

400

200

0

The value of cannabis harvested is the number one agricultural product (including livestock) in 37 states. It generates more money than 50% of all other agricultural product combined in 12 states, and exceeds 100% of the value of all other agriculture in four states.

100%

AK WV HI NH VT SC KY TN CT MT UT ME

Sources: USDA, DEA, NORML, EIR estimates for 1987

Cannabis Suspects' Assets Confiscated
Includes innocent people.

50

In $ Millions

40

30

20

10

0

1988 1989 1990 1991

Source: DEA

Prison: $42,889 per 17 months

California, 1 parole violation.

Source: State Assembly
Public Safety Committeee

Does not include costs of investigation, arrest, prosecution, etc.

40000

30000

20000

10000

0

$42,889 Average Cost

$1,658 ■ Parole
$5,265 ▨ Revocation
$6,200 ▨ Revocation time
$213 ▨ Pre-sentencing
$29,553 □ Incarceration

Ten Year California State Budget Savings From Cannabis Decriminalization

In $ Million

1000

800

600

400

200

0

1976-1985

■ Arrest costs
▨ Court costs
▨ Prison costs
▨ Parole costs

Source: State estimates

Prison Population Growth

Source: American Probation & Parole Assn.

120000
100000
80000
60000
40000
20000
0

Inmates

1980   1992

Prisoners of Prohibition:

Not More Crimes; Just More Federal Prisoners

■ Other Offense
□ Drug Offense

80

60

40

20

0

1985   1987   1989   1991

The real cost to business created by such testing through reduced employee morale, productivity, etc., has yet to be measured. Worker discontent appears to be quite high. The correlation between these two trends is not clearly established, but the late 1980s rise in urine testing did correspond with a drop in American industrial competitiveness in the global community.

A Healthy, Productive Society & Workplace

Do employers have the right to expect their employees not to be high on drugs on the job? Of course they do. Employers have the right to expect their employees not to be high, drunk, incompetent or asleep on the job. Job performance is the bottom line: If people cannot do the work, employers have a legitimate reason to fire them.

If someone is too impaired, by drugs or otherwise, to do their work, acuity and dexterity tests are the most accurate, prompt and cost-effective methods to determine that. A urine sample will not reveal emotional instability caused by an argument, for example—a potentially serious factor for someone operating heavy machinery.

In any event, employers have better ways to maintain high productivity, as well as to identify and help employees with drug problems. Competent supervision, professional counseling and voluntary rehabilitation programs may not be as simplistic as a drug test, but they are a better business investment. Good employee morale is extremely important, and urine testing demonstrably hurts that. Where businesses need to concentrate is in creating an atmosphere of trust and cooperation, not suspicion and fear. If the United States wants to regain its competitive edge, it must compete with other countries, not destroy its own workforce.

Escape From the Monkey Cage

Researchers tell of an experiment involving a roomful of monkeys. In the middle of the room is a tall stool. Suspended overhead is a banana on a wire.

The monkeys want the banana, but every time they climb up on the stool, a researcher appears with a hose and sprays all the monkeys with water.[84] After they've been hosed down a few times, the monkeys no longer allow each other up on the stool. If one monkey tries to get the banana, the others swarm all over him, pulling, punching and biting him to the ground before the hose is turned on them all. Eventually, this prohibition becomes the new "law."

One day, a monkey is taken out of the room and replaced with another who does not know the law. He enters the cage, sees the

---

[84]Paraphrased from Eddy Englesman, former head of Dutch drug policy. 1992

banana and makes a run for the stool, but is pulled down and beaten by banana enforcement monkeys until he gives up on the idea. This process is repeated, one monkey at a time, until the room is entirely populated with monkeys who have never been on the stool, never touched the banana, never been hosed down by the researchers. Now the law is sacred, an article of faith from an unknown law-giver. Experience is no longer at its base.

The prohibition takes on a life of its own. Logic no longer has a role to play. Nobody knows why they must not climb the stool or eat the banana. But all good monkeys strictly obey and enforce the law. The prohibitionists' job is not to stop the man with the hose. Their job is to beat up the monkey on the stool.

The free-thinking response would be to join together, grab the banana and the hose, and escape from the cage once and for all.

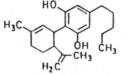

cannabidiol (CBD)

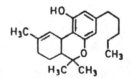

tetrahydrocannabinol (THC)

cannabinol (CBN)

olivetol (OL)

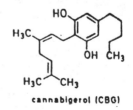

cannabigerol (CBG)

20

A NEW GENERATION OF ABOLITIONISTS

The divisions of white and slave, North and South once tore the United States apart. The Abolitionists of the 19th century rallied the nation to a higher moral ground to overturn the institution of slavery. Likewise now, the artificial divisions perpetuated by those who disrespect the principle of private choices are dividing a people meant to be as one. The new Abolitionist harkens back to the original intent of America: Unity in diversity.

Prohibition threw history and rationality out the window and replaced them with hardline ideology and brute force. Few people are aware of the corrupt conflicts of interest that initiated and sustain the suppression of hemp. Policy makers have built pot prohibition into an institution. But the resistance movement against cannabis criminalization goes back as far as the prohibition itself.

Post-Prohibition Cannabis Use in America

Time magazine noted in one article during the Second World War that "The United States (cannabis) vogue, precisely coincident with the vogue for hot jazz, began in New Orleans a generation ago, moved up the Mississippi to Chicago and thereafter spread east and west. Despite its lurid reputation, marijuana seems no more harmful than alcohol."[1] The LaGuardia Report of 1945 verified this, but national policy did not change. The doctors who did those studies were hounded by the Federal Bureau of Narcotics. The AMA was severely harassed and forced to reverse its support for cannabis, going so far as to call the landmark medical study "unscientific." Without a trace of irony, *Newsweek* called on Anslinger's FBN to act "as an umpire" to settle the public dispute.[2]

Facist McCarthyism signaled the mood of this era, the last time Republicans controlled Congress. Persecution was directed at political liberals. Actors like Robert Mitchum and jazz performers like Gene Krupa were arrested for smoking cannabis. Driven underground, the cannabis tradition was carried through the 1950s by the Beat generation, as described by poet Allen Ginsberg and by Jack Kerouac in a classic period piece, *On the Road.*

---

1 'The Weed.' in *Time*. July 19, 1943. p. 56
2 'Marijuana & Mentality.' in *Newsweek*, Nov. 18, 1946. p. 70

An Explosion of Interest in Herb

When the 1960s came along, the media rediscovered cannabis.

President John F. Kennedy fired Anslinger. In 1963 the President's Advisory Commission on Narcotics and Drug Abuse studied the evidence and said, "This Commission makes a flat distinction between the two drugs (cannabis and heroin) and believes that the unlawful sale or possession of marijuana is a less serious offense than ... of an opiate." Some say Kennedy planned to relegalize the herb after the 1964 election, based on this advice and his personal experience with cannabis for his back pain.[3]

If so, it was another plan cut short by his November 22, 1963 assassination in Dallas, Texas.

Both in America and in Europe, there came a period of high interest in cannabis during the 1960s. Hippie "flower children" sprouted across the globe with a message of peace and love. Freedom was their uniform, and cannabis was their ambassador of good will. Vietnam veterans brought back bags of the herb that had helped them cope with war and shared it with the young activists of the peace movement. Mick Jagger of the Rolling Stones spent six months in jail for possession of the herb. The Beatles took out a full page ad in the *London Times* in 1967 calling for cannabis relegalization. Three bandmembers were eventually arrested for cannabis.[4] Pop music charts were full of songs laced with lyrical imagery that alluded to cannabis and mind-altering experiences.[5]

President Lyndon Johnson's Commission on Law Enforcement and Administration of Justice reported in 1967 that[6]

> Marijuana is equated in law with the opiates, but the abuse characteristic of the two have almost nothing in common. The opiate produces physical dependence. Marijuana does not. A withdrawal sickness appears when use of the opiates is discontinued. No such symptoms are associated with marijuana. The desired dose of opiates tends to increase over time, but this is not true of marijuana. ... There are too many marijuana users who do not graduate to heroin, and too many heroin addicts with no known prior marijuana use, to support such a [gateway drug, or stepping stone] theory. Moreover, there is no scientific basis for such a theory.

In England a special government commission was launched to investigate the "drug" issue. Conservative parliamentarians were

[3]Herer, Jack. *Hemp & the Marijuana Conspiracy: The Emperor Wears No Clothes.* HEMP Publishing. Van Nuys, CA. 1991. pp. 56, 140
[4]John Lennon Oct. 1968, George Harrison March 1969 & Paul McCartney Jan. 1980.
[5]'Incense & Peppermints,' Strawberry Alarm Clock. 'White Rabbit,' Jefferson Airplane. 'Journey to the Center of the Mind,' Amboy Dukes. 'Are You Experienced?' Jimi Hendrix. 'A Day in the Life,' Beatles. 'One Toke Over the Line,' Brewer & Shipley. 'Rainy Day Woman (Everybody Must Get Stoned),' Bob Dylan. Etc.
[6]Cited in King, R. *The Drug Hangup.* C.C. Thomas. Springfield IL. 1974. pp. 94-95

shocked when the Wootton Report stopped just short of calling for the legalization of cannabis in 1968. Liberals were equally upset that the commission had succumbed to political pressure in not calling for its full legalization.[7]

Cannabis use became common on university campuses. Soon the herb smoking population numbered in the millions. The plant's public image shifted dramatically when it was said that its use at the gigantic 1969 Woodstock gathering kept it peaceful. People considered what might have happened if alcohol had been the "drug of choice" at the rock festival, instead of cannabis. They watched musicians who smoked the herb on stage and gave some of the greatest performances of their careers.

A Softening of Political Opinion & Tone

Cannabis smoking branched into the peace movement and the ecology and anti-nuclear movements. It spread across society and reached the highest levels of government and industry. Smokers and dealers alike were still occasionally arrested, but outlaw cannabis dealers became not only millionaires but heroes.[8]

With tens of millions of regular smokers in 1970, *Newsweek* ran a cover story, "Marijuana: Time to Change the Law?"[9] The question soon became "How long until they change the law?" A young lawyer, R. Keith Stroup, received a small grant and formed the National Organization for Reform of Marijuana Laws, or NORML.[10] The San Francisco-based Amorphia "cannabis cooperative" sold Acapulco Gold cannabis cigarette rolling papers to help finance marijuana initiatives in several states in 1972. A third of the voters in California said yes to legal cannabis that year.[11] Investigators found it difficult to link health problems to the herb, and a 1972 Presidential commission favored *decriminalization*. It was presented as a conservative version of legalization, designed to discourage experimentation and use.

In Holland, a policy of tolerance began in Amsterdam and spread throughout the land. Soon cannabis and hashish, labelled "soft drugs," were being sold openly in coffee shops throughout the nation. Back in America, one study after another proved that cannabis was no threat to society, and even had distinct medical

7Schofield, Michael. *The Strange Case of Pot*. Penguin. NY NY & London. 1970
8Warner, Roger. *Invisible Hand: The marijuana business*. Beech Tree/Morrow. New York NY. 1986
9'Marijuana: Time to change the law?' in *Newsweek*. Sept. 7, 1970
10From the Playboy Foundation. Anderson, Patrick. *High in America, The true story behind NORML & the politics of marijuana*. Viking Press. New York NY. 1981. p. 45
11*Ibid*. p. 100

value. Marijuana smuggler Tom Forçade founded *High Times* magazine to promote the issue. On August 2, 1977, President Jimmy Carter called for an end to penalizing cannabis use: "Penalties against possession of a drug should not be more damaging to an individual than the use of the drug itself."

Human rights was a political priority. The backyard cannabis plant became a fixture in the lives of young suburbanites and college students. Studies in Jamaica,[12] Costa Rica, and even the United States shed new light on the positive social and medical benefits of moderate cannabis consumption. Pushed by support for legalization, individual states adopted more lenient laws. Jamaican reggae music discovered America and Bob Marley sang "Get up, stand up for your rights," while Peter Tosh replied "Legalize it, and I will advertise it." Worried that legalization would further bolster the herb's popularity and lead to commercialization along the lines of tobacco and alcohol, the decriminalization concept caught on nationally. This approach served to divert cannabis smokers from the hard drug market, and policy makers sought to separate the issues.

Remove Penalties, Reduce Consumption

If the desire is to reduce cannabis consumption, a fundamental question must be asked. Do stiff penalties and jail terms accomplish this? Experience suggests that other factors are more effective and economical than the criminal penal system.

Cannabis use peaked in Colorado at about the time cannabis decriminalization was enacted in 1975. Afterwards, herb use fell sharply, especially among the youngest age groups. It essentially remained level in Oregon when a similar law was enacted in 1973. Likewise, in Maine cannabis use stayed flat after decriminalization.

When the California legislature debated the Moscone bill, similar to Colorado's, opponents said that abolishing jail terms would give a green light to potential cannabis users. A survey of street arrests and emergency room admissions 10 years later held that "the two best statistical indicators of drug use in California show that lowering penalties for marijuana possession did not cause a rise in the use."[13] Ann Arbor, Michigan, enacted an ordinance making cannabis possession a $5 fine,[14] overriding a state law making possession a felony. Despite the drastic reduction in the penalty, a survey of high school students showed no increase in cannabis use. A

---

[12]Sullivan, W. 'Marijuana study by US finds no serious harm.' in *New York Times.* July 9, 1975. p. C-2
[13]Kopel, D. 'Marijuana Jail Terms: Costly & hasty.' in *Independence Issue Paper.* Independence Institute. Golden CO. no 5-91. April 24, 1991. pp. 1-8
[14]Raised to $25 in 1990.

subsequent national study found that cannabis use rose and fell without any apparent relation to the severity of the law.[15]

The Addiction Research Foundation surveyed the studies:[16]

Decriminalization of marijuana does not appear to have had a major impact on the rates of use, as many people feared it might. ... (It) would appear that decriminalization measures have succeeded in reducing the costs without substantially increasing the health and safety hazards.

Most people thought that cannabis reform had won. Prosecutions dropped dramatically. Cannabis smokers joined the work ethic. Beer drinking and herb smoking went hand-in-hand. The plant's popularity and favorable public attitude peaked about 1978. The Gallup Poll in 1980 found that 53 percent of Americans polled favored the relegalization of small amounts of cannabis.[17]

Federal crime statistics chart a continuous drop in cannabis use that began in 1979, the period of greatest acceptance for cannabis. Complacency had set in. Official support for decriminalization and medical cannabis deflected the energy of legalization advocates.

The drive for full legalization lost its steam. Membership in support groups dried up. NORML diverted its resources to defend non-cannabis drug rights, particularly cocaine defendants. That decision came back to haunt them with a vengeance.

Drug Warriors' Counter-Offensive

At the end of the 1970s, the American economy began to falter, largely due to the dual pressure of a gas shortage, created by in ternational petroleum interests, and high inflation, caused by federal reserve board policies. Gabriel Nahas and friends controlled both national and international cannabis research and stepped up their disinformation effort. When Carter lost the 1980 election, the Reagan/Bush prohibition machine took power.

They fired up a low-burning witch hunt, with harsh penalties, urine tests, property seizures and a massive anti-cannabis propaganda campaign devoid of substance.[18] General anti-drug messages that were too inaccurate to be taken seriously began to gain credence through sheer repetition. Cannabis advocates found the charges too

15Comparing over an extended period of time states with harsh cannabis laws to states with milder ones & ones that reduced penalties. Saveland & Bray. 'American trends in cannabis use among States with different & changing legal regimes.' Bureau of Tobacco Control & Biometrics, Health & Welfare. Ottawa Canada. 1980

16Single, Eric. 'The Impact of Marijuana Decriminalization.' *Research Advances in Alcohol & Drug Problems*. Addiction Research Foundation. Plenum Pub. 1981. p. 423

17Musto, David. 'Opium, cocaine & marijuana in American history.' in *Scientific American*. July 1991. pp. 45-46

18"The one means that wins the easiest victory over reason: terror & force." Hitler, Adolph. *Mein Kampf*. Berlin Germany. 1924

absurd for comment. If they did comment, they found their remarks censored out of the press.

The slow process of attrition began with a bust here and a bust there. Shops which were the mainstay of support and a major site of networking among political liberals and cannabis activists were closed down because they sold pipes, papers and smoking utensils. In 1985, prices soared and growers bunkered down and moved indoors under full scale military attacks on their outdoor gardens. Reagan had been packing the federal courts with political hacks who would disregard the Constitution and rule on ideology.

Prohibitionists soon had secret police agents in every community and turned families inside out to uncover cannabis smokers. By 1986 only 27 percent of people surveyed would admit that they favored the herb's relegalization.[19]

The inner cities and suburbs were flooded with cheap and deadly white powders in the 1980s. Some asserted that the severe crackdown on the herb lead directly to the sharp increase in cocaine use.[20] At the same time, government officials engaged in the trafficking of hard drugs.[21] Prohibitionists used the crack cocaine epidemic as a smokescreen to deliberately confuse the public about cannabis. They used federal money and the mass media to psychologically link the herb with hard drugs. The DEA even imported cocaine and staged phony drug captures to rationalize its own excesses.[22]

Some legislators simply like the political message made by mandatory minimum jail terms for casual possession of cannabis, but they often have to resort to deceit and backroom deals to put it through. The federal ban was disguised as a tax revenue measure. An attempt to recriminalize cannabis in Colorado was hidden in a single sentence, deep inside a measure entitled "A bill for an act concerning elimination of substance abuse in the criminal justice system and making appropriations in connection therewith."[23]

Threats to withold millions of dollars in highway funds was used to extort California and other states to adopt "Smoke a joint, lose your license" bills to suspend drivers licenses of even non-driving "drug" offenders for 60 days.

---

[19]Those favoring penalties rose from 43-67%. Musto. op. cit.
[20]*Washington Times*. Washington DC. Sept. 11, 1990
[21]Cockburn, L. *Out of Control*. Atlantic Monthly Press. New York NY. 1987
[22]Associated Press. 'False Reports: US drug agency orders phony busts.' in *San Francisco Chronicle*. CA. Nov. 28, 1988
[23]Introduced in 1991. Kopel. op. cit.

Alternatives to the Failure of Prohibition

With all the distinctions that we have drawn between cannabis and other drugs, there is still one fateful link that holds them together: prohibition. Let's look now at the overall drug situation. "Government cannot be expected to solve the drug problem," the 1972 federal Commission report flatly stated. "Indeed, it is symbolic of a disturbing trend in American life that we have turned to the government to do so, not as a last resort but as a matter of habit."[24]

Twenty years experience shows it was right. A straightforward question that proponents of prohibition have never been able to answer is this: What good results can be directly attributed to their cherished policy? Apparently, there are none. Privately, more and more people have come to the conclusion that the only way to take the profits out of illegal "drugs" is to make them legal once again, so legitimate and honest businesses will be back in control.

Researchers at the Washington DC-based Drug Policy Foundation[25] offered this analysis: Stress causes drug use. The vast majority of those who use drugs are casual users. People who use drugs tend not to commit other crimes. Drugs in the workplace are not a serious burden on productivity. More problems are caused by making drug use a crime than by the use itself.[26]

While support for overall drug relegalization has grown, many people still oppose the open-market approach to drug sales. Sociologist Georgette Bennett, author of *Crime Warps: The future of crime in America,* proposed a system where only federally-licensed drug stores and clinics would sell hard drugs.[27] No advertising or brand name competition would be permitted. Driving while impaired and selling drugs on the black market would be subject to prosecution.

Eric Sterling of the Criminal Justice Policy Foundation in Washington DC proposed a more tightly controlled "Consulting Pharmacist Model." Hard drugs could only be purchased from a specially-trained pharmacist who would counsel people on how to use them safely and try to sell them the least harmful drugs. The pharmacy could sell only to those who have a "drug license" indicating they had been educated on safe drug use and were of legal age. Addicts would have special licenses and would be counseled each time they purchased drugs.

---

[24]*Report of the National Commission on Marijuana & Drug Abuse.* US Govt. Printing Office. Washington DC. 1973
[25]Drug Policy Foundation. 4801 Massachusetts Ave., NW # 400, Washington DC 20016-2087. 202-895-1634
[26]Morris, David. 'Drug Stories.' in *Anchorage Daily News.* May 12, 1991. p. J-1
[27]These would be taxed, but costs would be kept low. Poor addicts would receive free drugs, but treatment & employment training would be mandatory.

Another reform concept was developed by Tod Mikuriya, M.D., a consultant to the federal Shafer Commission in 1972 and the California Senate Select Committee on Control of Marijuana in 1974.[28] He proposed nine steps to "Drug Peace,"[29] based on the concept that "responsibility and accountability would be achieved through producers and users paying the costs of the side effects of the drug."

He recommends that drug tax rates and users' fees, including alcohol and tobacco, be based on actual use/morbidity factors indicating the relative risk of each substance. Transaction fees would be collected as sales tax. Since the DEA is already involved in identifying and preventing the use of precursor chemicals for the production of illicit substances, their international efforts to suppress the manufacture of and traffic in controlled substances suit them ideally to eradicate chemical and biological weapons.

"With the DEA data base and network of contacts, they could be quite helpful in this effort. Revising their list and distribution channels to be monitored would be an easy transition for a system that has been in place for some time."

Abolishing Prohibition & Controlling Drugs

What undermines prohibition is that it is based on a lie. Criminal "drug control" does not control drugs, dangerous or otherwise. To the contrary, it takes the market out of the normal scope of governmental control—the setting of age limits, issuing permits and licenses, collecting taxes, etc.—and puts it into the hands of the most dangerous and out-of-control groups in society: organized crime and corrupt law enforcement agencies.[30]

Legally licensed distributors, on the other hand, stand to lose lucrative incomes if their permits are revoked. British police sergeant Gordon Payne explained that relegalization will take the trade out of

---

[28]Mikuriya, member of the American & California Societies for the Treatment of Alcoholism & Other Drug Dependence, was the first director of federal cannabis research for the National Inst. of Mental Health Center for Narcotics & Drug Abuse Studies.

[29]1) Earmark alcohol/tobacco taxes for drug abuse prevention/treatment for a reliable source of funds. 2) Rescind alcohol & tobacco product liability exemptions. 3) Remove tobacco allotments & price supports. 4) Establish pharmacy-based drug users' voluntary co-ops. 5) Legalize personal home cultivation of cannabis; regulate its commercial market, like alcohol & tobacco. 6) Forbid warrantless searches & urine tests. 7) Test those who order drug tests for others. 8) Schedule steroids as controlled substances. 9) Redeploy DEA to eradicate chemical weapons. Mikuriya, Dr. Tod. 'A comprehensive proposal to legalize drugs.' in *California Physician*. CA. December 1989. p. 19

[30]Crack gets preference over marijuana because black marketeers prefer more profit for the same risk. To settle differences, they cannot turn to regulating agencies, so they resort to violence or work in organized criminal gangs. The criminal drug dealer has little more to lose by selling to a school child rather than an adult or by mixing dangerous fillers into drugs. Disgruntled customers have no recourse for their complaints.

the hands of criminals. "Legitimate businessmen would be responsible for production, processing, packing, distribution, retail and quality control, as they are for tobacco. Even allowing for profits and taxes, the price would be much lower."[31]

The 20th Annual California Attorney General's Report, 1989 studied the effects of drugs and criminalization on society. After a full review, the panelists still supported prohibition in principle, but noted that current policies did not control the availability or abuse of hard drugs. These experts criticized the contradictory nature of the law and advised a more consistent policy.[32]

> The first suggestions for demonstration legislation, rationalized and detailed herein are: 1) Permit the possession of syringes and needles. 2) Permit the cultivation of marijuana. 3) As a first step in projecting an attitude of disapproval by all citizens toward drug use, take a token action in forbidding sale or consumption of alcohol in state supported institutions devoted in part or whole to patient care and educational activity.

This suggestion made a number of advances over current policies. Perhaps most significantly, it recognized that cannabis is in a class by itself, and that alcohol is also a drug. The logical extension is to establish a uniform standard to apply for evaluation of cannabis, alcohol, tobacco, hard drugs and food additives and regulate them accordingly. A common recommendation, even among a growing number of police[33] and prohibitionists,[34] is to start the reform process by moving cannabis consumers out of the hard drug market by relegalizing or decriminalizing the herb. Public support for legalizing prescription medical cannabis has been strong for decades. A national telephone survey conducted by *Parade* magazine in June 1994 found that 76 percent of respondents agreed marijuana "should be as legal as alcoholic beverages."[35]

Two commonly offered models for regulation are the tobacco and wine models, both of which allow the individual to produce a limited amount of the product for their personal consumption. Further regulations apply to commercial production.

The distinction is that, while all illicit drugs are often used as frivolous pastimes, cannabis also has legitimate industrial, spiritual and medical uses. That brings us to still another crisis posed by the policy of cannabis prohibition.

---

[31]Payne, Sgt. Gordon. 'The drug problem upside down.' in *The Guardian*. Manchester England. Feb. 28, 1992
[32]California State Research Advisory Panel. *20th Annual Report*. State of CA Attorney General's office. Sacramento CA. 1990. Sections suppressed.
[33]Payne, Sgt. Gordon. 'Why drugs must be made legal.' in *Police Review*. London England. Feb. 28, 1992. p. 388-389
[34]California Research Advisory Panel. op. cit.
[35]'What readers say about marijuana.' in *Parade*. July 31, 1994. p. 16

The Great Marijuana Medical Debate

With a 5000 year medical history of widespread medical benefits and a nearly total lack of negative side effects, medical use of cannabis has only recently become a controversial subject.

The *United States Dispensatory* first listed cannabis in 1854. It was officially removed from the United States Pharmacopoeia and National Formulary in 1941. Incredibly, most European countries lack the medical cannabis exemption required by the preamble to the Single Convention Treaty,[36] which states, "The medical use of narcotic drugs continues to be indispensable for the relief of pain and suffering and ... adequate provisions must be made to ensure the availability of narcotic drugs for such purposes.... ." The right to effective medicine is also guaranteed by the Universal Declaration of Human Rights.[37]

The United States has many provisions for medical cannabis on the federal, state and local levels. The Controlled Substances Act of 1970 provided a comprehensive system of federal drug control laws in the United States. It established five schedules of controlled substances, with Schedule I containing those which meet the following criteria:

1) A high potential for abuse
2) No currently accepted medical use in treatment in the United States, and
3) A lack of accepted safety for use ... under medical supervision.

In 1975, the Secretary of Health, Education and Welfare reviewed data and reported that the most promising applications of cannabis were for treatment of glaucoma, for cancer patients receiving chemotherapy and possibly for asthmatics. "Applications as a sedative-hypnotic, an anti-convulsant, an antidepressant, an analgesic and in connection with the treatment of alcoholics have been attempted, but the results have either been inconsistent or highly preliminary."[38]

Congress took action in 1978. The Compassionate Investigational New Drug (IND) program was developed to provide doctors with legal supplies of cannabis provided by the federal government to treat patients suffering from life- or sense-threatening condi-

---

[36]*UN Single Convention Treaty on Narcotic Drugs*. 1961. Signed by the US in 1968
[37]Article 25.1. "Everyone has the right to a standard of living adequate for the health & well-being of himself & of his family, including food, clothing, housing & medical care & necessary social services."
[38]Secretary of Health, Education & Welfare. '*Marihuana & Health: In Perspective.*' US Govt Printing Office. 1975

tions.[39] This plan backfired, however, because it required the consent of multiple regulatory agencies to conduct research.

Furthermore, it ignored the entire scientific record and medical pharmacopeia accumulated over more than a century, and required researchers to start from the beginning as if cannabis was a new drug. In fact, the DEA treats all pre-1978 studies as folk medicine, and positive scientific studies are discounted.[40] Then the Costa Rican studies,[41] showing extraordinary health care potential for cannabis, were censored.[42] To prevent widespread exposure of its results, the NIH printed only 300 copies. The National Academy of Science next pronounced, "Marijuana has a broad range of psychological and biological effects, some of which, at least under certain conditions, are harmful to human health."[43] Its Committee on Substance Abuse and Habitual Behavior report recommended that possession and private use of small amounts of cannabis should no longer be crimes. That part of the NAS survey report was disavowed and censored.[44] Government arguments that cannabis posed serious health risks and had no acceptable, safe use were highly suspect, to say the least. In the years between 1978 and 1987, NIDA authorized, produced and oversaw the distribution of 477,507 cannabis cigarettes for human consumption.[45] No recipient has ever declined the herb or complained of intolerable side effects.

By the late 1980s, 33 states had enacted legislation recognizing the valid medical uses of cannabis.[46]

In May 1991, the United Nations re-scheduled delta-9-THC into Schedule 2 of the 1971 Convention on Psychotropic Substances, but failed to re-schedule the herb out of Schedule 1. The stated reason was that delta-9-THC has proven medical benefits and was "not

---

[39]MARS, Marijuana AIDS Research Service. A project of the Alliance for Cannabis Therapeutics & Richard J. Dennis

[40]The European Community, on the other hand, protects 'folk medicine' usage, but has not officially recognized cannabis as a folk remedy.

[41]Carter, Wm. ed. Cannabis in Costa Rica: A study in chronic marijuana use. Institute for the Study of Man. Philadelphia PA. 1980

[42]A copy was sneaked out to the National Organization to Reform Marijuana Laws (NORML). The Reagan administration & National Institute of Health refused the report three times, then gave up on the research scientists & rewrote it themselves.

[43]Institute of Medicine, National Academy of Sciences. Marijuana & Health. 1982. p.5

[44]in Time. July 19, 1982

[45]Below from: Mazur, Cynthia S. 'Marijuana as a Holy Sacrament.' Notre Dame Journal of Law, Ethics & Public Policy. vol 5:3. 1991. pp. 693-727

[46]Alabama, Arizona, Arkansas, California, Colorado, Connecticut, Florida, Georgia, Illinois, Iowa, Louisiana, Maine, Michigan, Minnesota, Montana, Nevada, New Hampshire, New Jersey, New Mexico, New York, North Carolina, Ohio, Oklahoma, Oregon, Rhode Island, South Carolina, Tennessee, Texas, Vermont, Virginia, Washington, West Virginia & Wisconsin. in 'Cannabis & Medicine.' ACT. Washington DC. Massachusetts added its name to the list in 1991.

widely used outside legitimate medical channels" while cannabis was "used illegally by millions of people worldwide." In other words, synthetic drug companies could control all the money from sale and distribution of THC, but not the herb.

Justices Say No to Criminalizing Medicine

Government autocrats have fought off the medical use of cannabis through various legal and bureaucratic delaying tactics since 1972, the year Alliance for Cannabis Therapeutics, NORML, McKinney, Olsen et al. filed a suit against the DEA. Sixteen years later, in September 1988, DEA Administrative Law Judge Francis Young, after two years of hearings on the case, finally concluded that the herb does have accepted medical use to treat nausea from chemotherapy, multiple sclerosis, spasticity and hyper-parathyroidism.[47]

> The cannabis plant considered as a whole has a currently accepted medical use in treatment in the United States, there is no lack of accepted safety for use under medical supervision and it may lawfully be transferred from Schedule I to Schedule II. The judge recommends the Administrator transfer cannabis. Based upon the facts established in this record and set out above, one must reasonably conclude that there is accepted safety for use of marijuana under medical supervision. To conclude otherwise, on this record, would be unreasonable, arbitrary and capricious.

The Agency had millions of dollars and 16 years to prove cannabis was not a safe natural medicine. They totally and utterly failed to do so. More than a year later, in December 1989, DEA Administrator John Lawn, who is not a doctor, simply refused to move cannabis out of Schedule I, the most restrictive. Millions of seriously ill people still are forced to go without, or to break the law and risk prison and assets forfeiture to find relief.

A 1991 Harvard University survey found that 44 percent of American cancer specialists have already recommended that their patients smoke cannabis to relieve chemotherapy side effects. Forty-eight percent said they would prescribe it in some cases, if it was legal, and 54 percent agreed that it should be legal to prescribe.[48]

The Appeals Court in April 1991 supported Judge Young, unanimously declaring that the DEA's Lawn had acted "with a vengeance" on his prerogative[49] to reject the recommended decision.

---

[47]Young, Francis L. DEA Administrative Law Judge. *in the Matter of Marijuana Rescheduling Petition*, Docket No 86-22. Sept. 6, 1988

[48]Ostrow, Ronald J. '48% of Cancer Specialists in Study Would Prescribe Pot.' in *Los Angeles Times*. May 1, 1991. p. A-12

[49]Under *Universal Camera Corp vs NLRB*, 340 US 474, 477 (1951). Lawn claimed that "the vast majority of physicians" do not accept marijuana as having a medical

Lawn had declared that the herb must meet an eight-part test from the Food, Drug and Cosmetic Act.[50] These criteria were ruled irrelevant to the DEA's mission. "Three of the factors in the Administrator's eight factor test appear impossible to fulfill and thus must be regarded as arbitrary and capricious ... perforce unreasonable."

The jurists asked how any Schedule I drug could be in general use or generally available. If a drug cannot be prescribed, "regardless of its safety or use—it will not appear in a pharmaceutical listing of medically useful drugs." They required the Agency to explain how all these factors were utilized in reaching its decision, and what role the eight criteria factors played in its decision.[51]

Renegade Bureaucrats Spur Public Outcry

The unilateral DEA decision to first delay and then disobey the law and all Congressional, international and judicial mandates to provide medical cannabis was not based on its therapeutic record, but to "send a message" that the Agency does not "condone" drug use, not even to save people's senses or to relieve the sick and dying. This delay has prolonged people's suffering from chronic pain and sense loss. When the role of cannabis in relief of AIDS symptoms was revealed, over 300 people with AIDS applied for medical access to it. Expressing "concern" about a sudden surge in applications from critically ill people, especially AIDS and cancer patients, the federal Public Health Service in 1991 stopped approving such requests unless another drug, Eli Lilly's *Marinol*, is tried first.[52] Even the White House Office of Drug Control Policy on January 30, 1992 recoiled at this, calling it "unconscionable" for the Health and Human Services Department to delay in deciding whether to lift a ban on cannabis for seriously ill patients. In a letter to Chief of Public Health Service James Mason, the office urged that cannabis be given immediately to 30 patients who had already been approved to receive it but had been put on hold in July 1990 while staff functionaries reviewed the program. "At this point it would be grossly unfair for the federal government to reverse its approval," wrote Ingrid Kolb, acting Deputy Director for Demand Reduction.

---

use: & it is "not recognized as medicine in generally accepted pharmacopoeia, medical references, journals or textbooks."
[50] Without Food & Drug Administration approval, the Appeals Court said, "commonly accepted medical use cannot be proven."
[51] Silberman, Buckley & Henderson, Circuit Judges. Opinion filed by Silberman. US Court of Appeals for the District of Columbia Circuit. *No 90-1019, ACT vs DEA. No 90-1020, NORML vs DEA*. Decided April 26, 1991
[52] Bear in mind that George Bush was a major stockholder in Eli Lilly. 'Marijuana for ill is curbed by US' in *New York Times*. June 23, 1991. p. 17. also Isikoff, M. 'HHS to phase out marijuana program.' in *Washington Post*. June 22 1991. p. A-14

In addition to the 30 patients, Kolb said dozens of eligible patients "are suffering from great pain—many are dying."

The DEA replied that the compassionate cannabis program had been set up by Congress "years ago" and the number of patients receiving the herb had dwindled to 12. "They don't have true proof [of cannabis's usefulness], but they had a doctor's opinion" and convinced judges they should receive it under the government program. "To treat this matter as just another bureaucratic decision ... shows an intolerable lack of compassion," Kolb said in her letter.[53] Robert Bonner, the new DEA administrator, then cut off the program completely, only providing cannabis to the handful of surviving recipients. The medicine was withheld from 28 people who had already been approved to receive it.[54]

The Alliance for Cannabis Therapeutics called for Chief Administrator James Mason's resignation in December, 1991. The federal program was officially cancelled in March, 1992. The Family Council on Drug Awareness demanded Mason be fired in March, 1992, and the International Human Rights Taskforce (I-Heart) supported the call. Congressman Henry Waxman promised to hold hearings on medical cannabis, stating "Health professionals want medical marijuana. ... Right Wing politicians don't." But, as of early 1993, Waxman had not even scheduled such hearings.

The Commonwealth of Massachusetts adopted a compassionate medical cannabis law in 1991. A citizen-sponsored initiative in the City of San Francisco ballot that same year, Proposition P, was overwhelmingly approved by almost four to one.[55] The proponents sought to responsibly implement the measure by setting up a comprehensive research project into the benefits and risks of hemp drugs.

In 1992, a public service group put forth an omnibus medical access bill proposal and began collecting Congressional sponsors.[56]

No law of the United States or of the individual states shall be construed so as to prohibit the prescription by a licensed physician of any mixture, admixture, poultice, tincture or derivative of, or the natural forms of the plant cannabis sativa or cannabis indica, known as marijuana or hemp, for diseases or conditions deemed beneficially treatable by the physician, to the patient. No law of the United States or of the individual states shall be held or construed so as to penalize in any way patients in posses-

---

[53]Ostrow, R. 'Delay in lifting pot ban to aid seriously ill is assailed.' in *LA Times*. Jan. 31 1992. p. A-13

[54]Cotton, Paul. 'Government extinguishes marijuana access, advocates smell politics.' in *Journal of the AMA*. vol. 267:19. May 20, 1992. pp. 2573-2574

[55]132,626 to 34,463

[56]Proposed Omnibus Law guaranteeing the right to prescribe cannabis by licensed physicians, right to possession of therapeutic amount of cannabis by patient. Initiated by BACH, Virginia. 1991

sion of both a lawfully issued active prescription and forms, derivatives of, or the natural plant cannabis sativa or cannabis indica.

The prescription shall so state the amount and form(s) of the derivations or natural plant prescribed and both the duration and frequency of intake by the patient. This law shall not be so construed as to apply to an aggregate amount in excess of that lawfully prescribed.

In early 1992, the California Medical Association noted that the "therapeutic use of cannabinoids may be appropriate for certain conditions."[57] It encouraged a comprehensive clinical study to establish protocols for prescriptive uses of cannabinoids.

In 1994, the Clinton administration extended the medical ban.

Medical Implications of Criminalizing a Plant

The medical use of cannabis should not be impeded by policies dictated by a handful of special interests, like the pharmaceutical companies and prohibitionists. Desperate patients say they would rather live by buying and using illegal marijuana than die by playing by the rules set by DEA autocrats.

Ken Jenks is a hemophiliac. He got AIDS through contaminated blood in 1980. He unknowingly infected his wife, Barbara. Both became too sick to work. They lived on disability, barely able to cope. Without cannabis, they probably would have wasted away and died, because of the nausea brought on by chemotherapy. But they found it really helped them eat and retain food like nothing else had. Then, one day, a new horror began. A police raid and arrest was added to their problems. They were charged with growing marijuana and possessing drug paraphernalia. In court their lawyer argued that they used the herb out of medical necessity. The prosecution agreed and even stipulated that it helped them and they would die without it.

The DEA has maintained for years that cannabis has no therapeutic value, that it's a dangerous drug and must remain illegal. However, no one from the DEA would come onto CBS's *Sixty Minutes* and respond to scientific evidence from those who say otherwise.[58] Dr. Ivan Silverberg in San Francisco works with cancer patients. "I have yet to hear of a patient who can't find it," he said. "... Morphine for example, Demerol, are far more hazardous drugs, in my opinion, than marijuana. I think part of it is an entrenched bureaucracy that doesn't want to admit it's wrong."

---

[57] Introduced to CMA by Tod Mikuriya, M.D. March 14-18, 1992
[58] Safer, Morley. 'Smoking to Live.' CBS News. *60 Minutes*. vol. 24:11. Dec. 1, 1991

As reformers gather momentum in their effort to reclaim the medicinal use of cannabis,[59] they must also recognize the validity of human consumption by others for religious sacrament and personal relaxation, as well as the importance of industrial hemp.

Convergence of Interest in Hemp Reform

The popular low point of support for cannabis reform seems to have hit in 1990, with the narrow vote in Alaska to recriminalize personal use of cannabis.[60] That same year, a new wave of support for hemp began to be felt.[61] Behind the scenes, new connections were being made between the cannabis movement and ecology, farm, industrial and civil liberties groups. In California, four prohibition bills on the ballot were rejected by state voters, and a government advisory commission publicly recommended that the State legalize cannabis growing.[62]

The *Los Angeles Times* reported on seven openly pro-cannabis candidates running for elective office.[63] The growing number of public advocates of cannabis legalization included economist Milton Friedman, former Attorney General Ramsey Clark, former Secretary of State George Shultz, Baltimore Mayor Kurt Schmoke and United States District Judge Robert Sweet of New York.[64]

In 1992, 50,000 people rallied for hemp reform in Atlanta, Georgia, the biggest such event held in the United States to date.[65] A national college newspaper reported that the movement for cannabis relegalization had once again burst onto the campuses, with rallies on hundreds of campuses around the country, at large and small schools, public and private alike.[66]

Holland has clung tenaciously to its successful policy of separating cannabis from hard drugs, despite strong pressure from its larger neighbors. Amsterdam is the only European city where nar-

---

[59]Bandow, Doug. 'Sometimes marijuana is the best medicine.' in *Wall Street Journal*, January 28, 1993. p. A-15

[60]By a margin of 54-46%. The Bush administration had threatened to withold highway construction funds from the state if it voted to retain legalization.

[61]Leland, J. 'Just say maybe.' in *Newsweek*. Nov. 1, 1993. See chart on p. 52

[62]California Research Advisory Panel. op. cit. also *LA Times*. Aug. 18, 1990

[63]1) KY gubernatorial candidate Democrat Gatewood Galbraith; 2) NH Congressional primary/GOP Michael Weddle; 3) KS Cong. candidate Demo Mark Creamer; 4) MI Cong. George Crockett, Jr., incumbent Demo; 5) MO State Rep Elbert Walton, incumbent Demo; 6) NY State Sen. Joe Galiber, incumbent Demo; & 7) NJ, Mercer County executive Bill Mathesius, incumbent GOP. in *LA Times*. CA. Aug. 18, 1990. Also, OR Libertarian gubernatorial candidate Dr. Fred Oerther. UPI. May 20, 1990

[64]*LA Times*. July 29, 1990

[65]Opdyke & Devault. 'A 60s style be-in without the angst." in *Atlanta Journal*. GA. April 12, 1992. p. D-1

[66]'Is Pot Making a Comeback?' in *U, The national college newspaper*. vol. 4. February 1991. p. 1

cotics addiction appears to be falling and its policy is catching on. A group of 17 cities and regions in Germany, Italy, Greece, Portugal, Switzerland and the Netherlands recently signed the Frankfurt Resolution, calling for the "decriminalization and depenalization" of drug use and users.[67]

In November 1991 the Swiss Supreme Court ruled that criminal penalties for cannabis use, in the absence of such penalties for alcohol, violated the equal protection clause of the Constitution. Around the same time, a German Superior Court made a similar ruling, sending shock waves through Europe. Even more exciting was the amount of support the decision brought from police and government officials. Hashish in Europe is generally smoked with tobacco. Herbal cannabis is still relatively hard to locate there, except in Holland. Cannabis is popular throughout Spain. Public consumption was only banned there in late 1991—a little-noticed clause in a sweeping anti-terrorism law. Privacy is still a cherished value in Spain, and personal possession within the household is still legal. However, cultivation of cannabis sativa is a governmental monopoly that requires a special license, and cultivation of indica is banned.

The Face of the New Abolitionist Movement

Working under a *de facto* media blackout by the major media, various pro-hemp and anti-prohibition groups have been moving on many different levels, independently but simultaneously. Cannabis supporters are organizing on new political and legal fronts. They recognize that smoking the herb is an act of nonviolent civil disobedience and are reaching out to the prisoners of conscience who are persecuted for doing so. The reformers have taken a major step by becoming better organized and more visible, by challenging myths and by holding out a consistent, multi-level vision.

Most importantly, they now acknowledge the full importance of the plant itself. After decades of discussing only civil liberties and the medical issue, the movement has at last expanded its base into its natural allies, the business and environmental communities. Any cost/benefit analysis demonstrates that change is inevitable; the question has become one of facilitation. Separate issues, like property forfeiture, school education, judicial prejudice, medical cruelty, political injustice, economic infrastructures and ecological necessity, are drawing together in one struggle.

Recent tactics have included people going before city councils and county boards to exempt the medical cannabis user from crimi-

---

67AP. 'Europeans leaning toward permissive Dutch drug policy.' in *Times Colonist*. April 7, 1992

nal charges and urge police to end cannabis enforcement in order to concentrate on violent crimes. Class action suits are being aimed at propaganda groups like PDFA and DARE for causing people direct financial harm, mental stress, damage to job prospects and reputation, alienation of family affection, fomenting social problems, violating their political tax exemptions, etc. Outraged parents have been going to school boards and PTA associations to demand accuracy of cannabis information in drug education, to monitor the programs and to get DARE-type propaganda banned from the schools. People today have seen how the lies about cannabis have backfired and led to increased use of hard drugs like cocaine, liquor, glue sniffing and so on. It is not enough to send kids a signal, give them the facts, show them the relative risks, and teach them personal responsibility.

There is talk of more ambitious plans, like enough sympathetic people moving into a selected state or municipality to create a voting majority and legalize hemp that way. Several plans are underway to develop a cannabis medical refuge outside the United States, such as in Holland, for those who cannot get the herb legally in America. Another proposal is to get thousands of cannabis smokers to turn themselves into police investigators on July 4, Independence Day, thereby overwhelming the court and penal systems.

The sheer unthinking brutality of police cannabis suppression has lent tragic eloquence to cries for justice. These cries carry the weight of Constitutional and international law, along with moral and religious conviction, to defend the principles of personal liberty and cultural diversity.

Why Not? The Other Side of the Argument

"Make the most of the *Indian hemp* seed," wrote President George Washington. "And sow it everywhere."[68]

When will the government follow this sage bit of advice? How long will it take? Why not right now? Much of the information on the benefits of hemp described herein is from government sources. Every independent panel of experts the government has ever commissioned has, without exception, opposed the penalization of cannabis.[69] Nonetheless, prohibitionists and government "experts"

---

[68]Washington, G. 'Note to Mt. Vernon Gardener.' *Writing of George Washington.* Library of Congress. 1794. vol 33. p. 270

[69]"The use of cannabis has been subject of many official enquiries. These enquiries have reached strikingly uniform conclusions on the effects of cannabis use both on the user & the community as a whole. The failure of legislators to accept these conclusions suggest that legislative responses are affected more by the perceived social status of users & the values & perhaps prejudices of powerful groups in the community than by careful evaluation of the pharmacological, medical or sociological evidence." Royal Commission into the Non-Medical Use of Drugs. South Australia. 1978

demand that all hemp be kept away from doctor, farmer and industry, even though a blind person can tell a field of herbal or seed cannabis from a field of industrial pulp and fiber hemp.[70] Shielded by a virtual mainstream news blackout on the benefits of hemp, most prohibitionists refuse to explain their opposition to reform. There have been a few exceptions. Let's look at some of the expert replies, when confronted by the press to explain that position.

Quentin Jones of the federal Agricultural Research Service told *Scientific American* in 1990 that, while hemp is certainly versatile, "other plants can fulfill its various roles more economically."[71] Note that he failed to name any crop or combination of crops that can do so, or even fill in for a third of the known uses of hemp. And his statement is contradicted by all available records.

Ohio State Representative Mary Abel (D-Athens) claimed that the "dangers" of cannabis as a drug may outweigh the value of hemp. After a 1989 Senate subcommittee hearing on hemp, she said, "People are concerned that drugs like marijuana really become a gateway drug. ... We know we've got an abuse problem that is growing. Changing the category of what is legal is not going to help the problem."[72] Let's compare her opinions to the facts. Abel did not name any problems directly caused by cannabis. Not illegal cannabis, but legal tobacco is the gateway drug recognized by virtually every drug abuse study on the topic.[73] Federal statistics report that alcohol and other hard drug use goes up as cannabis use goes down.[74] And, obviously, changing the categories would solve many problems in one stroke, by restoring hemp's horticultural, medical and industrial uses.

"There are all kinds of plants that can do exactly what they say marijuana can do without the hallucinogenic ingredient," said Marsha Keith Shuchard, co-founder of the propaganda group called Parents Resource Institute for Drug Education (PRIDE).[75] She could

---

[70]Industrial hemp is tall & planted so densely that it is extremely difficult to walk through a stand of it. The herbal (and seed) crops are branchier & need space around each plant, making it much easier to walk through. Furthermore, herbal cannabis is often pruned to a shorter height.

[71]Horgan, John. 'Going to Pot.' in *Scientific American*. Dec. 1990. pp. 23-24

[72]Phillips, Jim. 'Authorities Examine Pot Claims.' in *Athens News*. OH. vol 13:92. Nov. 16, 1989

[73]National Education Association, National Academy of Science, National Institute on Drug Abuse, National Institute on Mental Health, U.S. Surgeon General, et al.

[74]Drug use statistics 1985-1988. Justice Dep., NIDA, NIMH. also Cimons, M. 'Illegal drug use drops but crack addiction soars.' in *LA Times*. August 1989

[75]Gelb, Adam. 'Pro-pot forces rally, argue it's hip to grow hemp: Legalization said to hold commercial, environmental hope.' in *Atlanta Journal/Constitution*. GA. April 7 1991. p. C4. This group was originally funded with a federal ACTION/VISTA grant as part of a CIA anti-cannabis campaign. Hatch, R. 'Drugs, Politics & Disinformation.' in *Covert Action*. Washington DC. no. 28. Summer 1987. pp. 23-27

not, however, name any such plant. In fact, there is none. Few experts would agree that cannabis is a hallucinogen. It comprises its own distinct class of substance. At normal doses, the herb is a mood elevator and relaxant. Hallucinations only occur at the most excessive levels of consumption, and even then they are extremely rare. A pleasant sleepiness is the most common symptom of indulging in too much cannabis, or sometimes anxiety.

The most typical response of hemp's detractors is no response at all. No top government official has had the courage to debate with hemp advocates face to face, despite outstanding challenges going back for several years. No government official has been able to claim the $10,000 reward, first offered in 1990 by author Jack Herer, to disprove his assertion that hemp restoration can "save the planet."[76] The greatest marijuana prohibitionist of all, Federal Bureau of Narcotics' Harry Anslinger, acknowledged that hemp is "the finest fiber known to mankind. My God! If you ever have a shirt made of it, your grandchildren would never wear it out. You take Polish families; we used to see marijuana in the yards of Polish families. We'd go in and start to tear it up and the man came out with his shotgun, yelling, 'These are my clothes for next winter!'"[77] Yet he told the Women's National Exposition of Arts and Industries that the plant must be criminalized because, "If the hideous monster Frankenstein came face to face with the monster marijuana, he would drop dead of fright."[78] It's hard to argue with that.

So, there you have it. This is why they deprive us of the most versatile and valuable natural resource on the planet. "If marijuana wasn't illegal, I wouldn't be concerned about it," said Narcotics Task Force Supervisor Paul King. "But it is illegal, and until somebody changes the law, we're going to go after it. It's our job."[79]

What do you think President Washington would do about that?

What Form Should Relegalization Take?

While a wider reform of drug criminalization is clearly in order, reformers must not mix issues or fall back on prohibitionist equa-

[76]"A $10,000 challenge to the world to prove us wrong: If all fossil fuels & their derivatives, as well as the deforestation of trees for paper & agriculture are banned from use in order to save the planet & reverse the greenhouse effect: then there is only one known renewable natural resource able to provide the overall majority of our paper, textiles & food, meet all the world's transportation, home & industrial energy needs, reduce pollution, rebuild the soil & clean the atmosphere—all at the same time—our old stand-by that did it all before: Cannabis hemp ... marijuana." Herer. op. cit. Back cover

[77]Anslinger, Harry, commissioner of the FBN. in Frazier, Jack. *The Marijuana Farmers*. Solar Age Press. New Orleans LA. 1974

[78]NY Herald Tribune. Hearst newspapers. April 1937. Reproduced in Herer. op. cit.

[79]Kleffman, T. 'Don't try this at home.' in *New Times*. CA. Aug. 27, 1992. pp. 18-20

tions that lump industrial hemp with cannabis, and cannabis with hard drugs. We must not narrow our vision of the future. Hemp reform is distinct from, and largely peripheral to, other "drug" issues. Nonetheless, we must look at cannabis in the broader context of societal drug use. In the traditional American point of view, the policy which allows the most freedom is to receive preference. This is also the guiding principle of individual international human rights laws. The United Nations defines an ideal in which individual rights and freedoms are "subject only to such limitations as are determined by law solely for the purpose of securing due recognition and respect for the rights and freedoms of others."[80] However, the option of abrupt decontrol of the entire drug market seems unlikely to win the necessary public or political support in the immediate future.

The middle ground is one of progressive drug decriminalization, along with accurate education about the relative risks and benefits of different drugs, including legal ones. This gentle, reasoned approach begins by distinguishing between "hard drugs" and "soft drugs," meaning cannabis. Relegalizing the soft drugs to create a climate of acceptance and to separate people with a casual interest in the herb from street dealers of hard drugs will reduce opportunities to experiment with pharmaceuticals.

If society feels it needs to control cannabis, the answer is to permit open-market cannabis transactions and use government inspectors to verify the quality and dosages offered, and accountants to verify and audit the books and taxes. Consumers want cannabis, and merchants have a legitimate right to supply that demand. People who do not want it are free to not buy it. Competitive international trade in all forms of cannabis should give consumers the widest freedom of choice, with adequate guarantees of product quality.

Federal law permits personal production of up to 250 gallons of wine or beer in the home each year—a reasonable standard to apply to cannabis. For concessionaires, a license similar to that covering taverns and bars will be sufficient. It should, however, be distinct from the liquor license. Since failure to comply with the rules will lead to loss of the license, it is in the vendor's interest to comply with such controls. Limits can be set on what can be sold, as well as on the sizes of operations and sales or on the advertising methods of distributors. Vendors' permits can keep operations away from schools and require that customers present identification and be of legal age. Clearly labelling the shops with a leaf logo in the window will reduce the stigma of retail sales operations and will let people

---

[80] *Universal Declaration on Human Rights.* United Nations. New York NY. Article 29.2

know where to purchase a supply of cannabis. Situating outlets near entertainment zones will encourage people to wait until they arrive at the event before indulging. Replacing urine tests with impairment testing closes up loopholes in current public safety laws, regarding reckless driving. Personal responsibility should be emphasized.

The legal age for consuming cannabis, alcohol or tobacco can be held out to the young for what it is: a rite of passage into adulthood.

Facts About International Prohibition Law

Hemp is not banned by international law. In fact, not even personal cannabis use is banned. The preamble to the United Nations' Single Convention Treaty clearly protects the right to use cannabis for medicine. Article 28 specifically allows hemp industry and horticulture. Congress and the courts have a specific Constitutional duty to enforce international laws.[81]

Article 23 requires governments to set up bureaucracies who oversee and "interpret" the Treaty. Application of this or any treaty must be consistent with other elements of international law. If broadly interpreted, Article 23 permits social cannabis use, as long as a government board oversees production, distribution and sale. Well-intended bureaucrats can instantly transform the policy under Article 28:3. They simply determine that no steps beyond minimal record keeping are required to control "illicit traffic" in cannabis leaves; and no enforcement agency is necessary.

Any sovereign government can denounce the Treaty under Article 46. The Universal Declaration of Human Rights and the Anti-genocide Treaty offer a strong justification for such an action.[82] Hemp policy will then be handled by regional or local agricultural departments, like soybeans and grapes; its herb by regulatory agencies, like tobacco and wine. It's that simple.

The Fundamentals of National Restoration

Policy reform at the federal level can come from at least four different directions: through Congress, the executive branch, the courts or on a purely bureaucratic level.

Congress can repeal or enact laws. A general repeal of large sections of the criminal codes is in order and specific medical recognition and protection should be codified. Relegalization amendments

---

[81]"This Constitution...and all treaties made or which shall be made, under the authority of the United States, shall be the Supreme Law of the Land, & the judges of every State shall be bound thereby...laws of any state to the contrary notwithstanding." *US Constitution*. Article VI. 2. Under some interpretations, these groups have also violated the anti-genocide treaty.
[82]File such a petition with the UN Human Rights Committee Centre for Human Rights, Palais des Nations 1211, Geneva, Switzerland.

can be tacked onto unrelated bills. Congress should defund prohibition programs and enact truth in advertising laws with teeth to allow the public to sue groups like PDFA for lying about cannabis. Excesses of police force must be reigned in.

The President can veto legislation or initiate a helpful agency to supervise and facilitate cannabis distribution right down to the retail level. That agency can propose policy formulas that encourage commercial hemp to develop to its full potential. The President can also reassign the DEA to investigate new industrial chemical processes and environmental offenses. Federal attorneys general can refuse to prosecute cannabis offenders, then bring a test case to overturn prohibition. Many parts of the Bill of Rights can be reactivated to bring an end to hemp prohibition and the ways it is enforced.

Courts have great power to reverse the corruption of the past decade. Unfortunately, the current Supreme Court is an obstruction to justice. Respect must be restored for Constitutional rights,[83] along with a strict constructionist interpretation of governmental limits. Honest judges will eventually overturn prohibition and forfeiture laws on Constitutional grounds. They can fully inform jurors of their power of acquittal, hold policing agencies accountable for their excesses, and hear cases for damages against the government. First and foremost is to admit that the federal government exceeded its Ninth and Tenth Amendment limits and responsibilities when it criminalized personal gardening and use of cannabis hemp.

Bureaucrats wield a lot of power and can do a great deal of good. They can favorably reinterpret existing regulations and swiftly issue permits. They can reinterpret international treaties to allow full medicinal and industrial uses of hemp. The mobilization of hemp farmers and revival of the hemp industry for the 1940s was not a legislated change, but a policy shift by agreement between various governmental agencies. The Department of Agriculture got its Hemp for Victory program in high gear almost immediately. Its bulletin on how to grow hemp was reprinted in 1952, when Washington feared that the Chinese might invade the Philippines during the Korean War.[84] A similar shift can restore hemp today. The problem is that it gives a superficial appearance of reform while the cancer of prohibition continues to fester under the surface.

Finally, perhaps it is time for a Constitutional amendment to protect the people from this kind of fanatical despotism. The evil of prohibition must be purged once and for all from the nation's law

---

[83]The UN *Universal Declaration of Human Rights* protects many of these same items.
[84]Farmers Bulletin No. 1935. in Frazier, Jack. *The Marijuana Farmers*. Solar Age Press. New Orleans LA. 1974

books. An amendment forbidding prohibition of natural things should be adopted, written clearly and in plain English and not covering multiple issues. Politicians and police should be held liable for their criminal activity. Community-based laws can be designed to meet the needs of the local constituency rather than the whims of any oligarchy.

Mass Media, Not Just Mass Hysteria

Any publication might inadvertently cite a false report of harmful health effects from cannabis once, out of ignorance. Whatever happened to fact checking? But after the facts have been provided, use of these false statements is a libelous, irresponsible and malicious act, for which the publisher is responsible.

News media that knowingly report false information about cannabis should therefore be penalized and forced to make a retraction.

Changes In & Through the Courts

The Constitution is a legally binding contract between the government and its citizens. It gives the federal legislature no authority to enact criminal statutes, only revenue raising and commercial regulation. Not only has Congress adopted such statutes, it invented "mandatory sentencing guidelines" to strip the judiciary of its discretionary power to faithfully serve justice. This violates the separation of powers and due process and should be terminated.

Judges can overturn such requirements and reclaim substantial latitude to dismiss charges, to throw out evidence and to rectify many miscarriages of justice involving hemp prohibition. The goal of this process is to restore respect for personal responsibility and assure accountability for both the individual and government agencies. Sacramental and spiritual use of cannabis are technically legal under the First Amendment, which forbids laws that interfere with freedom of religion. So is the smokers' right to party, or "peaceably to assemble." The Fourth Amendment guarantees security and privacy both of home and person, which reasonably extends to possession, gardening and use of cannabis, as well as body fluids.

Taxation without legalization is contradictory and unjust. One law negates the other. Legislators voted to impose hemp taxes in 1937. Later tax bills have been adopted solely to take people's property for non-payment. These are not laws; they are traps. Since double jeopardy and self incrimination are banned under the Fifth Amendment, these tax laws have in effect already relegalized cannabis. Under strict Constitutional interpretation, states must now collect the designated tax and allow people to use cannabis.

The Sixth Amendment bans secret witnesses and the Seventh requires jury trials "where the value in controversy shall exceed $20." All the courts have to do is acknowledge that property seizure cases fall under common law. The Eighth Amendment forbids excessive fines and cruel and unusual punishment. The penalty must suit the "crime." Few cases of excessive penalties are more poignant than the attacks on this plant grown by the framers of the Constitution themselves. Moreover, the 14th Amendment's equal protection statute extends 21st Amendment safeguards to all intoxicants, not just alcohol. Therefore, cannabis, tobacco and alcohol would not be legal for minors, and could face similar regulations, such as labeling, advertising, licensing, etc.

The Swiss Supreme Court reduced the penalty there for casual dealers of hashish in 1991, saying it was no more dangerous than alcohol. The Court said that medical evidence showed that hashish did not directly harm the "physical and moral health of large numbers of people."[85] Those convicted of selling even large quantities of hashish will no longer be classed as "serious" offenders and will face a maximum three years' imprisonment.

Around that same time, a German judge ruled the laws against cannabis possession unconstitutional.[86] In his decision, Judge Nescovic ruled that keeping liquor legal while banning the herb violated the constitutional guarantee of equality before the law, and also a provision guaranteeing personal freedoms that do not infringe on the rights of others. The decision was praised by the justice and social welfare ministers in Lower Saxony, the health minister of Saarland and officials in other state capitals.[87] Germany's highest court ruled on April 28, 1994 that persons in possession of small amounts of cannabis should not be prosecuted, and left it to the states to decide the details.[88]

The Colombian Supreme Court then went even farther and removed penalties from use of all drugs, ruling that prohibition violates the rights to privacy, autonomy and "the free development of personality."[89] President Cesar Gaviria attacked the decision, but Prosecutor General Gustavo de Greiff praised it.

The Alaska Supreme Court relegalized cannabis in 1975 and held that the State Constitution's declared right to privacy permitted

[85]Nov. 7, 1991
[86]Wolfgang Nescovic, appeals court judge in Luebeck, Germany, overturned a case for a woman sentenced to 2 months in prison for 12 grams of hashish.
[87]A leading Social Democrat in Parliament, Gudrun Schaich-Walch, said that Germany should adopt a drug policy like the Netherlands. in *Bild am Sonntag*.
[88]Tomforde, Anna. 'Possession of cannabis is legalized in Germany.' in *Guardian*. Manchester England. April 28, 1994. p. 12
[89]Torres, C. 'Legalize it.' in *The Nation*. June 20, 1994. p. 857

cultivation and use of cannabis in the home.[90] Legislative hearings on April 13-14, 1988 found no compelling need to change the law, as was reiterated in 1989,[91] and in 1993, the Alaskan Supreme Court ruled the state's 1990 recrim bill unconstitutional, again under the right to privacy. Even judges from archconservative Orange County, California have come out in support of this position.[92]

Unfortunately, more and more judges are simply political appointees who misinterpret federal crime law as superseding state and Constitutional law. But there is a way to deal with them, too. Citizen monitors can catalog any judge's bias, prejudicial behavior, mistreatment of suspects, and unconstitutional or illegal decisions by sitting in at trials and keeping notes. Transmit the charges to build a case to the House Judiciary Committee through your Congressional representative to initiate the impeachment process and remove corrupt and incompetent judges from office.

Even more powerful will be the combination of a tough judge and district attorney holding a grand jury investigation into the possibility of criminal conspiracy by prohibitionists to deprive people of their Constitutional and human rights through cannabis prohibition.

Individual States Can Act Now

State legislatures can reduce prohibition penalties, create waivers and exemptions for certain cannabis users and re-prioritize law enforcement activity. In this era of government cost-cutting, an effective approach is to authorize only one dollar for the state prohibition enforcement budget. Another is to remove supervisory authority from police departments and put it under the Health Department.

The State of Minnesota put a special law on its books in the early days of prohibition, 1939, that technically allows farmers to grow hemp for commercial purposes.[93] Wisconsin has a similar law. The Minnesota Hemp Control Law further removes the county prosecutor's power to arrest someone for cultivating commercial hemp. This puts the matter into the hands of the Agriculture and Commerce Departments. There has been an increase in applications for such permits. Requests to operate under these statutes were denied in both states in 1991. Appeals continue, and lawyers advising the petitioners stated that neither state had legally valid reasons for rejecting the requests. The bizarre wordings of federal and other laws makes it somewhat nebulous as to when growing cannabis is "marijuana" or

---

[90]*Ravin vs. Alaska.* 1975. Citing Alaska State Constitution. Article 1:22
[91]This set the groundwork for the 1990 recriminalization initiative.
[92]Judges James B. Gray, James Smith & Ronald Rose. 1992.
[93]To protect farm interests after the 1937 federal ban. in Law 18.321: 'Growing hemp [cannabis sativa, l.] for commercial purposes; licenses.' MN. 1939

hemp. In states without an agricultural protection law, applicants must talk with the county prosecutor where they plan to grow hemp. A lot depends on attitude and interpretation, so tact is always in order. Show that growing industrial hemp is legal under international law and a common practice in other countries—and that hemp is a useful commercial crop, not a controlled dangerous substance.

Hemp farming is hostage to federal policy and, in the meantime, plants are cut down and destroyed at state taxpayer expense. The Minnesota-based Institute for Hemp has sought to privatize eradication by contracting out its services, so as to collect the stalks. When this was refused, it asked to purchase state-eradicated wild hemp stalks—so far without success—but any state can take advantage of this approach. To discourage human consumption, less than four percent THC strains of hemp might be preferred, although it seems pointless, since growing and handling techniques diminish the possibility of marketable smoking herb.[94] Furthermore, such burdensome over-regulation is unnecessary because when smoking cannabis is available, no one will want to ingest industrial grade hemp. Some politicians recognize the broader issue.

A bill to relegalize cannabis, with a specific reference to the commercial use of hemp, was introduced in the State of New York by Senator Joseph Galiber in 1991.[95] The Maine legislature unanimously voted sweeping changes in its cannabis control law in 1992 to broadly protect medical users of cannabis. But the good intentions of the legislature were subverted by a hard-line executive when the governor pocket-vetoed the legislation.

But, like the other 33 states that permit medical cannabis and the 11 that decriminalized social use of the herb, Maine has a problem. The problem is interference from the federal government. But any state can relegalize cannabis, then challenge federal meddling in their health and legal policies by suing it for violating Ninth and Tenth Amendment restraints. Alternatively, they can repeal state prohibition law, defund related police budgets and refuse to assist federal prohibition enforcement.

---

[94]"You'd probably have to smoke 100 kilos of it to get high, & you'd probably just end up with a sore throat," said Ian Wood, a non-wood fibers expert at Commonwealth Scientific & Industrial Research Organization. Brisbane, Australia. 1991
[95]Galiber, Sen. Joseph. 'An act to amend the alcoholic beverage control law, in relation to the sale, cultivation & processing of cannabis; & to repeal article 221 of the penal law relating to the sale & possession of marihuana.' in *SB 5778*. Senate Judiciary Committee. May 14, 1991. Not adopted.

An Initiative to Be Submitted to the Voters

Twenty-four states allow citizens' initiatives on the ballot.[96] The process begins when a citizen or organization writes a bill, then files the measure with the Secretary of State and qualifies it for the ballot by circulating petitions to collect a requisite number of valid signatures. The matter is then placed before the voters at the next election. Only certain states provide for this process. The following is adapted from the 1990 California Hemp Initiative, which incorporated many elements of reform, as a model for state legislation.

An Act to Amend the State Health and Safety Code
This act is an exercise of the police powers of the State to protect the safety, welfare, health and peace of the people and the environment of the State, to allow for the industrial and medicinal type uses of cannabis hemp, to eliminate the evils of unlicensed and unlawful cultivation, selling and dispensing of hemp drugs, and to promote temperance in the consumption of hemp as an intoxicant. It is hereby declared that the subject matter of this act involves in the highest degree, the economic, social and moral well-being, and safety of the State and all its people. All provisions of this act shall be liberally construed to accomplish these purposes.
I. Add this section to the Health and Safety Code, any laws or policies to the contrary not withstanding:
(1) Persons 21 years or older shall not be prosecuted, be denied any right or privilege, nor be subject to criminal or civil penalties for the cultivation, transportation, distribution or consumption of any of the following:
   (a) Industrial hemp products. Hemp farmers and manufacturers of industrial hemp products shall not be subject to any special zoning or licensing fees that are discriminatory or prohibitive.
   (b) Hemp medicinal preparations.
   (c) Hemp products for nutritional use.
   (d) Hemp products for personal use in private. No permit or license may be required for non-commercial cultivation, transportation, distribution or consumption of any hemp product.
(2) Hemp preparations are hereby restored to the available list of medicines. Physicians shall not be penalized for, or restricted from, prescribing hemp preparations for medical purposes to patients of any age.
(3) Hemp intoxicants shall be regulated according to the State wine industry model. For purposes of distinguishing personal from commercial production under the Business and Professions Code, 15 grams of cured hemp flowers and/or leaves shall be held equivalent to one gallon of dry wine.
II. The legislature is authorized to enact legislation, using reasonable standards to determine impairment, to regulate or prohibit persons from operating a motor vehicle or heavy machinery, or from otherwise engaging in conduct which may affect public safety. Testing for inert cannabis metabolites shall not be considered in determining impairment, nor be required for employment or insurance.
III. No State personnel or funds shall be used to assist enforcement of federal prohibition laws against these acts which are no longer illegal here.

---

[96]Salem, D. 'Bypassing the politicians.' in *LA Times*. Oct. 19, 1994. p. A5

Local Jurisdictions & Individual Actions

Frustrated with the retrograde policies of federal and state policies, some local governmental bodies have begun to take action on their own. In 1991 and 1992, the counties of San Francisco, Santa Cruz and Marin, California, all opted to create havens for medical users of cannabis, even protecting cultivation of small herb patches. A town in Maine voted to legalize cannabis within its borders. Proponents of the Frankfurt Resolution are reaching out to American cities to adopt their policy of *harm reduction*.[97]

Concerned citizens throughout America have been seeking a solution to the problems raised by criminalizing cannabis. The trick is to make it good and find a legislator to introduce it. The power of the individual is largely untapped as a reserve of potential change. Thousands of individuals and groups are disseminating information and lobbying for change. This is the source of honest police, good judges and honest policy makers. Half or more of all college graduates tried cannabis from about 1970 right up through the 1980s. The greying of the baby-boomer generation is being felt. They are now in positions of power and old enough to run for office.

Long-term approaches will identify allies and groom candidates for high office. Candidates won't need to campaign on the issue, as long as their supporters know who they are: hemp "stealth" candidates. Abolitionists must assume jobs in the police, legislative and judicial bureaucracies. They must seek out and work with police, judges and officials who support restoration of hemp. Parents and teachers can work within the PTAs and school governance bodies. Students can form campus groups, do related research projects, bring speakers and hemp events to campus and so on. Anyone can join neighborhood watch groups, churches, civic groups like Kiwanis, Rotaries and political groups to help shape policies with far-reaching consequences. Any civic group or elected body can adopt resolutions in support of abolition and forward it to their legislators.[98] The news blackout on the subject can be turned into an advantage by allowing people to work quietly for reform. The story remains "new" to the media, and whichever major news source "breaks" the Hempgate story will pick up a big audience share when they take up the issue. Meanwhile, this allows information to be spread quietly into an ubiquitous base of support, creating a 'grey

---

[97]*Frankfurt Resolution*. European Cities on Drug Policy. WalterKolbstrasse 9-11, D60594 Frankfurt am Main, Germany. 069-62-0701

[98]A memorial to Congress is a resolution by a state legislature calling on Congress to take an action. It is a standard means of communications between States & Congress. Typically these are submitted by citizen groups, & have been effective in shaping law & policy; for example, to end slavery.

force' for change that is backed up with relentless political pressure. Everyone should send letters to office holders and publications, telephoning talk radio shows and passing on information about the many uses of hemp and the many avenues of hemp reform. Get on the internet and network with other hemp advocates.

Businesses can explore investment options, pursue necessary permits and exemptions to work with hemp, network with Chambers of Commerce and such. Writers, producers and artists can use their skills to present information as entertainment.

It's time to identify and target prohibitionists—first to persuade them of the rightness of hemp restoration, then to eliminate incorrigible hardliners. Armed with facts and carefully selected rhetoric, reformers must not be afraid to expose prohibitionists and hold them personally responsible for the death and misery they have caused. This will send the message that they must separate hemp from hard drugs and follow a course of progressive decriminalization tied to each substance's relative risks.

Any citizen can initiate the impeachment of a bad judge, can draft relegalization legislation and see it through the legislature, can file a lawsuit on the subject or can, in some states and localities, draft and circulate a voters' initiative to directly write law. One need not even be a citizen to write, circulate or sign advisory petitions for legal reforms. Where communities do not have police review operations, the International Community Watch Program "CrimeStoppers" offers some possibility. Directors are volunteers who are nominated to and appointed by members of an existing board.[99] Programs are developed by citizens, police and existing CrimeStoppers programs in other communities. The volunteers' basic duties include advertising, organizing community events, discussion of local crimes and suggesting law enforcement policies and priorities. This offers a unique opportunity to monitor police conduct and misconduct.

Hemp Restoration & Cannabis Relegalization

In light of the foregoing, it is clear that, sooner or later, hemp restoration and cannabis relegalization will have occurred. Vegetable criminalization will look petty and ridiculous in retrospect.

The irrationality of "marijuana" criminalization is holding society hostage. Criminalization disrupts and injects itself into the lives of ordinary American citizens and creates the very problems it is intended to solve. However, a change may well be at hand.[100] United

---

[99]To find out about available positions, call your local police station & ask for Community Watch information.
[100]'Drug policy: It's time to try something very different.' editorial in *LA Times*. LA CA. Jan. 4, 1991. p. B-6

States District Judge Robert Sweet spoke to the concerns of those who can't imagine a world without a legal wall of repression between people and their personal freedom and responsibility over their personal time. He said in a 1989 speech on the drug war:[101]

> What we ought to do is try to get at the source of this problem, which is poverty and disillusion, and put our resources behind that and turn it around. I suggest it is time to abolish the prohibition; to cease treating indulgence in mind-altering as a crime. The result would be the elimination of the profit motive, the gangs, the drug dealers. Obviously, the model is the repeal of (Alcohol) Prohibition and the end of Al Capone and Dutch Schultz.

The lingering problem of alcohol abuse does not compare with the crime caused by its criminalization: the gangs, public shootouts, etc. Problems of aggression, violence, physical degeneration, poor job performance and social dissipation, all associated with alcohol abuse, have no parallels among cannabis users. It is important to recognize that there has been no violence on the part of the cannabis industry that even remotely compares to that of alcohol or cocaine prohibition.

The ban on the cannabis herb raises questions and contradictions that criminalizers cannot resolve. What danger is presented to society by cannabis but not tobacco or alcohol? If escaping from reality is inherently wrong, why are television and movies legal? Why should police spend more time and money going after peaceful cannabis smokers than they do on murderers and rapists? Who put police in charge of medicine and personal activities, instead of doctors and social workers? How can a plant be illegal? Of all plants, why make the world's most useful sustainable resource illegal?

Take heart in the words of Ronald Reagan's 1986 drug policy speech. "Remember this when your courage is tested: You are Americans. You're the product of the freest society mankind has known. No one—ever—has the right to destroy your dreams and shatter your life." Remember the Berlin Wall. For almost 30 years it was considered a permanent fixture on the international landscape: a symbol of authoritarian repression. At the end of 1988, no one believed it could ever change. Six months later, people wondered if it might happen within a decade.

On November 9, 1989, the Wall came tumbling down.

---

[101]Speech at the Cosmopolitan Club. New York NY. Dec. 12, 1989

21

REAPING THE REWARDS OF REFORM

The new era began quietly, with a few reports, studies and meetings that changed the way this commodity has since been discussed. There has been an explosion of revelations about the commercial potential of hemp, its history and medical benefits.

The new hemp reform movement includes ordinary people from all walks of life with a wide variety of concerns. It includes people seeking a source of tree-free paper and clean energy alternatives. People who care to can see solutions to the environmental and manufacturing crises and for a sustainable and profitable crop to save farms. It includes people looking for a way to save our civil liberties and budgets from the ravages of a half century of prohibition, and looking for affordable health care and maintenance and for better treatment of AIDS and other critical illnesses.

It includes working people who want respect, parents who want an end to prohibition-related violence and a return to the values of family privacy and personal responsibility, and police who want to reduce crime, not merely increase prison populations, and—yes— some people who only want to get high legally.

The arrest of eight million citizens over the past two decades has made cannabis suppression a national tragedy.[1] In 1988, Americans spent around $30 to $40 billion purchasing 35.7 million pounds of cannabis from South America and Mexico. It is illogical to allow those transactions to go unregulated and untaxed. It is time to discard failed policies and have the courage to make a serious change. The growing recognition that many social problems are a direct result of the evil of prohibition rather than drug use, plus a rapidly changing public attitude toward hemp, allow us to finally and fully consider the real economic impact in store.

The picture has taken a form most people did not expect. In 1991 Australia and Holland began cultivating industrial hemp for paper. In 1992, 17 European cities signed the Frankfurt Resolution, agreeing to once again tolerate social cannabis use. On Feb. 19, 1993 Great Britain officially eased its restrictions on hemp farming. The momentum continues. America is behind the curve on this one.

---

[1]After the relegalization of cannabis, arrest records should be immediately expunged so their detrimental effects can be minimized.

How Will Restoration Affect Society?

What is life like beyond the prison of cannabis prohibition? Perhaps most notable will be the lack of spectacular overnight changes. Society's problems will probably not vanish, and long-term benefits for society will take some time to be felt. But there will be steady improvements, like renewed economic vigor, major ecological gains and better public health.

When America comes home to hemp, we will again see something that our ancestors took for granted: the brilliant foliage, massive stalks and impenetrable density of a hemp field. Restoring hemp to its traditional role as a source of paper, textile, food, fuel, cordage, fabrication, medicine and other products will put money into local communities in an ecologically sound, financially stabilizing manner.

The Business Alliance for Commerce in Hemp[2] identified four key areas of social concern: the industrial/horticultural uses of hemp; the medicinal use of the herb; personal/social consumption; and regulation of concessions. None harbors serious obstacles to reform.

Hemp will be fully integrated as an agricultural resource for industry and food services. Banks will handle loans, and business will make private capital investments, as in any other industry. It will be grown commercially, traded on the commodity exchanges and regulated by the Department of Agriculture and Interstate Commerce Commission, like other crops. Publicly-owned company investments will be traded on the stock markets. Taxes will be collected through normal governmental channels.

Farms will be first to feel the financial benefits. Since hemp is an annual crop, it can make a major impact on the economy in just two seasons—one to yield an acclimated seed line, and one for full-on hemp production. People will largely be doing the same jobs of product design, development, production, transportation, marketing and distribution, just as they always have. There will simply be more hemp goods, lower prices, more people working, and more economic stability.

Cannabis medicines will immediately benefit millions of people, especially the critically ill and those in chronic pain, but also the rest of us with mundane aches and pains. Extracts and tinctures would be available at pharmacies. People will have few negative side effects. The cost of health care—to the individual, to the providers and to insurance carriers—will decline dramatically. Equally important, we can finally have scientific studies into the health benefits of this

---

[2]BACH. PO Box 71093, Los Angeles CA 90071-0093. 310-288-4152

amazing herb and/or any negatives, assessed without all the hype and hysteria.

Social consumption of the herb will probably rise slightly and level off. Cannabis use will not escalate indefinitely, because not everyone likes it. Many people will grow their own[3] and the market price will drop significantly, freeing up discretionary-spending dollars. Some people are concerned that relegalizing cannabis might create "another problem like alcohol." While alcohol poses significant problems for society, cannabis does not. The herb is simply not a hard drug. Researchers thoroughly tested both mental functions[4] and perceptual motor skills.[5] Even "long-term use of marijuana produces insignificant effects."[6] And since cannabis use reduces alcohol consumption,[7] alcohol-related problems will probably go down.

Cultural tolerance reduces social tensions and expands the sense of belonging to a greater community.[8] Research has shown that cannabis smokers, non-smokers and former smokers "did not differ from each other in terms of social or emotional adjustment, alienation, aggression or reactions to frustrations."[9]

There will be subtle changes in attitude as prejudices are removed and economic prosperity returns. Workers' self-respect will rebound with the end of urine testing. In Costa Rica, "marijuana use was often correlated with employment stability, low unemployment and acquisition of material goods."[10] Businesses will save on overhead and enjoy improved worker morale. There could be a net gain in creativity, according to NIDA, which found cannabis users displayed attributes reflecting "unconventionality, non-traditionality or non-conformity. Users tend to be more open to experience, more aesthetically oriented and more interested in creativity, play, novelty or spontaneity than non-users."[11]

---

[3]The precedent is the wine law, which permits production of up to 250 gal./yr. for personal use & as gifts, but requires licenses for further production & sale.
[4]Like cognition, motivation & memory
[5]Such as physical coordination, sustained attention & reaction time
[6]Hall, F.B., Klein, A.L. & Waters, J.E. 'Long-term effects of marijuana smoking.' *Journal of Altered States of Consciousness*. vol. 2:2. 1975-76. p. 161-170
[7]Passell, P. 'Less marijuana, more alcohol?' *NY Times*. June 17, 1992. p. C-2
[8]Legalization will "remove a serious source of conflict between the police & a section of society which is in danger of seeing itself as an underclass, & the police as mere guardians of white, middle-class values." Payne, Sgt G. 'The drug problem upside down.' in *The Guardian*. Manchester England. Feb. 28, 1992
[9]Pascale, Hurd & Primavera. in *Journal of Social Psychology*. no 110:273-283. 1980
[10]Carter, W.E., ed. *Cannabis in Costa Rica: A study of chronic marijuana use.* Institute for the Study of Human Issues. Philadelphia PA. 1980
[11]Jessor, R. 'Marihuana: A review of recent psycho-social research' in *Handbook on Drug Abuse*. NIDA. US Govt. Printing Office. 1979. p. 337-355.

These subtle differences may have a profound impact. Police can return to solving crimes, directing traffic, helping children get safely home from school, and enforcing industrial health and safety regulations—and governments to addressing the core issues of the day, not just spewing political rhetoric. Instead of testing urine, and hair to determine peoples' lifestyles, medical labs can help sick and dying people. Bureaucrats can face up to our health, environmental, economic and social problems. Scientists can restore local environments and support the communities that support them.

But how will people get the cannabis to smoke? Not everyone wants to grow their own. There were 1200 smoking parlors in New York City in 1926 and 500 in 1945. Jazz clubs and coffee houses lined Central Avenue in Los Angeles before prohibition hit. We can regulate new American cannabis cafes as earlier generations have, just as beer and alcohol concessions are licensed today.

Many United States shops will wish to provide herb without dealing liquor, so separate permits will be issued. This creates a mechanism for control and taxation at the retail level, and an opportunity to set age limits on consumption. Cannabis cafes will decorate to attract regular clients. They will offer products that are labelled for quality and freedom from contaminants.[12]

The Coffee House That Cannabis Hemp Built

There are 400 cannabis shops in Amsterdam and 2000 throughout the Netherlands. No advertising is allowed, but most shops serve both herb and hash, along with non-alcoholic beverages, cigarette papers, snacks and other concessions.[13] These coffee shops are the equivalent of the American bar, providing thousands of good jobs in the tavern and concessions industries and as sales outlets for "soft drugs," meaning cannabis.

Possession of up to 30 grams (just over an ounce) of herb or derivatives has been tolerated there since 1976. Sales of small amounts are also allowed. There is a "Hash Taxi" cannabis delivery service for the homebound infirm who cannot get out to the cafes.

Coffee shops in Amsterdam became venues for dealing without license to do so. Governmental permission was an after-the-fact occurrence. Perhaps such a Gandhian non-cooperation civil disobedience is the quickest and most effective way to open the market. There is the ground work of coffee shop openings expanding exponentially these last few years.

---

[12]List potency & freedom from paraquat contamination, chemical pesticides, etc. For purity, emphasis may be given to organic approaches to growing.
[13]Jansen, A.C.M. *Cannabis in Amsterdam*. Dick Coutinho. Muiderberg Holland. 1991

Growing your own is not legal but still widely done. "We don't know exactly how big the domestic harvest of cannabis is, but we tend not to worry about it as long as it is not for export," explained Leo Zaal, head of the Amsterdam municipal police narcotics division. California growers took potent seed lines to Holland in the mid-80s. Dutch gardeners exercise their traditional horticultural touch in growing the herb. There are dozens of seed lines, and various seed banks provide high quality seed stock. A strain called "skunk" sells for around $1600 per pound,[14] and is one of the favorites of thousands of connoisseurs called "marijuana tourists." Cured skunk buds have a strong, unmistakable smell. They are sold over the counter in measured quantities, among a selection of sativas and indicas, and an earthy rainbow of blonde, red, brown and black hashish. Coffee shops, cafes and hash bars make a nice profit on cannabis resales, as well as on food and beverage concessions to satisfy the palate.

Neighborhood souvenir and specialty shops sell cannabis wares and smoking paraphernalia, along with arts and crafts. A side industry has grown up around the small scale growers: grow stores that sell lamps, rockwool, nutrients and, of course, seeds. Their lists of fertilizers run from the standard cow manure and fish emulsion to exotic fossilized pigeon, hamster and even pelican droppings. Boxes of tiny spiders are sold to growers to control aphids and avoid pesticides.

A Policy of Controlled Relegalization

Once we look beyond the emotional bias attached to all the disinformation, it is clear that cannabis is simply an agricultural product with tremendous demand in every city in the United States.[15]

Since not everyone can or will want to grow their own, this portends a huge market for commercially grown cannabis. Growing and processing top-grade bud is not a care-free process by any means. It requires experience and expertise. The *Kentucky Marijuana Feasibility Study*[16] encourages a small-scale industry, rather than large corporate control. Under the Kentucky plan, the primary step is to declare cannabis totally legal to grow and possess for personal use. The approach uses a two-tiered system of govern-

---

[14]$3,500 per kilo. in *Contours*. vol. 5:4. Germany. December 1991. p. 26-27. also in *Bangkok Post*. Thailand. Oct. 6, 1991

[15]Burly tobacco was $1.50-$1.60/lb in 1988. The black market price of low-grade cannabis was $800/lb and up to $3,000/lb for excellent herb in the large urban markets.

[16]Galbraith, Gatewood, et al. *The plan for taxing & controlling hemp in Kentucky*. KY Marijuana Feasibility Study. POB 1438, Lexington KY 40501. 1977, 1988. 21 p

ment agencies. In many ways this plan simulates the tobacco allotment program.

Anyone could legally grow a certain number of plants for their own use, or to give to friends. To market cannabis as a cash crop, however, will require a license from the agriculture department. This license allows farmers to grow a specified allotment.[17] This system will benefit the greatest number of farmers and will greatly increase the average farm income throughout the region. No major capital outlay is needed to begin production of excellent herb for market. A relatively small farm structure will handle even the largest allotment allowed. To implement this plan, the agriculture department needs a warehouse at the end of the growing season, centrally located to maximize the growers' convenience. A two or three month period is long enough for every grower to move their product to that location. The same warehouse may house both the packaging and distribution operations. Unlike tobacco, there is no need to grind the leaf, and to do so may actually reduce the resale value! The herb should merely be set into one ounce plastic bags, topped and closed with an official seal denoting the grade, weight, date and recommended selling price, much as packaged liquor and tobacco products are. Labelling information would describe potential side effects of consumption.

The produce will be tested to determine its grade category and, consequently, its value. These criteria include color, texture, aroma, taste, overall appearance and, most importantly, its potency.[18] Cannabis will be categorized into several grades, with different price ranges set for each. A review board will hear any complaints from farmers and subject the product to another inspection before resale. It is foreseeable that the farmer will receive from $100 to $400 a pound for his crop. This revenue will brighten the outlook of many rural homes and have an economic "ripple effect."

Distribution at the Retail Level

The state agency then resells the herb at a profit to retailers, also licensed by the State, who resell the ounces of cannabis (or portions thereof) to the public. With up to 10 pounds a month distributed to each permit bearer to retain at a markup of $300 per pound, the State will create a new population of middle-class wage earners to satisfy an existing market demand, each having a net taxable income gain of between $2000 to $3000 a month. Thousands of people already supplement their incomes by dealing cannabis. As with bootleggers

---

[17]At 30 lbs/producer, 75,000 licenses in KY will allow about 500 farmers. County to bring in $6000-$9000/yr. Other plans would set limits at an acre or less.
[18]Tests developed at the University of MS Agriculture Research Center & elsewhere can be used to accurately measure active ingredients.

at the end of Alcohol Prohibition, dealers could "go legal" by supplying, among other things, affidavits from long-time, satisfied customers that their dealings have been honest and above board.

Licenses should be let on a population ratio basis, and sales can be handled informally from the home or on a storefront basis. In Holland, the local government has licensing power to control the number and location of cannabis outlets. Cannabis can be sold in bulk, as loose herb, as hashish, or rolled into cigarettes. People will lose their vending license if they abuse their status, defraud consumers or violate the regulations imposed on them. Licenses will specify whether the herb is to be sold on a to-go basis, like a liquor store, or for on-site consumption, like taverns and bars.

Brand names will allow customers to identify the product blend they prefer. The ratio of sativa to indica in the seed line should probably be indicated.[19] While cannabis advertising should be allowed, limits can be set, such as stipulating that it not be directed at the pre-teen market.

There will probably be an age limit on those to whom retail dealers may sell, as per alcohol and tobacco. The purchaser would have to present proof of age. Some propose setting age limits at 18 or 21 years, consistent with state alcohol consumption law, while others attach it to the age of sexual consent, around 16 years in some states. Parents might have similar discretion in sharing cannabis with their children as they have with sharing a sip of wine.

Young adults at the age of 19 are the second largest group of cannabis users in the nation. They are generally treated as adults, have finished with public schooling and often live outside their parents' homes. The Kentucky plan recommends that the legal age to buy cannabis be 19 years, with consumption limited to inside the home or on private property.[20]

In a liberated America, people will once again have the option to open a corner cannabis cafe for concessions of herb, pastries and beverage. The market will blossom with economic potential, and crafts will flourish as people begin to make creative, artistic and healthier smoking contraptions.

Manufacturers of indoor-grow equipment will operate in a climate without fear, and the news media will be able to report factually on the cannabis issue. There will also be tremendous opportunities to research the medical potential of cannabis. Legal cannabis is a windfall in every aspect.

---

[19] At least in general terms, such as *pure sativa, some indica & mostly indica.*
[20] Galbraith. op. cit.

Creating a Simple Buffer Against Habitual Use

Large tobacco processing and marketing corporations are well aware that the major reason for the huge consumption of cigarettes is that they are pre-rolled, encouraging habitual usage.

In light of this fact, many people oppose marketing cannabis in a pre-rolled fashion. Because the herb does alter an individual's consciousness, it recommended that a small ritual remain attached to the preparation of cannabis for smoking.[21] One approach is this simple device: do not allow pre-rolled cannabis cigarettes. It is unlikely that cannabis will be sold from vending machines, as are cigarettes, because it is too difficult to enforce age limits.This forces smokers to roll their own cigarette, to load a pipe, etc., to use or pass around. The extra effort also discourages cannabis smoking while driving.

This would also stimulate another side industry. The smoking paraphernalia industry that has grown up around the use of cannabis grossed $4 million in 1982 and $2 million in 1987. The bulk of those sales were by the rolling paper companies, along with thousands of individual craftspersons who hand manufacture smoking apparatus.

Taking a Hard Line on Criminal Misconduct

It is hypocritical that human law allows strip mining, clear cutting, the forced insemination and mutilation of mammals, toxic pollution, *ad nauseum*, yet criminalizes the growing and ingestion of a gentle flower. How can Governments tolerate such ecological violence and political corruption yet afford zero tolerance of personal life style choices like what to grow in your garden.

At some point, society must come to grips with the excesses and crimes committed by government officials in the name of prohibition enforcement. Grand juries and government commissions need to investigate corruption and to consider where restitution is due to citizens—and in which cases criminal prosecution of public officials and groups is in order.

A bureaucratic purge—with all due process to protect the innocent—to make examples of a few high-placed, corrupt officials will send a message throughout the system that society finally is getting tough on crime. Furthermore, the House Judiciary Committee of Congress has a duty to impeach judges who violate the basic Constitutional rights of the people. Such judges are also

---

[21]Galbraith. op. cit.

accountable for violating the right to equal treatment before the law, as guaranteed by both Constitutional and international law.[22]

The 1970s reforms did not work simply because of a lack of will among government officials. Police bureaucrats chose to impose their political priorities rather than obey the law. This includes their failure to obey mandates for medical compassion, violation of civil rights, etc. Under their own creed of "zero tolerance" for crime, corrupt officials must be indicted, prosecuted and given a dose of law-and-order medicine: long, hard sentences and seizure of their property for crimes committed in office.

In a colonial era plan called "Hempshire"[23] the convicts were placed on a prison farm to cultivate and manufacture hemp products. The idea was that the hard, honest labor of working in hemp fields and factories improves moral fiber, puts people back in touch with nature and at the same time teaches them a useful job skill. These are lessons that corrupt political functionaries need to learn. This would also employ these felons for our better supply of products of all sorts, as long as it doesn't take jobs away from the innocent.

Who Benefits From Relegalization?

Many distinct categories of people will benefit from declaring cannabis legal.[24] All businesses and consumers who want to have high quality, affordable products on the market will benefit from the revival of the hemp industries. Those with nutritional deficiencies benefit from access to nature's most perfect food, the hempseed.

For the public-at-large, abolition frees up billions of dollars of their tax money, making it available to upgrade other state services, like education, sanitation, transportation and so on. This will have a major and much needed effect on several state services. It will help restore public confidence that the government can react to new insights in ways that benefit those whom they serve.

For government agencies, it frees up money spent on unnecessary equipment and will allow departments to provide higher wages for personnel, a less extensive work week, etc. Most importantly, perhaps, it would greatly lessen the stigma attached to many police officers for arresting decent and respectable cannabis users, who categorically view their pastime as enjoyable and harmless; and it will allow law enforcement the time and resources to concentrate on

---

[22]"Everyone is entitled in full equality to a fair & public hearing by an independent & impartial tribunal, in the determination of his rights & obligations & of any criminal charge against him." UN. *Universal Declaration of Human Rights.* Art 10.
[23]Jones, Hugh. *Present State of Virginia.* p. 122. in Moore, Brent. *The Hemp Industry In Kentucky.* Press of James E. Hughes. Lexington KY. 1905. pp. 11, 13, 14
[24]Galbraith. op. cit.

real crimes. Beyond this are all the schoolteachers, children and parents who gain a more honest education system. Also benefitting will be all the politicians who no longer will have to spend time voting on useless laws and squandering taxes, so they can get on with their job of enacting sound social policies.

For current cannabis consumers and suppliers, it removes the risks and problems of operating in a black market economy and the fear and stigma of prosecution. It allows them to be honest about their life styles and pastimes with their friends, families, employers, doctors, elected officials, etc.

Another group to benefit are all the new entrepreneurs and businesses who will engage in the honest business of supplying a good quality product to meet the consumer demand. Add to that the sick and suffering whose lives will be improved by medical cannabis, all the hungry to be fed with hempseed products, the homeless who can be housed, the future generations who have better air, cleaner water and a wealthier, more wholesome society.

When you come right down to it, everybody benefits from legalizing cannabis except prohibitionists and organized criminals. Well, it's either them or us. The time is growing short, and the choice is clear. The hempen lifeline is dangling before us, waiting to be taken up so it can lift us back to the American dream of life, liberty, property and pursuit of happiness.

In return, hemp asks only one thing—that we let it grow—that governments allow their people to again grow hemp. To reap the bounty you must sow the seed. Today the world is on the verge of a pro-hemp backlash against pollution and prohibition. This point must be driven home: that this outrageous crime known as *marihuana prohibition* will never be committed again.

I respect the force of history and hold great hopes for the future of both our species. It was in the hope of speeding up this process that I wrote this book. Now it is in your hands. Talk about it, write about it, pass it on. The future of humanity is at stake.

Hemp for victory.

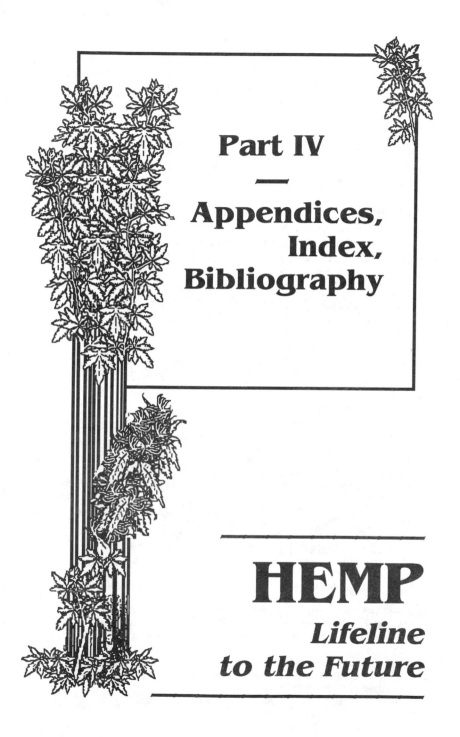

Part IV
—
Appendices,
Index,
Bibliography

HEMP
*Lifeline
to the Future*

22
—
GLOSSARY OF SPECIAL TERMINOLOGY

acre *n.* measure of land 1/640 sq.mi.; 43,560 sq.ft.; 4046.9 sq.m
bast fiber *adj.* long bark fiber from a plant; line fiber
biofuel *n.* any plant cellulose used for biomass conversion, often grown as a farm crop
break *v.* to fracture a retted hemp stalk in order to separate the fiber from the hurds
broadcast *v.* to sow seed by hand; to scatter
bushel *n.* a dry measure of 32 quarts; 4 pecks; approx. 44 lbs. of hempseed
calyx *n.* the green pod surrounding the hemp seed
cannabis *n.* a genus of plant having industrial and pharmaceutical uses
canvas *n.* a heavy, waterproof fabric made of hemp, a name derived from the Greek root word *kannabis* and the Latin *cannabis*
cellulose *n.* a carbon-based raw material found in vegetable pulp that is used for industrial fabrication; $C_6H_{10}O_6$
cook *v.* to reduce fibrous raw materials to a residue of cellulose pulp by means of a chemical and heat process
cure *v.* to dry an item in such a manner as to retain its essential qualities of aroma, strength, color, texture, etc.
digest *v.* to break down organic matter
dioecious *adj.* class of plant having distinct sexual characteristics
duck *n.* waterproof, lightweight canvas made of hemp, sometimes blended with cotton or other fibers, and used for ship sails, Conestoga wagon covers, the first Levi Strauss jeans, etc.
edestin *n.* highly digestible protein globulin found in hempseed
extruder *n.* machine used in the extrusion process
extrusion *n.* an operation whereby fibrous raw materials are altered by extreme pressure, usually with heat, chemical and mechanical treatment
feedstock *n.* a raw material used for industrial fabrication
fossil fuel *n.* an industrial feedstock derived from prehistoric lifeforms, mostly plants, and usually extracted as coal, petroleum, etc. by drilling or mining.
hackle *v.* to split and comb out the bast fiber from retted or broken hemp stalks; also *heckle*
hackle *n.* an instrument set with paralel pins for hackling, or combing, line
harrow *v.* to rake the ground smooth after plowing
hashish *n.* extracted, compressed resin of hemp flowers; *hash, charas*.
hectare *n.* a measure of land 10,000 sq. meters; 2.47 acres
hemp *n.* any plant of the genus cannabis, but usually cannabis sativa; the fiber derived therefrom
hermaphrodite *n.* an individual with both male and female characteristics
high *n.* psychological effect of elevated consciousness, etc. from consuming cannabis
high *adj.* to be in a cannabis influenced psychological state
hurds *n.* extracted raw cellulose; also *hards, pulp* or *wood*
joint *n.* cannabis cigarette, usually hand rolled with or without tobacco; also *reefer, split, doobie*, etc.
lignin *n.* glue-like organic substance that binds plant cells together
line *n.* post-hackled fine and long stapled fibers of hemp or flax after hackling and separated for spinning; "good" fiber
linen *n.* high quality cloth made from either flax (lin) or hemp

lint *n*. cleaned vegetable fibers prepared for spinning; refuse of the same

monoculture *n*. agricultural term for cultivation of only a single crop

peck *n*. dry measure of 8 quarts; 1/4 bushel; about 11 lbs. of hempseed

pistillate *adj*. refers to seed bearing, or female, dioecious plant

polymerize *v*. to convert matter into an impermeable plastic mass

potash *n*. potassium carbonate, often derived from plant ash

pulp *n*. extracted raw cellulose; also *hards*, *hurds* or *wood*

roach *n*. a butt of a marijuana cigarette; also *la cucaracha*

ret *v*. to soak in water or expose in moisture to soften and season or to break down the lignin binding together hemp or flax fibers from the pulp; derived from the English *rot*

ropewalk *n*. factory for making hemp cordage

scutch *v*. to dress hemp by beating, sometimes using a thrashing machine; to clean and further separate hurd from fiber

scythe *n*. long handled tool with a curved blade for hand mowing

scythe *v*. to harvest a crop by using a scythe in a swinging motion

shock *n*. a bundle of shocked stalks

shock *v*. to gather cut stalks into an upright, teepee shaped configuration, with butt end extended out and tops close together

spin *v*. to twist fiber into thread

staminate *adj*. refers to pollen bearing, or male, dioecious plant

THC *n*. tetrahydracannabinol; the major active medicinal alkaloid in the cannabis herb

tow *n*. post-hackled short or broken strands of hemp fiber prepared for spinning; "inferior" fiber

weave *v*. to work thread into cloth using a loom

23
—
A CHRONOLOGY OF CANNABIS

8,000 BC — Civilization, agriculture & hemp textile industries begin in **Europe & Asia**, simultaneously.

3727 — Cannabis called a "superior" herb in world's first medical text, or pharmacopeia, Shen Nung's *Pen Ts'ao*, in **China**.

1500 — Cannabis-smoking **Scythians** sweep through **Europe & Asia**, settle down everywhere & invent the scythe.

1400 — Cultural & religious use of ganga, or cannabis, and *charas*, or resin (hashish), recorded by **Hindus** in **India**.

c.800 — **Zoroastrians, Therapeutia, Coptics, Essenes** & other African & Eurasian religions adopt cannabis.

c.500 — Gautama **Buddha** survives by eating hempseed.

450 — **Herodotus** records **Scythians & Thracians** as consuming cannabis & making fine linens of hemp.

300 — **Carthage & Rome** struggle for political & commercial power over hemp & spice trade routes in Mediterranean.

100 BC — **Chinese** make paper with hemp & mulberry.

c. 0 — **Jesus** teaches. "Not that which goeth into the mouth defileth a man; but that which cometh out of the mouth, this defileth a man." Matthew 15:11.

100 AD — **Roman** surgeon **Dioscorides** names the plant *cannabis sativa* & describes various medicinal uses. Pliny tells of industrial uses & writes a manual on farming hemp.

500 — First botanical drawing of hemp in *Constantinopolitanus*.

c. 600 — **Germans, Franks, Vikings,** etc., all use hemp fiber.

c. 800 — **Mohammed** allows cannabis, but forbids alcohol use.

1000 — The **English** word 'hempe' first listed in a dictionary.

— **Moslems** produce **hashish** for medicine & social use.

1150 — **Moslems** use hemp to start Europe's first **paper** mill. Most paper is made from hemp for next 850 years.

1484 — Inquisitor **Pope Innocent VIII** outlaws hashish.

1492 — Hempen sails, caulking & rigging ignite Age of Discovery & help **Columbus** & his ships reach **America**.

1545 — Hemp agriculture crosses the continent overland to **Chile**.

1564 — **King Phillip** of Spain orders hemp grown throughout his empire, from modern-day Argentina to Oregon.

16-17th c. — **Dutch** achieve Golden Age through hemp commerce.

— Explorers find "wilde hempe" in **North America**.

1619 — **Virginia** colony makes hemp cultivation mandatory, followed by most other colonies. Europe pays hemp bounties.

1631 — Hemp used as **money** throughout **American** colonies.

1776 — **Declaration of Independence** drafted on hemp paper.

1791 — President **Washington** sets duties on hemp to encourage domestic industry; **Jefferson** calls hemp "a necessity" & urges farmers to grow hemp instead of tobacco.

1800s — **Cotton gins** make cheaper fiber than hemp.

1841 — **Dr. W.B. O'Shaughnessy** of Scotland works in India, then introduces cannabis to Western science.

1850s — **Petrochemical** age begins. Toxic sulfite & **chlorine** processes make **paper** from trees, steamships replace sails, tropical fibers introduced.

1860 — First governmental commission study of cannabis & health conducted by **Ohio State Medical Society**.

1876 — Hashish served at **American Centennial Exposition**.

1890 — **Queen Victoria**'s personal physician, **Sir Russell Reynolds**, recommends using cannabis therapies for "mental, ... sensorial ... & ... muscular" disorders.

1894 — **Indian Hemp Drugs Commission** (British) studies social use, comes out firmly against its prohibition.

1895 — First known use of the word '**marijuana**' for smoking, by Pancho Villa's supporters in Sonora **Mexico**.

1910 — African-American 'reefer' use reported in **jazz** clubs of New Orleans, said to be influencing white people.

— Mexicans reported to be smoking marijuana in Texas.

1911 — Hindus reported to be using 'gunjah' in San Francisco.

1916 — USDA *Bulletin 404* calls for new program of expansion of hemp to replace uses of timber by industry.

1920s — **Alcohol Prohibition** takes effect, **Anslinger** heads prohibition enforcement; **Mellon** is secretary of treasury; **DuPont** experiments with petrochemicals. Gang war as **Al Capone**'s Chicago mob takes over alcohol industry.

1930s — **New machines** invented to break hemp, process the fiber & convert pulp, or hurds, into paper, plastics, etc. 1200 hash bars in New York City. Racist fears of Mexicans, Asians & African-Americans leads to outcry for cannabis to be outlawed.

1935 — Compressed Agricultural Fiberboard invented in Sweden.

1937 — **Marijuana Tax Act** forbids hemp farming. Du Pont files patent for **nylon**.

1943-45 — **Hemp for Victory** program urges farmers to grow it.

1955 — Hemp farming again banned.

1960s — **Hippies, pop music** & **Vietnam** vets adopt cannabis.

1970s — Social use of cannabis receives widespread acceptance & policy of legal **decriminalization** sweeps the USA.

— **CIA**-sponsored 'experiments' claim to show new risks from marijuana smoking. Tax money shifted from jobs programs to sponsor disinformation groups.

1976 — Holland adopts tolerance.

1980s — **Reagan/Bush** war on cannabis: 'Head shops' that sell smoking apparatus outlawed. Urine testing, recriminalization, asset & property seizure, armed forces, prison camps, Just Say No, PDFA, DARE, tobacco & nuclear subsidies, etc. imposed. Price-per-ounce of cannabis higher than gold. It is the **biggest cash crop** in many states. DEA's chief administrative judge rules the government should allow the herb's medical use.

1990s — **Voters** pass regional medical cannabis measures. Interest in this & industrial hemp add new support to campaign for legal right to social use. Hemp Movement takes off.

1992 — Australia licenses hemp farm. Bush loses race for US president to admitted ex-pot smokers **Bill Clinton & Al Gore**.

1993 — England eases restrictions on hemp farming. News media declare hemp clothes and cannabis leaf logo hottest new fashion.

1994 — Canadian government permits hemp farm in Ontario province.

Hemp Agrotech plants first commecial research crop in the United States since the post WWII era, but the crop is destroyed by prohibition agents just a week before harvest.

November 15 declared Medical Marijuana Day

Hemp Industries Association founded.

24

—

WASHINGTON & JEFFERSON ON HEMP

That the States' Founders grew and promoted hemp is a fact frequently brought up in the discussion of prohibition, along with various kinds of conjecture. We were not able to find any comments about smoking that can resolve this debate about whether or not they may have smoked cannabis, however it is quite clear that Washington and Jefferson intended for American farmers to produce hemp for commercial purposes and that they held the personal liberty of the individual to be of paramount importance.

Excerpted below are references to hemp made by Presidents Washington and Jefferson that we encountered during the research of this book.

Thomas Jefferson: Hemp is a "necessity."

Thomas Jefferson advocated and acted on behalf of hemp many times in keeping his farm journals and writing numerous letters on the topic, illegally smuggling rare seeds into America and refining the hemp break. Jefferson allotted a few acres each to hemp and flax to satisfy the needs of his home manufactures, a need that varied from year to year. He grew much more hemp than flax and was interested in several mechanized devices for breaking hemp, removing the fibers from the woody stalk. Among his comments on hemp were:

Supplies: "Wrote to Tom Stewart of Augusta for 10 bushels of flax seed & 10 co. of hemp seed. Wrote to James Black for 2 flax-wheels, such hackles etc., as he thinks necessary. 100 lb. fine flax and 100 lb. of hemp ready dressed for spinning." (*Account Book.* December 29, 1774)

Comparison with Tobacco: "The culture (of tobacco) is pernicious. This plant greatly exhausts the soil. Of course, it requires much manure, therefore other productions are deprived of manure, yielding no nourishment for cattle, there is no return for the manure expended.... It is impolitic. The fact well established in the system of agriculture is that the best hemp and the best tobacco grow on the same kind of soil. The former article is of first necessity to the commerce and marine, in other words to the wealth and protection of the country. The latter, never useful and sometimes pernicious, derives its estimation from caprice, and its value from the taxes to which it was formerly exposed. The preference to be given will result from a comparison of them: Hemp employs in its rudest state more labor than tobacco, but being a material for manufactures of various sorts, becomes afterwards the means of support to numbers of people, hence it is to be preferred in a populous country. America imports hemp and will continue to do so, and also sundry articles made of hemp, such as cordage, sail cloth, drilling linen and stockings." (*Farm Journal.* March 16, 1791)

Home Industry: "We clothe ourselves chiefly, and our laborers entirely in what we spin and weave in our family." (letter to Charles Peale. March 21, 1815)

Comparison and Invention: "Flax is so injurious to our lands and of so scanty produce that I have never attempted it. Hemp, on the other hand, is abundantly productive and will grow forever on the same spot, but the breaking and beating is, which has always been done by hand, is so slow, so laborious and so much complained of by our laborers.... (but recently) a method of removing the difficulty of preparing hemp occurred to me, so simple and so cheap. I modified a threshing machine to turn) a very strong hemp-break, much stronger and heavier than those for the hand. By this the cross arm lifts and lets fall the break twice in every revolution of the wallower. A man feeds the break with hemp stalks... where it is more perfectly beaten than I have ever seen done by hand.... I expect that a single horse will do the breaking and beating of ten men." (letter to George Fleming. December 29, 1815)

Invention: "In a former letter I mentioned to you that I had adapted a hemp break to my sawmill, which did good work. I have since fixed one to my threshing machine in Bedford." (letter to Charles Peale. May 8, 1816)

George Washington: "Make the most of the hempseed."

George Washington is called the "Father of our country," and was surely the friend of the hemp farmer. He himself engaged in the commercial production of hemp, both for home consumption and for export, and hemp was often on his mind.

Trade with Europe: "I am prepared to deliver ... hemp in your port watered and prepared according to Act of Parliament." (letter to Robert Cary & Co, London England. Sept. 20, 1765.)

Economic Policy: "How far... would there be propriety, do you conceive, in suggesting the policy of encouraging the growth of cotton and hemp in such parts of the United States as are adapted to the culture of these articles? The advantages which would result to this country from the produce of articles which ought to be manufactured at home is apparent." (October 1791 letter to Secretary of the Treasury Alexander Hamilton, vol. 31, p. 389)

"Much hemp might be raised in these countries were there the proper encouragement. The foreign hemp gluts the market and there is not sufficient protecting duty to spur the farmer to raise this useful article. Our hemp lands would average a 700 weight to the acre [that which is called broken hemp]. ... Rich fresh bottom lands yield 500 or 600 and highly manured land 6, 8 or 900 pounds to the acre." (letter to Arthur Young, 1795, vol. 34, p. 146)

Washington's Diary Notes:
"Sowed hemp at muddy hole by swamp." (May 12-13, 1765). "Began to separate the male from the female plant at do [sic] — rather too late." (August 7, 1765). "Pulling up of the (male) hemp. Was too late for the blossom hemp by three weeks or a month." (Aug. 29, 1766). (from *The Diaries of George Washington*. Houghton Mifflin Pub. 1925)

Hemp Seed: "Make the most you can of the Indian Hemp seed and sow it everywhere." (1794 note to Mt. Vernon's gardener, vol. 33, p. 270) "I cannot with certainty recollect whether I saw the India hemp growing when I was last in Mt. Vernon, but I think it was in the Vineyard, somewhere I hope it was sown, and therefore desire that the seed may be saved in due season and with as little loss as possible." (1794, vol. 33, p. 469)

Seed Lines: "What was done with the seed saved from the India Hemp last summer? It ought, all of it, to have been sewn again; that not only a stock of seed sufficient for my own purposes might have been raised, but to have disseminated the seed to others, as it is more valuable than the common hemp." (vol. 35, p. 72)

Hashish?: "I thank you as well for the seeds as for the pamphlets which you had the goodness to send me. The artificial preparation of hemp, from Silesia [a region shared by Germany and Poland], is really a curiosity." (letter to Dr. James Anderson, May 26, 1794, vol. 33, p. 384)

25

INDEX

26

BIBLIOGRAPHY

— Refer to footnotes for a more complete source listing. —

Abel, E.A. *Marijuana, The First 12,000 Years.* Plenum Press. New York NY. 1980
Adams, James T., ed. *Album of American History.* Charles Scribner's Sons. New York NY. 1944. p. 116.
Allen, J.L. *The Reign of Law, A Tale of the Kentucky Hemp Fields,* MacMillan Co. New York NY. 1900.
Anderson, Patrick. *High in America.* Viking Press. New York NY. 1981.
Andrews, George & Vinkenaog, Simon, editors. *Book of Grass, The.* Grove Press. Inc. New York NY. 1967.
Anicia Juliana. Roman. 512 AD
Annual Report, 1937. Du Pont Company. Wilmington DE. 1937.
Anslinger, Harry & Oursler, F. *The Murderers.* Farrar, Strauss & Cudahy. New York NY. 1961.
Anslinger, Harry Jacob. The Protectors: The heroic story of the narcotics agents, citizens, & officials in their unending, unsung battles against organized crime in America & abroad. Farrar, Straus. New York NY. 1964
Beatty, A. *Southern Agriculture.* C.M. Saxton & Co. New York NY. 1843. p. 113.
Berton, Hal; Kovarik, William & Scott Dklar. *Forbidden Fuel.* Boyd-Griffin. New York NY. 1982.
Bidwell, Percy Wells, Ph.d. *History of Agriculture in the Northern US, 1620-1860.* Carnegie Institution. Washington DC. May 1925.
Bonnie, R. & Whitebread, C. *The Marijuana Conviction.* U of VA Press. Richmond VA. 1974.
Bonnie, Richard & Whitebread, Charles. "The Forbidden Fruit & the Tree of Knowledge: An inquiry into the legal history of American marijuana prohibition." in *Virginia Law Review.* vol. 56:6.
Boyce, S.S. *Hemp.* Judd & Orange. New York NY. 1900.
Brecher, Edward 'Marijuana: The Health Questions.' in *Consumer Reports.* March 1975. p. 149.
Brecher, Edward M. & the editors of Consumer Reports. *Licit & Illicit Drugs: The Consumers Union Report.* Little Brown & Co. 1972.
Bromberg, Dr. W. 'Marihuana: A Psychiatric Study.' in *Journal of the AMA.* vol. 113. 1939. pp. 4-12.
Brown, Michael. *Brown's Second Alcohol Fuel Cookbook.* Tab Books. Blue Ridge Summit PA. pp. 125-129.
Burbank, Luther. "How Plants Are Trained To Work For Man," in *Useful Plants.* P. F. Collier & Son Co. New York NY. 1921. vol. 6. p. 48.
Caius Plinius II. De Historia Natura. Roman. 23-79 AD. 19.57 & 20.97
Carter, Edward W. *Cannabis In Costa Rica: A study in chronic marijuana use, 1980-82.* Institute for the study of Human Issues. Philadelphia, PA. 1982.
Carter, President James. "Statement on National Drug Policy." August 2, 1977.
Cherniak, Laurence. The great books of Cannabis & other drugs, or Researching the pleasures of the high society. Cherniak/Damele Pub. Co. Oakland, CA. 1982.
Clark, V.S., *History of Manufacture in US.* McGraw Hill. New York NY. 1929. p. 34.
Clark, Victor S. History of manufactures in the United States. Carnegie Institution of Washington. McGraw-Hill. 1929
Clarke, Robert Connell. Marijuana botany: an advanced study, the propogation & breeding of distinctive Cannabis. And/Or Press. Berkeley, CA. 1981.
Cockburn, L. *Out of Control.* Atlantic Monthly Press. New York NY. 1987.
Cohen, Dr. S. & Stillman, R. eds. *Therapeutic Potential of Marijuana, The.* Plenum Press. New York NY. 1976
Colby, Jerry. *Dupont Dynasties, The.* Lyle Stewart. 1984.
Colvin, James. 'Du Pont.' in *American Peoples Encyclopedia.* Sponsor Press. Chicago IL. 1953.
Compilations including or reprints for any or all of these:
Coxe, Tench. A statement of the arts & manufactures of the United States of America, for the year 1810 [microform]. A Cornman, Jr. 1814
Crosby, A.W., Jr. *America, Russia, Hemp & Napoleon.* OH State U. Press. Columbus OH. 1965.
"Dagga: A review of fact & fancy." in *Medical Journal.* no 44. 1970.
Dewey, L. "Hemp Industry in the US." in *USDA Yearbook, 1901.* DC. 1902.
Dewey, L. "Hemp." in *USDA Yearbook, 1913.* Washington DC. 1914.
Dewey, L. & Merrill, Jason. "Hemp Hurds as a Papermaking Material." in *Bulletin #404.* US Dept. of Agriculture. Washington DC. 1916.
Dewey, Lyster H. "Cultivation of hemp in the United States." in *US Plant Industry Bureau Circ. #57.* 1910.
Dickson, D.T. 'Bureaucracy & Morality.' in *Social Problems.* vol. 16. 1968. pp. 143-156.
Dioscorides Pedanius, of Anazarbos. La "Materia medica" de Dioscorides; transmision medieval y renacentista, por Cesar E. Dubler. Tipografia Emporium. Barcelona, Spain. 1952-1959
Drug Use in America: Problem in Perspective.' *Report of the National Commission on Marijuana & Drug Abuse.* US Federal Printing Office. 1973.
Erasmus, Udo. Fats & oils: the complete guide to fats & oils in health & nutrition. Alive. 1986
Facts for Farmers. Robinson, S., ed. Johnson & Ward. New York NY. 1865.

Fairbanks, E., editor. *Compilation of Articles Relating to the Culture & Manufacture of Hemp in the US*. Jewett & Porter. St. Johnsbury VT. 1829.

Fink, Max M.D. 'Study of long-term hashish users in Greece.' in *Hashish: Studies of Long-Term Use*. Raven Press. New York NY. 1977. pp. 153-154.

Frank, T. *An Economic Survey of Ancient Rome*. Pageant. Patterson NJ. 1959.

Frazier, Jack. *Great American Hemp Industry, The*. Solar Age Press. Peterstown WV. 1991.

Frazier, Jack. *Marijuana Farmers, The*. Solar Age Press. New Orleans, LA. 1972.

Galbraith, G. *Kentucky Marijuana Feasibility Study*. Lexington KY. 1977, 1988.

Galen, Claudius. De Facultatibus Alimentorum. Roman. c.150 AD 100.49

Godwin, H. 'The Ancient Cultivation of Hemp.' in *Antiquity*. no 41. 1967. pp. 42-49.

Gray, Lewis Cecil. *History of Agriculture in the Southern US to 1860*. Carnegie Institution of Washington. Washington DC. 1933. vol. 1.

Grierson, G.A. 'On References to the Hemp Plant Occurring in Sanskrit & Hindi Literature." in *Indian Hemp Drugs Commission Report*. vol. 3. Simla India. 1894.

Hatch, Richard. 'Drugs, Politics & Disinformation.' in *Covert Action*. No. 28. Washington DC. Summer 1987. pp. 23-32.

Hemp for Victory. USDA film. Washington DC. 1942.

Hemp, the Barometer of War." in *Literary Digest*. Jan. 27, 1923. p. 26

Herer, Jack. *Hemp & the Marijuana Conspiracy: The Emperor Wears No Clothes*. HEMP Publishing. Van Nuys CA. 1990.

Herodotus. *Histories, The*. Book IV (Melpomene). University Press. Cambridge MA. 1906. p. 74-76.

High Times Encyclopedia of Recreational Drugs. Trans High/Stonehill Publishing. New York NY. 1978.

Holy Bible, The. King James edition.

Hopkins, James F. "The production of hemp in Kentucky for Naval Use." in *Filson Club History Quarterly*. January 1949. pp. 34-51.

"How Heads of State Got High." in *High Times*. April 1980.

Indian Hemp Drugs Commission. *Report of the Indian Hemp Drugs Commission,1893-1894*. T. Jefferson Pub. Silver Spring. MD. 1969.

Jefferson, T. *Writings of Thomas Jefferson*. J.B.Lippincotts Co. Philadelphia PA. 1871.

Kaplan, John. *Marijuana: The New Prohibition*. World Publishing Co./Pocket Books. New York NY. 1970.

King, R. *The Drug Hangup*. C.C. Thomas. Springfield IL. 1974. p. 101.

Kmmens, A.C., ed. *Tales of Hashish*. Wm. Morrow. New York NY. 1977. p. 228.

Latimer & Goldberg. *Flowers in the Blood*. Franklin Watts. New York NY. 1981.

Lawther, Marcia, ed. *Hemp in America: A History & Critical Survey*. Van der Marck Press. New York NY.

Lee, M. & Shlain, B. *Acid Dreams*. Grove Press. New York NY. 1985.

Levine, Michael. *Deep Cover: The inside story of how DEA infighting, incompetence & subterfuge lost us the biggest battle of the drug war*. Delacourte Press. 1990.

Lower, George. "Hemp & Flax." in *Mechanical Engineering*. February 1938

Lydon, J.; Teramura , A.H. & Coffman, C.B. "UV-B radiation effects on ... cannabis sativa chemotypes." in *Photochemistry & Photobiology*. vol. 46:2. p. 201-206.

Malone, Dumas & Rauch, Basil. *War & Troubled Peace: 1917-1939*. Meredith. 1960.

Mann, Peggy. *Marijuana Alert*. McGraw Hill. New York NY. 1985.

Marcandier, M. *A Treatise on Hemp*. Edes & Gill. Boston MA. 1766.

Marijuana & the Bible. Ethiopian Zion Coptic Church. PO Box 1161, Minneda FL 34755-1161.

Mikuriya, Tod H., M D., ed. *Marijuana: Medical Papers, 1839-1972*. Medi Comp Press. Oakland CA. 1973.

Miller, C. & Wirtshafter, D. *Hemp Seed Cookbook*. Ohio Hempery, Inc. Athens OH. 1992. 21 p.

Mills, Ogden Livingston (1884-1937). 'On Liberty.' in Addresses & Essays. [S.1. s.n., 1935-1936]

Moore, Brent. *The Hemp Industry In Kentucky, A study of the past, the present & the possibilities*. Press of James E. Hughes. Lexington KY. 1905.

Morris, B. "Higher Ground." in *Details*. February 1993. pp. 26-31+

Morton, Thomas (1575-1646). New English Canaan or New Canaan. Containing an abstract of New England, composed in three books. The first books setting forth the original of the natives, their manners & customes, together with thier tractable... J. F. Stam. Amsterdam, Netherlands. 1637. also in New English Canaan of Thomas Morton. Introductory matter & notes by Charles Francis Adams, Jr. New York, B. Franklin. 1967

Musto, David F., M.D. *The American Disease: Origins of Narcotic Control*. Colonial Press. Clinton MA. 1973.

"New Billion Dollar Crop." in *Popular Mechanics*. February, 1938

New York Mayor's Committee Report. *The Marihuana Problem in the City of New York*. State of NY. 1946. Scarecrow Reprint. Metuchen NJ. 1973.

"No Marijuana, Plenty of Hemp." in *New Scientist*. November 13, 1980.

Novak, William. *High Culture*. CIA Pub. Boston MA. 1980.

O'Shaughnessy, W.B. 'On the Preparation of Indian Hemp, or Gunjah.' in Translations of the Medical & Physical Society of Calcutta. vol. 8:2. 1842

O'Shaugnessy, W.B. "On the preparation of Indian hemp, or gunjah." in *Transactions of the Medical & Physical Society of Bengal, 1838-1849*. p. 421-461.

Ohio State Medical Society. *Transcript of 15th annual meeting, June 12-14, 1860*. p. 75-100.

Osburn, Lynn. *Energy Farming in America*. Access Unlimited. Frazier Park CA. 1989.

Ostrowski, James. 'Thinking About Drug Legalization.' *Policy Analysis No. 121*. Cato Institute. Washington DC. 1989. pp. 1-2.

Oxford English Dictionary. Oxford U. Press. Oxford England. 1982.

Pimentel, David & Marcia. Food, Energy, & Society. Edward Arnold. London, England. 1979
Pliny the Elder (Caius Plinius Secundus). Natural History. vol. 19:57.
Relman, Arnold, M.D., ed. Marijuana & Health. National Academy Press. Washington DC. 1982.
Report of Senate Intelligence Committee Subcommittee on Terrorism & Narcotics, 1989. Kerry, Sen. John (MA), Chairman. Washington DC.
Report of the CA State Research Advisory Panel. 20th Annual Report. 1989. Commissioned by the State of CA Attorney General. Sections suppressed. 1990.
Report of the Canadian Government Commission of Inquiry into the Non-Medical Use of Drugs. Canadian Government Printing Office. Toronto Canada. 1972.
Reuter, Crawford, Cave, Murphy, et al. Sealing the Borders: Effects of increased military participation in drug interdiction. Rand Corp. Santa Monica, CA.1988
Roffman, Roger, Ph.D. Marijuana as Medicine. Medrone Books. Seattle WA. 1982.
Rogers, James Edwin Thorold, (1823-1890) The Economic Interpretation of History: lectures delivered in Worcester College Hall, Oxford. T. Fisher Unwin. London, England. Putnam's Sons. New York NY. 1888
Rubin, Dr. Vera & Comitas, Lambros, eds. Ganja in Jamaica: A medical anthropological study of chronic marijuana use. Mouton & Co. The Hague Netherlands. 1975.
Rubin, Dr. Vera, ed. Cannabis & Culture. Mouton & Co. The Hague Netherlands. 1975.
Rubin, Dr. Vera, ed. Jamaican Studies. Institute for the Study of Man. Philadelphia PA. 1975.
Sackett & Hobbs. Hemp; A war crop. Mason & Hanger. New York NY. 1942.
Scientific American. "American Hemp Industry." vol. 87. Nov. 29, 1902. p. 356. Dacy, G.H.. "Revolutionizing an Industry: How modern machinery is minimizing hand labor in hemp production." June 4, 1921. p. 446. Dodge, G.R., "Growing Hemp in America." May 15, 1915. "Kentucky Hemp." vol. 71. October 6, 1894. p. 210. "Making Paper Pulp From Hemp Hurds." vol. 116. Feb. 3, 1917. p. 127.
Siegel, Dr. Ronald K. Intoxication: Life in Pursuit of Artificial Paradise. Dulton Press. 1989.
Siler Commission. Canal Zone Papers. US GPO. Washington DC. 1931. p. 106.
Silver, G. & Alderich, M. The Dope Chronicles. Harper & Row. San Francisco. 1979.
Single Convention Treaty on Narcotic Drugs. United Nations. NY. 1961, 1968.
Sloman, Larry. Reefer Madness, Marijuana in America. Grove Press. New York NY. 1979.
Solomon, David, ed. The Marijuana Papers. Bobbs-Merrill. New York NY. 1966.
Stafford, Peter. Psychedelics Encyclopedia. And/Or Press. Berkeley CA. 1977.
Transcript of Hearing before a subcommittee of the Committee on Finance HR 6906. US Senate. 75c, 2s. Library of Congress. July 12, 1937.
Transcript of Hearings on HR 6387. House Committee on Ways & Means. US Congress. 75c, 1s. 1937.
Universal Declaration on Human Rights. United Nations. New York NY. 1980. Article 18.
US National Narcotics Intelligence Consumers Committee (NNICC) Annual Reports. El Paso TX.
'US to produce big hemp crop in '43.' in Barron's. vol. 22:6. Nov. 23, 1942.
USDA Agricultural Indices. 1916-1982. Washington DC.
USDA Yearbooks. Dept. of Agriculture. Washington DC.
War on Drugs: Arrests burdening local criminal justice systems. Report no. GAO/GGD 91-40. US GPO. Washington DC. April 3, 1991.
Warner, Roger. Invisible Hand: The marijuana business. Morrow & Co./ Beech Tree. New York NY. 1986.
"The Weed." in Time. July 19, 1943. p. 56.
Werf, Hayo van der. Crop Physiology of Fibre Hemp. PProefschrift Wageningen. Wageningen Netherlands. 1994
Wirtshafter, Don. The Schlichten Papers. Ohio Hempery. Athens OH. 1994.
Wolfe, S.M., M.D. & Coley, C. Pills That Don't Work. Public Citizen. Research Project 1981.

We invite your input for future editions of

Hemp: Lifeline to the Future

For bulk orders of this book, or to send your comments, write to:

Creative Xpressions Publications c/o BACH
PO Box 1005, Novato CA USA. Postal Code: 90071-0093
310-288-4152
Book order line: 1-800-HEMPMAN